Whose
American
Revolution
Was It?

Whose American Revolution Was It?

Historians Interpret the Founding

Alfred F. Young and Gregory H. Nobles

NEW YORK UNIVERSITY PRESS
New York and London

NEW YORK UNIVERSITY PRESS
New York and London
www.nyupress.org

References to Internet websites (URLs) were accurate at the time of writing. Neither the author nor New York University Press is responsible for URLs that may have expired or changed since the manuscript was prepared.

Library of Congress Cataloging-in-Publication Data
Young, Alfred Fabian, 1925–
Whose American revolution was it? : historians interpret the founding /
Alfred F. Young and Gregory H. Nobles.
p. cm.
Includes index.
ISBN 978-0-8147-9710-5 (cl : alk. paper) — ISBN 978-0-8147-9711-2 (pb : alk. paper)
ISBN 978-0-8147-9743-3 (e-book)
1. United States—History—Revolution, 1775–1783—Historiography. 2. United States—History—Revolution, 1775–1783—Influence. 3. United States—History—Revolution, 1775–1783—Social aspects. I. Nobles, Gregory H. II. Title.
E209.Y684 2011
973.3—dc22 2011015712

New York University Press books are printed on acid-free paper, and their binding materials are chosen for strength and durability. We strive to use environmentally responsible suppliers and materials to the greatest extent possible in publishing our books.

Manufactured in the United States of America

c 10 9 8 7 6 5 4 3 2 1
p 10 9 8 7 6 5 4 3 2 1

Contents

Introduction

Gregory H. Nobles and Alfred F. Young

Whose American Revolution Was It? speaks to the different ways Americans at the time of the Revolution might have answered this question and to the different ways historians in the twentieth and twenty-first centuries have interpreted the Revolution for our own time. On one level, the answer to the question in either era might seem quite obvious: Whose American Revolution was it? It was the Americans', of course, a successful War for Independence from Great Britain. Americans made—and won—their revolution. But no sooner has one said the word "Americans" than other questions immediately come up: Which Americans? Who were the Americans who made the political Revolution of 1776? Who fought to win the War for Independence? And who within America benefited from the results of the Revolution?

The meaning of the American Revolution as both a political and a popular movement has always been a measure of the ways the United States has progressed as a society, particularly in fulfilling its promise in the Declaration of Independence of liberty and equality. Asking "Whose American Revolution was it?" forces us to think about the Revolution in ways that do not offer simple answers but that make for a much more vital and engaging line of inquiry. The question remains contested, and the stakes are still high. Every generation has to come to terms with the Revolution in the context of its own time, looking back to the founding era as a historical touchstone that tells us where we have come from, how far we have come, and perhaps where we still ought to be going. The more we invoke the symbols of the Revolution today, or glorify its famous leaders, the more we need to know it well in its own time, embracing a broad view that encompasses all its inherent contradictions and sometimes unclear outcomes.

Asking "Whose American Revolution was it?" makes some present-day Americans uncomfortable, however. It implies that the Revolution may not have been everybody's Revolution, that there may have been an underside to it that could undermine, or certainly complicate, the standard narrative that puts the "Founding Fathers" at the head of an all-embracing, consensual movement. Yet that supposed "underside" has hardly been invisible to anyone who reflected on the Revolution. However uncertain average Americans may be about the specific events of the Revolutionary era, they still have a general sense of who was there and of the very significant differences among the people of the era. They know that slavery existed and that some of the most prominent political leaders of the Revolution, such as George Washington and Thomas Jefferson, were slave owners. They might not grasp the full extent of slavery, that in a population of 2.5 million there were five hundred thousand enslaved African Americans and that tens of thousands fought with the British and several thousand others on the side of the Americans. They also have a sense, perhaps from the iconic image of the statue of the "Minute Man" at Concord—one hand on the plough, the other holding his rifle—that at a time when most of the country was agricultural, most of the white soldiers on the patriot side, some two hundred thousand men, came from farm families and that their way of life was far different from that of the leaders who lived at Mount Vernon or Monticello. So too it is not hard to imagine that John Hancock, whose signature was first and largest on the Declaration of Independence—and who was also the wealthiest merchant in New England—lived a life in Boston that was very different from the craftsmen who built his ships and the sailors who manned them. They also can intuit that women, no matter what their class or race, were not accepted as full citizens after the Revolution and did not even get the vote until the twentieth century. Finally, it is common knowledge that that there were Native Americans within the colonies and new nation—actually no less than one hundred thousand Native Americans in the area east of the Mississippi River—who would be displaced and decimated by the expanding nation. Thus, even with a basic knowledge of such differences among Americans at the time, it should not be hard for Americans today to imagine that not everyone experienced the Revolution in the same way. It seems reasonable to ask "Whose American Revolution was it?"

In 1994, a group of historians and educators framed essentially the same question to help teachers and students explore American history in the nation's classrooms. The committee that developed the National Standards for United States History in the Schools asked "how revolutionary the Revolution actually was," which was another way of asking what the Revolution did to change American society, and for whom? To answer this question, the Standards suggested that students would have to look beyond the familiar focus on the Founding Fathers and would "necessarily . . . have to see the Revolution through different eyes—enslaved and free African Americans, Native Americans, white men and women of different social classes, religions, ideological dispositions, regions and occupations."[1] Gary Nash, a leading historian of the Revolution, was co-chair of the committee that drew on three years of discussion by hundreds of historians, teachers, and educators on all levels, delegated by some thirty national educational organizations. Intended as a guide for middle and high school teachers, the Standards as a whole addressed a problem recognized by a wide political spectrum of people alarmed by the declining state of knowledge of American history. Soon after the report was released, the Standards became the target of a massive right-wing assault, allegedly for giving less attention to George Washington and other great men than to the groups previously left out of the national narrative. After some revision and a decade of classroom application, the current version of the Standards met with wide approval by high school teachers.

That does not mean, however, that the debate over what to teach in American history has disappeared. Indeed, the continuing controversy speaks to a central concern of this book. Some people still feel uneasy in recognizing that not all historians explain the Revolution the same way, and to ask the question posed by this book—Whose American Revolution was it?—means asking whose *interpretations* of the Revolution are valid. The very notion that teachers might teach different ways of looking at the past raises the hackles of those Americans who say they want only "the facts" about history, assuming that there is some finite, never-changing body of "facts" about a historical event that comes down to us free from interpretation. In 2006, for example, the state legislators of Florida were so riled up by the apparent menace of historical interpretation that they drafted legislation that would have required the history of the United States to "be taught as genuine history and shall not follow the revisionist or postmodernist viewpoints of relative truth." They passed a law mandating that in the state's schools "history shall be viewed as factual, not as constructed,

[1] National Center for History in the Schools, *National Standards for United States History* (Los Angeles, 1994).

shall be viewed as knowable, teachable, testable, and shall be defined as the creation of a new nation based largely on the universal principles stated in the Declaration of Independence."[2] Woe, then, to the unfortunate Florida high school teacher who wanted to take the National Standards seriously about looking at the Revolution through different eyes. A few years later, in 2010, the Texas Board of Education turned against the principal author of the Declaration of Independence because, as the *New York Times* reported, "Jefferson is not well liked among conservatives on the board because he coined the term 'separation between church and state.'"[3] In a 10–5 vote on the required contents of the state's history textbooks, the board excised Jefferson from a list of writers whose words helped inspire revolutionaries in the late eighteenth century. Thus, the gatekeepers of the state's history curriculum, who doubtless were outraged by the alleged diminution of the most famous Founders in the National Standards, had little compunction about engaging in their own form of revisionism by banishing a leading figure in the Revolution when it suited their political purposes.

In reality, so-called revisionist history is not new, nor is it by any means the sole creation of the proponents of "postmodernist viewpoints of relative truth," the so-called relativists. The Council of the American Historical Association pointed out in 2007 that revisionist history "has been practiced for almost a century—since 1913 when Charles Beard published his economic interpretation of the American Constitution." Revisions "have been applied to the Industrial Revolution, the Revolution, the Civil War, the First and Second World Wars, the bombing of Hiroshima and Nagasaki, the Cold War and many other historical issues and problems." Revisionists, the AHA Council points out, "are for the most part the opposite of relativists. They argue that standard accounts of a given event are incorrect and that new documents or new interpretations of known documents can prove this is true."[4] Indeed, most historians believe that the business of their profession is to examine previous versions of history found to be wanting, to ask new questions about familiar subjects, and to open up new subjects long neglected.

Sometimes fresh questions arise when new original primary source

[2] J. L. Bell, "History 101: Florida's Flawed Lesson Plan," *History News Network*, July 17, 2006, http://hnn.us/articles/28095.html (accessed July 30, 2010).

[3] "Texas Conservatives Win Curriculum Change," *New York Times*, Mar. 12, 2010.

[4] Council of the American Historical Association, "Statement on the 2006 Florida Education Bill," Jan. 7, 2007, http://www.historians.org/perspectives/issues/2007/0703/0703aha6.cfm (accessed July 30, 2010).

materials—the essential "facts," the building blocks of historical evidence —are discovered. New biographies of the most prominent men of the Revolution, for example, have appeared in such profusion in recent years in good part because the documentary record available to researchers has increased exponentially as a result of the projects assembling and publishing their papers, which began more than half a century ago. (The Massachusetts Historical Society has now published forty-two volumes of the papers of John Adams and his family, and the Library of Congress has made available online over sixty-five thousand documents from George Washington's papers and twenty-seven thousand from Thomas Jefferson's—with more to come for all three.) Libraries are also digitizing thousands of other sorts of primary sources formerly found only in the files of a single archive. At the same time, many books, both old and new, now appear on the Internet in their entirety, and scholarly articles are easily searchable in electronic databases. The possibilities of Web-based research have expanded enormously in only a few years, and anyone with a computer can get almost immediate access to materials that used to require time, travel, and sometimes considerable expense to find. The dream of the historian Carl Becker—"Every man his own historian"—is within reach for men, women, and students at all levels.[5]

But new sources alone are not the only reason for new inquiries. Often the historian's questions arise from perceived gaps in knowledge: if thousands of slaves fled from their plantations in Virginia in 1775–76 in response to the appeals of British generals, one might ask what the impact was on plantation owners such as Washington and Jefferson who lost numerous slaves. Sometimes questions emerge from the powerful examples set by the recovery of people's stories that had previously been thought all but lost: Laurel Ulrich's decoding of the diary kept by Martha Ballard, a midwife, physician, and farm housewife on the Maine frontier for twenty-seven years, from 1785 to 1812, demonstrates "the way the political revolution and social revolution that accompanied it were related." "By restoring a lost substructure of eighteenth-century life," Ulrich rightly claims, a diary long dismissed as replete only with trivia "transforms the nature of the evidence upon which much of the history of the period has been written."[6] The list of the reasons for new inquiries could go on and on, because the

[5] Carl Becker, "Every Man His Own Historian," *American Historical Review* 37 (1931): 221–36, http://www.histyorians.org/info/aha.

[6] Laurel Thatcher Ulrich, *A Midwife's Tale: The Life of Martha Ballard, Based on Her Diary, 1785–1812* (New York, 1990), 27.

everyday reality of the historian's life as a researcher is that, whatever the subject, large or small, he or she has no alternative but to select from a vast array of facts in an ever-expanding body of evidence. That is what writing or teaching history is all about.

Inevitably, the historian's life exists within history itself. As the influential English historian Edward Hallett Carr has put it, "The historian, before he begins to write history, is the product of history." But because truth is relative to the historian—the meaning of relativism, simply put—it does not mean, in Carr's words, that "one interpretation is as good as another and the facts of history are in principle not amenable to objective interpretation." One interpretation can be better than another because it takes into account more evidence or is based on source materials not previously available or because the historian may be inspired to greater insight by something in his or her own time. "Great history," Carr argued, "is written precisely when the historian's vision of the past is illuminated by insights into the problems of the present."[7]

Thus, the questions asked by historians are often in response to significant changes in society that push them, as they do other citizens, to rethink parts of the past that have been overlooked, buried, or little appreciated. The effectiveness of the mass movements of the 1960s and 1970s for racial and gender equality contributed to historians' awareness of movements "from the bottom up" and the role of ordinary people who helped shape such struggles in the past. By the same token, the widespread disillusionment with national political leaders in recent decades contributed to an emphasis on the presumably superior "character" of the leaders of the Revolutionary era in the many new biographies of the famous Founders.

Recognizing the influences of the world scholars live in does not distort our perspective on the past or diminish the validity of historical discoveries. To realize, for instance, that movements for civil rights and women's rights in our own time helped inspire the recovery of objective facts about African Americans or women in the past does not mean that scholars have skewed the evidence. Nor does it follow that the emphasis on "history from the bottom up" means that the more traditional, top-down way of looking at the Revolution as a political event leading to Independence and the formation of a nation-state is irrelevant. Quite the opposite. There are now new dimensions to political history. "In the last quarter century,"

[7] Edward Hallett Carr, *What Is History? The George Macaulay Trevelyan Lectures Delivered in the University of Cambridge, January–March 1961* (London, 1961), 34–38.

as Linda Kerber writes, the research of "a new generation of historians . . . has tended to restore *rebellion* to histories of the American Revolution, by dealing with the ways in which marginal people—blacks, women, the impoverished—shaped the Revolution and were in turn affected by it."[8] The Revolution historians know today is less skewed than it was when the focus was on the great men.

While some historians recovering underlying long-range trends have avoided formal political history, others have drawn on social history to broaden our understanding of what we mean by "political." Recent research has redefined the political. The wave of runaway slaves in Virginia in 1775–76, for example, shaped the political decision of planters in Virginia and in the Continental Congress in Philadelphia to adopt independence as a goal: faced with what the Declaration of Independence called "convulsions" within, they became "forced founders," supporting the rebellion against Great Britain in the hope of establishing a government that could quell the rebellion in their midst.[9] Even quieter forms of rebellion had a political impact. When Abigail Adams was managing the family farm while her husband, John, was absent for years and calling herself a "farmeriss," she was implicitly making a political claim for equality—one that she also made more explicitly to her husband in the Continental Congress. We need to see them together—John and Abigail Adams, Washington and Jefferson and their slaves, James Madison and Daniel Shays—as part of a larger political process. Arguably, understanding the presence and potential power of the groups once dismissed as being marginal has brought us much closer to the political world American leaders experienced at the time.

In this spirit, this book approaches historians' interpretations of the American Revolution from several different angles of vision, beginning at an important point in time—the plea, in 1925, of the historian J. Franklin Jameson, a historian then at the peak of the profession, to "consider the American Revolution as a social movement." It was a fresh challenge to historians, and it opened, as Jameson presciently suggested, "a field of history deserving further and deeper study." Those who originated the Revolution, Jameson held, "had no other than a political program and would have considered its work done when political independence of Great Britain had

[8] Linda K. Kerber, "The Revolutionary Generation: Ideology, Politics, and Culture in the Early Republic," in Eric Foner, ed., *The New American History*, rev. and exp. ed. (Philadelphia, 1997), 31–59, quotation at 32.

[9] The phrase "forced founders" comes from Woody Holton, *Forced Founders: Indians, Debtors, Slaves, and the Making of the American Revolution in Virginia* (Chapel Hill, NC, 1999).

been secured." But, he asked, "who can say to the waves of Revolution: Thus far shall we go and no farther? . . . The stream of Revolution, once started, could not be confined within narrow banks but spread abroad upon the land."[10]

The two essays in this book explore the ways historians have interpreted the impact of those "forces thus let loose." The first essay, by Alfred F. Young and originally published in 1995, was written for a scholarly conference devoted to reconsidering the Jameson thesis about the "transforming hand of revolution," the conference in itself testimony to the staying power of the thesis. Surveying the scholarship of the last three quarters of the twentieth century, it takes the reader through successive schools of interpretation: the Progressive interpretation more or less dominant to about 1945; the consensus or counter-Progressive view, sometimes called the ideological interpretation of the Revolution, which emerged in the 1950s and '60s to dominate the field; the "new social history," which accelerated in the 1970s and '80s, devoted to long-range trends in early American society; the "New Left" history that ran parallel with it, arguing for examining the Revolution as a whole from the bottom up; and the diverse efforts in the 1980s and early '90s to synthesize the many strands of what had become very large bodies of scholarship.

The second essay, by Gregory H. Nobles, picks up where the first leaves off and deals with scholarship since about 1995. It focuses especially on how present-day historians interpret the major groups that the no longer "new" social history has brought onto the stage of the Revolution, groups long regarded as only bit players or extras: farmers and artisans who made up the vast majority of white Americans of English and European descent, African Americans, Native Americans, and women of all social classes. Focusing on these groups does not mean ignoring the traditional "stars" of the show, the leading men who have long stood at the center of the stage. Rather, the emphasis of the second essay is on seeing the whole cast of characters together as an ensemble production, seeking to appreciate how the players formerly considered marginal actually helped determine the outcome of the historical drama.

Recent historians of the social history of the Revolutionary era no longer frame their questions around Jameson, and he has receded from sight, even while these scholars pursue his themes. Why, then, organize an account of

[10] J. Franklin Jameson, *The American Revolution Considered as a Social Movement* (Princeton, 1926; reprint 1967), 8–9.

historians of the Revolution around a question advanced by one scholar so long ago? For several reasons. First, social history has so obviously become a major focus of scholarship of the Revolutionary era, and historians would agree with Gordon Wood's assessment that Jameson "is the starting point for appreciating the social changes of the revolutionary era."[11] Second, because so many historians weighed in on Jameson in the twentieth century, he provides an excellent frame of reference to track the successive schools of interpretation. His claim for the significance of social change ran parallel to the arguments of his influential fellow Progressive historians, Carl Becker and Charles Beard. Becker framed the political history of the Revolution as not only a struggle war for "home rule" but as a struggle among Americans "for who shall rule at home," and Beard offered *An Economic Interpretation of the Constitution*, portraying the political capstone of the Revolution as a product of a clash of classes and economic interests he saw running through the period. The three were instrumental in directing historians to the "internal" history of the Revolution—as opposed to the "external" one, which focused on the break with Great Britain—and as a consequence focused attention on results as opposed to "causes."

Third, Jameson's insights have been remarkably enduring among historians, even while they have subsequently opened up subjects he did not envision. Jameson and his fellow Progressives, for all their insight about internal conflict within American society, did not address the historical significance of the social groups that historians have since moved to the center of the stage: Native Americans, African Americans, and women. Jameson's emphasis on long-range social change has also challenged historians to think about the Revolution in ways that break through the traditional boundaries for the Revolution, beginning in 1763 and ending in 1789, bracketed by political events. Seeking to assess the significance of the American Revolution as a social movement—or movements, plural, to be more precise—has meant locating the larger cast of historical actors on a much longer chronological continuum, reaching from the colonial period well into the era of the early republic into the 1790s and well beyond. Historians who now write of the "long" Revolution thus implicitly acknowledge Jameson's approach. Those who take the measure of the Revolution's success by exploring the success of the various seekers of liberty and equality similarly build on Jameson's awareness of different outcomes for both the agents and opponents of change. People who might have been on the

[11] Gordon Wood, *The American Revolution: A History* (New York, 2002), 172–73.

same side of the fence when it came to American independence often had dramatically differing notions about how far the ideals of the Declaration might extend, and to whom. Jameson opened up areas of contention that have remained central to the interpretation of the Revolution.

Controversy over interpreting the Revolution can appear in surprising places. Some years ago it stole some scenes in a popular Hollywood movie, *Good Will Hunting*, which won an Academy Award for screenwriting in 1998 for Matt Damon and Ben Affleck. Will Hunting, a twenty-year-old, Irish, working-class guy from South Boston (played by Damon), and Chuckie, his fellow "Southie" (Affleck), are visiting the Bow and Arrow bar in Cambridge, Massachusetts, frequented by Harvard students. Will is a math genius who also reads widely in history but by choice works as a janitor at MIT sweeping floors: he has a class-conscious chip on his shoulder about elite universities. At the bar, Chuckie, a construction worker who, like his friend, never went to college, fakes it to a Harvard history graduate student that he attended a class in early American history at Harvard, and the grad student calls his bluff: "I was just hoping that you could give me some insight into the evolution of the market economy in the Southern colonies," the grad student says with sneering condescension. "My contention is that prior to the Revolutionary War the economic modalities *especially* in the Southern colonies could most aptly be characterized as agrarian, pre-capitalist. . . ."

Will, springing to the rescue of his cornered buddy, interrupts with a breathless put-down: "Of course that's your contention. You're a first-year graduate student. You just got finished readin' some Marxian historian—Pete Garrison prob'ly. You're gonna be convinced of that 'til next month, when you get to James Lemon, and then you're gonna be talking about how the economies of Virginia and Pennsylvania were entrepreneurial and capitalist way back in 1740. That's gonna last until next year—you're gonna be in here regurgitating Gordon Wood, talking about, you know, about the pre-Revolutionary utopia and the capital-forming effects of military mobilization."

The hapless grad student tries a comeback: "Well, as a matter of fact I won't, because Wood drastically underestimates the impact of . . ." But Will breaks in again, finishing the student's sentence: "Wood drastically underestimates the impact of social distinctions predicated upon wealth, especially inherited wealth. You got that from Vickers, *Work in Essex County*, page 98, right? Yeah, I read it too. Do you have any thoughts of your own on this matter?" The student backs off, they avoid a fight, and the barroom debaters part peacefully. Will has impressed a woman student at the bar (played by Minnie Driver), who gives him her phone number and will later become his girlfriend—all things considered, not a bad ending for a scholarly conversation about American history.

In a later scene, Will, who as a condition of a suspended sentence for fighting has been ordered by a judge to spend time with a psychiatrist, again shows off his knowledge of historical interpretations in a confrontation with his therapist, Sean Maguire (played by Robin Williams). Will, looking at Sean's office walls lined with books, asks if he has read them all. "I did," Sean replies. Scanning the titles on one shelf and spotting *A History of the United States, Volume 1*, Will blurts out, "If you want to read a real history book, read Howard Zinn's *A People's History of the United States*. That book will knock you on your ass."

These two scenes establish Will Hunting's character as a rebel; they also invite viewers to think about why American history might matter to him. Damon, who attended Harvard College before he became a movie star and screenwriter, got his historians right. Three of the scholars named in the barroom dialogue—James Lemon, Daniel Vickers, and Gordon Wood—do indeed exist, and they all figured more or less in a longstanding debate about how capitalist the colonies were and in effect how much inequality there was in early American society—all matters very much relevant to the question of whose Revolution it was. The name of the Marxian historian Will uses is made up, but there are real historians of early America who write from a left perspective. There was certainly a real Howard Zinn, whose *People's History* has sold more than two million copies; the book challenges the celebratory view of the American past, championing defiant class-conscious movements from below, which might well have caught Will's sympathies.

But that still begs the question, Why would anyone take the time and trouble to read all this stuff? For the Harvard grad student, the answer is easy: he is an academic historian in training, and devouring the books on his reading list is part of his preparation for entering the profession (or at least for getting through his comprehensive exams). For the psychiatrist, the display of big volumes of serious history on his office bookshelves underscores the breadth of his knowledge. But for Will, a class-conscious Southie who does not aspire to professional status like the others, his engagement with historical debates suggests more interesting answers. It is not just an academic exercise to him, not just a game of memorization or showing off. The differing interpretations of historians matter to him, an angry young man who thus far in his life has wound up on the wrong side of authority. Knowing that there are differing interpretations of history that challenge the traditional top-down, celebratory narrative helps give him a better perspective on his relationship with the powers that be and his place in society. And perhaps knowing that the interpretations that offer a bottom-up approach emphasizing the role of ordinary people in shaping the course of history makes it possible for someone like Will Hunting to see himself as an actor in a much larger story.

We cannot claim that the discussion of historical interpretations in this book will provide a guide to current historical movies. We hope, though, that this book may be useful for a number of audiences: historians and would-be historians, including grad students at Harvard and elsewhere, who want to get their bearings on the large and growing body of scholarship about the American Revolution; conscientious middle school and high school teachers who have to make decisions about how to squeeze the Revolution into a shrinking American History curriculum that allows less time for the early period; and curators and guides at historic sites and museums who need to establish historical contexts and introduce different interpretations to their visitors; and maybe future screenwriters. We also hope this book may stimulate the appetite of readers who have been brought to the Revolution by the absorbing biographies of the famous men and who sense there may have been other important actors on the scene.

There is no getting around the American Revolution. It will always matter, because it will always define the founding of our national history. For that reason, we will always need to come to terms with the world of the Founders. To do so, however, means expanding our very definition of who were "Founders." Founders of all sorts played different roles in the American Revolution, and they often differed on how far the Revolution should go and on whose Revolution it would ultimately be. In the end, we hope that this book will inspire readers to think through their own way of looking at the American Revolution.

American Historians Confront "The Transforming Hand of Revolution"

Alfred F. Young

Introduction

In August 1926 Charles A. Beard published an enthusiastic review of John Franklin Jameson's book *The American Revolution Considered as a Social Movement* in the *New Republic.* Jameson sent him a warm letter of appreciation and clarification, and Beard responded with even more lavish praise.[1] The exchange is a convenient point from which to launch an inquiry into the achievement of Jameson in the context of the scholarship of his day, the remarkable durability of his little book of four lectures, and the way American historians have dealt with the Jameson thesis and the larger, still unresolved issue of what Jameson called "the transforming hand of revolution." Beard has since been battered and some would say buried, but his ghost still haunts historical studies, and were he to appear, he might be tempted to borrow the comment John Adams allegedly made about Thomas Jefferson from his death bed, on July 4, 1826, when he was told that Jefferson, who also lay dying, was still alive: "J. Franklin Jameson still survives."

In 1950, when a historian published the results of a poll of 103 scholars (drawn from "an approximate cross section of the profession") as to the ten

[1] J. Franklin Jameson to Charles A. Beard, Aug. 10, 1926, and Beard to Jameson, Aug. 14, 1926, in Elizabeth Donnan and Leo F. Stock, eds., *An Historian's World: Selections from the Correspondence of John Franklin Jameson* (Philadelphia, 1956), 319–320.

"best" works in American history published between 1920 and 1935, Jameson's book came in fourteenth, with 26 votes. At the head of the list were Vernon Louis Parrington's *Main Currents in American Thought* (84 votes) and Frederick Jackson Turner's collection of essays on the frontier (83), followed by Charles and Mary R. Beard's *Rise of American Civilization* (58), Carl L. Becker's *Declaration of Independence* (51), and Arthur M. Schlesinger Sr.'s *New Viewpoints in American History* (32). Jameson clearly held a place on the hit parade of Progressive historians. Counter-Progressive "consensus" history was only a cloud on the historical horizon.[2]

Four years later Frederick B. Tolles, in a full-dress reevaluation of Jameson's book in the *American Historical Review*, summarized the serious challenges to Jameson's hypotheses but concluded that "basically the 'Jameson thesis' is still sound, and what is more important, still vital and suggestive, capable of further life, still greater usefulness." The tide, however, was already turning. Edmund S. Morgan, in what became the most influential short work of synthesis on the American Revolution, *The Birth of the Republic* (1956), recognized Jameson's "influential essays" as a book that "helped focus attention on the internal conflicts that accompany such changes" as the American Revolution. But he was convinced there was "no radical rebuilding of social institutions at this time," the Revolution bringing only "a host of incalculable, accidental, and incidental changes in society." A decade later Jack P. Greene pronounced the Progressive interpretation of the Revolution associated with Beard, Becker, Schlesinger Sr., and presumably Jameson, "shattered and deeply discredited."[3]

Scholars continued to pay deference to Jameson, however, even as they substituted alternative syntheses of the Revolution. Gordon S. Wood called Jameson "the starting point for appreciating the social changes of the Revolution." James A. Henretta thought the book "remains a good summary of the social changes of the revolutionary era." In 1987 Richard B. Morris, one of the few senior historians who kept the door open to the Jameson thesis in the 1960s, summed up his own reflections on social change in the era by entitling a chapter in his last book "A Cautiously Transforming

[2] John W. Caughey, "Historians' Choice: Results of a Poll on Recently Published American History and Biography," *Mississippi Valley Historical Review* 39 (1952): 293, 299.

[3] Frederick B. Tolles, "The American Revolution Considered as a Social Movement: A Re-evaluation," *American Historical Review* 60 (1954): 1–12; Edmund S. Morgan, *The Birth of the Republic, 1763–1789* (Chicago, 1956), 96, 98; Jack P. Greene, "Social Origins of the American Revolution: An Evaluation," *Williams and Mary Quarterly* 88 (1973): 1–22, quotation at 3; also see Greene, *The Reappraisal of the American Revolution in Recent Historical Literature* (Washington, DC, 1967).

Egalitarianism." Greene in the late 1980s paid Jameson the ultimate homage by devoting a conference to defining the "limits" of change in the Revolutionary era.[4]

Jameson's thesis was diffused and widely accepted (1920s–1950s), then rejected (1950s–1960s), and finally revived in very different guise (1960s–1990s). "In the last quarter century," Linda K. Kerber wrote in 1990, "responding in part to the pressing questions of our own time, a new generation of historians have offered their own rich interpretations of the experience of the revolutionary generation." This new research "has tended to restore *rebellion* to histories of the American Revolution" by dealing with "the ways in which marginal people—blacks, women, the impoverished—shaped the revolution and were in turn affected by it." To this list others would add farmers, middling artisans, and American Indians. Historians, she writes, have also developed "broader conceptualizations of political ideology." What unites this diverse scholarship is an appreciation of "the radicalism—both social and intellectual—of the American Revolution."[5]

As a consequence, the issue of "the transforming hand of revolution"—Jameson's provocative concept—after a long exile, has been restored to a central place in the historiography of the era. An examination of how historians have dealt with a single historian may be of value if it takes us to the heart of this larger issue his scholarship raised, the extent to which the American Revolution was a transforming event. It also sheds light on how a historian, in Edmund Morgan's words, "may reflect, however remotely, the needs of his time."[6]

In this essay I propose, first, to summarize the Jameson thesis; second, to locate and analyze Jameson's achievement and limitations in the context of the scholarship of his own time; and third, to analyze the way successive schools of historical interpretation have considered the thesis. In the course of this discussion I will take up the alternative ways in which historians have dealt with the larger question of transformation in the

[4] Bernard Bailyn, Robert Dallek, David Brion Davis, David Herbert Donald, John L. Thomas, and Gordon S. Wood, *The Great Republic: A History of the American People* (New York, 1992), 296; see also Gordon S. Wood, *The American Revolution: A History* (New York, 2002), 172; James A. Henretta, David Brody, and Lynn Dumenil, *America's History* (Chicago, 1987), 207; Richard B. Morris, *The Forging of the Union, 1781–1789* (New York, 1987), chap. 7; Jack P. Greene, ed., *The American Revolution: Its Character and Limits* (New York, 1987), 1–13.

[5] Linda K. Kerber, "The Revolutionary Generation: Ideology, Politics, and Culture in the Early Republic," in Eric Foner, ed., *The New American History* (Philadelphia, 1992), 25–49, quotations at 26, 44.

[6] Edmund S. Morgan, *The Challenge of the American Revolution* (New York, 1976), x.

American Revolution, which alone justifies such a long voyage through twentieth-century historiography.

I. J. Franklin Jameson

1. The Jameson Thesis: The Text

The Jameson thesis is disarming in its simplicity, as is the form of the book: four short lectures, no more than thirty thousand words, the equivalent today of a hefty journal article, without footnotes, without a bibliographic essay, and with only hints within the text as to the evidence he was drawing on. Delivered as lectures at Princeton in 1925, published the next year by Princeton University Press, it was something that only Jameson at age sixty-six, "the wise and honored elder statesman of the historical profession," as John Higham has called him, could get away with.[7]

The American Revolution, Jameson argued, was "a political revolution" that had "social consequences." This was the gist of the thesis. It was "vain to think of the Revolution as solely a series of political or military events." The Revolution began one way and ended another. At no point did Jameson claim there was either "a social revolution," "a revolution within," or an "internal revolution"—these were the phrases of later scholars. He argued by metaphors heavy with physical analogies. The Revolution was "a stream." "But who can say to the waves of revolution: Thus far shall we go and no farther? . . . The stream of revolution, once started, could not be confined within narrow banks, but spread abroad upon the land. Many economic desires, many social aspirations were set free by the political struggle, many aspects of colonial society profoundly altered by the forces thus let loose." This was perhaps his fullest statement of his overall thesis.[8]

He expressed his underlying assumption in another analogy: "The various fibres of a nation's life are knit together in great complexity. It is impossible to sever some without loosening others, and setting them free to combine anew in widely different forms." He also offered the physical analogy of heat: "Whatever . . . was outgrown or exotic seemed to be thrown into the melting-pot, to be recast into a form better suited to the work which

[7] J. Franklin Jameson, *The American Revolution Considered as a Social Movement* (1926; reprint ed., Boston, 1956); John Higham, *History: The Development of Historical Studies in the United States* (Englewood Cliffs, NJ, 1965).

[8] Jameson, *American Revolution as a Social Movement*, 8, 26, 9.

the new nation had before it. The hot sun of revolution withered whatever was not deeply rooted in the soil."[9]

Mystical as these analogies seem at first glance, they represented Jameson's quest for a vocabulary to express an analysis of a process of revolution that did not exist outside the framework of Marxism. He posited generic stages in revolution, and while the physical analogy of the stream overrunning its banks seemed to deny agency, he left no doubt that different groups of people moved revolutions from one stage to another. "Therefore the social consequences of a revolution are not necessarily shaped by the conscious or unconscious desires of those who started it, but more likely by the desires of those who came into control of it at later stages of its development. . . . Certain it is that, in some of our states at least, it [the American Revolution] fell ultimately into quite other hands than those that set it in motion." He then asked, "who were in favor of the Revolution, and who were against it?" offering a short analysis that took into account class, occupation, race, nationality, and age. "The strength of the revolutionary party," he concluded, "lay most largely in the plain people, as distinguished from the aristocracy. It lay not in the mob or rabble" of the cites "but in the peasantry, substantial and energetic though poor, in the small farmers and frontiersmen."[10]

After devoting most of his first lecture, "The Revolution and the Status of Persons," to sketching these broad outlines of his thesis, Jameson devoted a few pages to the political changes that brought social change, in particular, the suffrage that he believed was "much extended" and led to the elevation of voters "in their social status" and a decline of deference. He then devoted the remainder of his attention to slavery as an issue, focusing on the growth of antislavery sentiment among whites that led after the war to emancipation in the northern states, individual acts of manumission in the South, and the checking of slave importation. His emphasis was on the "leaven" of the Revolution leading to "very substantial progress."[11]

Jameson's second lecture was on "The Revolution and the Land," which he summed up as "the freeing of the soil from all connection with the feudal land-law, the breaking up of large estates, [and] the universal extension, in the North at least, of that system of small or moderate farms, cultivated by the owner's own hands." In his judgment, "we may properly give a place

[9] Ibid., 9, 32.
[10] Ibid., 12, 18.
[11] Ibid., 18–19, 25–26.

of great prominence to the land" because "political democracy came to the United States as a result of economic democracy."[12]

Jameson devoted his third lecture, "Industry and Commerce," using "industry" in the broad sense of productive economic activity, to the ways in which the stimulus of war and the liberating effects of Independence benefited agriculture, manufactures, and maritime trade. He considered the war not as a disruption; for most Americans "industrial life went on during these seven years . . . without cessation in its development." Farmers, "their minds . . . widened by the war," supported "much-needed" agricultural improvement societies. The prewar anti-importation movement and the war itself "called into existence or stimulated" a variety of manufactures and spurred household or domestic production as well. Maritime commerce was stimulated by privateering that overshadowed both the navy and commercial ventures. Independence provided a "release from fetters" that led to the opening of "new channels of trade." The only drawback to this litany of progress was the "weakness" of the Articles of Confederation government, which is why the architects of stronger federal government "found their best helpers among the commercial classes." The American Revolution, Jameson concluded, "brought ultimate benefit to the agriculture, the manufactures, and the commerce" of the nation.[13]

In his fourth and final lecture, a grab bag called "Thought and Feeling," Jameson attempted to suggest "the imponderable effects" of the Revolution "in the field of public opinion and popular emotion." Sketching the growth of humanitarian reform, nationalist feeling, and education, he devoted most of his attention to religion—the organization of denominations on a national basis and the disestablishment of church from state that made "religious freedom and equality . . . America's chief contribution to the world's civilization." Jameson closed the lecture and the book by mentioning the denominations of the future whose growth he suggested might be correlated with "the idea of the natural equality of all men." He offered it as an illustration of the underlying holistic assumption of the lectures: "The thesis that all the varied activities of men in the same country and period have intimate relations with each other, and that one cannot obtain a satisfactory view of any one of them by considering it apart from the others."[14]

[12] Ibid., 49, 27, 29.

[13] Ibid., 49, 51, 59, 69, 71, 73.

[14] Ibid., 74, 90, 100.

2. The Jameson Thesis: The Context

This was the thesis, deceptively simple in the lectures, simplified still further by any summary. On what scholarship was it based? Jameson provided no footnotes and made almost no internal references to scholars. He revealed some of his primary sources—European travelers' accounts, the letters of leaders, an occasional memoir or diary. But he gave no sign of having gone through any major bodies of sources; he offered examples but made no effort to pile proof on proof; his evidence was, in the best sense, impressionistic. And his erudition was clear. To understand on what it was based one must attempt an archaeology of the layers of his hitherto unpublished writing of the 1890s that the recent edition of his papers makes possible.[15]

What was it about Jameson's little book that inspired such admiration among so many scholars over so many decades? The exchange between Beard and Jameson helps to situate Jameson in the context of the scholarship of their time. Beard welcomed the book because it was "by one of the first scholars in America, . . . a master of the older generation." It marked "the definitive close of the Bancroftian or romantic era" in scholarship that Beard had tried to deflate. Beard's review, with the barbed caption "A Challenge to Windbags," was written from outside the academy, appearing in the *New Republic*, the founding magazine of Progressive politics. Beard identified himself as among those who "have long been watching eagerly the flight of birds at the annual meetings of the American Historical Association hoping for new signs." He read each chapter as supporting his own economic interpretation. "The Status of Persons" was "a euphemistic title employed to cover the class arrangements of American society"; the "substance" of the business was economic; "the line-up of forces was essentially economic." In chapter two on the land system Beard seized on Jameson's argument that "political democracy came to the U.S. as a result of economic democracy"; "the abundance of cheap land was the prime factor." Chapter three he saw as supporting a thesis of *An Economic Interpretation of the Constitution*. "The grooms of the sacred cow will not thank him for his page on privateering" or for seeing that "the pathway to the creation of a firmer union led through considerations of commercial regulations." Only chapter four—on humanitarian reform, ideas, and

[15] Morey D. Rothberg and Jacqueline Goggin, eds., *John Franklin Jameson and the Development of Humanistic Scholarship in the United States*, 3 vols., vol. 1, *Selected Essays* (Athens, GA, 2001).

religion—Beard thought "shows how much hard preliminary work must be done before culture can be geared with economics and war." "A truly notable book," he concluded, "carefully organized, cut with a diamond point to a finish, studded with novel illustrative materials, gleaming with new illumination, serenely engaging in style, and sparingly garnished with genial humor."[16]

Jameson wrote to Beard to thank him—with one exception, it was "the only serious review" he had seen—but he discreetly distanced himself from Beard. He was appreciative but clearly wanted to take up the insinuation that he was "a late convert to the economic interpretation of history." First of all, he wrote, "I will tell you confidentially that the four lectures only convey the substance of six that I gave to a small audience at Columbia University in 1895." His Princeton sponsors knew this; that was not the point. What struck Jameson as he set about revising his lectures of 1895 and surveyed the books, dissertations, and articles published in the previous thirty years was "how little had been done to illuminate that period from the social and economic point of view—how little needed to be changed in [his] statements." Strictly speaking, this was not true, but he wanted Beard to know he had formulated his thesis long before the landmark monographs of Charles Henry Lincoln (1901), Becker (1909), Beard (1913), and Schlesinger (1918) had appeared. Second, Jameson resisted Beard's effort to pigeonhole him in a passage that has been echoed by countless scholars over the years. "There is some tendency to classify historical scholars particularly rigidly as of new and old schools, as if one must be distinctly of one school or the other and as if there had been a sharp transition, whereas I should think there has been a gradual one, and the new history does not seem so altogether new to me as many represent."[17]

In his reply Beard was mildly apologetic. "I quite understand how you feel about being driven into any particular corner, such as an economic interpretation, and it is far from my desire to drive anyone there." But he doubled his appreciation. "I wish that some rich man or wise college president (if such there be) had in 1895, when you first drafted these lectures, emancipated you from all routine work, freed your powers, and given you unlimited mechanical service and permitted you to devote your talent to

[16] Charles A. Beard, "A Challenge to Windbags," *New Republic*, Aug. 11, 1926, 344.

[17] Jameson to Beard, Aug. 10, 1926, in Donnan and Stock, eds., *Correspondence of Jameson*, 319–20; Charles Henry Lincoln, *The Revolutionary Movement in Pennsylvania, 1760–1776* (Philadelphia, 1901); Robert Gough, "Charles H. Lincoln, Carl Becker, and the Origins of the Dual-Revolution Thesis," *William and Mary Quarterly*, 3d ser. 38 (1981): 97–109.

the theme of the book. . . . If that had been done we should now have at least one great historical work in America lifted above 'was uns alle bandigt das Gemeine.'" He ended by agreeing "that there is a lot of embattled nonsense in the chatter about old schools and new."[18]

Beard's reaction was based on who Jameson was and on the gulf between them. Beard, the iconoclast, had become the consummate gadfly. As author of *An Economic Interpretation of the Constitution* (1913), he had incurred the wrath of conservatives, including the trustees of Columbia University, who misread the book—as have so many scholars since—as indicting the pocketbook motives of the Founding Fathers and questioning their sincerity and patriotism. In 1917 he had resigned from Columbia to protest the firing of two political opponents of the war from the faculty. In 1926 a gentleman farmer on his Connecticut diary farm, he and his wife, Mary Ritter Beard, were in the final stages of their monumental two-volume *Rise of American Civilization* (1927), with its breathtaking, Olympian economic interpretation of the sweep of American history. A public intellectual, he published his review in the organ of the "new liberalism" to which he was a regular contributor.[19]

By contrast, Jameson at sixty-seven in 1926 was at the peak of the American historical establishment he had helped bring into being. Recipient of the first Ph.D. in history from Johns Hopkins University in 1882, Jameson was a founder of the American Historical Association (AHA), its president in 1907, and managing editor of the *American Historical Review* from 1895 to 1901 and 1905 to 1928. After teaching for twenty-three years at Hopkins, Brown, and the University of Chicago, in 1905 Jameson became the second director of the Carnegie Institution's Bureau (later Department) of Historical Research in Washington. He served there for twenty-two years, until 1927 (continuing as managing editor of the *American Historical Review*), and then served as chief of manuscripts at the Library of Congress until his death in 1937. Over his lifetime there was not a major institutional historical project in American history—*The Dictionary of American*

[18] Beard to Jameson, Aug. 14, 1926, John Franklin Jameson Papers, Box 59, Manuscript Division, Library of Congress, kindly provided by Morey D. Rothberg. See Donnan and Stock, eds., *Correspondence of Jameson*, 320, for an excerpt. The only prior exchange between the two was in 1914 over a review Beard thought was marked by "personal animus" (Beard to Jameson, Oct. 8, 1914, and Jameson to Beard, Oct. 10, 1914, Jameson Papers, Box 279).

[19] Richard Hofstadter, *The Progressive Historians: Turner, Beard, Parrington* (New York, 1968), chap. 6; for Beard's writings, see Howard K. Beale, ed., *Charles Beard: An Appraisal* (Lexington, KY, 1954), 265–86.

Biography, the National Historical Publications Commission, the National Archives—that did not bear his mark. He was Mr. History, a tall, dignified, somewhat austere man with a neatly trimmed beard who wore a winged collar.[20]

Professionalizing American history came at a price. As Peter Novick has demonstrated, Jameson "drove out the amateurs" with a vengeance. He not only "turned the profession over to academics"—as opposed to the patricians, antiquarians, and social scientists who had dominated it—but to two or three dozen professors in half a dozen elite universities in the Northeast who in 1907 could not even abide the founding of the Mississippi Valley Historical Association (now the Organization of American Historians).[21] Jameson managed the *American Historical Review* in an autocratic style and dominated the AHA to such an extent that he became a principal target of an insurgency in 1913–15 opposed to "an oligarchy" and "an Eastern establishment" and favoring a more democratic governance and ownership of the *Review* by the AHA. Jameson later fobbed off the rebellion as an "interesting tempest in a teapot," but at the time he devoted enormous energy to quelling it. Beginning in 1917, each summer for twenty years Jameson convened a private "convivium historicum" at a New England resort to set policy for the profession. He learned how to reform in order to conserve, a tactic a later AHA establishment repeated in 1969 to quell a far more serious rebellion.[22]

Politically Jameson was at first a mugwump, then a conservative Progressive in tune with Teddy Roosevelt and Woodrow Wilson, whom he

[20] Higham, *History*, 20–25. For a brief biography, see Richard Schrader, "J. Franklin Jameson," in Clyde N. Wilson, ed., *Twentieth-Century American Historians* (Detroit, 1983), 236–40; for brief articles by fourteen contributors, see Ruth Anna Fisher and William Lloyd Fox, eds., *J. Franklin Jameson: A Tribute* (Washington, DC, 1965); for a chronological bibliography of Jameson's writings by Donald Mugridge, see Fisher and Fox, eds., *J. Franklin Jameson: A Tribute*, 103–37, expanded in Rothberg and Goggin, eds., *Selected Essays*, 355–57; Morey D. Rothberg, "'To Set a Standard of Workmanship and Compel Men to Conform to It': John Franklin Jameson as Editor of the *American Historical Review*," *American Historical Review* 89 (1984): 957–75.

[21] Peter Novick, *That Noble Dream: The "Objectivity Question" and the American Historical Profession* (Cambridge, UK, 1988), 183–85; Mary Furner, *Advocacy and Objectivity: A Crisis in the Professionalization of American Social Science, 1865–1905* (Lexington, KY, 1975).

[22] Ray Allen Billington, "Tempest in Clio's Teapot: The American Historical Association's Rebellion of 1915," *American Historical Review* 78 (1973): 348–69; Billington, *Frederick Jackson Turner: Historian, Scholar, Teacher* (New York, 1973), 338–43; for the "convivium historicum," see Jameson to "Dear Colleague," Aug. 10, 1934, Jameson Papers. "This annual gathering of professors of history (taking place for the 18th time, I think) will be held. . . . This notice and invitation is sent to all 'full professors' of history in New England and adjacent parts."

especially admired. He was a Brahmin by adoption. His social values, captured by Morey D. Rothberg with exquisite skill, were those of a New England, Anglo-Saxon elitist; he was anxious in the 1880s about the hordes of working-class immigrants from southern and eastern Europe and fearful in the 1890s of the Populists as spokesmen for the "unintelligent farmers" (as he was of the Shaysites in the 1780s for their "plebeian" and "lawless insurrection").[23] He had a touch of genteel anti-Semitism and of noblesse oblige to African Americans. He published an article by W. E. B. Du Bois in the *American Historical Review* in 1907 (the only article by a black person to appear in that journal until John Hope Franklin's presidential address in the 1970s). But Jameson, although the grandson of an abolitionist, was self-righteous when Du Bois requested that he capitalize "Negro."[24]

In his politics his brand of Progressivism was very different from Beard's, contrary to the facile critics of the 1950s who lumped historians of that era in a single Progressive political stereotype (even while scholars were rapidly revising it). If young Charles Beard taught worker's education courses in London, was a founder of the labor college Ruskin Hall, and campaigned in New York City for the Jewish socialist Morris Hillquit on the Lower East Side, young Jameson in Baltimore recoiled from the urban masses at political rallies and from a Jewish candidate he found loud and vulgar. If Beard brought down the wrath of Columbia's wealthy trustees for his iconoclasm, Jameson was appointed a department chairman at Chicago at a time when such appointments had to be acceptable to John D. Rockefeller and then became the head of a department in Andrew Carnegie's Institution and a fund-raiser par excellence among wealthy philanthropists. Jameson defended academic freedom at Brown.[25] In World War I, while Beard supported both the war and the right to dissent from it, Jameson unabashedly fine-tuned the *American Historical Review* to patriotism. With other Progressives, he enlisted in George Creel's Committee on Public Information, where he was responsible for authenticating *The German*

[23] Rothberg and Goggin, eds., *Selected Essays*, 29, 56–57, 227, 228.

[24] Jameson to W. E. B. Du Bois, July 22, 1910, in Donnan and Stock, eds., *Correspondence of Jameson*, 133. W. E. B. Du Bois, "Reconstruction and Its Benefits," *American Historical Review* 15 (1910): 781–99. See also August Meier and Elliott Rudwick, "J. Franklin Jameson, Carter G. Woodson, and the Foundations of Black Historiography," *American Historical Review* 89 (1974): 1005–15.

[25] Morey D. Rothberg, "In the 1890s . . . a young professor named Jameson initiated graduate study in history and struck a blow for academic freedom," *Brown Alumni Monthly* (May 1987): 18–22, 29.

Bolshevik Conspiracy, "a pseudohistorical certification of manifestly forged documents."[26] Thus, if Beard was in a wing of Progressivism "which shaded off into reformist socialism,"[27] Jameson was in the centralizing, professionalizing wing, reforming in order to conserve the system from threats of radicalism.

Yet Jameson was complex. He had an intellectual passion for social history that linked him to Beard and the "New History" of James Harvey Robinson. The terms "social" and "economic" were then used loosely; well into the twentieth century universities offered courses in the "social and economic history" of the United States or medieval Europe. In graduate school Jameson was smitten with the European and English scholars who suggested the potential of the field, especially by Henry Thomas Buckle and Hippolyte A. Taine. In one of his first lectures as an instructor at Hopkins in 1885 he expressed his critique of conventional history in classical imagery: "Our political histories have for the most part been Iliads; they are filled with the deeds of chieftains . . . while the well-greaved Achaians stand in their ranks unnoticed and unsung." Later he used the same passionate rhetoric of others who discovered this gap: "No view is truthful that leaves out of account ideals which animated these toiling millions." There was no "paucity" of sources; he counseled a young scholar to do the history of "the less articulate classes" for colonial America.[28]

At Hopkins he took from Herbert Baxter Adams's seminars the canons of the new scientific history—mastery of the documents, analysis, presentation in scientific monographs or journal articles, and the eventual assembling of these "bricks" into works of synthesis. But he was impatient with Adams's "germ theory" of the evolution of American institutions from Germany and Anglo-Saxon England. He had arrived at a frontier interpretation of American history at about the same time as Frederick Jackson Turner. In fact, Jameson's unpublished lectures of 1885 and 1891 anticipated Turner's "Significance of the Frontier" paper of 1893, and his own 1895 lecture at Barnard, "The West in the American Revolution," was as rhapsodic about the influence of the frontier as anything Turner ever wrote. The timing suggests that Jameson, who left Hopkins in the fall of 1888, and Turner, who received his degree there in 1890, had developed their ideas

[26] Novick, *That Noble Dream*, 64, 519, 521, quotation at 124.

[27] Ibid., 96; Hofstadter, *Progressive Historians*, chap. 5.

[28] J. Franklin Jameson, "An Introduction to the Study of the Constitutional and Political History of the States," in Rothberg and Goggin, eds., *Selected Essays*, 18, 24; Jameson to Caroline Hazard, Oct. 8, 1926, in Donnan and Stock, eds., *Correspondence of Jameson*, 320.

concurrently. Jameson consistently was an admirer of Turner's "fruitful" mind and brought him into the inner circle of the AHA.[29]

Jameson's view of the American Revolution also owed much to the imperial school of historians taking shape in the 1890s in a mood of Anglo-American rapprochement that was consummated in World War I. Like them, he was steeped in English and European history and cool to George Bancroft's patriot-charged narrative. The imperial scholars—George Louis Beer, Herbert L. Osgood, and later Charles M. Andrews and Lawrence Henry Gipson—were trying to look dispassionately at the Revolution from the vantage point of Britain and the loyalists. A major part of Jameson's first lecture in 1895 (given again in 1920 but abandoned in 1925) was devoted to rehabilitating the loyalists. In centering his attention on internal American developments, however, he clearly parted company with the imperial school.[30]

With the recent publication of Jameson's early lectures of 1885, 1890, and 1891, and the only two 1895 lectures at Barnard that have survived, it is possible to see how Jameson's prior scholarship fed into *The American Revolution as a Social Movement*, the name he originally gave to his 1895 lectures. The states provided the framework as he developed the constitutional and political history of the colonial and Revolutionary eras (1885), the history of political parties (1890), and a constitutional and political history of the South (1891). He began with constitutions and laws, but by 1891 he was dealing with the subjects that were to become central in 1895—entail and primogeniture, the separation of church and state, the suffrage, land policy. He was also discovering intense political conflict. Massachusetts, he concluded, experienced "a social as well as a political revolution, new strata everywhere came to the surface." In Virginia he focused on the "radical reformers," looking through the lens of Jefferson's memoirs at the disestablishment of the church and reforms of the land system. His studies of the South were suffused with a sense of class but strangely devoid of the presence of slavery. In his research, judging by internal evidence, he worked outward from politics into the society not through any systematic

[29] J. Franklin Jameson, "Lectures on the Constitutional and Political History of the South" (1891), and Jameson, "The American Revolution as a Social Movement: Lectures on Slavery and the West" (1895), in Rothberg and Goggin, eds., *Selected Essays*, 62–165, 203–30; for the origins of the frontier thesis, see Lee Benson, *Turner and Beard: American Historical Writing Reconsidered* (New York, 1960), parts 1 and 2; Billington, *Frederick Jackson Turner*, chap. 5.

[30] Rothberg and Goggin, introduction to Rothberg and Goggin, eds., *Selected Essays*, xxvii–xlvii.

investigation but through such sources as the diary of Devereux Jarrett or David Ramsay's contemporary history.[31]

In 1895 his six lectures, built on this array of incompletely shaped essays on state polity and parties, moved squarely into social and economic history. For the next decade he seems to have done no new research on these topics. At Chicago (1901–5), where he taught graduate courses on the constitutions of the states and on political parties, he very likely embellished his earlier lectures, finding new examples. After 1905, in his new position at the Carnegie, he did no sustained research on the themes he began in the 1890s. But he now had a scholarly institution in which to fulfill his passion for social history.[32]

In 1907 he devoted his presidential address to the AHA to a plea to study religion for its potential to reach "the lives of out of the way communities or of inarticulate classes not represented in literature. . . . Millions have felt an interest in religion where thousands have felt an interest in literature or philosophy, in music or art."[33] In 1912 he made an ardent plea to the Carnegie trustees for the utility of social history. "What information regarding the past," he asked, "will be demanded by a socialized, probably in some sense socialistic America?"—using the term in the loose way many contemporaries applied it, as reform that expanded the role of government. The "drum and trumpet" historian "has his place." But "social and economic history will surely assume a greater place than political history. Where hitherto men have interrogated the past concerning the doings of generals and politicians, they will be more prone to interrogate it concerning"—and here he reeled off a list of topics that "the new history" was addressing—"the holdings of public and private land, the course of prices, the migration of settlers and of crop areas, the rise of trade unions, the development of new religions, the status of the negro, the advance of education or of missions, or of the spirit of toleration."[34]

At the Carnegie a major thrust of the projects he initiated and supervised was social: a guide to archives for religious history, multivolume documentary collections on the slave trade and the laws on slavery, a collection

[31] Jameson, "American Revolution as a Social Movement," in Rothberg and Goggin, eds., *Selected Essays*, 203–30.

[32] Jameson letters, 1901–5, in Donnan and Stock, eds., *Correspondence of Jameson*, 78–89, and letters, 1915–24, in ibid., 176–302.

[33] Jameson, "The American Acta Sanctorum," in Rothberg and Goggin, eds., *Selected Essays*, 166–82, quotation at 179.

[34] Jameson, "The Future Uses of History," in Rothberg and Goggin, eds., *Selected Essays*, 314–15.

of sources on privateering and piracy (which he himself edited), Charles O. Paullin's *Atlas of the Historical Geography of the United States*, which mapped, besides political boundaries, the distribution of populations, land patterns, and a host of social factors.[35]

Thus, in the long interim between 1895 and 1925, while he did not pursue the social history of the Revolution per se, his intellectual activities contributed to the 1925 lectures. As managing editor of the *American Historical Review* he stayed on top of the scholarship of the Revolution, assigning book reviews, reviewing all submissions, and editing documents. In 1925, in response to a query from Britain, he could evaluate in detail the work of a dozen major colonialists.[36] And if he had not himself turned the manuscripts, through the Carnegie projects he had a perspective on a range of social themes.

Why did it take Jameson thirty years to revise and publish his 1895 lectures? The subject is worth pursuing for what it reveals about the way historians are shaped by their life experiences and capacities, the canons of the profession, and the politics of their time.[37] Rothberg offers the insightful suggestion that trapped between his conservative political values and his passion for social history, Jameson "suppressed" the lectures, instead promoting the study of social history by others.[38] He may have been trapped in three other ways. In the late 1890s the book probably fell victim to his own intense careerism, one of the bitter fruits of the new academic professionalism. Jameson's early academic career was less than brilliant. He was an "associate," then an instructor at Hopkins for six years after receiving his degree in 1882 and published little. Brown, where he landed his first job, was then a small Baptist school. He was in pursuit of a job at Barnard when he gave the lectures there in 1895. Barnard made him an offer, but Jameson took umbrage at the salary and turned it down. Immediately after, he was

[35] Rothberg and Goggin, introduction to Rothberg and Goggin, eds., *Selected Essays*, xxxv; Morey D. Rothberg, "The Brahmin as Bureaucrat: J. Franklin Jameson at the Carnegie Institution of Washington, 1905–1928," *Public Historian* 8 (1986): 47–60; John Tracy Ellis, "American Religious History," and John K. Wright, "The Atlas of the Historical Geography of the United States," in Fisher and Fox, eds., *J. Franklin Jameson: A Tribute*, 9–23, 66–79.

[36] Jameson to J. Holland Rose, Sept. 19, 1925, in Donnan and Stock, eds., *Correspondence of Jameson*, 311.

[37] Ray Allen Billington, "Why Some Scholars Rarely Write History: A Case Study of Frederick Jackson Turner," *Mississippi Valley Historical Review* 50 (1963): 3–27.

[38] Morey D. Rothberg, "J. Franklin Jameson and the Creation of *The American Revolution Considered as a Social Movement*," in Ronald Hoffman and Peter J. Albert, eds., *The Transforming Hand of Revolution: Reconsidering the American Revolution as a Social Movement* (Charlottesville, VA, 1995), 1–26.

appointed the first managing editor of the new *American Historical Review*, then a part-time job that he held while at Brown. Still in the job market, in 1901 he was appointed head of the University of Chicago's department of history. He helped plan the Department of Historical Research at the Carnegie Institution with himself in mind and was disappointed when someone else was appointed as the first director. *The American Revolution as a Social Movement* was too bold and too inchoate a book to have helped his career between 1895 and 1905.[39]

He may also have been trapped, secondly, by the conventions of publication of the new scientific history: presentation for an audience of specialists either as an annotated monograph or article. The interpretive analytical essay, a form Turner pioneered in 1893 in "The Significance of the Frontier," was not yet established.[40] In 1895 Jameson seems not to have been prepared to commit himself to the kind of sustained research in primary sources necessary to document so innovative a thesis. He had never published a monograph; his doctoral thesis on the origin of municipal institutions in New York City, in the early Hopkins mode when dissertations were less formidable than they later became, was no more than an extended essay.[41] At Brown he gave lectures to supplement his income, organized a collection of essays by others, and prepared a potboiler, the *Dictionary of United States History*. His only published book, *The History of Historical Writing in America* (1891), was a collection of deftly turned lectures on major historians.[42] But in none of these efforts had he brought a large, diverse mass of primary materials under control. Nor was he prepared to issue a rousing call to arms for the study of his subject, as had Turner. Had he risked publication in the late 1890s, he would have been out on a limb. The landmark monographs of the Progressive interpretation of the Revolution did not appear until the first two decades of the twentieth century.[43]

[39] Jameson letters, 1888–1901, in Donnan and Stock, eds., *Correspondence of Jameson*, 44–77.

[40] Hofstadter, *Progressive Historians*, chap. 1.

[41] Donnan and Stock claim the subject of the thesis was the common lands of Easthampton (*Correspondence of Jameson*, 25n. 50); I am indebted to Morey Rothberg for correcting this (Rothberg, conversation with author, Feb. 1993).

[42] J. Franklin Jameson, *The History of Historical Writing in America* (New York, 1891); Jameson had also written *William Usselinx, Founder of the Dutch and Swedish West India Companies* (New York, 1987) and edited two volumes in the series *Original Narratives of American History*, 19 vols. (New York, 1906–7), for which he was the general editor.

[43] Lincoln, *Revolutionary Movement in Pennsylvania* (1901); Carl L. Becker, *The History of Political Parties in the Province of New York, 1760–1776* (Madison, WI, 1909); H. J. Eckenrode, *The Revolution in Virginia* (Boston, 1916); Charles A. Beard, *An Economic Interpretation of the Constitution of the United States* (New York, 1913); Beard, *Economic Origins of Jeffersonian Democracy*

Jameson was also caught, thirdly, in a trap of his own making, namely, his perception of himself as a historian. "I know I am not good in many branches of historical work," he confided to his best friend in 1903, at age forty-four, after two years at the University of Chicago. "I could never be an excellent historian, I am not a first-rate teacher, I am not making a success of my present position. My own talent, if I know myself, lies in the direction of Heuristik," a term he used to mean suggesting lines of inquiry for other scholars to pursue. Not until 1905 did he achieve the job he had created to suit his talents—director of the Carnegie's new research department.[44]

After fifteen years at the Carnegie Jameson defined himself as "an historical powder monkey." "That is what I am for," he eagerly replied to a request for bibliographic help from the ailing Woodrow Wilson in 1922, "to help real historians . . . to pass forward ammunition to historical gunners, or gunmen." The self-demeaning answer was poignant—as if exercising scholarly judgment as editor of a journal and initiating massive publications and archival projects was not functioning as a "real historian." He had internalized the self-abasing hierarchy of values of the profession that assigned the highest status to publication of a book. "You know I have never written a book," he said ruefully to Allan Nevins some years later. He probably accepted Princeton's offer to do the 1925 lectures (which required publication) because it was as close as he would get to producing what the profession would accept as a book. And he turned to the American Revolution as a social movement because it was the only large subject that he had more or less laid out.[45]

Undoubtedly, if Jameson was not more conservative in 1925 than he was in 1895, he was more calculating. He was a consummate strategist who had learned how to anticipate and deflect criticism. He had watched the storm over Beard's economic interpretation of the Constitution; he was aware that Turner's lyricism about the frontier played better in Madison than in the Ivy League. Scarred in quelling the rebellion in the AHA, after 1920 he was in trouble at the Carnegie. The traditional skepticism among the natural scientists there toward history as a science was out in the open under a new director, a paleontologist, and was to lead the trustees to let Jameson

(New York, 1915); Arthur M. Schlesinger Sr., *The Colonial Merchants and the American Revolution* (New York, 1918).

[44] Jameson to Francis A. Christie, Mar. 6, 1903, in Donnan and Stock, eds., *Correspondence of Jameson*, 85–86.

[45] Jameson to Woodrow Wilson, May 12, 1922, in ibid., 270; Allan Nevins, "The Sage and the Young Man," in Fisher and Fox, eds., *J. Frederick Jameson: A Tribute*, 43.

go and close the Department of Historical Research in 1927. In 1925 Jameson may have felt he was under scrutiny. All of this, taken together, may account for the unmistakable caution in the lectures.[46]

He talked and wrote as if he was protecting his flanks from hidden adversaries. *The American Revolution as a Social Movement* of 1895 became *The American Revolution Considered as a Social Movement* in 1925. He reduced his interpretive thesis to a heuristic, that is, a suggestion to pursue a hypothesis. The revised title simply asked the reader to "consider" the American Revolution as a social movement. Of course, he never claimed it was a "social revolution" or an "internal revolution," a phrase Merrill Jensen turned in 1940. To Jameson it was a political revolution that "had important social consequences," softened still further to "some social consequences." He would be content, he said in a final retreat in closing, "if some who hear him are convinced that here is a field of study deserving further and deeper study."[47] The choice of the word "social" undoubtedly was also deliberate. The distinction between social and economic may have been vague, but Jameson knew how explosive Beard's analysis of the Founding Fathers had been, even after he tried to soften the blow by making the title *An Economic Interpretation of the Constitution*, implying it was one among other possible interpretations. Jameson's avoidance of documentation may also have been conscious; he thereby skirted the burden of the monograph for proof, turning to a genre, a short collection of reflective essays, that overcame the procrustean demands of "scientific" history.

Jameson may have been accurate in claiming to Beard that "everything that is a matter of doctrine was already in the text read in 1895."[48] Yet in condensing his 1895 lectures, as the two surviving drafts reveal, he pulled back from his sweeping claims. Slavery as an issue to which he devoted an entire lecture in 1895 he reduced to several pages. The argument was the same, stressing the positive gains of the Revolution, but the subject had lost its importance by eliminating the intense debate and was reduced to a minor episode in American history, as Jameson, Turner, and others in flight from the liberal commitments of abolitionism, the Civil War, and Reconstruction believed it should be. Jameson also eliminated his lyrical chapter on the West, retaining some of its argument here and there in his discussion of land and democracy; he saluted the frontiersman but abandoned

[46] Jameson letters, 1925–28, in Donnan and Stock, eds. *Correspondence of Jameson*, 303–31.

[47] Jameson, *American Revolution as a Social Movement*, 10–11.

[48] Jameson to Beard, Aug. 10, 1926, in Donnan and Stock, eds., *Correspondence of Jameson*, 319.

the original Turneresque tone. Most important of all, when Jameson told Beard that nothing had been written on the subject in the thirty years gone by, he was reading political history out of his interpretation: it was as if the work of Becker, Schlesinger, and Beard that had introduced the internal political dimension had no bearing on the Revolution as a social movement. By shunting aside politics (which had been uppermost in his history in the early 1890s), Jameson eliminated conflict from his analysis.

Yet two major political events of the intervening years impinged on Jameson, sharpening his analysis. World War I was on his mind, enabling him at several points to draw an important distinction between the influence of the war and the influence of the Revolution on late eighteenth-century America. So was the Russian Revolution, which he called "the greatest of all revolutions, the one destined evidently to be the most momentous in its consequences." He was emboldened in his interpretation of the "natural history" of revolution by the phases through which it had passed.[49] Thus, if in 1925 he adopted a strategy that in many ways retreated from 1895, he also tightened his argument by focusing on a single unifying theme, demonstrating at age sixty-six a grasp of the Revolution as a whole that had eluded him at age thirty-six.

3. Jameson's Achievement

What was Jameson's achievement in the context of the scholarship of his own time? It was both more and less than Beard recognized. Had Jameson published the lectures in 1895 soon after he had delivered them, conceivably his book might have had an effect on studies of the American Revolution comparable to Frederick Jackson Turner's "The Significance of the Frontier," delivered 1893. But then again, judging by the two lectures of 1895 that have survived, they would not have been as good a book as the lectures he released in 1925—focused, finely honed, and suggestive, rather than diffuse, sweeping, and strident. Coming as it did in the mid-1920s, the book was a coda to the meteoric works of Becker, Schlesinger, and Beard while it might have been a prologue. Yet Jameson accomplished something the other Progressive historians did not.

First, he shifted the focus of scholarly attention from the origins of the Revolution to the results. Up to then all "schools" focused on the origins. Andrews, to Jameson the "chief authority on the colonial period," focused

[49] Jameson, *American Revolution as a Social Movement*, 11.

exclusively on the imperial relationship. Gipson, his successor, took thirteen volumes to get to 1776.[50] Schlesinger took the colonial merchants only through the making of the Revolution, while Becker presented the "struggle for who shall rule at home" in New York only from 1765 to 1776. Turner, while not concerned with the Revolution per se, called attention to the importance of land, sectional conflict, and western state-making in the post-Revolutionary era. Among the Progressives, Beard alone focused frontally on the results, treating the contest over the Constitution and the Hamiltonian-Jeffersonian conflicts as the capstone of the Revolution.

Second, Jameson dared to analyze the American Revolution in the generic category of revolutions. "Is there such a thing as a natural history of revolutions" through various "stages?" he asked. He drew on three revolutions for his answer. "The English Revolution" of the 1640s (his phrase) at first was "the affair of moderate statesmen, like Pym and Hampden"; then it "fell into the hands of men like Cromwell"; and finally, in the Commonwealth, "men of far more advanced views, . . . radicals had come into control of the movement." As for the French Revolution, "everyone knows how its history is marked by distinct successive periods." And he had no fear in 1925 of adding to his roster the Russian Revolution, which had passed from one stage to another, transforming Russian society by 1925 "to an extent which no one would in 1913 have dreamed to be possible."[51] Jameson never explored the "radicals" of the American Revolution and disassociated himself from the Jacobins of the French Revolution (but felt no need to make clear he was not a Communist). Yet he clearly attempted to rescue the American Revolution from conservative filiopietists who by the 1890s, as Michael G. Kammen points out, had reduced it to a War for Independence and a unique American experience.

Third, without denigrating the leaders of the Revolution, Jameson shifted attention from elites to the "plain people." True, he defined them solely as small-property-holding farmers, distancing himself from what he called "the mob and rabble" of the cities, and he had nothing to say about slaves, women, or the propertyless rural classes. But Beard and Schlesinger studied elites, and Schlesinger and Becker focused on merchants and middling leaders who mobilized mobs. Jameson was closer to Turner and scholars of the South who dealt with a sectional clash of frontier and

[50] Jameson to Rose, Sept. 19, 1925, in Donnan and Stock, eds., *Correspondence of Jameson*, 311; Lawrence Henry Gipson, *The British Empire before the American Revolution*, 14 vols. (New York, 1936–79).

[51] Jameson, *American Revolution as a Social Movement*, 11.

tidewater aristocracy. And if he was more comfortable framing his history around abstract issues, he made it possible for others to study the people themselves—to go from antislavery to the slaves, from religious liberty to the Baptists, from the expanding economy to the rising middling men.

Finally, Jameson tried to grasp the American Revolution in a holistic way. That "all the varied activities of men in the same country and period have intimate relations with each other, and that one cannot obtain a satisfactory view of any one of them by considering it apart from the others" was not a self-evident truth to historians.[52] In flight from Becker's factional and class conflict and Beard's economic-interest conflict, Jameson played down political activity but did not jettison it. Schlesinger took social history in the direction of history with the politics left out—not Jameson, whose thesis rested on the impact of the political on the social. By distinguishing his thesis from the more political, conflict-driven theses of the other Progressives, he won more of a hearing for the American Revolution considered as a social movement.

If there was a certain pose in Jameson's tentativeness, there was also a certain wisdom. He was asking scholars to "interrogate the past" with questions they had not asked in fields of study that did not exist. His book was an invitation to an inquiry, a door-opener in the study of American history.

II. Progressives and Counter-Progressives

4. The Progressive Historians

To enter the domain of historiography one has to pass through the thorny thicket in which scholars are sorted out by "schools." The dangers in such exercises have been persistently deplored by scholars of almost all persuasions. Jameson's lament to Beard in 1926 of the tendency rigidly to classify historians is recurrent. Four decades later Merrill Jensen was convinced "that the moment we start pasting labels on historians and groups of historians mental rigor mortis sets in." By 1974 Jensen thought it would be in order to abandon "such labels as 'Progressive,' 'consensus,' 'new conservative,' 'neo-whig,' 'New Left' and the like." Writing at the same time, Bernard Bailyn was critical of the "uncontrollable inner dynamic" of bibliographic essays on the Revolution in which "trends or schools are detected and criticized before they are fully developed" and "general interpretations

[52] Ibid., 100.

are pounced upon before the ink has dried." Moreover, the entire process, as Richard Morris complained, frequently leads to distortion, to setting up straw men to knock down.[53]

Yet for all the pitfalls of bad historiography—pigeonholing, dismissive labeling, and distortion—it remains true, as Edmund Morgan, another foe of lumping, remarked in 1976, that "historical understanding of the Revolution has proceeded in a series of reactions, one generation emphasizing problems and espousing views that the previous generation seemed to neglect or reject." Morgan's contention that "the successive reactions have carried us to new levels of perception" smacks of the whig history he has deplored. "The so-called consensus historians," Morgan argued, "could scarcely have reached their own understanding of the Revolution without attention to the Progressives who emphasized the internal conflicts of the Revolution. Similarly New Left historians, while returning to the themes of conflict have also built on the work of those with whom they disagree." Yet it is reassuring to be reminded that "since the time needed to produce a historian is a good deal less than a lifespan, a lively dialogue has been possible among generations of scholars."[54] It is only unfortunate that more scholars have not accepted Morgan's invitation to a dialogue and that leading historians were often more interested in closing doors than in opening new ones.

For a quarter of a century after Jameson's book appeared in 1926, his thesis stayed alive largely on the strength of the Progressive paradigms for American history as a whole advanced by Beard, Turner, and Vernon Parrington and on the strength of the Progressive synthesis of the Revolution. He was the arch in the bridge between the interpretations of the origins of the Revolution, introduced by Becker and Schlesinger, and its consequences, offered by Beard. While Jameson may have "thrilled younger scholars," as John Higham writes, "by publishing an almost radical economic and social interpretation of the American Revolution," there was no Jameson school. He had no graduate students to pursue or test his insights, and as the powerful dean of the historical profession, he had few challengers. Indeed, judging by the number of copies of his book sold over

[53] Merrill Jensen, "The American People and the American Revolution," *Journal of American History* 57 (1970): 10; Jensen, *The American Revolution within America* (New York, 1974), 221–24; Bernard Bailyn, "Lines of Force in Recent Writings about the American Revolution" (paper presented at the Fourteenth International Congress of Historical Sciences, San Francisco, 1975), 3–4; Richard B. Morris, *The American Revolution Reconsidered* (New York, 1967), 177.

[54] Morgan, *Challenge of the American Revolution*, 174–75.

twenty-five years—a scant 1,356—one wonders how many scholars read Jameson; then again in those quaint days before paperbacks, teachers put required reading on library reserve shelves. But over the 1930s and early 1940s scholars tested a number of his themes. And by the end of the interwar period a number of works synthesized the results of the Revolution, carrying his argument in different directions.[55]

The first generation of Progressive historians, Jameson's contemporaries, publicized his thesis but contributed little to exploring his hypotheses. Jameson's thesis passed rapidly into both the stream of scholarship and the popular perception of the American Revolution through Charles and Mary Beard's magisterial *Rise of American Civilization* (1927). Over time it sold at least 130,000 copies and shaped the outlook of several generations of left and liberal intellectuals; in the late 1930s the *New Republic* ran a series of articles on "the books that changed the world" in which Beard was considered along with Thorstein Veblen and John Dewey. The Beards, in six well-turned pages in which they uncharacteristically acknowledged Jameson and his work by name, summed up "a far-reaching transformation in the land system" and the "shocks" felt by the clergy as well as the landed gentry. "In nearly every branch of enlightened activity, in every sphere of liberal thought," the Beards wrote, "the American Revolution marked the opening of a new humane epoch." "If a balance sheet is struck," they concluded, "then it is seen that the American Revolution was more than a war on England. It was in truth an economic, social, and intellectual transformation of prime significance."[56]

For the other leading Progressive historians, Turner and Parrington, Jameson's book came too late to be absorbed into their scholarship. But they did not need him; they sustained Jameson. Frederick Jackson Turner (1861–1931) published little in the two decades before his death, but his collected essays on the frontier (1921) and his essays on sectionalism (1932) gave a long afterglow to the argument he had first advanced in 1893. His glorification of the traits of the frontiersmen and western influences on democracy sustained Jameson's rather Turnerian interpretation of the Revolution.[57] Vernon Louis Parrington in *Main Currents in American Thought*,

[55] Higham, *History*, 185; W. Stull Holt, "Who Reads the Best Histories?" *Mississippi Valley Historical Review* 40 (1954): 617.

[56] Charles A. Beard and Mary Beard, *The Rise of American Civilization*, 2 vols. (1927; reprint ed., New York, 1930), 1:291; Hofstadter, *Progressive Historians*, 291–96.

[57] Frederick Jackson Turner, "The Old West," in *The Frontier in American History* (New York, 1920), 67–125; Turner, *The Significance of Sections in American History* (New York, 1932).

published in 1927 but written some years before, had already reached the conclusion that the Revolution brought the triumph of "the republican" ideal over monarchy and aristocracy, and "out of this primary revolution came other revolutions, social and economic, made possible by the new republican freedom."[58]

Arthur M. Schlesinger Sr. and Carl L. Becker, who began their scholarship with pathbreaking monographs on the origins of the Revolution, evaded the Jameson question of transformation for the rest of their careers. Schlesinger admired Jameson: he introduced the 1956 paperback edition of the book as "an epoch-marking if not epic-making event," linking it to the publication in 1927 of the Beards' *Rise* and the first volume in his own *History of American Life* series in social history. But after his book on the merchants in 1918 and a few essays, Schlesinger did not return to the Revolution for more than thirty years. Then he elaborated the Progressive interpretation at its weakest point, the theme of propaganda. The first generation of Progressive historians, suspicious of ideas as rationalizations of interests and devoid of empathy with urban laboring classes, never rose above the conception of the people as "the mob," manipulated by the propaganda of whig leaders. Schlesinger was responsible for the metaphor likening the mob to "Frankenstein's monster," created by their betters but "impossible to control," an image that foreclosed scholarship on the subject. Thus, there was a logic to his devoting one of his last books to the newspaper war against Britain from 1764 to 1776, based on his old assumption that propaganda aroused the masses. In his *History of American Life* volumes Schlesinger took American history to the extreme of a depoliticized social history. "I thought it was a mistake to write social history with politics omitted," Becker wrote to him; "I never understood why politics is not social."[59]

Becker, for his part, took the Revolution in the direction of an intellectual history that left out both the politics and social history. After his

[58] Vernon Louis Parrington, *Main Currents in American Thought: An Interpretation of American Literature from the Beginnings to 1920*, 3 vols. (1927; reprint ed., New York, 1930), 1:190–93; Hofstadter, *Progressive Historians*, chaps. 10–11.

[59] Arthur M. Schlesinger Sr., introduction to Jameson, *American Revolution as a Social Movement*, vii–xii; Schlesinger, "The American Revolution," in *New Viewpoints in American History* (New York, 1922), 172; Schlesinger, *Prelude to Independence: The Newspaper War on Britain, 1764–1776* (New York, 1958); Carl L. Becker to Arthur M. Schlesinger Sr., Feb. 14, 1933, quoted in Novick, *That Noble Dream*, 178–79; Higham, *History*, 194–95.

1909 work on New York Becker suggested gingerly that his dual revolution thesis applied to other colonies. He dramatized his thesis brilliantly in "The Spirit of '76," an imaginative essay in the guise of a fictitious memoir of a conservative New York whig confronting a radical whig to his left and a loyalist aristocrat on his right. His forays into intellectual history produced a masterful analysis of the Declaration of Independence and another on the "climate of opinion" of eighteenth-century intellectual life, but almost all of his work ended the Revolution in 1776. Then from the mid-1930s on he devoted himself to well-honed essays defending the liberal democratic tradition confronted with totalitarianism and to espousing historical relativism. Self-defined as a historian of European intellectual history, he trained students who worked in European, rather than American, history.[60]

Gradually in the 1930s and early 1940s the mills of academic history ground out doctoral monographs taking up Jameson "heuristics." Not surprisingly, this afterglow of Progressive scholarship was bright at Columbia University, where Beard and the "New History" had flourished and where Schlesinger had done his thesis and Becker had studied. Evarts B. Greene, who had shifted from institutional to social history, directed a number of theses in the Revolutionary era, and Columbia appointed Allan Nevins, a warm admirer of Jameson whose solid 1924 book on the political history of the American states in the Revolutionary era anticipated Jameson but lacked his flair.[61] In addition, Columbia gave doctorates to a handful of Marxist students drawn to early American history in the 1930s.

One focus of Columbia dissertations was land policy in the Hudson Valley. Irving Mark established the long history of agrarian conflict between tenant and landlord that continued during the Revolution, and Harry B.

[60] Carl L. Becker, *The Eve of the Revolution* (New Haven, CT, 1918); Becker, *The Declaration of Independence: A Study in the History of Political Ideas* (New York, 1922); Becker, *The Spirit of '76 and Other Essays* (Washington, DC, 1927), 9–58; Becker, *The Heavenly City of the Eighteenth-Century Philosophers* (New Haven, CT, 1932); Milton M. Klein, "The Dilemma of Carl Becker," in Alden T. Vaughan and George A. Billias, eds., *Perspectives on Early American History: Essays in Honor of Richard B. Morris* (New York, 1973), 120–66. Burleigh T. Wilkins, in *Carl Becker: A Biographical Study in American Intellectual History* (Cambridge, MA, 1961), 121, summarizes Louis M. Hacker's criticism, "namely, that Becker was in effect a timid academician who always stopped on the *eve* of revolutions instead of following their entire course" (Hacker, "Historians of Revolution," *New Republic*, Jan. 8, 1936, 260–61).

[61] Allan Nevins, *The American States during and after the American Revolution, 1775–1789* (New York, 1924). Nevins reviewed Jameson's book very favorably in the *American Historical Review* (32 [1926–27]: 167–68), in a section entitled "Minor Notices," another sign of Jameson's self-deprecation.

Yoshpe found the distribution of confiscated land from loyalist landlords far less democratic than Jameson hypothesized. Postwar social and economic change was another theme. Sidney I. Pomerantz's book on New York City from 1783 to 1803 was a case study of the "leaven" of the Revolution in humanitarianism, social policy, religion, and culture. Jameson's third chapter on industry and commerce was fleshed out by Robert A. East's depiction of postwar business corporations, banks, and large-scale speculation. Others added dimensions missing in Jameson: the transformation of eighteenth-century deism from a gentlemen's cult to a popular movement, the emergence of a body of opinion about women, and the development of indentured servitude.[62]

With scholarship such as this available by the late 1930s and early 1940s scholars began producing syntheses of the transformations of the Revolution that were more empirically based and more tough-minded than Jameson's. Among them were Evarts P. Greene, "a scholar and gentleman of the older generation," as Richard Morris called him, and Curtis P. Nettels and Merle Curti, both second-generation Progressives. Greene's volume in the *History of American Life* series took synthesis in the direction Schlesinger promoted—social history with very little politics. Politics, while there, was lost in a catalog of information on social, economic, and intellectual subjects without any integrating themes stronger than growth, progress, and the development of an American nationality. Greene, who spoke of Jameson's volume as no more than "a suggestive brief survey," gave himself a broad canvas. He took nine chapters to survey prewar colonial society and culture to provide a base for measuring change, devoted two to the war, and then five to the postwar years. He fleshed out Jameson's themes but lost the thread. On the other hand, in summarizing social change he was more balanced than Jameson: "The young republic made some progress towards realizing the Revolutionary ideal of equality. . . . Yet the conservative classes were still strong. The antislavery efforts of Southern

[62] Irving Mark, *Agrarian Conflict in Colonial New York, 1711–1775* (New York, 1940); Harry B. Yoshpe, *The Disposition of Loyalist Estates in the Southern District of the State of New York* (New York, 1939); Sidney I. Pomerantz, *New York, an American City, 1783–1803: A Study of Urban Life* (New York, 1938); Robert A. East, *Business Enterprise in the American Revolutionary Era* (New York, 1938); Herbert Morais, *Deism in Eighteenth Century America* (New York, 1934); Mary S. Benson, *Women in Eighteenth-Century America: A Study of Opinion and Social Usage* (New York, 1935). For scholarship at other universities, see Tolles, "American Revolution Considered as a Social Movement."

liberals failed save in the prohibition of Negro importations by the border states. Property qualifications [to vote] though somewhat reduced, were still general, and Jefferson's efforts to equalize educational opportunities came to nil."[63]

By contrast Curtis P. Nettels, in *The Roots of American Civilization* (1938), a textbook that was more than a text, offered the first socioeconomic, conflict-oriented analysis of the colonial era as well as the origins and results of the Revolution. In the chapter "The Revolution Within"—the first use of this telling phrase—Nettels acknowledged Jameson's book as "the best general discussion of themes of this chapter." But unlike Jameson, Nettels depicted a sharp conflict between a "democratic or popular party" and "a conservative party," linking struggles over forming the new state governments, the currency question, and the distribution of land. More class-oriented than Jameson, Nettels recognized that "most of the gains of democracy were made at the expense of British interests and Loyalists rather than at the expense of the conservatives who supported the revolutionary cause. The latter held their own."[64]

Merle Curti, in *The Growth of American Thought* (1943), a book marking the coming of age of American intellectual history, presented a new synthesis of the "thought and feeling" of the Revolutionary era that Jameson had not grasped. Curti was the epitome of the second generation of Progressive historians; a student of both Turner and Schlesinger, he thanked Beard for his "searching criticisms" of his manuscript. But unlike his mentors, Curti elevated the history of ideas, reaching down especially to ideas of the "plain people" that had eluded even Parrington. Using a rich array of ephemeral original sources, he called attention to such neglected grassroots spokesmen of the Revolutionary era as Ethan Allen and William Manning. His analytical framework took a sense of conflict from Beard rather than Jameson. There was "a revolutionary shift in emphasis" and an "expanding enlightenment" followed by a "conservative reaction." The

[63] Richard B. Morris, "History over Time," *William and Mary Quarterly*, 3d ser. 41 (1984): 455–63; Evarts B. Greene, *The Revolutionary Generation, 1763–1790* (New York, 1943), 328–29 and chaps. 11–16; see also Richard B. Morris, ed., *The Era of the American Revolution: Studies Inscribed to Evarts Boutell Greene* (New York, 1939), a collection of essays, some of which showed "class overtones in the Revolution," by Morris, Morais, Pomerantz, East, Michael Kraus, and others.

[64] Curtis P. Nettels, *The Roots of American Civilization: A History of American Colonial Life* (New York, 1938), chap. 24, quotation at 386; Nettels, *The Money Supply of the American Colonies before 1720* (Madison, WI, 1934), his doctoral thesis; for Nettels's acerbic commentary on Harvard historians in 1937 and his radical politics, see Novick, *That Noble Dream*, 181–82, 244–45.

Revolution in Curti's judgment "did not democratize American intellectual life," but "it did much to democratize American thought."[65]

These three early syntheses summed up one era of inconclusive scholarship but could not anticipate another. They were harbingers of the postwar era in which the University of Wisconsin overtook Columbia as the center of the second generation of Progressive historians and as the creator of a third. Nettels taught at the University of Wisconsin from 1933 to 1944; Curti, from 1942 to 1968 in a department whose leading Americanists were all Progressives.[66]

At Wisconsin (1944–76), Merrill Jensen was regarded as "the leading, currently active spokesman for the Becker-Beard school," as E. James Ferguson, a student long close to him, wrote in 1975. "Jensen does not repudiate this categorization, but he is rather amused by it; he does not regard himself as a member of any school. . . . Jensen over a long period has merely stuck, as he would say, to recording the facts, aware of but undistracted by shifting fashions of interpretation." To Ferguson he was "essentially pragmatic, disdainful of ideology" yet "vaguely populist, combining a sympathy for the common man with a realistic sense of human motives and a hardheaded recognition of how the loaves and fishes are divided." Born and bred in rural South Dakota, where he taught a one-room grade school, Jensen received his B.A. and M.A. at the University of Washington and his Ph.D. in 1934 from Wisconsin, where Nettels was his teacher.[67]

For forty years Jensen made the issue of internal transformation and the divisions within the Revolutionary generation the focus of his scholarship. He had his students read Jameson, but he and they drew their problematics from Becker and Beard, not Jameson. "Even the historians who have seen the Revolution as a social movement," he wrote in criticism of Jameson, "have not tied that movement to the political history of the times."[68] In the

[65] Merle Curti, *The Growth of American Thought* (New York, 1943), chaps. 6–8, quotations at 153, 129; for Curti's radical politics, see Novick, *That Noble Dream*, 242, 247, 318–19, 325, 346, 369.

[66] Curtis P. Nettels, "History Out of Wisconsin," *Wisconsin Magazine of History* 39 (1955–56): 113–24. In this brag sheet of scholars who had studied, received their Ph.D.s, or taught at Wisconsin and had made their mark on the profession, for early American history there were Turner, Becker (a student of Turner), Orin G. Libby, Nettels, Jensen, Curti, and Robert E. Brown. For the spirit of postwar Progressivism, see Paul Buhle, ed., *History and the New Left: Madison, Wisconsin, 1950–1970* (Philadelphia, 1990).

[67] E. James Ferguson, "Merrill Jensen: A Personal Comment," in James Kirby Martin, ed., *The Human Dimensions of Nation Making: Essays on Colonial and Revolutionary America* (Madison, WI, 1976), 5–6.

[68] Merrill Jensen, *The Articles of Confederation: An Interpretation of the Social-Constitutional History of the American Revolution, 1774–1781* (Madison, WI, 1940), 5; the book sold two thousand

first phase of his scholarship Jensen dealt with the Confederation era, first the shaping of the Articles of Confederation adopted in 1781, then the fruits of the Revolution in the period from 1781 to 1789. His consistent goal was to rescue the period from historians who looked at it through Federalist eyes from the hindsight of the victorious Constitution of 1787.

In 1940 Jensen introduced the phrase "the internal revolution" and stayed with the concept, if not the term, which he rephrased in 1974 as *The American Revolution within America*. Jameson's milder social interpretation was confused with this sweeping concept; Jameson was caught in the heavy cross fire leveled against Jensen by his critics. Jensen argued that the political revolution of 1776 was "predominantly an internal revolution carried on by the masses of the people against the local aristocracy," achieved by victories of "radicals" over "conservatives." In effect, he added an element of class conflict to Becker's thesis and extended it colony by colony. The "radical ascendancy was of brief duration, but while it lasted an attempt was made to write democratic ideals and theories of government into the laws and constitutions of the American states. Fulfillment was not complete, . . . and once independence was won, the conservatives soon united in undoing, so far as they could, such political and economic democracy as had resulted from the war." The major part of the book was devoted to the writing and ratification of the Articles of Confederation. The Revolution, ran Jensen's thesis, was "essentially, though relatively, a democratic movement," and the Articles of Confederation "were the constitutional expression of this movement." Thus, radicalism for Jensen, unlike Jameson, was not a spillover from the political revolution into other fields but a democratizing political movement that made the Revolution of 1776 possible.[69]

In his second book, Jensen took up Beard's battle to deflate John Fiske's filiopietist interpretation of the postwar era as *The Critical Period* (1888), a time of stagnation and disaster from which the Federalist saviors rescued the country. Ostensibly he paid homage to Jameson by devoting two chapters to "the spirit of the new nation" and "the betterment of humanities" and five chapters to the expanding economy—all fuller and richer than Jameson's account. But he framed these within a political narrative in which interest groups of all sorts fought over the fruits of the Revolution.

copies by 1959 and thirty-eight thousand by its eighth printing in 1981. Michael Stevens, "Merrill Jensen," in Wilson, ed., *Twentieth-Century American Historians*, 237.

[69] Jensen, *Articles of Confederation*, chap. 1, quotations at 5, 14–15.

The subtext was that the achievements of the era did not justify the political consolidation of 1787. It was not a time of social or economic instability; Shays's agrarian rebellion was a tempest in a teapot used by nationalists. Thus, if Jensen could not explain why it was indeed a "critical period" for hard-pressed Shaysite farmers and desperate urban mechanics, he gave the fullest, most balanced picture of the era.[70]

Fortified with a sense of how the Revolution turned out, in the next phase of his scholarship Jensen turned back to how it began. In 1955 he published a massive collection of documents on the colonial era in which he balanced sources for the internal history of the colonies with sources for the imperial relationship. With some 225 documents that included not only the standard acts, petitions, and resolutions but also correspondence drawn from unpublished manuscripts, newspaper accounts, and statistical tables, all accompanied by introductions and concise bibliographic essays, the book was a scholar's guide to the history of the Revolution. Jensen published a detailed narrative history of the coming of the Revolution in 1968; it is the fullest one-volume narrative of the period, embracing both the imperial and internal politics of the Revolution. His aim was "not a search for causes or principles" but "a political history" that emphasized "the deeds of men rather than their motives." Because this book was "necessarily a history of thirteen separate colonies," many of which "were divided into 'factions' or 'parties,'" the history that emerged was "one of extraordinary intricacy," which probably dismayed critics who had stereotyped the Progressive interpretation as simplistic.[71]

In his last book in 1974, based on four lectures, Jensen returned to the theme of transformation over the entire era from 1765 through 1787. And in retirement he rounded out his long exploration of divisions within the Revolutionary generation by turning to the debates capping the era, directing two large-scale documentary projects, one on the first federal elections and the second on the history of the debates on the ratification of the Constitution. The latter, still in progress, piling up the debates over the Constitution state by state and day by day, in the public forum in newspapers and

[70] Merrill Jensen, *The New Nation: A History of the United States during the Confederation, 1781–1789* (New York, 1950).

[71] Merrill Jensen, ed., *American Colonial Documents to 1776*, English Historical Documents, vol. 9 (London, 1955); Jensen, *The Founding of a Nation: A History of the American Revolution, 1763–1776* (New York, 1968), xiii.

pamphlets as well as in official conventions, opened new vistas to popular political thought that scholars have only begun to explore.[72]

Over the years Jensen modified his original interpretation in response to his critics. In 1959, in the third printing of the *Articles of Confederation*, he confessed that had he called his chapter "Discontent within the Colonies, 1763–1774," he might have avoided the acrimony over the term "internal revolution." But while he stuck to his central assumption, namely, that colonial political society was undemocratic, he shaded his argument: "The war for independence was accompanied by *a degree* of democratization, and . . . *in part* . . . was the result of demands for political and social change both before and after 1776" (my emphasis). Insisting that "it matters little whether one calls the political and social process 'internal revolution' or 'political and social change,' change there was."[73] He concluded, second, that the "new men" he had identified as "radicals" might better be called "popular leaders," because "few if any men such as Samuel Adams, Patrick Henry, and Christopher Gadsden had any interest in a program for 'internal' reform.'" It was a clarifying distinction, since widely adopted. Third, he eased away from the old Progressive stereotype of the manipulated mob. "The mob was a political power to be reckoned with," he wrote in 1974, and "mass meetings accustomed ordinary people to take part in politics as they never had before." While thus open to "popular participation," he continued to stress the effective but often opportunistic leadership of the popular leaders, as had Becker.[74] Fourth, he clarified the timing of radicalism. Prior to 1774–75, the movement for revolution was not, he granted, a democratic movement "except by inadvertence"; from 1776 on, democratic thought flowered as Americans confronted the restructuring of their governments. Fifth, he gave greater recognition to social radicalism, to what he called the "elusive undercurrents" or the "levelling spirit"—the "idea of an equal distribution of property"—and the erosion of deference to men of property, currents that helped make the Revolution "in part a 'people's' revolution."[75]

[72] Merrill Jensen, *The American Revolution within America* (New York, 1974); Jensen et al., eds., *The Documentary History of the First Federal Elections, 1788–1790*, 4 vols. (Madison, WI, 1976–89); Jensen et al., eds., *The Documentary History of the Ratification of the Constitution*, 26 vols. to date (Madison, WI, 1976–2008).

[73] Merrill Jensen, *The Articles of Confederation: An Interpretation of the Social-Constitutional History of the American Revolution*, 3d printing (Madison, WI, 1959), xix.

[74] Jensen, *American Revolution within America*, 26–27 and chap. 2.

[75] Jensen, "The American People and the American Revolution," *Journal of American History* 57 (1970): 5–35.

Jensen was sometimes his own best critic. He regretted that he had not paid more attention to political ideas that shaped democratic action.[76] Other criticisms eluded him. He was indifferent to theory. Jensen equated "historical materialism" with "economic determinism" and read Beard as favoring not economic determinism but "the economic interpretation of politics."[77] In the 1960s he was impatient with historical methods drawn from the social sciences; he dismissed the quantitative analysis of the distribution of wealth pursued by his student Jackson Turner Main as "sociology."[78] And while he welcomed the new practitioners of "history from the bottom up" who studied mechanics and seamen, the midwestern farm boy joked about them as "asphalt flowers" for their seeming eastern, urban bias.[79] Confronted from the 1960s on with obituaries burying the Progressive interpretation as in "erosion" and then as "shattered and discredited," he was not in a mood to face its weaknesses or suffer graduate students who questioned fundamental Progressive assumptions.[80]

Challenging the Progressive paradigm in Madison was difficult; the "three parts of the god-head here at Wisconsin—the Father, the Son, and the Holy Ghost," Warren Susman wrote in 1950, were Turner, Beard, and Parrington.[81] The department's graduate system encouraged a master-disciple relationship. Jensen's doctoral students, some fifty in all, worked within the Progressive paradigm, yet they often modified or amplified Progressive themes, strengthening them. Among his early students, E. James Ferguson made a major revision in Beard's argument about the way funding and assumption worked, while sustaining the relevance of the issue. He also established a full-blown nationalist agenda as early as 1783, which gave a firmer

[76] Merrill Jensen, introduction to Jensen, ed., *Tracts of the American Revolution, 1763–1776* (Indianapolis, 1967), xiii–lxix.

[77] Merrill Jensen, "Historians and the Nature of the American Revolution," in Ray Allen Billington, ed., *The Reinterpretation of Early American History* (San Marino, CA, 1966), 122.

[78] Jackson Turner Main, "Main Travelled Roads," *William and Mary Quarterly*, 3d ser. 41 (1984): 444–54.

[79] Comment on papers by Jesse Lemisch and Alfred F. Young presented at Conference on Early American History, Newberry Library, Chicago, 1974, typescript in author's possession. Earlier William B. Hesseltine, a Wisconsin Progressive, dismissed Richard Hofstadter's *Age of Reform* (New York, 1955) as "asphalt-oriented"; see Novick, *That Noble Dream*, 340.

[80] Jack P. Greene, "The Flight from Determinism: A Review of Recent Literature on the Coming of the American Revolution," *South Atlantic Quarterly* 61 (1962): 235–59; for Greene's essays in 1967 and 1968, see Greene, *Reappraisal of the American Revolution*, and Greene, ed., *Reinterpretation of the American Revolution*.

[81] Warren Susman to Paul W. Gates, Jan. 14, 1950, quoted in Novick, *That Noble Dream*, 346–47; for a list of Merrill Jensen's doctoral students and their theses, see Martin, ed., *Human Dimensions of Nation Making*, 365–67.

base to an economic interpretation of the Federalists of 1787 than Beard's immediate pocketbook thesis. Jackson Turner Main and Van Beck Hall developed hypotheses about party divisions in the states in the 1780s around dichotomies of "cosmopolitan" and "localist" that were more complex than Beard's. Among Jensen's later students, Joseph A. Ernst and Marc Egnal pushed the study of the economic origins of the Revolution into the field of political economy. Ronald Hoffman's sophisticated study of the Revolution in Maryland added new dimensions to the struggle within elites as well as between elites and poor farmers. Hoffman portrayed a gentry frightened by the threat of social revolution and ready to sacrifice part of their wealth to preserve their power, a theme Jensen incorporated in his last book.[82]

Jackson Turner Main, grandson of Frederick Jackson Turner and Jensen's most productive and innovative early student, was alone in making social as well as political transformation in the Revolutionary era the central focus of his scholarship. In *The Social Structure of Revolutionary America* (1965), a pioneering work in the new social history, Main attempted to measure social change nationally, making use of massive numbers of probate records and tax lists. "He told me," Main wrote of Jensen, "my book on the social structure was sociology, which damned it, and as far as I know he didn't read it." Comparing colonial society in the 1750s and 1760s with society in the late 1780s, Main examined the economic class structure, North and South, social mobility, social classes and their cultural patterns, as well as contemporary opinions about class. He concluded with candor that "the effects of the Revolution seemed on the whole to have been less than I expected"; change had to be traced over a longer period of time, and he later deprecated the book as "at once pioneering and obsolescent." When he returned to the question a few years later he felt that subsequent research had still not resolved the issue. Yet looking at the overall picture, Main, with the strongest base of evidence yet assembled, affirmed Jameson. "The Revolution

[82] E. James Ferguson, *The Power of the Purse: A History of American Public Finance, 1776–1790* (Chapel Hill, NC, 1961); Ferguson, "Political Economy, Public Liberty, and the Formation of the Constitution," *William and Mary Quarterly*, 3d ser. 40 (1983): 389–412; Van Beck Hall, *Politics without Parties: Massachusetts, 1780–1791* (Pittsburgh, 1972); Joseph A. Ernst, *Money and Politics in America, 1755–1775: A Study in the Currency Act of 1764 and the Political Economy of Revolution* (Chapel Hill, NC, 1973); Marc Egnal, *A Mighty Empire: The Origins of the American Revolution* (Ithaca, NY, 1988); Joseph A. Ernst and Marc Egnal, "An Economic Interpretation of the American Revolution," *William and Mary Quarterly*, 3rd ser. 29 (1972); Ronald Hoffman, *A Spirit of Dissension: Economics, Politics, and the Revolution in Maryland* (Baltimore, 1973). For changes in elites, see James Kirby Martin, *Men in Rebellion: Higher Government Leaders and the Coming of the American Revolution* (New Brunswick, NJ, 1973).

contributed to the decline of deference, delayed the trend towards an economic and social aristocracy, and momentarily reversed the growing concentration of wealth. Whether intended or not, and whether permanent or not, these changes registered a clear gain for social democracy."[83]

In his analysis of political change Main was more confident of a pattern of democratization. In a second large-scale quantitative project comparing the socioeconomic composition of the state senates before and after the war and in an article on the assemblies, Main amassed impressive evidence for the democratization of the state legislatures. Turning to an analysis of voting patterns in the legislatures in the 1780s, Main found evidence of distinct blocs which, when correlated with his socioeconomic findings on the members, suggested a division between what he dubbed "cosmopolitan" and "localist" parties. In the late 1780s Main saw this alignment coming into play in the conflict over ratifying the proposed federal Constitution.[84]

The Wisconsin school sustained a sophisticated, complex political side of the Becker-Beard interpretation but, save for Main, more or less passed by the Jameson themes about the society and "thought and feeling." Jensen found the counter-Progressive interpretation that assigned causation to a set of ideas such as the belief in a conspiracy "a form of intellectual determinism" which he did "not find any more satisfactory than economic determinism." He was anything but simplistic. "Complexity, conflict and change," Thomas P. Slaughter observed, are the hallmarks of Jensen's narrative work, as he "piles fact upon fact, nuance upon nuance, variation upon variation," so much so that the "evidence can bewilder."[85] If there is a place for the analysis of politics and conflict in the Revolutionary era, there is a resiliency to Jensen's tough-minded analysis. As the smoke of the barrage cleared—a barrage to which we will next turn—he remains one of the few scholars with an imposing command of large bodies of original sources who worked out a vision of the Revolutionary era that linked its transformations to its origins.

[83] Jackson Turner Main, *The Social Structure of Revolutionary America* (Princeton, NJ, 1965); Main to author, Aug. 5, 1993; Main, "Main Travelled Roads," 451; Main, *The Sovereign States, 1775–1783* (New York, 1973), 348.

[84] Jackson Turner Main, *The Upper House in Revolutionary America, 1763–1788* (Madison, WI, 1967); Main, "The American Revolution and the Democratization of the Legislatures," *William and Mary Quarterly*, 3d ser. 23 (1966): 391–407; Main, *Political Parties before the Constitution* (Chapel Hill, NC, 1973).

[85] Merrill Jensen, "Commentary on Bernard Bailyn's Paper at the AHA Meeting, Philadelphia, 1963," typescript in author's possession; Thomas P. Slaughter, "In Retrospect: Merrill Jensen and the Revolution of 1787," *Reviews in American History* 15 (1987): 691–701.

5. The Counter-Progressives: Part 1

"If one had to choose a single term to characterize the dominant tendency in postwar American historical writing," writes Peter Novick in his exhaustive survey of the "objectivity question" and the historical profession in the United States, " 'counterprogressive' would seem the best choice, for no project was more central to historians from the late 1940s onward than the revision and refutation of the alleged deficiencies of the progressive historians who had preceded them." He adds, "As is usual in such revisionist projects, the new school constructed something of a straw man to battle against"; the revisionists "exaggerated" the dominance of Turner, Beard, and Parrington and often "vulgarized" their theses "so as to present a broader target." Richard B. Morris said the same thing at the time about the treatment of Jameson, who "said many sensible things, but it is now fashionable to exaggerate his thesis in order to decapitate a straw man."[86]

Postwar historians were adamant that their own scholarship, unlike that of their Progressive forebears, was not "disfigured by presentism," as Novick puts it. As Edmund S. Morgan reviewed his long, fruitful career, he insisted that "the whole school of consensus history, if there is a school, is sort of accidental." It was "simply the result of historians looking closely at episodes that had not been looked at so closely before and saying 'Hey, I don't see this happening.' "[87] A decade before, however, while reflecting on the shifts in the direction of his own scholarly interests since the Second World War, Morgan pointed out that "the influence of the present upon [the historian] is so strong, albeit so subtle, that he may not be aware of it." When "different historians have found different things in the same records," he observed, "the differences may come simply from keener perception or from taking a closer look, but they are also affected, consciously or unconsciously, by the time and place in which the historian lives and by the people who live there with him. . . . An historian's understanding of the Revolution may thus reflect, however remotely, the needs of his time,

[86] Novick, *That Noble Dream*, 332; see the influential contemporary analysis by John Higham, "The Cult of the American Consensus: Homogenizing Our History," *Commentary* 27 (1959): 93–100, and Higham, "Beyond Consensus: The Historian as Moral Critic," *American Historical Review* 67 (1962): 609–25, reprinted in Higham, *Writing American History: Essays on Modern Scholarship* (Bloomington, IN, 1970), chap. 8; Higham, *History*, chaps. 5–6; Morris, *American Revolution Reconsidered*, 77. I recall Higham as coining the term "consensus history."

[87] Novick, *That Noble Dream*, 321; David T. Courtwright, "Fifty Years of American History: An Interview with Edmund S. Morgan," *William and Mary Quarterly*, 3d ser. 44 (1987): 336–69, quotation at 360–61.

which may differ from the needs of earlier times and differ also from year to year within his own lifespan."[88]

How a historian of the Revolution "may . . . reflect, however remotely, the needs of his time" is a subject most scholars have been reluctant to address in their contemporaries. Historians have no hesitation in pointing out how George Bancroft's version of the Revolution "reflected" his Jacksonian convictions, or Charles Beard's, his Progressivism. But they are not comfortable with books such as Michael G. Kammen's exploration of the Revolution in "the American historical imagination" or his magisterial survey of "the transformation of tradition in American culture" that imply the current cultural and political context in which historians function. Yet a much adopted research handbook advises students to read historians "by a sort of triangulation: here I stand; there to the left or right, stands Macaulay [or whoever]; and beyond are the events that he reports" and warns that doing this "is not the same as dismissing an author having 'doped out' that he is a Whig, a Catholic, [etc.]." This kind of relativism is obviously a two-edged sword; no historian wants to see his or her scholarship reduced to a reflection of the time. Only recently have a minority of scholars been willing to grant that their questions are inspired by the "needs" of their own time or to claim their history is the better for their own life experiences or convictions.[89]

Reading Peter Novick's deeply researched, evenhanded study of the published writings and revealing private correspondence of historians early in the Cold War, it is remarkable not how remotely but how directly leaders of the profession responded to and indeed shaped "the needs of [their] time." "In the late forties and early fifties," which, as Novick writes, was "the height of the cold war," "a sense of urgent crisis, and impending Armageddon, was widespread" among scholars. The crusade against Communism abroad, with its correlate, an inquisition into political heresy at home, settled a pall on emerging postwar academic communities.[90]

Conyers Read's presidential address to the AHA in 1949, "The Social Responsibilities of the Historian," was a call to arms. "Total war, whether it be hot or cold, enlists everyone and calls upon everyone to assume his part. The historian is no freer from this obligation than the physicist." In 1950

[88] Morgan, *Challenge of the American Revolution*, x.

[89] Michael G. Kammen, *A Season of Youth: The American Revolution and the Historical Imagination* (New York, 1978); Kammen, *Mystic Chords of Memory: The Transformation of Tradition in American Culture* (New York, 1991); Jacques Barzun and Henry F. Graff, *The Modern Researcher* (1957; rev. ed., New York, 1970), 183–84.

[90] Novick, *That Noble Dream*, chap. 10, quotation at 314.

Samuel Eliot Morison (a rear admiral by virtue of his multivolume history of United States naval operations in World War II) issued a jeremiad in his AHA presidential address: the historian "owes respect to tradition and folk memory. . . . Historians, deal gently with your people's traditions." The years 1920 to 1940, he continued, were "two woeful decades" in which "historians were robbing the people of their heroes, . . . insulting their folk memory of great figures they admired." He issued a call for "a sanely conservative history of the United States." Daniel Boorstin, expiating his brief sin as a Communist in the 1930s, explained to the House Committee on Un-American Activities in 1953 his form of opposition to Communism: "[It] has been an attempt to discover and explain to my students, in my teaching and in my writing, the unique virtues of American democracy."[91]

Other scholars conformed. On the left, disassociation from Marxism was obligatory. Merle Curti, in his presidential address to the Mississippi Valley Historical Association, included a passage disavowing Marxism, "to be on the safe side." In these "dark and wintry times," Curti wrote to Thomas C. Cochran, "I can't swim with the current and being a notoriously poor swimmer I can't swim against it." While Cochran remained convinced "of the essential soundness of most of historical materialism," he too was "disinclined to try to swim against the overwhelming current" and concluded, "I guess what I've done is to build an ivory tower called the Social Science approach to history." Younger scholars without tenure were more vulnerable. Lee Benson, who wrote from an "implicit Marxist standpoint," fearful of making it explicit, said, "during the 1950s, and for some time thereafter, I for one—was intellectually terrified."[92]

Graduate students were especially vulnerable. At Columbia in 1947 I chose to do an M.A. thesis on "New York City in the Hysteria of the Alien and Sedition Laws, 1798–1800," because I wanted to see if I could learn

[91] Ibid., 318 (Read), 315–16 (Morison), 328 (Boorstin). For an analysis written in the 1960s, see Jesse Lemisch, *On Active Service in War and Peace: Politics and Ideology in the American Historical Profession* (Toronto, 1975), initially presented at the AHA Convention, Dec. 1969.

[92] Novick, *That Noble Dream*, 330 (Curti), 325 (Cochran), 332 (Benson). For heresy hunting in the academic world, see ibid., chap. 11, and Ellen Schrecker, *No Ivory Tower: McCarthyism and the Universities* (New York, 1986). For diverse historians affected, see the references in Schrecker's index to Daniel Boorstin, John W. Caughey, Natalie Zemon Davis, Sigmund Diamond, Moses Finley, Philip S. Foner, Sidney V. James, Richard Schlatter, Vera Shlakman, and Dirk Struik, an incomplete list. For the experiences of three left historians with inquisitorial committees, see the interviews with Natalie Zemon Davis, William Appleman Williams, and Herbert G. Gutman in Henry Abelove et al., eds., *Visions of History* (New York, 1983), 97–122, 125–46, 187–216; Sigmund Diamond, *Official Stories, Little Secrets: On the Trail of the Intelligence Agency–University Complex, 1944–55* (New York, 1991).

how the country responded to what Jefferson called "the reign of witches." I suppose this made me suspect. I can remember standing in front of a newspaper kiosk before the Columbia subway entrance on Broadway and catching out of the corner of my eye my thesis director staring at me to see which newspaper or magazine I would choose. I left Columbia (overcrowded with four hundred history graduate students) for Northwestern, where Lawrence "Bill" Towner and I (with an assist from George McGovern) cranked out leaflets against some new threat of a federal witch hunt on a departmental mimeograph machine with the blessings of our advisor, Ray Allen Billington.

For a number of reasons Charles Beard (1874–1948) and to a lesser extent Carl Becker (1873–1945) were the prime targets of a generalized attack on Progressive history. Their philosophy of history and their politics were under fire long before the 1950s, when their scholarship on the Revolution came under review. In the interwar years Beard and Becker were the leading advocates of historical relativism. "The attack on moral relativism," Novick points out, "was part of an effort to rearm the West spiritually for the battle with totalitarianism," first against fascism in the late 1930s and during World War II and then against Communism in the late 1940s. As early as 1938 Howard Mumford Jones lamented Beard's "unfortunate influence . . . from the point of view of keeping alive a necessary patriotic glow in the juvenile breast." J. H. Hexter, Novick writes, "saw an intimate connection between Becker's relativism and Nazi historical practice." Later Robert E. Brown, chief prosecuting attorney of Beard and Becker, recycled the old charge that Becker's moral relativism and liberalism led him to skate "on the thin ice of communism," a red-baiting accusation J. Franklin Jameson in the 1930s found beneath contempt.[93]

Second, by the onset of World War II, Beard's "isolationist" politics had made him a pariah among internationalist-minded liberals and antifascist leftists. Beard's economic analysis of the internal domestic forces that shaped foreign policy led him to oppose Roosevelt's interventionist foreign policies. He devoted his last book in 1948 to proving Roosevelt's complicity in bringing on America's entry into the war.[94]

[93] Novick, *That Noble Dream*, 283 (Jones and Hexter); Robert E. Brown, *Carl Becker and the American Revolution* (East Lansing, MI, 1970), chap. 7; Jameson to Mrs. Grattan Doyle, Dec. 9, 1935, in Donnan and Stock, eds., *Correspondence of Jameson*, 358–59.

[94] Hofstadter, *Progressive Historians*, chap. 9.

Third, during the postwar onslaught against Marxism, Beard's economic interpretation was equated with economic determinism, which was equated with Marxism, and in the absence of influential Marxist intellectuals in the United States, Beard became a surrogate for Marxism. Merely to raise the subject of the economic interests of the patriots of 1776 or of the Framers of 1787 was to question their "sincerity" or their "motives." In 1913 in Marion, Ohio (home of Warren G. Harding), the *Ohio Star* ran a banner headline in response to Beard's book on the Constitution: "Scavengers, Hyena Like, Desecrate the Graves of the Dead Patriots We Revere."[95] A half century later, Barry Goldwater, the conservative candidate for president, wrote columns in the same vein. With such celebration the touchstone of loyalty, Beard, a relentless explorer of interests that lay behind official cant, was a dangerous model.

By the early 1950s a number of books popular among intellectuals were setting the new parameters of historical inquiry. David M. Potter told us we were *A People of Plenty*, and the economist John Kenneth Galbraith wrote that we were *An Affluent Society*, which led the historian Jack P. Greene to conclude that "the absence of serious internal economic problems and the general levelling of society [since the war] has enabled [historians] to avoid that central preoccupation with economic questions that led many scholars of the progressive school to wrench Revolutionary events out of context by superimposing some of the a priori assumptions and tenets of economic determinism." The sociologist Daniel Bell intoned *The End of Ideology* and the theologian Reinhold Niebuhr warned against "utopian visions of historical possibilities" and "Jeffersonian illusions about human nature," which may be why Cecelia M. Kenyon was so little challenged when she dismissed Thomas Paine as the "Peter Pan of the Age of Reason" who could not see the "dark side of human nature." "The outburst of McCarthyism"—of guilt by accusation and guilt by association—Richard Hofstadter points out, "instead of provoking a radical response, aroused in some intellectuals more distaste than they had ever thought they would feel for popular passions and anti-establishment demagogy. The populism of the right inspired a new skepticism about the older populism of the left." Such distaste for what Hofstadter called *The Paranoid Style in American Politics* turned most scholars away from examining the urban mobs, agrarian riots, slave insurrections, evangelical Great Awakenings, millennialist outbursts, and other

[95] Quoted in Ellen Nore, *Charles A. Beard: An Intellectual Biography* (Carbondale, IL, 1983), 63.

forms of "enthusiasm" or "fanaticism" that in the eighteenth century were sources of radicalism.[96]

By the mid-1950s the major interpretive works in American history were slamming the door to the questions the Progressive historians had opened up about the Revolution. If Hofstadter was right in 1948 that liberal and conservative antagonists shared a consensus of values through American history, then there was more reason to explore agreements rather than disagreements in the founding generation. If Daniel Boorstin was right in *The Genius of American Politics* (1953), his offering of loyalty, that "the most obvious peculiarity of our American Revolution is that in the modern European sense of the word, it was hardly a revolution at all." And if Louis Hartz was right in *The Liberal Tradition in America* (1955) that America was "born free" because it had no feudal past, then Jameson's destruction of "feudal relics" in the land system was no more than "a mopping up operation."[97] If Robert E. Brown was right in 1955 that colonial Massachusetts was an equalitarian "middle-class" society and a political democracy, then there was no need for change and Becker's and Jensen's dual revolution went out the window. And if Brown was right in 1956 and Forrest McDonald right in 1958 in their demolition jobs on Beard's interpretation of the Constitution, then the entire Progressive temple was in a state of collapse and by implication Jameson's piece of the arch had fallen in.[98]

The climate of opinion among leading early American historians changed with a speed that suggests that "the needs of [their] time" may have predisposed their response. The angry, one-sided polemics by Brown and McDonald against Beard were not surprising. McDonald's sympathetic biographer speaks of him as "unabashedly conservative" (and in 1964 he was chairman of the Goldwater for President committee in Rhode Island).

[96] Greene, "Flight from Determinism," 258; Cecelia M. Kenyon, "Where Paine Went Wrong," *American Political Science Review* 45 (1951): 1086–99; Hofstadter, *Progressive Historians*, 438; Hofstadter, "The Paranoid Style in American Politics," *Harper's Magazine*, Nov. 1964, reprinted in Hofstadter, *The Paranoid Style in American Politics and Other Essays* (New York, 1967).

[97] Richard Hofstadter, *The American Political Tradition and the Men Who Made It* (New York, 1948), 15, 18; for his second thoughts twenty years later, see Hofstadter, *Progressive Historians*, chap. 12; Daniel Boorstin, *The Genius of American Politics* (Chicago, 1953), chap. 3, 68–69; Louis Hartz, *The Liberal Tradition in America: An Interpretation of American Political Thought since the Revolution* (New York, 1955).

[98] Robert E. Brown, *Middle-Class Democracy and the Revolution in Massachusetts, 1691–1780* (Ithaca, NY, 1955); Robert E. Brown and B. Katherine Brown, *Virginia, 1705–1786: Democracy or Aristocracy?* (East Lansing, MI, 1964); Robert E. Brown, *Charles Beard and the Constitution: A Critical Analysis of "An Economic Interpretation of the Constitution"* (Princeton, NJ, 1956); Forrest McDonald, *We the People: The Economic Origins of the Constitution* (Chicago, 1958).

He was a business historian who had written one book about the utilities industry of Wisconsin that was financed by the industry and went on to write a biography that rehabilitated the utilities magnate Samuel Insull. What was surprising was the speed with which these prosecuting attorney historians were canonized by liberal scholars who valorized balance and a judicious temperament. "Negative writing is always unpleasant," Morgan remarked, which perhaps is why he left it to others. The response among graduate students was more critical. Gary B. Nash writes, "I remember vividly how enthusiastically [at Princeton] we deplored Brown and McDonald when we were graduate students in the early 1960s."[99]

The contrast between Frederick B. Tolles's evenhanded, sympathetic appraisal of the state of the Jameson thesis in 1954 and Morgan's dismissal of the Progressives in his synthesis of the Revolution in 1956 measures the shifting tide. Tolles, a Quaker who had written a biography of George Logan, the Quaker resister to the Quasi War with France in 1798, pointed to the serious shortcomings in Jameson's hypotheses. On the status of persons, he had simplified what happened to the old aristocracy and the loyalists and overlooked such dependent classes as women and indentured servants. The Revolution "made less difference in the status of persons than Jameson believed." On the bedrock subject of land, the changes in entail, primogeniture, and quitrents were largely symbolic, and the distribution of confiscated loyalist estates led to "considerably less diffusion and democratization of landownership . . . than Jameson supposed." The economic changes in commerce and industry were both more and less than Jameson perceived. In his chapter "Thought and Feeling," Jameson in general "overlooked or underestimated the dynamic forces already present in the society of colonial America." Yet Tolles could forgive Jameson "a few oversights" and "overstatements." He pronounced the thesis "still sound, and what is more important, still vital and suggestive, capable of still further life, still greater usefulness."[100]

[99] For McDonald's value judgments of modern revolutions, see his *E Pluribus Unum: The Formation of the American Republic, 1776–1790* (Boston, 1965), 235–56; for his politics and other scholarship, see Justus Doeneke, "Forest McDonald," in Wilson, ed., *Twentieth-Century American Historians*, 258–59; for Brown's political judgments, see his *Carl Becker*, 265–67, and his *Reinterpretation of the Formation of the American Constitution* (Boston, 1963), 56–63; see also Courtwright, "Interview with Morgan," 367; for a thoughtful analysis of the "dualism" in Beard's concepts of economic interest and class ignored by his critics, see Benson, *Turner and Beard*, 95–150; Gary B. Nash to author, Jan. 1994.

[100] Tolles, "American Revolution Considered as a Social Movement," 1–12; Tolles, *George Logan of Philadelphia* (New York, 1953).

Morgan's *The Birth of the Republic, 1763–1789*, in the Chicago History of American Civilization series commissioned by Daniel Boorstin, "drew together and consolidated all of the emerging scholarship opposed to Charles Beard," as three of his students put it in introducing his festschrift. This well-honed, readable short synthesis was nothing if not counter-Progressive, explicitly critical of Becker, Beard, Jameson, and Jensen; in tone it was remarkably defensive, assuming that the "motives" of the Founding Fathers were under attack. At every point Morgan seized on the most extreme version of the Progressive interpretation to deflate it. Regarding Becker: "To magnify the internal conflict in the same proportion as the revolt against England is to distort it beyond recognition." Regarding Jameson: there was "no radical rebuilding of social institutions"—a claim Jameson had never made—but only "a host of incalculable, accidental and incidental changes in society many of which tended towards a redistribution of wealth." Regarding Beard: if the Framers of the Constitution had "self-interest" or "selfish interest," it was "undeniable" that their personal economic interests were involved, but the delegates to the Constitutional Convention also had a "selfish interest in bringing about a public good." Indeed, this was the thrust of Morgan's entire interpretation; in each crisis "self-interest led to the enunciation of principles which went far beyond the point at issue."[101]

Morgan may have been slaying more than the Beard-Becker-Jameson hydra. He had grown up in Cambridge, where his father was a professor of law at Harvard and where he earned his B.A. in 1937. He spent 1938 at the London School of Economics, where his mentors included Harold Laski, England's leading socialist intellectual, and R. H. Tawney, celebrated for *Religion and the Rise of Capitalism*, and where, he said, "most of the people I knew were, I guess, what would be called 'fellow travellers,' that is sympathetic to the Communist party and the Marxists." He was "disillusioned," however, by the politics of the left and regarded Marxist analysis as "simplistic." For a time a conscientious objector, he spent the war as a skilled tool and die maker. Back to Harvard for graduate school, he admired most Samuel Eliot Morison, who had long been engaged in rehabilitating the

[101] David D. Hall, John M. Murrin, and Thad W. Tate, introduction to Hall, Murrin, and Tate, eds., *Saints and Revolutionaries: Essays on Early American History* (New York, 1984), xi; Morgan, *Birth of the Republic*, 100 (Becker), 96, 98 (Jameson), 94–95, 190 (Beard); Morgan, "The American Revolution: Revisions in Need of Revising," *William and Mary Quarterly*, 3d ser. 14 (1957): 3–15, reprinted with a preface in Morgan, *Challenge of the American Revolution*, 43–44, and with an author's postscript in *In Search of Early America: The William and Mary Quarterly, 1943–1993* (Williamsburg, VA, 1993), 44–53.

Puritans as "a courageous, humane, brave, and significant people," and Perry Miller, who admired "the majesty and coherence of Puritan thinking" and was convinced that "the mind of man is the basic factor in human history." Both were bent on rescuing intellectual history from the degrading embrace of social history and the Puritans from economic-determinist stereotypes fostered by Parrington and James Truslow Adams.[102] Morgan thus turned away from the analytical path that led Tawney and Max Weber to explore Protestantism in its relation to capitalism and away from the path that led another admired Harvard teacher and friend, F. O. Matthiessen, a socialist, to left activism and a social interpretation of the great writers of the American Renaissance, a seminal work in American Studies.[103] Morgan had his own crusade; Miller and Morison "made it necessary to take Puritanism seriously," to "address what they said and wrote and read and taught," as he put it in 1966. He approached the American Revolution in the same spirit—to pursue "the American Revolution as an intellectual movement," the title of an essay that laid down the gauntlet to supporters of Jameson. The "distinguishing feature of the new historians"—among whom he numbered himself—in revising the Progressives, he wrote in 1992, "was not really their assumption of consensus among Americans but their insistence on taking seriously what the colonial leaders said they were fighting about."[104]

Morgan's first foray into the American Revolution in 1953—"my first real book after my dissertation" on the Puritan family—was a richly researched study in collaboration with Helen M. Morgan, his wife, of the two years of the Stamp Act crisis, 1765–66. One of the most influential books on the Revolution, the thrust was counter-Progressive. The Morgans rejected the prevailing interpretation that the colonists in responding to

[102] Courtwright, "Interview with Morgan," 336–69; for the historiographic context, see Robert Allen Skotheim, *American Intellectual Histories and Their Historians* (Princeton, NJ, 1966), chap. 5, quotations at 174 (Morison) and 187 (Miller).

[103] Edmund S. Morgan, "The American Revolution as an Intellectual Movement," in Arthur M. Schlesinger Jr. and Morton White, eds., *Paths of American Thought* (Boston, 1963), 11–33; F. O. Matthiessen, *American Renaissance: Art and Expression in the Age of Emerson and Whitman* (New York, 1941); Paul Sweezy and Leo Huberman, eds., *F. O. Matthiessen, 1902–50: A Collective Portrait* (New York, 1950).

[104] The quotations are from Edmund S. Morgan, "The Historians of Early New England," in Billington, ed., *Reinterpretation of Early American History* (1966), 51, and Morgan, "The Second American Revolution," review of *The Radicalism of the American Revolution*, by Gordon S. Wood, *New York Review of Books*, June 25, 1992, 23; for analysis of Morgan, see Marian J. Morton, *The Terrors of Ideological Politics: Liberal Historians in a Conservative Mood* (Cleveland, 1972), chap. 5, and Higham, *History*, 224.

British taxation drew a distinction between internal and external taxation. They also rejected the Progressive contention that it was the economics and not the principle of taxation that was at stake and that the patriots, as Becker wrote, "step by step, from 1764 to 1776 . . . modified their theory to suit their needs." The Morgans found that the colonists always objected on principle to all forms of parliamentary taxation and not simply to internal taxes. Second, in vivid accounts of the resistance led by the Sons of Liberty, they concluded that "the episodes of violence . . . were planned and prepared by men who were recognized at the time as belonging to the 'better and wiser part,'" who never lost direction of events. Frankenstein had not created a monster, as Schlesinger had argued; the mob had little agency. Third, to "show the other side of the picture and thus achieve a kind of balance," they offered sympathetic chapter-length portraits of five leading loyalist officials, "sufferers from that resistance," among them Thomas Hutchinson. The book was thus a peculiar blend, rescuing whig thought from the economic interpretation of the Progressives while embracing the imperial school's sympathies with suffering loyalist gentlemen and a distaste among conservatives and liberals for the mob.[105]

These conclusions in 1953, based on the opening crisis of 1765–66, cast a long shadow over Morgan's interpretation of the entire Revolutionary era in *The Birth of the Republic* (1956). The Revolution "was a history of the Americans' search for principles." The first, "the principle that taxation was the exclusive right of their own elected representatives," was held consistently through the entire era. The colonists' attachment was "sincere" and "genuine," and there was "no incongruity in their coupling of principle and self-interest"; they held to the principle of liberty "as a way of safeguarding the property which they regarded as the only security for life and liberty." The second principle they discovered was "equal rights" asserted in the Declaration. In the years that followed, while there was no "rebuilding of society," it was "possible to see the ideal [of equality] beginning to take shape and operating, if only fitfully, against the grosser social inequalities of the day." The third principle was national union achieved in the Constitution of 1787, "the final fulfillment" of the struggle to make property secure and to link representation with taxation and equal rights.[106]

[105] Edmund S. Morgan and Helen M. Morgan, *The Stamp Act Crisis: Prologue to Revolution* (1953; 2d rev. ed., New York, 1962); Edmund S. Morgan, "Colonial Ideas of Parliamentary Power," *William and Mary Quarterly*, 3d ser. 5 (1948): 311–41; Becker, *Declaration of Independence*, chap. 3.

[106] Morgan, *Birth of the Republic*, 51–52, 88–89, 96, 100, 132, 156–57.

After a decade and more devoted to exploring the Puritans, when Morgan turned once again to the Revolution in 1967, he linked it to Puritanism. The Revolution in all of its phases, he argued, "was affected, not to say guided, by a set of values inherited from the age of Puritanism." The Puritan ethic stressing frugality and frowning on extravagance, encouraging productive manufactures and discouraging speculation, informed the prewar movements for nonimportation and nonconsumption, the divisions during the war over corruption, and the movement to encourage American manufacturing and independence during the 1780s and 1790s.[107]

In the early 1970s, as Morgan turned from New England to Virginia to explore the origins of the labor system, he was struck by the fact that "the rise of liberty and equality in this country was accompanied by the rise of slavery." The "central paradox in American history," he said in his presidential address to the Organization of American Historians in 1972, was "that two such contradictory developments were taking place simultaneously . . . from the seventeenth century to the nineteenth." The book that resulted from this exploration, *American Slavery, American Freedom: The Ordeal of Colonial Virginia* (1975), the three editors of Morgan's festschrift claimed, was "perhaps a more profound and desperate story of social conflict than anything the Progressives had ever written about colonial America." They wondered if perhaps the book was "a response to the war in Vietnam, a war replete with senseless massacres and exploitation." The Progressives, it was true, had never come to grips with slavery, but as Peter H. Wood pointed out, "the action and the anguish" in Morgan's Virginia "continue to belong largely to Europeans," not African Americans.[108]

Surprisingly, this discovery of "the central paradox" led to no changes in Morgan's consensus interpretation of the Revolution. Quite the contrary, he thought that "the development of slavery is perhaps the key to the

[107] Edmund Morgan, "The Puritan Ethic and the American Revolution," *William and Mary Quarterly*, 3d. ser. 24 (1967): 3–43, reprinted in *In Search of Early America*, 78–108. Morgan's books on the Puritans were *The Puritan Dilemma: The Story of John Winthrop* (Boston, 1958), *The Gentle Puritan: A Life of Ezra Stiles, 1727–1795* (New Haven, CT, 1962), *Visible Saints: The History of a Puritan Idea* (New York, 1963), *Puritan Political Ideas, 1558–1794* (Indianapolis, 1965), and *Roger Williams: The Church and the State* (New York, 1967).

[108] Edmund Morgan, "Slavery and Freedom: The American Paradox," *Journal of American History* 59 (1972): 5–29; Morgan, *American Slavery, American Freedom: The Ordeal of Colonial Virginia* (New York, 1975); Hall, Murrin, and Tate, introduction to Hall, Murrin, and Tate, eds., *Saints and Revolutionaries*, xii; for Morgan's reaction, see Courtwright, "Interview with Morgan," 358–59; Peter H. Wood, "'I Did the Best I Could for My Day': The Study of Early Black History during the Second Reconstruction, 1960 to 1976," *William and Mary Quarterly*, 3d ser. 35 (1978): 185–225.

consensus that prevailed in colonial America, for slavery meant the substitution of a helpless, closely guarded lower class for a dangerous, armed lower class that would fight if exploited too ruthlessly." This prevented the recurrence in 1776 of the class conflict of Bacon's Rebellion in 1676. So too did the "extraordinary social mobility" in the colonies and the war against Britain, which "tended to suppress or encompass social conflict." "With a majority of laborers in chains and with the most discontented freemen venting their discontent in loyalism, the struggle over who shall rule at home was unlikely to bear many of the marks of class conflict." The social system contained the conflict.[109]

He left the argument of the *Birth of the Republic* intact in a second edition in 1976. In discussing the results of the Revolution, he added a page on slavery, acknowledging that "the blessings of liberty had grown side-by-side with the burdens of slavery, and the two were locked in an embrace not easily broken." But he let stand his earlier optimistic summary; he could still see the ideal of equality taking shape and beginning to take effect "against the grosser social inequalities of the day." Slavery, an issue that David Brion Davis, Winthrop D. Jordan, and a host of scholars were moving to a central place in the history of the Revolution, remained unobtrusive in Morgan's narrative, and African Americans as actors were not a presence.[110] In his third edition in 1992 Morgan saw no reason to change this sunny appraisal. He now added one sentence—a response to the "needs of his time"?—granting that the ideal of equality did not operate effectively against the inequality of women. "Although the Revolution called upon women to undertake jobs formerly reserved to men, and though they emerged from it with an enlarged view of their role in society, they did not achieve any fundamental change in the inferior status English and colonial law had allotted them." But these racial and gender paradoxes were not allowed to intrude on his original evaluation of the Revolution as a successful search for the principles of liberty and equality. It was a Revolution without losers, save for suffering loyalist émigrés, or at least it was a world where the principle of equality would eventually trickle down to the unequals.[111]

[109] Edmund Morgan, "Conflict and Consensus," in Stephen G. Kurtz and James H. Hutson, eds., *Essays on the American Revolution* (Chapel Hill, NC, 1973), 289–309.

[110] Morgan, *The Birth of the Republic*, 2d ed. (Chicago, 1977); David Brion Davis, *The Problem of Slavery in Western Culture* (Ithaca, NY, 1966); Davis, *The Problem of Slavery in the Age of Revolution, 1770–1823* (Ithaca, NY, 1975); Winthrop D. Jordan, *White over Black: American Attitudes toward the Negro, 1550–1812* (Chapel Hill, NC, 1968).

[111] Morgan, *Birth of the Republic*, 3d ed. (Chicago, 1992), 95–96.

Perhaps this is what Daniel Boorstin may have had in mind in his editor's foreword to the third edition in 1992 when he praised Morgan for avoiding "fashionable atomizing fads [which] obscure the wisdom and heroism" of the Founders, the "fads," presumably, of black history, women's history, or artisan or agrarian or Indian history. Boorstin also pointed to "recent events abroad in what was once the Soviet Union [which] have dramatized the weakness of dogmatic empires and a priori ideology as the cement for a changing society." In his bibliographic essay in 1992 Morgan still defined the historians' debate over the Revolution in terms of Beard and his critics, by then a debate long faded and redefined. Morgan concludes a later book with an analysis of the decline of deference, which he attributes to the experience of the war. But the internal conflict, as he put it in his 1987 interview, remains "pretty small potatoes compared to the contest with Great Britain." An admirer of men of consistent principles, Morgan thus remained consistent in his interpretation.[112]

"No Morgan school exists," his students insist, "no point of view sustained by generations of disciples," although their work reflects "his confidence in intellectual history and his long standing interest in the Puritans." He concurs. Among over fifty doctoral students, more have written about the Puritan "saints" than the "revolutionaries," and among the latter several have mapped territory uncharted by Morgan. Especially in recent decades many have responded creatively to the "needs of their times."[113] But with notable exceptions they have not challenged the interpretation he has presented with an unmatched cogency and consistency for over forty years.

6. Against the Grain

When an old paradigm is under assault and a new one vying to replace it, books often appear that do not fit the ascendant trend and seem to be a voice from the past. They often are the work of an older generation; sometimes they are the voice of a graduate student not caught up in prevailing

[112] Ibid., ix (Boorstin), 191–92 (Morgan); Courtwright, "Interview with Morgan," 361 ("small potatoes"); Morgan, *Inventing the People: The Rise of Popular Sovereignty in England and America* (New York, 1988); Morgan's other recent works include *The Meaning of Independence: John Adams, Thomas Jefferson, George Washington* (New York, 1976), and *The Genius of George Washington* (New York, 1980).

[113] Hall, Murrin, and Tate, introduction to Hall, Murrin, and Tate, eds., *Saints and Revolutionaries*, xiii; for a list of Morgan's students and their theses, see ibid., 373–79.

fashions. Such voices against the grain are often not appreciated when they appear and are not recognized years later.

In the 1950s it took a while for the Cold War to freeze scientific inquiry in the ice of consensus history. If the prospect of a nuclear armageddon made coexistence unlikely among the superpowers, a strange kind of co-existence flourished in the uniquely American, publisher-driven books in the "Problems of Interpretations" anthologies, the first of which was known as "the Amherst series," which presented students with arrays of conflicting historical views. Students were asked to evaluate spokesmen for the various schools: Andrews or Gipson for the imperial school, Louis M. Hacker for economic-determinist Marxism, Jameson and Tolles for the Revolution as a social movement, Morgan for the Revolution as an intellectual movement, and, after the 1960s, Bailyn for the ideological interpretation and Jesse Lemisch for history "from the bottom up." The pattern was similar in the Bobbs-Merrill series in the 1960s that reprinted single articles at a cheap price, very popular in an age before xeroxing. For the Revolutionary period, for which Morgan was the juror, students (and their teachers) could read articles by Jensen, Ferguson, and Main and by their critics Bailyn, Brown, Greene, Kenyon, McDonald, Morgan, Tolles, and Wood, as well as by William Appleman Williams, Staughton Lynd, and Lemisch of the New Left, and scholars who fit no categories. These publications are a reminder of the healthy skepticism of many historians to all determinisms, the desire to explore different interpretations, and an eclectic willingness to borrow a little from this interpretation and a little from that.[114]

Scholarly works appeared during these years that were not incorporated into counter-Progressive paradigms. Books by Elisha P. Douglass, Benjamin Quarles, Curtis P. Nettels, and Robert R. Palmer and the scholarly career of Richard B. Morris are examples of scholarship that did not fit and actually enhanced older interpretations, including Jameson's.

Douglass is an example of a doctoral student trying to pursue an old hypothesis that had not died. He introduced his book on the struggle for political democracy state by state, initially a thesis at Yale directed by Leonard W. Labaree, as an effort to deal with an aspect of the social

[114] Earl Latham, ed., *The Declaration of Independence and the Constitution* (Boston, 1956), and John C. Wahlke, ed., *The Causes of the American Revolution* (Boston, 1962), both volumes in the much used "Amherst series"; George A. Billias, ed., *The American Revolution: How Revolutionary Was It?* (New York, 1965); *Index to the Bobbs-Merrill Reprint Series in American History* (Indianapolis, 1973).

movement Jameson had neglected: "The struggle of certain less privileged groups within the ranks of the revolutionary party to obtain equal political rights." He was extending Becker's internal struggle past 1776. While Douglass stressed the conservatism of the outcome and halted at constitutions rather than political practice, he portrayed conflicts over the structure of government that were intense, widespread, and often class oriented. More sympathetic to the democrats than to the conservative whigs, Douglass offered a yardstick by which to measure achievement of the democratic ideal, for example, Thomas Jefferson, who emerged more moderate than radical when contrasted to grass-roots democrats.[115]

Benjamin Quarles's *The Negro in the American Revolution* (1961) was simply a book ahead of its time by a pioneer African American scholar. In the 1950s and early 1960s the scholarly debate on slavery spun around the axis of what slavery did to African Americans, with Kenneth M. Stampp's northern abolitionist view challenging Ulrich B. Phillips's benevolent racism, and after 1959 around Stanley M. Elkins's interpretation of the slave system as a concentration camp that infantilized blacks. Quarles's carefully researched study focused on what blacks did in the war from 1775 to 1783, fighting as bearers of arms in the American militia or army or serving as spies and laborers or taking flight from slavery to fight "in the king's service" and after the war evacuating to Nova Scotia with the British. Such a book built around the agency of blacks in resistance to slavery fit not at all into any framework of the Revolution or of slavery and lay fallow.[116]

Curtis P. Nettels's *The Emergence of a National Economy, 1775–1815* (1962) was a voice from the past—the magnum opus of a second-generation Progressive published twenty-five years after his initial scholarship. A thorough, almost encyclopedic inventory of the economic changes wrought in the Revolutionary era, it seemingly pursued no themes. But it provided ample evidence for the changes in the land system Jameson had suggested in his second chapter and for the burgeoning of commerce and manufacturing, the theme of Jameson's third chapter. It was an economic history of the Revolution, not an economic interpretation, but coming as it did when

[115] Elisha P. Douglass, *Rebels and Democrats: The Struggle for Equal Political Rights and Majority Rule during the American Revolution* (Chapel Hill, NC, 1955).

[116] Benjamin Quarles, *The Negro in the American Revolution* (Chapel Hill, NC, 1961). Quarles received his Ph.D. at Wisconsin in 1940; for the historiography of slavery, see August Meier and Elliott Rudwick, *Black History and the Historical Profession, 1915–1980* (Urbana, IL, 1986), and for Quarles, see ibid., 115–16; see also David Brion Davis, "Slavery and the Post–World War II Historians," *Daedalus*, Spring 1974, 1–16.

intellectual and ideological interpretations were in vogue, it was probably used more as a work of reference than interpretation.[117]

Robert R. Palmer's ambitious work of synthesis in the late 1950s, a magisterial two-volume comparative study of the late eighteenth-century revolutions in Europe and United States, sustained the ailing Jameson thesis in unexpected ways. A scholar of the French Revolution, a student of Carl Becker, Palmer offered the first comparative history of revolutions since Crane Brinton's and one of the last to include the American Revolution. Very much aware that he was writing at a moment when "those who discount the revolutionary character of the American Revolution seem to be gaining ground," Palmer asserted, "my own view is that there was a real revolution in America and that it was a painful conflict in which many were injured."[118]

To gauge the extent of social change Palmer offered two "quantitative and objective measures: how many refugees were there from the American Revolution, and how much property did they lose in comparison to the [émigrés from the] French Revolution." Estimates of the number of loyalist refugees ranged from sixty thousand to one hundred thousand. Taking the lower figure, Palmer calculated that this represented twenty-four émigrés per thousand population, compared to five per thousand in the French Revolution. Then, taking conservative figures for both countries to measure the confiscation of property, Palmer concluded that "revolutionary France, ten times as large as Revolutionary America, confiscated only twelve times as much property from its émigrés." Looking at the political impact of loyalist migration, Palmer wrote, "It must always be remembered that an important nucleus of conservatism was permanently lost in the United States." French émigrés, by contrast, returned to France.[119]

In examining the political dimensions of change, Palmer emphasized the way Americans institutionalized the concept of "the people as constituent power" in creating state constitutions. The Revolution "was revolutionary because it showed how certain abstract doctrines, such as the rights of man and the sovereignty of the people, could be 'reduced to practice' as [John] Adams put it." Palmer found the Revolution as a whole "really a revolution" but cloaked in "ambivalence." "It was conservative, it was also revolutionary, and vice versa. It was conservative because colonial Americans had

[117] Curtis P. Nettels, *The Emergence of a National Economy, 1775–1815* (New York, 1962).

[118] Robert R. Palmer, *The Age of the Democratic Revolution: A Political History of Europe and America, 1760–1800*, 2 vols. (Princeton, NJ, 1959–64), 1:187–88.

[119] Ibid., 188–90.

long been radical by general standards of Western Civilization. . . . It was conservative because the colonies had never known oppression, excepting always for slavery—because, as human institutions go, America had always been free." If these conclusions fell in with the thrust of consensus scholarship, the rest did not. The Revolution "was revolutionary because the colonists took the risk of rebellion, because they could not avoid a conflict among themselves, and because they checkmated those Americans who as the country developed most admired the aristocratic society of England and Europe. . . . Elites, for better or for worse, would henceforth be on the defensive against popular values."[120]

Richard B. Morris was a scholar who moved away from the Progressive interpretation of the Revolution without closing the door to Jameson and the issue of transformation. He received his degree in legal history from Columbia in 1929 and taught at the City University of New York until he received the call from Columbia. He was an outsider; a Yale professor described him to Jesse Lemisch, a Yale undergraduate on his way to Columbia graduate school, as "an energetic little man of your religious persuasion." In 1946 Morris published *Government and Labor in Early America*, a massive study of the white colonial laboring classes, free and indentured, based on ten years of research in twenty thousand court cases from Maine to Florida. Its importance was not apparent at the time to scholars either of the Revolution or of labor history. In a lengthy chapter Morris richly documented "concerted action among workers," including "political action by working-class groups," before, during, and after the Revolution. Morris located the urban classes the Progressive historians were unable to recognize, identifying the first American labor movement and filling in the missing "plain people" in the Revolution who Jameson could only see as "peasant proprietors." His mammoth two-volume documentary history of the Revolution, coedited with Henry Steele Commager, emphasized the experiences of the common people during the war—it is still unmatched —and included a chapter on the Progressive theme, "The Struggle for Democracy at Home."[121]

[120] Ibid., 235.

[121] Leonard W. Labaree to Jesse Lemisch, summer 1957, cited in Jesse Lemisch, "Radicals, Marxists, and Gentlemen: A Memoir of Twenty Years Ago," *Radical Historians' Newsletter* 59 (Nov. 1989); Richard B. Morris, *Government and Labor in Early America* (New York, 1946); Morris and Henry Steele Commager, eds., *The Spirit of 'Seventy-Six: The Story of the American Revolution as Told by Participants* (New York, 1958), chap. 10; Morris, *American Revolution Reconsidered*, chap. 2, 76, 84; Morris, "History over Time," 461.

"As I read more deeply into the American Revolutionary period," Morris reminisced, "I came to feel that the fashionable Populist-Progressive interpretation represented an oversimplification of the facts, and I parted company with much of the interpretation as regards the Confederation period." But in the mid-1960s, despite his sharp differences with Merrill Jensen, he held to the formulation that there were "the two Revolutions," one against Great Britain, the other internal, which was "marked by liberative currents, class currents, and egalitarian urges. . . . Clearly there is something more to the Spirit of '76 than 'redcoats go home.' "[122]

Earlier he had abandoned a massive study of slavery—not yet a fashionable field—shifting his energies to elites, editing the papers of John Jay and producing a full study of the diplomacy of the Revolution. But he did not abandon his earlier concerns. His own scholarship on the Confederation, he felt, focused "on the people rather than the leaders." "This is where my interpretation of the period departs from both the Populist-Progressive school and the consensus historians." In 1976, in his presidential address to the AHA, citing the scholarship of the New Left and new social history of the decade gone by, he spoke with verve of "a people's revolution" that began "an era of innovation unprecedented in that day and age." He laid stress, as did Palmer, on the "new men" who rose in the era of the Revolution. While he felt that "the case for significant social change during the Revolution still needs to be made," he was confident that "indubitably reform in . . . diverse categories helped create a more egalitarian and pluralistic society."[123]

A decade later, in his last book, he encapsulated these changes in the chapter "A Cautiously Transforming Egalitarianism," half of which he devoted to "persons forgotten," namely, "poor whites," "black people," "native Americans," and "women." "After more than half a century of interpreting the past," Morris offered a "confession": "Honest historians must be prepared to concede that new situations, additional documentation and further reflection may modify our earlier views." His openness to new trends

[122] Morris, "History over Time," 462.

[123] Richard B. Morris, *The Peacemakers: The Great Powers and American Independence* (New York, 1965); Morris, ed., *John Jay: Unpublished Papers, 1745–1784*, 2 vols. (New York, 1975–80); Morris, " 'We the People of the United States': The Bicentennial of a People's Revolution," *American Historical Review* 82 (1977): 1–19; for Morris's career, see Peter Coclanis, "Richard B. Morris," in Wilson, ed., *Twentieth-Century American Historians*, 307–14; for a bibliography, see Vaughan and Billias, eds., *Perspectives on Early American History*, 376–85.

was testimony to the persisting pull of a social interpretation of the Revolution, if not of Jameson.[124]

Reviewing recent reactions among scholars to the works of Douglass, Quarles, Nettels, Palmer, and Morris, it is striking how historians now testify to their durability despite the rising tides of the consensus era. Douglass's book in Gordon Wood's judgment is "important in emphasizing the radical and populist impulses in the states." Quarles's study is to Peter Wood "the judicious and pathbreaking study," and the editors of a volume of essays on slavery in the Revolution dedicated the book to Quarles and three other pioneer African American scholars. The standard survey of the literature on the economy takes it for granted that Nettels's thorough study of the impact of the war raises questions that merit further exploration. A scholar of the new history of colonial labor speaks of Morris's 1946 book as "a neglected classic . . . at the zenith of labor history." A survey in the 1990s of a score of historians of the Revolution for their opinions of Palmer's book finds a near consensus on his "amazing ability" to transcend the historiography of his time and enthusiasm for his interpretation. Such belated recognition should give heart to scholars who go against the grain; it is also a warning to judge each piece of nonconforming scholarship on its merits.[125]

7. The Counter-Progressives: Part 2

"This book," Bernard Bailyn wrote in 1974 in introducing his biography of Thomas Hutchinson, the leading loyalist of the American Revolution, "which depicts the fortunes of a conservative in a time of radical upheaval and deals with the problems of public disorder and ideological commitment, was not written as a tract for the times. . . . But it would be foolish to deny that I have been influenced in writing it by the events of the late

[124] Morris, *Forging of the Union*, chap. 7; Morris, "History over Time," *William and Mary Quarterly* 41 (1984): 455–63, quotation at 463.

[125] On Douglass: Bailyn et al., *The Great Republic*, 319; on Quarles: Wood, "I Did the Best I Could for My Day"; on Nettels: John J. McCusker and Russell R. Menard, *The Economy of British North America, 1607–1789* (Chapel Hill, NC, 1985), 360–61; on Morris: Marcus Rediker, "Good Hands, Stout Hearts, and Fast Feet: The History and Culture of Working People in Early America," in Geoff Eley and William Hunt, eds., *Reviving the English Revolution: Reflections and Elaborations on the Work of Christopher Hill* (London, 1988), 222n. 2; on Palmer: William Pencak, "A Second Look: R. R. Palmer's *The Age of the Democratic Revolution*: The View from America after Thirty Years," *Pennsylvania History* 60 (1993): 73–92.

1960's, when the original drafts were written. . . . My understanding of all of this has undoubtedly been sharpened by the course of American politics in the 1960's and early 1970's."[126]

If the first wave of counter-Progressive interpretations of the Revolution was shaped in the 1950s in the Manichean atmosphere of the Cold War and the need to lay the ghost of Charles Beard, the second wave associated with the ideological interpretation of Bernard Bailyn and Gordon Wood was more complex. It unfolded in the early 1960s in an atmosphere where revisionist scholarship was more secure and the nation, guided by the best and the brightest in Washington, seemed headed toward Arthur M. Schlesinger Jr.'s "vital center" and a renewal of the reform impulse. Then as the civil rights movement became Black Power and the movement against the Vietnam War and the youth counterculture turned reform into rebellion, the ideological interpretation seemed to veer off into opposition to "radical upheaval" and "public disorder."

If Edmund Morgan rejected Jameson's thesis of "the transforming hand of Revolution" outright, Bernard Bailyn and Gordon Wood cast a new interpretive mold in which "the transforming radicalism of the revolution" (Bailyn's phrase) flowing from the dominant ideology became a central theme. It was this latter theme that Bailyn later seemed to abandon but which Wood pursued.

The weight Bailyn attached to ideas in his ideological interpretation of the Revolution surprised his graduate students, who, as Wood wrote in a festschrift in 1991, thought of him in the 1950s and early 1960s as a historian of colonial America for whom "society itself" was "the central subject of study and analysis." His research had illuminated the merchant class of colonial New England, the social context of early American education, and the relation of politics to social structure in Virginia. In the study of politics they thought of him as committed to a "hard-boiled Namierism," skeptical of the causal role of ideas. Bailyn dedicated his edited volume on the pamphlets of the Revolution to his Harvard mentor and colleague, Oscar Handlin, a historian who had led social history into new terrain.[127]

[126] Bernard Bailyn, *The Ordeal of Thomas Hutchinson* (Cambridge, MA, 1974), vii–viii.

[127] Gordon S. Wood, "The Creative Imagination of Bernard Bailyn," in James A. Henretta, Michael G. Kammen, and Stanley N. Katz, eds., *The Transformation of Early American History: Society, Authority, and Ideology* (New York, 1991), 16–50; Jack N. Rakove, "'How Else Could It End?' Bernard Bailyn and the Problem of Authority in Early America," in ibid., 60–62. On the "vital" place of the Hutchinson biography in Bailyn's interpretation of the Revolution, see Bernard Bailyn, *The New England Merchants in the Seventeenth Century* (Cambridge, MA, 1955); Bailyn,

Bailyn's ideological interpretation of the Revolution was unmistakably counter-Progressive. Earlier he had distanced himself from some of the shapers of consensus scholarship. He characterized Daniel Boorstin's study of colonial America as an "apologia for his disillusioned conservatism." He regarded Robert Brown's claim that colonial Massachusetts was a middle-class democracy as "very confusing" for its failure to distinguish between the legal existence of a relatively wide franchise and its exercise and as "anachronistic" in its use of the concept of democracy. But Bailyn had accepted the Hartzian premise of the counter-Progressive critique. "Reforms that made America seem to the enlightened world like the veritable heavenly city of the eighteenth-century philosophers had been matters of fact before they were matters of theory and revolutionary doctrine," he wrote. In the Revolution the leaders "undertook to complete, formalize, systematize, and symbolize what previously had been only partially realized, confused, and disputed matters of fact."[128]

The Ideological Origins of the American Revolution (1967), originally published in 1964 as the extended introduction to the first of four projected volumes of pamphlets of the Revolution, was the outgrowth of Bailyn's study of over four hundred pamphlets, some seventy-two of which he chose to edit for the John Harvard Library. The Progressive historians from Schlesinger on had read the pamphlets as propaganda. Philip Davidson called his book *Propaganda and the American Revolution*; John C. Miller subtitled his biography of Samuel Adams *Pioneer in Propaganda*. "The more I read," Bailyn wrote, "the less useful it seemed to me, was the whole idea of propaganda in its modern meaning when applied to the writings of the American Revolution." Reading the pamphlets from the "interior" view, he was convinced "that the fear of a comprehensive conspiracy against liberty throughout the English-speaking world . . . lay at the heart of the Revolutionary movement." His study of the pamphlets, he wrote, "confirmed my rather old-fashioned view that the American Revolution was above all else an ideological, constitutional, political struggle

"Politics and Social Structure in Virginia," in James M. Smith, ed., *Seventeenth-Century America* (Chapel Hill, NC, 1959), 90–115; Bailyn, *Education in the Formation of American Society: Needs and Opportunities for Study* (Chapel Hill, NC, 1960).

[128] Bernard Bailyn, review of *The Americans: The Colonial Experience*, by Daniel Boorstin, *New Republic*, Dec. 15, 1958, 18, cited in Novick, *That Noble Dream*, 334; Bailyn, "The American Revolution," in John Garraty, *Interpreting American History: Conversations with Historians*, 2 vols. (New York, 1970), 1:85–86; Bailyn, "Political Experience and Enlightenment Ideas in Eighteenth-Century America," *American Historical Review* 67 (1962): 339–51.

and not primarily a controversy between social groups undertaken to force changes in the organization of the society or the economy"—a formulation in which the words "primarily" and "undertaken" made for a needlessly overstated antithesis.[129]

But if Bailyn's reading of the pamphlets confirmed his "old-fashioned" view of the origins of the Revolution, it suggested a newfangled view of the consequences or arguably a new version of J. Franklin Jameson's old-fashioned interpretation. The book in its original form in 1964 was called "The Transforming Radicalism of the American Revolution,"[130] and, if Bailyn retreated to a less threatening title, he did not abandon his bold formulation. Chapter 6, "The Contagion of Liberty," explored the impact of political ideas on antislavery thought, the disestablishment of religion, and the decline of deference, a terrain Jameson had opened, and on radical democratic thought, a subject Jameson had avoided.

To Jameson the Revolution had been inadvertently radical, a stream overflowing its banks; to Bailyn it was inherently radical, the consequence of the "logic of revolutionary thought" and of the "intellectual dynamism" of ideas. Bailyn posited two major intellectual transformations. The first was "a new world of political thought," which "crystallized in effect three generations of political experience" of the eighteenth century. "The radicalism the Americans conveyed to the world in 1776 was a transformed as well as a transforming force." Then, beginning in 1775–76, the movement of thought "swept past boundaries that few had set out to cross, into regions few had wished to enter." In an array of rich metaphors, in which agency was lost, this process was sometimes mechanical ("a spillover"), sometimes a disease ("the contagion of liberty"), sometimes a firestorm ("defiance of constituted authority leaped like a spark from one flammable area to another, growing in heat as it went"), and sometimes altogether mysterious (conditions were "touched by the magic of revolutionary thought"). Thus, while "in no obvious sense was the American Revolution undertaken as a social revolution"—"undertaken" offering another misleading caricature of Progressive claims—"the order of society" was "transformed as a result of the Revolution," or at least a basis for transformation was laid in "changes in

[129] Bernard Bailyn, with the assistance of Jane N. Garrett, ed., *Pamphlets of the American Revolution, 1750–1776: Volume 1, 1750–1765* (Cambridge, MA, 1965), vii–xii; Philip Davidson, *Propaganda and the American Revolution, 1763–1783* (Chapel Hill, NC, 1941); John C. Miller, *Sam Adams: Pioneer in Propaganda* (Stanford, CA, 1936); Schlesinger, *Prelude to Independence*; Bailyn, *The Ideological Origins of the American Revolution* (Cambridge, MA, 1967), vi.

[130] Bailyn, ed., *Pamphlets of the American Revolution*, xv.

the realm of belief and attitude."[131] In defending his interpretation, Bailyn later insisted that "it does not minimize the social and political changes that the Revolution created; it does not deny—indeed it alone explains—the upsurge of reformist zeal that is so central a part of the Revolution."[132]

Bailyn did not explore the "spillover" of the radicalism of Revolutionary thought. He edited only the first volume of pamphlets, which went to 1765, leaving in limbo the pamphlets of the mid-1770s that would have demonstrated the "contagion of liberty" in full epidemic. And the thrust of his own scholarship in these years lay entirely in amplifying the proof of the ideological origins of the Revolution, whether he was dealing with whig leaders; Thomas Hutchinson, the chief American loyalist; Protestant ministers; or the intellectual world of an ordinary man, Harbottle Dorr, a Boston shopkeeper.[133]

In the late 1960s and early 1970s Bailyn's argument and tone shifted. Earlier he portrayed the radical patriots as principled, rational, and ideological, even when driven by a paranoid conception of conspiracy.[134] He and his students, especially Pauline Maier, building on the pioneering work of George Rudé, rescued the mob from the accusations of contemporary loyalists and historians of all schools that rioters "were mindless instruments, passive tools of unscrupulous demagogues like [Ebenezer] McIntosh," the shoemaker prominent in the Boston Stamp Act demonstrations. Bailyn argued that, "far from being empty vessels," the rioters, albeit one-sidedly, "shared actively the attitudes and fears of the intellectual leaders of the Revolutionary movement."[135] Now Bailyn seemed to identify himself with Thomas Hutchinson, as had Edmund Morgan in *The Stamp Act Crisis*, and to distance himself from the radicals. In Bailyn's biography of Hutchinson, Hutchinson's radical whig opponents became "demagogues" and "malcontents" who included "wild men, alarmists, the political paranoids, the

[131] Bailyn, *Ideological Origins*, 161–62, 230, 236, 271, 302, 305.

[132] Bernard Bailyn, "The Central Themes of the American Revolution," in Kurtz and Hutson, eds., *Essays on the American Revolution*, 15.

[133] The essays are assembled in Bernard Bailyn, *Faces of Revolution: Personalities and Themes in the Struggle for American Independence* (New York, 1990).

[134] Bernard Bailyn, "A Note on Conspiracy," in Bailyn, ed., *Pamphlets of the American Revolution*, 86–89.

[135] Bernard Bailyn, introduction to Benjamin Church, *Liberty and Property Vindicated*, in ibid., 583; Pauline Maier, "Popular Uprisings and Civil Authority in Eighteenth-Century America," *William and Mary Quarterly*, 3d ser. 27 (1970): 3–35, reprinted in *In Search of Early America*, 138–61, with author's postscript, 161–62; Maier, *From Resistance to Revolution: Colonial Radicals and the Development of American Opposition to Britain, 1765–1776* (New York, 1972).

professional agitators." They were "paranoics" driven by "passion and personal discontent" to make a "scapegoat" of Hutchinson. Bailyn thus reduced to a crude psychological determinism a group he had previously portrayed as rational. And the mob now appeared as "brutal," "savage," "more and more savage," and in effect mindless.[136] The historian reaches the "ultimate stage of maturity," Bailyn wrote, "where partisanship is left behind, and the historian can find an equal humanity in all the participants, the winners and the losers."[137] Between 1964 and 1974 Bailyn's winners, the patriots, top and bottom, lost some of their humanity.

This shift in Bailyn's value judgments of radicals was striking in his commentary on Thomas Paine. In 1964, in the comparative context of the pamphlets, Bailyn considered *Common Sense* "that brilliant pamphlet," agreeing explicitly with the socialist Harold Laski that Paine, "with the exception of Marx," was "the most influential pamphleteer of all time." In the late 1960s *Common Sense* was still "a brilliant rhetorical production" and "a brilliant pamphlet by any measure." But by 1973 Paine was "savage," "enraged," "an ignoramus," "a bankrupt corset maker," whose writing was "slapdash," "crude," and "slightly insane," and by 1975 Bailyn dismissed his writings as "marginal."[138]

In his attitude to other historians by the 1970s Bailyn demonstrated what Gordon Wood calls an "aversion" and a "particular antipathy" to a social interpretation of the Revolution "which confused and troubled even some of his former students." "He has been apparently unwilling to entertain any sort of social interpretation of the Revolution," Wood wrote. "Since his discovery of ideology, Bailyn has repeatedly denied that the Revolution had social origins and social impulses and has gone out of his way to refute those historians who have tried to find any."[139]

A contextualist analysis of Bailyn's own writings—the only source open to outsiders—suggests he was obsessed with the emergence of a wide range of historians who had not fallen in with either an intellectual or an ideological reading of the Revolution. He lumped together as "neo-progressives" second- and third-generation Progressives, the first wave of the New Left

[136] Bailyn, *Ordeal of Thomas Hutchinson*, 15, 72–73, 125, 133–34, 139, 182.

[137] Ibid., viii–xii; Bailyn, "Central Themes," 15.

[138] Bailyn, *Ideological Origins*, 285–86; Bailyn, "American Revolution," in Garraty, *Conversations with Historians*, 1:87–88; Bailyn, "Common Sense," in *Fundamental Testaments of the American Revolution*, Library of Congress Symposia on the American Revolution (Washington, DC, 1973); Bailyn, "Lines of Force," 10.

[139] Wood, "Creative Imagination," 35.

and the new social history, and even other consensus scholars and heretics among his students. In a paper he delivered in 1971 to a conference of scholars of the Revolution, one had to guess who were his contemporary targets from the arrows of "nots" he shot from his quiver. "The outbreak of the revolution was not the result of social discontent, or of economic disturbances, or of rising misery [Gary Nash? Kenneth Lockridge? James Henretta?], or of those mysterious social strains that seem to beguile the imaginations of historians straining to find peculiar predispositions to upheaval [Jack Greene? Gordon Wood?]. Nor was there a transformation of mob behavior or of the lives of the 'inarticulate' [Jesse Lemisch? Staughton Lynd?] in the pre-revolutionary years that accounts for the disruption of Anglo-American politics."[140] Earlier he thought that "there can be some benefits from what the New Left historians are attempting to do"; the study of the mob "should yield some useful social data."[141] In 1975, in a paper before an international congress of historians, he pilloried scholars pursuing the study of "the mob," "the helpless and inarticulate," seamen, and slaves as being for the most part "hopelessly presentist" or driven by "extreme and polemical presentism." He felt compelled to reassure scholars still steeped in the comparative study of revolutions that in the American Revolution "there was no massive challenge from below," as in the English civil war, and "no peasant uprising, no millenarian or anarchistic or jacobin communistic rebellion." Bailyn attempted to withdraw the American Revolution altogether from the generic category of revolutions.[142]

What accounts for Bailyn's differences with his critics hardening into "aversion" and his judgment of the radical whigs changing from principle to paranoia? The events of 1968 and 1969 that might have impinged on a professor at Harvard University writing about rioters who had destroyed Thomas Hutchinson's manuscript history of Massachusetts in 1765 while demolishing his house were many: students storming University Hall in Harvard Yard bent on uncovering the dean's files, students at Columbia University occupying buildings and destroying a scholar's manuscript, liberal and left historians mounting a serious challenge to the historical establishment at the AHA's annual convention in 1969—one could go on. Kenneth Lynn, a Harvard professor of American Civilization, believes Bailyn

[140] Bailyn, "Central Themes," 12–13. The identification of the scholars is made explicit in Bailyn, "Lines of Force."

[141] Bailyn, "American Revolution," in Garraty, *Conversations with Historians*, 1:86–87.

[142] Bailyn, "Lines of Force," 8–20, 24–34. This essay was not published or reprinted in Bailyn, *Faces of Revolution*.

"learned a great deal from his experience in the Harvard Bust. He learned what it felt like to be an establishment insider who knows that the social order he is fighting for has made grave mistakes, but whose first duty is to preserve its integrity from the onslaughts of anarchy." An obsession with presentism in other scholars has its own presentist roots.[143]

Bailyn never published his angry polemic of 1975, and in 1981, after a semblance of equilibrium was restored to American society, Harvard, and the historical profession, in an expansive mood in his presidential address to the AHA Bailyn said, "We are all Marxists in the sense of assuming that history is profoundly shaped by underlying economic or 'materialist' configurations and by people's responses to them." This together with his massive "Peopling of British North America" studies led Gordon Wood to conclude that "he has returned to social history with a vengeance and has reminded us that he is still the social historian he always was." In 1992, with the radicalism of the American Revolution on the agenda of historians, Bailyn in the preface to the second edition of *Ideological Origins* reminded readers, "In fact I called the book when it was first published *The Transforming Radicalism of the American Revolution*." He expanded the volume to include a chapter on the Constitution of 1787 as "the final and climactic expression of the ideology of the American Revolution" but left in limbo "the contagion of liberty." It was a theme he had asserted but not pursued.[144]

If Bailyn did not pursue his hypothesis about the "the transforming radicalism of the Revolution," Gordon Wood did. Of all Bailyn's numerous, talented, independent-minded students, Wood did the most to expand and at the same time challenge his mentor's interpretation. While Wood's book *The Creation of the American Republic, 1776–1787* (1969) took a place alongside *Ideological Origins* in the canon of the ideological interpretation, Wood was persistently in tension with Bailyn. In an influential article in 1966 Wood argued that the very success of the Bailyn thesis pointed to the need

[143] Kenneth Lynn, "The Regressive Historians," *American Scholar* 47 (1978), reprinted in Lynn, *The Airline to Seattle: Studies in Literary and Historical Writing about America* (Chicago, 1983), 190–93; for events of the 1960s, see Todd Gitlin, *The Sixties: Years of Hope, Days of Rage* (New York, 1987); for events at Harvard, see Lawrence E. Eichel, Kenneth W. Jost, Robert D. Luskin, and Richard M. Neustadt, *The Harvard Strike* (New York, 1970); for scholarship and politics at Harvard, see John Trumpbour, ed., *How Harvard Rules* (Boston, 1989), 379–97; for the activities of radical historians, see Jonathan M. Wiener, "Radical Historians and the Crisis in American History, 1959–1980," *Journal of American History* 76 (1989): 399–434, and Novick, *That Noble Dream*, chap. 13.

[144] Bernard Bailyn, "The Challenge of Modern Historiography," *American Historical Review* 87 (1982): 1–24, quotation at 6; Wood, "Creative Imagination," 44; Bailyn, *Ideological Origins of the American Revolution*, enlarged ed. (Cambridge, MA, 1992), v, 321–79.

for a new socioeconomic interpretation of the Revolution. Wood rejected the scholarship of the Progressive historians because it "explicitly rejected the causal importance of ideas"; for Bailyn "ideas counted for a great deal."

Indeed, Wood wrote, for Bailyn "the ideas of the Revolutionaries take on . . . a dynamic self-intensifying character that transcended the intentions and desires of the historical participants." He "has ended by demonstrating the autonomy of ideas as phenomena where the ideas operate as it were over the heads of the participants, taking them in directions no one could have foreseen." Whig thought showed "fear and frenzy," "enthusiastic extravagance," and a "paranoic obsession." "The very nature of the Americans' rhetoric," Wood argued, "reveals as nothing else apparently can the American Revolution as a true revolution with its sources lying deep in the social structure. For this kind of frenzied rhetoric could only spring from the most severe sorts of social strain." The sources of the strain therefore required investigation. "It may be," Wood concluded, "that the Progressive historians in their preoccupation with internal social problems were more right than we have recently been willing to grant."[145]

In his own book that followed, Wood did not fulfill the promise of this hypothesis; but if he did not take on the challenge to portray the "reality" that underlay "the rhetoric," as did several other scholars of politics, his analysis of the rhetoric restored conflict in the realm of ideas to the period from 1776 to 1787. Accepting Bailyn's ideological construct of the origins of the Revolution, he argued that after 1776 the Revolution "broadened into a struggle among Americans themselves for the fruits of independence, [and] became in truth a multifaceted affair with layers below layers." Some deep-going, underlying social conflict was implicit in this rhetorical conflict. "How to keep them down" was a "central question" to whigs after Independence, and while Wood never defined "them," through his dense forest of quotations from contemporary sources one caught occasional sight of an agrarian rebel, an urban mechanic, or more likely a self-interested "new man" of the middling sort pushing into politics.[146]

[145] Gordon S. Wood, "Rhetoric and Reality in the American Revolution," *William and Mary Quarterly*, 3d ser. 23 (1966): 3–32, reprinted in *In Search of Early America*, 54–77. For a list of Bailyn's students and their theses, see Henretta, Kammen, and Katz, eds., *Transformation of Early American History*, 261–66.

[146] Gordon S. Wood, *Creation of the American Republic, 1776–1787* (Chapel Hill, NC, 1969), 83; for Wood's subsequent analysis, see Wood, "The Democratization of Mind in the American Revolution," in *Leadership in the American Revolution*, Library of Congress Symposia on the American Revolution (Washington, DC, 1974), 63–88, and see the works by Wood discussed in section 11 of this essay.

This interpretation of 1776–87 as a period of intense ideological conflict, however undefined the interests, raised serious questions about Bailyn's interpretation of 1765–76. "The dominant fact of the earlier years," wrote Bailyn, "had been the intensification of the ideological passions first ignited by the Stamp Act crisis and their final bursting into open insurrection." Thereafter the ideas "were turned to positive uses in the framing of the first state constitutions [and] in the transforming of regressive social institutions." But "passions cooled as ordinary life reasserted itself and cultural, sectional, and social difference . . . became important." As Wood argued, "Bailyn's notion that ideas are ascendant and important at particular ideologically exciting times in the past—until social conditions reassert themselves—suggests a kind of seesawing up-and-down fluctuation between ideology and social behavior that . . . does violence to the full reality of human action."[147]

As Wood reached 1787, his analysis of the rhetoric implied a Progressive-like reality. The crux of the movement for the Constitution of 1787 was an effort by the elite to control the "vices of the political system," which Wood, like James Madison, located in the volatile, popular politics of the state legislatures, responsive to "the people out of doors." The Constitution thus was "in some sense an aristocratic document designed to curb the democratic excesses of the Revolution." This rattled Beard's ghost. At the conclusion of his magnum opus, Wood asked other scholars to "assess the immense consequences of the social forces released by the Revolution," an invitation that beckoned Jameson from the grave.[148]

The Bailyn-Wood thesis wedded to J. G. A. Pocock's "civic humanism" was rapidly absorbed into a "Republican synthesis" that, as Wood writes, was not at all Bailyn's intention and "is an object lesson in the unanticipated consequences of purposive action."[149] Joyce Oldham Appleby likened the discovery of republicanism "to the response of chemists to a new element. Once having been identified, it can be found everywhere." It was also challenged convincingly by Appleby's own analysis of liberalism as an ideology competing with republicanism, a "second language" that was equally revolutionary but more "modern" than republicanism and that had special resonance among the "upwardly mobile" seeking their own "self-interest."[150]

[147] Wood, "Creative Imagination," 37.

[148] Wood, *Creation of the American Republic*, 626–27.

[149] Wood, "Creative Imagination," 28–29; Bailyn, *Ideological Origins*, 2d ed., v–viii.

[150] Joyce Oldham Appleby, "Republicanism and Ideology," *American Quarterly*, 3d ser. 37 (1985): 461–73, reprinted in Appleby, *Liberalism and Republicanism in the Historical Imagination*

By 1982 Robert Shalhope, who in 1972 considered the republican synthesis pervasive, found that the research of the ten years gone by made clear that "it is no longer possible to see a single, monolithic ideology characterizing American thought on the eve of the Revolution."[151] And in 1992 Daniel T. Rodgers's review of "the career of a concept" summed up what was missing: "It squeezed out massive domains of culture—religion, law, political economy, ideas of patriarchy, family and gender, ideas of race and slavery, class and nationalism, nature and reason—that everyone knew to be profoundly tangled in the revolutionary impulse." John Shy summed up the longstanding skepticism of a wide range of scholars when he said in an interview, "What is troubling me at this moment about the state of American historical writing and thinking about the revolutionary period is the assumption that there is a single unitary culture that holds something that can be accurately described as an ideology. . . . And frankly I just don't believe it. I am ready to be *convinced*, I think, but I *have* not been convinced."[152]

Almost all of this challenge dealt with the argument on terrain Bailyn and Wood had staked out in the realm of ideas or at the point of origins. "The transforming radicalism of the revolution" went untested at the point of consequences and in the social and economic terrain until the emergence of historians of "the New Left" and "the new social history."

III. New Left, New Social History

8. The New Left

Among historians there were two New Lefts: the first around *Studies on the Left* (1959–67), a journal founded by graduate students in history at

(Cambridge, MA, 1992), quotation at 277; see also Appleby, "Liberalism and the American Revolution," and Appleby, "The Social Origins of American Revolutionary Ideology," in Appleby, *Liberalism and Republicanism*, 140–60, 161–87.

[151] Robert Shalhope, "Toward a Republican Synthesis: The Emergence of an Understanding of Republicanism in American Historiography," *William and Mary Quarterly*, 3d ser. 29 (1972): 49–80; Shalhope, "Republicanism and Early American Historiography," *William and Mary Quarterly*, 3d ser. 39 (1982): 334–56, quotation at 346.

[152] Daniel T. Rodgers, "Republicanism: The Career of a Concept," *Journal of American History* 79 (1992): 11–38, quotation at 17; for a critique in the Progressive tradition, see Colin Gordon, "Crafting a Usable Past," *William and Mary Quarterly*, 3d ser. 46 (1989): 679–95; Loretta Valtz Mannucci, "Four Conversations on Future Directions in Revolutionary War Historiography," *Storia Nordamericana* 2 (1985): 118–19 (John Shy).

the University of Wisconsin associated with William Appleman Williams and the "radicalism of disclosure," the second, beginning later in the 1960s, associated with Staughton Lynd and Jesse Lemisch and "history from the bottom up." The two groups shared a distaste for the politics and historiography of the Old Left but were in tension with each other. Eventually, as Peter Novick has pointed out, "the new, left-oriented historians who became visible within the profession during the 1960s came to be capitalized, reified and often tacitly homogenized as 'New Left historians.' This was a largely empty and misleading designation, lumping together individuals of the most diverse orientation, and often, innocently or maliciously, associating them with the most extreme wing of the student movement." Yet distortions aside, there were New Left historians of the Revolution who laid out contrasting radical visions of the transformations of the era that challenged Progressives as well as counter-Progressives.[153]

New Left historians found few models in an Old Left American historiography dating to the 1930s either for doing history or for interpreting the Revolution. The Old Left scholarship on the Revolution was in different ways a tail on the Progressive kite. In the late 1930s, on the one hand, was Louis M. Hacker's *Triumph of American Capitalism*, a highly schematic economic-determinist Marxism with no sense of agency, which saw the Revolution as the triumph of mercantile capitalism leading inevitably to the victory of industrial capitalism. Hacker was an economist at Columbia whose interpretation circulated in the 1950s (long after he recanted his youthful exuberance), probably because it fit the caricature of Marxism as economic determinism. At the other pole was a book by Jack Hardy, *The First American Revolution*, brought out by International Publishers; Hardy read the Sons of Liberty radicals as if they were a vanguard party leading the masses to revolution. Becker's dual revolution and Jameson's social movement were understated in Hacker and overstated in Hardy. The most important Marxist monograph of the era, Herbert Aptheker's pathbreaking study of slave revolts (1943), had far-reaching implications for the study of

[153] Novick, *That Noble Dream*, chap. 13, quotation at 417–18; Wiener, "Radical Historians," 399–444. For the first New Left, see *Studies on the Left* (1959–67). For the second New Left, see Barton J. Bernstein, ed., *Towards a New Past: Dissenting Essays in American History* (New York, 1968); *Radical America* (1967–); Paul Buhle, "History, United States," and "New Left," and Elliot Shore, "Radical Professional and Academic Journals," in Mary Jo Buhle, Paul Buhle, and Dan Georgakas, eds., *Encyclopedia of the American Left* (New York, 1990). For a contemporary critique, see Irwin Unger, "The 'New Left' and American History: Some Recent Trends in United States Historiography," *American Historical Review* 72 (1967): 1237–63, and Unger, ed., *Beyond Liberalism: The New Left Views American History* (Waltham, MA, 1971).

both the Revolution and slave resistance that were not integrated into an analysis either by Marxists or by any other historians. The Old Left of the popular-front era fell into a kind of whig history celebrating liberal democratic heroes such as Thomas Jefferson and radicals such as Samuel Adams and Thomas Paine as forerunners of their own radical tradition.[154]

William Appleman Williams was the most important scholar of elites in the New Left and one of the few to devote major attention to the founding era. His influential synthesis, *Contours of American History*, suggested a new conceptualization for American history. The first third of this book was devoted to "The Age of Mercantilism, 1740–1828," the second to "The Age of Laissez Nous Faire, 1819–1896," and last third to "The Age of Corporate Capitalism, 1882–."[155] The idea of the third age won more converts than the idea of the first. A graduate student at Wisconsin, then a member of the Department of History (1957–68) at its Progressive ebbtide, Williams drew from Progressive scholarship; an article by Curtis Nettels was an inspiration for Williams's conceptualization. But Williams was more left than his Progressive colleagues. Active in the early civil rights movement, he was hounded by the House Committee on Un-American Activities and was probably the only historian to have the honor of having the manuscript of a book subpoenaed by that committee. Williams was also more theoretical. An admirer of Beard as a "Tory radical," he attempted to dissolve a major theoretical impasse in the debate over Beard by shifting attention from the pocketbook interests of elites to the political economy

[154] Louis M. Hacker, *The Triumph of American Capitalism: The Development of Forces in American History to the End of the Nineteenth Century* (New York, 1940); Hacker, "The American Revolution: Economic Aspects," *Marxist Quarterly* 1 (1937): 46–67, widely reprinted in the 1950s; Jack Hardy, *The First American Revolution* (New York, 1937); Elizabeth Lawson, ed., *Samuel Adams: Selections from His Writings* (New York, 1946); Paul Buhle, *Marxism in the United States* (London, 1987), chaps. 5–7; Buhle, "American Marxist Historiography, 1900–1940," *Radical America* 4 (1970): 5–36; Herbert Aptheker, *American Negro Slave Revolts* (New York, 1943); Aptheker, *Essays in the History of the American Negro* (New York, 1945); Herbert Morais, *The Struggle for American Freedom: The First Two Hundred Years* (New York, 1944); Philip S. Foner, ed., *The Complete Writings of Thomas Paine*, 2 vols. (New York, 1945); for postwar Marxist scholarship, see Aptheker, *The American Revolution, 1763–1783* (New York, 1960); Foner, *Labor and the American Revolution* (Westport, CT, 1976); see also Harvey Kaye, "Capitalism and Democracy in America: Leo Huberman's *We the People*," chap. 6 in *The Education of Desire: Marxists and the Writing of History* (New York, 1992).

[155] William Appleman Williams, *Contours of American History* (1961; reprint ed., New York, 1988); Michael Wallace, interview with William Appleman Williams (1980), in Abelove et al., eds., *Visions of History*, 125–46; Williams, "My Life in Madison," in Buhle, ed., *History and the New Left*, chap. 28; Herbert G. Gutman and Warren Susman, "Memories of Madison in the Fifties," *Radical History Review* 36 (1986): 101–9.

and world outlook of their class. "Reality is not economics vs. ideals or of politics vs. either," he argued. "Reality instead involves how a political act is also an economic act, of how an idea of freedom involves a commitment to a particular economic system."[156]

Williams saw the leaders of the Revolution as a coalition of interest groups among the "gentry," who in breaking from the British Empire wanted to establish their own mercantilist empire. Expansion had a central place in American policy from the outset. The leaders were bent on building "a rising empire" or an "empire of liberty" (phrases common to men such as Franklin and Jefferson), dedicated both to landed expansion across the continent and commercial expansion overseas. Very much aware of the radicalism of the era, Williams saw James Madison's effort to "extend the sphere" of the republic in 1787 as the gentry's solution to "the long pattern of discontent and unrest among the middle and lower classes." But he reinterpreted radicals of the Revolution; he saw Samuel Adams, for example, as "a true Calvinist and thoroughgoing mercantilist" who was "dedicated to the ideal and reality of a corporate Christian commonwealth" and thus was "a revolutionary without being a radical." To Williams the true radicals in American history were those who dissented from empire as a way of life.[157]

Williams, who directed some forty doctoral dissertations, won recognition as "the single most important figure in the reconceptualization of the history of American foreign policy." His insight into the political economy of the Revolution was picked up by scholars anxious to break out of a narrow economic determinism, but his emphasis on the centrality of expansion probably was little appreciated by historians of the Revolution who generally compartmentalized foreign from domestic policy.[158]

[156] William Appleman Williams, "Confessions of an Intransigent Revisionist," *Socialist Review* 17 (Sept.–Oct. 1973): 94, reprinted in Henry Berger, ed., *A William Appleman Williams Reader* (Chicago, 1992), 336–44; Williams, "Charles Austin Beard: The Intellectual as Tory Radical," in Harvey Goldberg, ed., *American Radicals: Some Problems and Personalities* (New York, 1957), reprinted in Berger, ed., *Williams Reader*, 105–15.

[157] Williams, *Contours*, chaps. 3–5; Williams, "The Age of Mercantilism: An Interpretation of American Political Economy, 1763–1828," *William and Mary Quarterly*, 3d ser. 15 (1958): 419–37; Susman to Gates, Jan. 8, 1961, cited in Peter Novick, "American Leftist Historians" (paper presented at the American Historical Association, San Francisco, Dec. 1978); Williams, "Samuel Adams: Calvinist, Mercantilist, Revolutionary," *Studies on the Left* 1 (1960), reprinted in Williams, *History as a Way of Learning* (New York, 1973).

[158] Novick, *That Noble Dream*, 446; Egnal, *Mighty Empire*; Ernst, *Money and Politics in America*; Ernst and Egnal, "An Economic Interpretation of the American Revolution"; John Nelson, *Liberty and Property: Political Economy and Policymaking in the New Nation, 1789–1812* (Baltimore, 1987); for an echo of the expansionist theme, see Drew R. McCoy, *The Elusive Republic: Political*

Lynd and Lemisch were characteristic of the other trend in the historiography of the New Left—an emphasis on the agency of the common people, an avowed identification of the historian with movements for radical change in contemporary society, and a sense of moral passion in the presentation of history. Each focused on the Revolutionary era, initially exploring groups that were blanks in the books of almost all historians —Lynd on tenant farmers and urban mechanics, Lemisch on the merchant seamen.

Both began their scholarship as graduate students in the "bottom of the fifties and the bad times before the sixties became *The Sixties*," as Lemisch has put it in a memoir, a statement which is less a puzzle than it seems. Both grew up in "Old Left" families in New York. Lynd's parents were the critical sociologists Helen and Robert Lynd of *Middletown* and *Middletown in Transition* fame. Lemisch's mother was a rank-and-file Communist "totally unschooled in Marxism," Lemisch writes, "who bred in me a street level variety which may have been better than the real thing." As undergraduates, Lynd at Harvard (1946–51) and Lemisch at Yale (1953–57) were members of the student left. At Columbia, Richard Morris, sui generis for his interest in colonial labor history, directed Lynd's doctoral thesis and Lemisch's master's work before Lemisch returned to Yale to do his doctoral thesis under Edmund Morgan. While becoming a historian, Lynd was contributing articles to *Studies on the Left*, the *New Republic*, *Commentary*, and *Liberation*, where he interpreted Henry David Thoreau as "an admirable radical," a forerunner of his own Quaker commitments; Lemisch wrote for the *Nation*.[159]

Not until both were well into their scholarship did the mass political movements emerge in which they took part. Each acknowledged the interrelatedness of their experience as historians and activists. From the mid-1960s "the civil rights and anti-war movements," Jonathan M. Wiener

Economy in Jeffersonian America (Chapel Hill, NC, 1980); for Williams's general influence, see "Excerpts from a Conference to Honor William Appleman Williams," *Radical History Review* 50 (1991): 39–70, and Bradford Perkins, "*The Tragedy of American Diplomacy*: Twenty-five Years After," *Reviews in American History* 12 (1984): 1–18.

[159] Jesse Lemisch, "Looking for Jack Tar in the Scholarly Darkness, or, The Political Context of History from the Bottom Up at the End of the '50s" (paper presented at the "Jack Tar in History" conference, Halifax, Nova Scotia, Oct. 1990), in possession of the author; Staughton Lynd, "Father and Son: Intellectual Work outside the University," *Social Policy*, Spring 1993, 4–11; Lynd, "Henry Thoreau: The Admirable Radical," *Liberation*, Feb. 1963, 21–26; Lemisch, "Who Won the Civil War, Anyway?" *Nation*, Apr. 9, 1961; for the context, see Maurice Isserman, *If I Had a Hammer: The Death of the Old Left and the Birth of the New Left* (New York, 1987).

writes, "gave participants an experience of making history from below. . . . The revival of political opposition among the most oppressed (blacks) and the most incorporated (students) required analysis; it suggested a different sense of how history was made, not simply by elites, from the top down, but in the interaction of social groups holding power in different forms." Lynd's shift of attention to the Founding Fathers and slavery and to the abolitionists paralleled his activity as director of the Mississippi Freedom Schools in 1964 and as a teacher at Spelman, a historically black college. His exploration of the intellectual roots of American radicalism paralleled his role in the movement against the war in Vietnam and his citizens peace mission to Hanoi in 1965. Lemisch, who had been arrested for civil disobedience in 1963 and 1965, writes that he came "to a deeper understanding of the phenomenon of 'riot'" in August 1968 in Chicago as he made his way across the chaos and tear gas of Michigan Avenue after the police broke up a demonstration at the Democratic Party convention. The movements, as Wiener put it, "rapidly *became* a source of intellectual energy for those developing critical perspectives on consensus history."[160] So did the powerful examples of the recovery of plebeian history by the English revisionist Marxist scholars—of George Rudé on the crowd, Eric Hobsbawm on "primitive rebels," Christopher Hill on Puritan radicals, and especially E. P. Thompson, who sought to rescue the "agency" of the common people from "the enormous condescension of posterity."[161]

Staughton Lynd epitomized left historians trying to break out of the Progressive paradigm. Looking back in 1967, he wrote, "My own initial attitude toward the Progressive historiography of Turner, Beard, Becker, and Parrington, was uncritical. I did not expect to be driven beyond Beard, to lay greater stress than he did upon city artisans, upon slavery, upon the role of ideas. These themes were imposed, one at a time, by the subject matter itself." "Beyond Beard" was the title he gave to his essay in synthesis; "After Carl Becker," the title he and I gave to the introduction to a brace of articles

[160] Wiener, "Radical Historians," 412–13, emphasis added; Staughton Lynd and Thomas Hayden, *The Other Side* (New York, 1966); Lemisch, "Looking for Jack Tar."

[161] George Rudé, *The Crowd in History* (New York, 1964); Eric Hobsbawm, *Primitive Rebels: Studies in Archaic Forms of Social Movements in the 19th and 20th Centuries* (New York, 1965); Christopher Hill, *The World Turned Upside Down: Radical Ideas during the English Revolution* (New York, 1972); E. P. Thompson, *The Making of the English Working Class* (1963; reprint ed., New York, 1966); see the interviews with Thompson (1976, 1978) in Abelove et al., eds., *Visions of History*, 3–46; Harvey Kaye, *The British Marxist Historians: An Introductory Analysis* (Oxford, UK, 1984); and for George Rudé, see Kaye, *Education of Desire*, chap. 2.

on the mechanics of New York City, his dealing with 1775 to 1787, mine focusing on 1788 to 1801.[162]

Lynd used a single locale, Dutchess County, New York, as a microcosm to test Becker and Beard and implicitly Jameson, pioneering a case study approach long before it become commonplace. Dutchess County on the east bank of the Hudson River, with its vast estates of landlord aristocrats and tenants and a small middling class of farmers and entrepreneurs, while atypical, was a rich laboratory. What he found was a complex picture in which "the same economic groups, to a striking extent the same leaders, confronted each other in the tenants' rising of 1766, the struggle during the Revolution over the confiscation and sale of loyalist lands, and in the battle over ratification of the Constitution." Tenants fought for the confiscation and then the sale of the land they farmed, winning a struggle in which the middling gentry foes of the landlords (the Antifederalists to be) supported them. Thus, Lynd added agency to Jameson's lifeless discussion of the redistribution of land and complexity to Beard's simplified analysis of the alignments in New York on the Constitution.[163]

In New York City, Lynd found the faceless "rabble" of Becker and Jameson to be composed of politically conscious mechanics, who after 1775 developed a radical democratic program and after the war, as "a mechanic interest," formed an alliance with merchants behind the Constitution of 1787 in support of their own manufacturing and commercial needs. He thus explained a group Beard could not account for. Interested in the interplay of elites with subordinate classes, he saw the New York gentry in 1787 as "a governing class on the defensive," who turned to national power to curtail the state power they had lost to the new middling men, an alternative

[162] Staughton Lynd, *Class Conflict, Slavery, and the United States Constitution: Ten Essays* (Indianapolis, 1967), 8–9; Lynd and Alfred F. Young, "After Carl Becker: The Mechanics and New York City Politics, 1774–1801" (Lynd, "The Mechanics and New York City Politics, 1774–1788"; Young, "The Mechanics and the Jeffersonians, 1789–1801"), *Labor History* 5 (1964): 215–76. Lynd and I presented the papers at a session of the Organization of American Historians in 1962; I later worked with him as general editor of the American Heritage Series, for which he edited *Nonviolence in America: A Documentary History* (Indianapolis, 1966); in 1967–68 I served with Christopher Lasch as cochair of the Ad Hoc Committee to Defend Academic Freedom in Illinois, formed to defend Lynd in the Chicago cases.

[163] Staughton Lynd, "Who Should Rule at Home? Dutchess County, New York, in the American Revolution," *William and Mary Quarterly*, 3d ser. 18 (1961): 330–59; Lynd, *Anti-Federalism in Dutchess County, New York: A Study of Democracy and Class Conflict in the Revolutionary Era* (Chicago, 1962), quotation at 4. The thesis won Loyola University Press's William P. Lyons Masters Essay Contest for 1960.

to Beard that substituted a viable analysis of class for narrow economic interest.[164]

Lynd went "beyond Beard" most sharply in the importance he attached to slavery in the making of the Constitution and Jeffersonian democracy. Beard's dichotomy between "personalty" (liquid capital) and "realty" (land), he argued, had submerged a more fundamental distinction between slaveholding southern planters and northern yeomen. "The slave, though he spoke few lines, should be moved front and center" because "to whatever extent the Constitution betrayed the promise of the Declaration of Independence, it did so most of all for the Negro." Lynd grappled with the puzzle of the old Confederation Congress in New York passing an ordinance banning slavery in the Northwest with the consent of the South shortly after the delegates at the Philadelphia Constitutional Convention ninety miles away broke the impasse between North and South by adopting the three-fifths compromise over representation in the House. This, he argued, as have other scholars since, was the result of an accommodation over slavery, the fundamental compromise of 1787.[165]

Lynd's search for the eighteenth-century intellectual origins of the radical tradition that found fulfillment in the higher-law radicalism of Thoreau and Martin Luther King Jr. took him beyond Becker and beyond Bailyn. In a book-length "exploratory sketch," he located in the English dissenting radicals of the 1760s and 1770s, especially James Burgh and John Cartright, a cluster of beliefs not addressed in the prevailing view of the Commonwealthmen. "Dissenting radicalism raised awkward questions about the absolute right of private property," which found echoes in Jefferson's doctrine that "the earth belongs to the living." And the dissenting belief in

[164] Staughton Lynd, "Capitalism, Democracy and the United States Constitution: The Case of New York," *Science and Society* 27 (1963): 385–414, reprinted as "A Governing Class on the Defensive: The Case of New York," chap. 5 in Lynd, *Class Conflict*, 109–32.

[165] Staughton Lynd, "Beyond Beard," in Bernstein, ed., *Towards a New Past*, 46–64, quotation at 58; Lynd, "The Compromise of 1787," *Political Science Quarterly* 81 (1966): 225–50, "On Turner, Beard, and Slavery," *Journal of Negro History* 48 (1963): 235–50, and "The Abolitionist Critique of the United States Constitution," in Martin Duberman, ed., *The Antislavery Vanguard: New Essays on the Abolitionists* (Princeton, NJ, 1965), 209–39, all three reprinted in Lynd, *Class Conflict*, chaps. 6–8, 135–213; for recent scholarship, see Paul Finkelman, "Slavery and the Constitutional Convention: Making a Covenant with Death," in Richard R. Beeman, Stephen Botein, and Edward C. Carter II, eds., *Beyond Confederation: Origins of the Constitution and American National Identity* (Chapel Hill, NC, 1987), 188–225; and Gary B. Nash, *Race and Revolution* (Madison, WI, 1990), 204.

"active freedom of conscience," grafted onto Quaker sensibilities, led to the justification of individual resistance to unjust laws.[166]

Reflecting on "the elements" that a future synthesis of the Revolution based on findings such as his own might include, Lynd offered a tentative New Left synthesis. The American Revolution "was waged by a coalition of diverse social groups." "Internal conflict," he believed, was "a secondary aspect of the revolution of 1776 which in fact was primarily a war of national independence." This was Becker with the proportions changed. Second, "the popular elements in this coalition often clashed with their upper-class leaders," and this fear among the elites of domestic insurrection "was a principal motive for the formation of the United States Constitution." So much for consensus history. Third, "the upper-class leaders . . . were themselves divided into two basic groups, Northern capitalists and Southern plantation owners, and the Constitution represented not a victory for one over the other but a compromise between them." This was Beard fundamentally revised. There was "a second revolution which determined what kind of society the independent nation would become, . . . a bourgeois revolution comparable to the French Revolution, but it was directed not against England but against slavery and took place not in 1776 but in 1861." Here was the Beard of *Rise of American Civilization* cast in a different conceptual framework. Thus, to Lynd the American Revolution was both less and more of a transforming event than portrayed by either the Progressives or their critics.[167]

These insights were the product of a meteoric decade for Lynd as a historian and activist. The target of national right-wing political attacks, the victim of a bruising academic freedom fight at two Chicago colleges in 1967–68, denied tenure at Yale in 1968, his appointment by history departments in a host of Illinois and Indiana institutions blocked by administrators, Lynd was blacklisted.[168] In 1969, at a tumultuous annual meeting of the AHA attended by some two thousand, he led an unsuccessful effort

[166] Staughton Lynd, *Intellectual Origins of American Radicalism* (1968; reprint ed., Cambridge, MA, 1982).

[167] Lynd, *Class Conflict*, 13–14; see also Lynd, "Beyond Beard," in Bernstein, ed., *Towards a New Past*, 50–54.

[168] On Lynd at Yale, see Staughton Lynd, "Academic Freedom: Your Story and Mine," *Columbia University Forum* 10 (Fall 1967): 23–28; Edmund S. Morgan and C. Vann Woodward, "Academic Freedom: Whose Story?" *Columbia University Forum* 11 (Spring 1968): 42–43, with a reply by Lynd, 50–51.

to condemn the war in Vietnam; then, as an opposition candidate for the presidency, he won 396 votes to 1,004 for Robert Palmer, a rebellion that led the AHA to more far-reaching reform than under Jameson in 1913.[169] Lynd, without much choice and never convinced that a radical activist historian should commit himself to a lifetime in academia, left early American history. He became a lawyer and began a second creative career as a labor lawyer and labor activist, applying his New Left insights as a historian of twentieth-century labor history and American law.[170]

Jesse Lemisch was the godfather of "history from the bottom up," a phrase used by Turner in 1923 and Caroline F. Ware in 1940 that did not come into common parlance until the movements of the 1960s gave it resonance.[171] It was in currency in the circles of the Students for a Democratic Society in which Lemisch moved. The subtitle of Lemisch's thesis, "Jack Tar vs. John Bull: The Role of New York's Merchant Seamen in Precipitating the Revolution," announced his bold theme. The heart of it was a reexamination of the Stamp Act crisis, not as an event in the search for principle, the theme of his mentor, Edmund Morgan, but as an event in the emergence of a popular movement. The seamen were the true "radicals" who pushed "liberal" leaders into action.[172]

[169] Wiener, "Radical Historians," 399–434; Novick *That Noble Dream*, chap. 13; Lemisch, "Radicals, Marxists, and Gentlemen," 2, 7–9. The AHA subsequently established three divisions, Research, Teaching, and Professional; in 1970 it established the Ad Hoc Committee on the Rights of Historians, in response to a resolution I introduced with others in the annual meeting. I served on this committee, chaired by Sheldon Hackney, and on the subcommittee responsible for the investigation of individual violations of academic freedom, in the course of which I read the documents in the Lynd and Lemisch cases and some forty others. For the report and the "Statement of Professional Standards" adopted by the AHA, see *AHA Newsletter* 12 (Dec. 1974): 9–13.

[170] Interview with Lynd (1977), in Abelove et al., eds., *Visions of History*, 149–65; Lynd, "Intellectuals, the University, and the Movement," with a response by Lemisch, "Who Will Write a Left History of Art While We Are Putting Our Balls on the Line?" (1968), reprinted in *Journal of American History* 76 (1989): 479–86; Lynd and Alice Lynd, eds., *Rank and File: Personal Histories by Working-Class Organizers* (1973; 3d ed., New York, 1988); Lynd, *The Fight Against Shutdowns: Youngstown's Steel Mill Closings* (San Pedro, CA, 1982); Lynd, "The Genesis of the Idea of a Community Right to Industrial Property in Youngstown and Pittsburgh, 1977–1987," *Journal of American History* 74 (1987): 926–58.

[171] Turner to Carl Blegen, Mar. 16, 1923, cited in Novick, *That Noble Dream*, 442; I recall encountering the term in Caroline F. Ware, ed., *The Cultural Approach to History* (New York, 1940); Lemisch, "Towards a Democratic History," Students for a Democratic Society Radical Education Project Occasional Paper (1967).

[172] Jesse Lemisch, "Jack Tar vs. John Bull: The Role of New York's Merchant Seamen in Precipitating the Revolution," Ph.D. diss., Yale University, 1962, published with a foreword by Marcus

His since-famous "Jack Tar" article of 1968 broadened the scope of the argument in time and place. Challenging the stereotype of "jolly Jack Tar" and Samuel Eliot Morison's image of the seaman as "a clean young farm boy on the make," Lemisch suggested there were many sailors like Ishmael in Herman Melville's *Moby Dick* "who left the land in flight and fear, outcasts, men with little hope of success ashore, . . . dissenters from the American mood." He revealed a long history of struggle against colonial impressment, often in spectacular riots that made more credible the large-scale participation of seamen in crowd actions in Atlantic seaports after 1765. In effect he uncovered a new cause of the Revolution, illuminating a forgotten clause of the Declaration of Independence. Lemisch felt he had tested the contention of the loyalist historian Peter Oliver that "the Mobility of all Countries, [were] perfect Machines, [that could be] wound up by any Hand that might take the Winch." He found that "the seaman had a mind of his own and genuine reasons to act, and that he did act purposefully." He also felt that Bailyn's claim that the "demonstrations by transient sailors and dock workers" were "ideologically inert" was not proven. Granting that "it might be extravagant to call the seamen's conduct and sense of injustice" ideological, yet, he argued, "there are many worlds and much human history in the vast area between ideology and inertness."[173]

Lemisch's essay "The American Revolution Seen from the Bottom Up," appearing about the same time, was akin to Turner's ardent appeal to scholars in 1893 to do the history of an unexplored subject and to Jameson's "heuristic." What might the history of the Revolution look like if scholars approached it from a different vantage point? Lemisch conceded that, insofar as the elite was concerned, the Revolution may well have been as conservative as Daniel Boorstin claimed but pounded on the assumptions that there was a consensus behind the elite or that the actions of the lower classes could be explained by "manipulation, propaganda, and the mindlessness of the people." The "inarticulate" "had adequate reason to act on

Rediker (New York, 1997); Lemisch, "New York's Petitions and Resolves of December 1765: Liberals vs. Radicals," *New-York Historical Society Quarterly* 49 (1965): 313–26.

[173] Jesse Lemisch, "Jack Tar in the Streets: Merchant Seamen in the Politics of Revolutionary America," *William and Mary Quarterly*, 3d ser. 25 (1968): 371–407. This essay was reprinted as "The Radicalism of the Inarticulate: Merchant Seamen and the Politics of Revolutionary America," in Alfred Young, ed., *Dissent: Explorations in the History of American Radicalism* (DeKalb, IL, 1968). For Lemisch's impact, see Colin Howell and Richard J. Twomey, eds., *Jack Tar in History: Essays in the History of Maritime Life and Labour* (Fredericton, Canada, 1991).

their own, [and] had the capacity to act on their own." The history of "the powerless, the inarticulate, the poor," he concluded, "has not yet begun to be written."[174]

He next made "a struggle to get inside Jack Tar's head," attempting "an experimental history" in which he treated the British prisons as a laboratory to study the behavior of ordinary men without the presence of elites or outside political leaders. Sailors set up self-government, established a code of ethics, and voiced their patriotism in songs and celebrations. All but a few rejected the opportunity to go free by becoming turncoats. Putting "inarticulate" in quotation marks to correct a misreading of his earlier essay, he relied on little-used memoirs of seamen to construct a collective portrait of articulateness.[175]

Lemisch's contribution to the debate over transformation in the Revolution was to establish a consciousness among ordinary people. To trace consciousness over time he attempted a full-scale biography of Andrew Sherburne, a seaman and prisoner of war. The youthful son of a New Hampshire carpenter, Sherburne was lured to sea on a privateering vessel, was taken prisoner of war, returned from a British prison broken in health, eked out a living on the Maine frontier, and became a preacher in the Baptist church where he found community akin to what he had experienced as a prisoner. He went to Ohio to farm worthless land, received a veteran's pension, lost it in red tape, and went to Washington to fight for it. He ended his life in poverty, writing his autobiography and selling it door to door for two dollars—a painful reminder of the broken promises to the losers of the Revolution.[176]

To advance history from the bottom up Lemisch moved in several directions. He wrote critical analyses of other historians; he offered an influential critique of the government's historical-publications programs for failing to support the editing of papers other than those of "great white men." In response to those who dismissed the New Left as presentist, he offered in 1969 a scathing indictment of the present-mindedness of the historical establishment since World War II, an article that the *American*

[174] Jesse Lemisch, "The American Revolution Seen from the Bottom Up," in Bernstein, ed., *Towards a New Past*, 3–43, quotation at 29.

[175] Jesse Lemisch, "Listening to the 'Inarticulate': William Widger's Dream and the Loyalties of American Revolutionary Seamen in British Prisons," *Journal of Social History* 3 (1969): 1–29.

[176] Jesse Lemisch, "The American Revolution and the American Dream: A Short Life of the Reverend Andrew Sherburne, a Pensioner of the Navy of the Revolution" (paper presented at a conference in honor of Edmund S. Morgan, New Haven, CT, 1979).

Historical Review and the *Journal of American History* refused to print and that was published in Canada in 1975.[177] And finally he engaged in a series of exchanges with his critics on the Marxist left, responding to charges that he romanticized the masses, failed to acknowledge the hegemony of ruling classes, and treated the bottom in isolation from the top.[178]

In 1966 the history department at the University of Chicago did not renew Lemisch's appointment. Daniel Boorstin found Lemisch's "sea stories" interesting but deplored his emphasis on class. In 1968 the chairman, William H. McNeill, informed him, "Your convictions interfered with your scholarship." Lemisch continued in academia, but, as he put it, "Great Institutions began to shun me."[179]

At the time the three pathbreakers of the New Left probably had a greater impact on young historians of modern rather than early American history. The *William and Mary Quarterly* under Lawrence Towner published articles by Williams (1961) and Lynd (1962) and under Thad W. Tate published Lemisch (1968). It published a critique of "Jack Tar" that questioned only whether seamen were typical, as well as Lemisch's response. The gatekeeping journal in the field, it reviewed only one of Lynd's three books and ignored Williams's book as out of scope. In 1971 the Institute of Early American History and Culture invited neither Lemisch nor Lynd to a conference of representative scholars on the bicentennial of the Revolution. "Why didn't they invite Jesse and Staughton?" I remember Edmund Morgan asking me at lunch. Nor was there a welcome mat in Williamsburg for the seminal British New Left historians. The Council of the Institute long reserved a slot for someone in British history, but in 1977, when as chair of the nominating committee I brought in the name of Christopher

[177] Jesse Lemisch, "Bailyn Besieged in His Bunker," *Radical History Review* 3 (1976): 72–83; Lemisch, "Radical Plot in Boston (1770): A Study in the Use of Evidence," *Harvard Law Review* 84 (1970): 485–504 (a critique of Hiller Zobel, *The Boston Massacre*); Lemisch, "The American Revolution Bicentennial and the Papers of Great White Men," *AHA Newsletter* 9 (1971): 7–21; Lemisch, "The Papers of a Few Great Black Men and a Few Great White Women," *Maryland Historian* 7 (1975): 60–66; Lemisch, "Present-Mindedness Revisited: Anti-Radicalism as a Goal of American Historical Writing since World War II" (paper presented at the AHA, Dec. 1969), published as *On Active Service in War and Peace: Politics and Ideology in the American Historical Profession* (Toronto, 1975).

[178] Aileen Kraditor, review of *Towards a New Past*, ed. Bernstein, *American Historical Review* 74 (1968): 528–29; response by Lemisch and rejoinder by Kraditor, *American Historical Review* 75 (1969): 1766–69; Joan Scott and Donald Scott "Toward History," with a rejoinder by Lemisch, "New Left Elitism," *Radical America* 1 (1967): 35–53.

[179] Jesse Lemisch, author's postscript to "Jack Tar in the Streets," reprinted in *In Search of Early America*, 136–37.

Hill, they voted it down. Rudé was later a visiting professor at the College of William and Mary. The Institute's 1989 volume listing recommended reading carries some eighty-five titles in British history, but not one by Hill, Thompson, Rudé, or Hobsbawm. Recently Lynd, whose books have been reprinted, has appeared as a reviewer in the *Quarterly*, and the journal's readers voted Lemisch's "Jack Tar" one of the most influential articles in the past fifty years.[180]

Lynd demonstrated that it was possible, by substituting class for economic interest and exploring subordinate classes, to arrive at a more sophisticated version of the dual revolution than in Becker, Beard, or Jensen. In pushing slavery to the center of the Revolutionary stage, he was joined in time by a host of scholars. Lemisch's "Jack Tar" essay was a tour de force. Scholars have told me that after reading it as undergraduates, they decided to become historians. It created a subject that scholars did not know existed, demonstrating in a tone that was genuinely exploratory that there were sources to do history from the bottom up. Edmund Morgan likes to tell the story that it was the last time he would tell a graduate student there were no sources for a subject.

Lemisch was a founder of the early American crowd as a field of study. Rudé created the field for England and Europe. Bailyn, Gordon Wood, and Maier broke the stereotype of the mindless, manipulated mob, but before there was sufficient evidence, they substituted for it a single type of crowd sharing the mind of the whig pamphleteers.[181] Lemisch opened the door to what later research has shown to be a wide range of crowds. Lynd and Lemisch showed it was possible to find agency and consciousness below, if not ideology. And both challenged the complacent celebration of the Revolution, allowing scholars who followed to come to grips with its dark side, whether of slaves abandoned by the Founding Fathers or the Ishmaels and Andrew Sherburnes of America.

[180] Ibid.; James H. Hutson, "An Investigation of the Inarticulate: Philadelphia's White Oaks," *William and Mary Quarterly*, 3d ser. 28 (1971): 3–25; Lemisch with John K. Alexander, "The White Oaks, Jack Tar, and the Concept of the 'Inarticulate,'" *William and Mary Quarterly*, 3d ser. 29 (1972): 109–34; Lynd, *Intellectual Origins*; Lynd, review of *Anti-Racism in U.S. History*, by Herbert Aptheker, *William and Mary Quarterly*, 3d ser. 50 (1993): 631–34; David L. Ammerman and Philip D. Morgan, comps., *Books about Early America: 2001 Titles* (Williamsburg, VA, 1989), 12–14.

[181] Thomas P. Slaughter, "Crowds in Eighteenth-Century America: Reflections and New Directions," *Pennsylvania Magazine of History and Biography* 115 (1991): 3–34; for a reassertion of the communitarian interpretation, see Paul A. Gilje, *The Road to Mobocracy: Popular Disorder in New York City, 1763–1834* (Chapel Hill, NC, 1987).

9. The New Social History

The "new" social history of the 1960s and 1970s laid a basis for reopening the question of transformation in the American Revolution by beginning a systematic analysis of colonial society. The new social history paralleled the development of New Left history, sharing the same interest in "history from the bottom up" yet diverged from it in intellectual sources, focus, and methodology.

In the "old" social history epitomized by the volumes in the *History of American Life* series edited by Schlesinger and Dixon Ryan Fox, successive unlinked chapters described society, education, recreation, literature, and so on, with what Beard called an "impressionistic eclecticism." "It represented the New History [of the early twentieth century] at its worst," Peter Novick writes, "shapeless and sprawling; 'liberal' in its avoidance of the issues of power (social history as 'history with the politics left out'); 'progressive' in its emphasis on rapid social change with no attention to long-range structural dynamics."[182]

At its best, in focused monographs, the old social history actually was more solid. Scholars who were steeped in their sources organized their subject empirically. Usually they fit no paradigm; indeed that may have been their source of strength. Examples are Carl Bridenbaugh's two volumes on the colonial cities, Morgan's studies of the family in New England and Virginia, studies of colonial women by Julia Cherry Spruill or Elizabeth Anthony Dexter, of the laboring classes by Morris and Towner, or of African Americans in colonial society and in the Revolution by Lorenzo Johnston Greene and Benjamin Quarles. Such works survived and are still consulted by scholars.[183]

The "new social history," James Henretta wrote when its trends had become clearer, "does not resemble a coherent subdiscipline but rather a

[182] Novick, *That Noble Dream*, 178–80; Higham, *History*, 194–95.

[183] Carl Bridenbaugh, *Cities in the Wilderness: The First Century of Urban Life in America, 1625–1742* (New York, 1938); Bridenbaugh, *Cities in Revolt: Urban Life in America, 1743–1776* (New York, 1955); Edmund S. Morgan, *The Puritan Family* (Boston 1944); Morgan, *Virginians at Home* (Williamsburg, VA, 1952); Julia Cherry Spruill, *Women's Life and Work in the Southern Colonies* (Chapel Hill, NC, 1938); Elizabeth Anthony Dexter, *Career Women of America, 1776–1840* (Francistown, NH, 1950); Morris, *Government and Labor*; Lawrence W. Towner, "A Good Master Well Served: A Social History of Servitude in Massachusetts, 1620–1750," Ph.D. diss., Northwestern University, 1955; Lorenzo Johnston Greene, *The Negro in Colonial New England, 1620–1776* (New York, 1942); Quarles, *Negro in the American Revolution*.

congeries of groups." One group drew especially on the French *Annales* school, with its emphasis on achieving "total" history and on the trends of long duration that provided an underlying structure to eventful history and with its use of methods of quantification to achieve rigorous statistical analysis. A second group, which included the New Left, drew intellectually from the liberated revisionist Marxism of England; it was untraditional in focusing on agency and consciousness but traditional in its methods.[184]

Politically both groups were moved by the unprecedented popular movements of the late 1960s and early 1970s to recover the common people left out of conventional history. By 1975 Jack Greene, the perennial chronicler of historical trends who, the decade before, thought he was viewing the wake of the social interpretation of the Revolution, wrote enthusiastically about the way the new history "reorders our priorities about the past." "It has become clear that the experience of women, children, servants, slaves and other neglected groups are quite as integral to a comprehensive understanding of the past as that of lawyers, lords, and ministers of state."[185]

The two histories had a common foe—so-called elitist history that ignored the vast majority and was excessively political, constitutional, and ideological; they parted company in focus. The New Left was concerned with movements and redefining the political to include the crowd, "primitive rebels," and cultural resistance. For colonial American history the new social historians by contrast were interested in the uneventful *longue durée* that captured trends in demography, family patterns, social structure, social mobility, social stratification, and literacy.[186] Both were interested in consciousness, but the new social historians were apt to deduce consciousness from behavior, and their methods usually were quantitative. Dealing with what they could count, perhaps unconsciously, they perpetuated the notion that the common people were inarticulate and the historian had to speak for them, after Lemisch, for example, had pulled back from the concept.

The contribution of the first wave of new social historians was to open up two large subjects, the contours of the small community—typically the New England town—and class stratification in the large seaboard cities.

[184] James A. Henretta, "Social History as Lived and Written," *American Historical Review* 84 (1979): 1293–1322, quotations at 1295–96.

[185] Jack P. Greene, "The 'New' History: From Top to Bottom," *New York Times*, Jan. 18, 1975.

[186] Daniel Scott Smith, "A Perspective on Demographic Methods and Effects in Social History," *William and Mary Quarterly*, 3d ser. 39 (1982): 442–69; for recent surveys of this scholarship, see Jack P. Greene and J. R. Pole, eds., *Colonial British America: Essays in the New History of the Early Modern Era* (Baltimore, 1984).

Initially few scholars of the small towns were interested in the Revolution, much less the Jameson thesis; indeed, the town studies usually stopped before the Revolution. Jackson Turner Main's social history, discussed earlier, was doubly exceptional in studying the social structure of the country as a whole both after as well as before the Revolution.[187]

The foray into the social structure of the major cities was opened up by James Henretta's analysis of tax records in Boston showing the growing class stratification in the colonial era (followed a few years later by Allan Kulikoff's analysis of the continuation of these trends after the war).[188] But Gary Nash led the first full-scale inquiry taking on the three largest communities, New York, Philadelphia, and Boston, with statistical analysis of a massive array of estate inventories, tax lists, and poor-relief records that enabled him to measure social change over the century before the Revolution. The picture that emerged was of a growing concentration of wealth, "the crumbling of economic security for the lower middle class," and below that, widespread, chronic poverty. Unlike most other social historians, Nash went on to explore the "linkages" between this "restructuring of society" and the transformation of urban politics before and during the Revolutionary crisis, providing a dimension hitherto missing to explain urban radicalism. Unlike others at the time in the new social history, Nash gave major attention to race, measuring, for example, changing patterns of slaveholding in colonial Philadelphia. And in the first work of its kind, *Red, White, and Black*, he explored the interactions of American Indians, Europeans, and African Americans in colonial America.[189]

Whether or not they were disciples of the new social history, historians continued to find the social themes of the Revolution compelling. Several

[187] Richard R. Beeman, "The New Social History and the Search for 'Community' in Colonial America," *American Quarterly* 29 (1977): 442–43; an exception was Robert A. Gross, *The Minute Men and Their World* (New York, 1976).

[188] James A. Henretta, "Economic Development and Social Structure in Colonial Boston," *William and Mary Quarterly*, 3d ser. 22 (1965): 75–92; Allan Kulikoff, "The Progress of Inequality in Revolutionary Boston," *William and Mary Quarterly*, 3d ser. 28 (1971): 375–412.

[189] Gary B. Nash and James T. Lemon, "The Distribution of Wealth in Eighteenth-Century America: A Century of Change in Chester County, Pennsylvania, 1693–1802," *Journal of Social History* 2 (1968); Nash, ed., *Class and Society in Early America* (Englewood Cliffs, NJ, 1970); Nash, *Red, White, and Black: The Peoples of Early America* (Englewood Cliffs, NJ, 1974); Nash, "Urban Wealth and Poverty in Pre-Revolutionary America," *Journal of Interdisciplinary History* 4 (1976): 545–84; G. B. Warden, "Inequality and Instability in Eighteenth-Century Boston: A Reappraisal," *Journal of Interdisciplinary History* 4 (1976): 585–620; Jacob M. Price, "Quantifying Colonial America: A Comment on Nash and Warden," *Journal of Interdisciplinary History* 4 (1976): 701–9; Nash, "Up from the Bottom in Franklin's Philadelphia," *Past and Present* 77 (1977): 57–83.

essayists in the volume sponsored by the Institute of Early American History, in a consensus sandwich between the essays of Bernard Bailyn and Edmund Morgan's, obdurately explored Jamesonian hypotheses. John Shy, a military historian, was convinced that "no question has aroused more interest and drawn more scholarly energy than the one posed by Jameson 'did the Revolution change American society?'" Focusing on the triangularity of the struggle in which "two armed forces contended less with each other than for the support and control of the civilian population," he saw a "great middle group of Americans" who were "almost certainly a majority of the population, . . . people who were dubious, afraid, uncertain, indecisive." "A great many of these people were changed by the war," and "the revolutionary war, considered as a political education for the masses, helps to fill the explanatory gap" contributing to "the rapid erosion of deferential political behavior."[190]

William G. McLoughlin, dealing with the growth of religious liberty, thought that the Revolution "provided so many changes in so short a period that Jameson may have rightly described it as social revolution, as least in the area of religion." Unlike Jameson or his critics, McLoughlin located the agency of change in the dissenters, especially the Baptists of New England, whose long war against the standing order he unfolded in a small library of books.[191]

Rowland Berthoff and John M. Murrin, with characteristic iconoclasm, rejected as conjectural the hypotheses of the new social historians about the social origins of the Revolution to return to an old question central to Jameson, the effects of the Revolution on the land system. Skeptical of historians who reduced the abolition of entail and primogeniture to an issue of only symbolic importance, Berthoff and Murrin argued that "most colonies in the eighteenth century experienced what European specialists would recognize as a 'feudal revival.'" Challenging Louis Hartz's rarely questioned

[190] John Shy, "The American Revolution: The Military Conflict Considered as a Revolutionary War," in Kurtz and Hutson, eds., *Essays on the American Revolution*, 121–56, quotations at 126, 147, 154; Shy, *A People Numerous and Armed: Reflections on the Military Struggle for American Independence* (New York, 1976).

[191] William G. McLoughlin, "The Role of Religion in the Revolution: Liberty of Conscience and Cultural Cohesion in the New Nation," in Kurtz and Hutson, eds., *Essays on the American Revolution*, 197–255; see also McLoughlin, *Isaac Backus and the American Pietistic Tradition* (Boston, 1967); McLoughlin, *New England Dissent, 1630–1833: The Baptists and the Separation of Church and State*, 2 vols. (Cambridge, MA, 1971); McLoughlin, *Revivals, Awakenings, and Reform: An Essay on Religion and Social Change in America, 1607–1977* (Chicago, 1978); and McLoughlin, ed., *The Diary of Isaac Backus*, 3 vols. (Providence, RI, 1980).

assumption that America had no feudal past, they contended that "feudal projects [that] collapsed in the seventeenth century, not because America was too progressive to endure them but because it was too primitive to sustain them," took on new life in the eighteenth century. "Between 1730 and 1745," old claims were revived and consolidated from Carolina to New York "not to restore feudal relationships but for the income they might produce" from tenancy. Outside New England this feudal revival "was as diverse as it was profitable, provoking more social violence after 1745 than perhaps any other problem." "We can only guess what sort of society the feudal revival might have produced had it gone unchecked for another half century. . . . But because the Revolution happened when it did the feudal revival was truly destroyed." If Jameson thus underestimated the dimensions of this issue, he overestimated the democratizing effect of the sale of confiscated loyalist land. "The long-term tendency," Berthoff and Murrin concluded, was "towards greater inequality with marked class distinctions."[192]

The consequence of all these forays into colonial society was to reopen analysis of the transformation question not at the point of consequences, Jameson's focus, but at the point of origins. The systematic analysis of late colonial society began to provide insight into the social origins of the Revolution as well as a base line for measuring change after the Revolution.

In the early 1970s the social-science-oriented historians who generalized about these trends—Jack P. Greene, Kenneth A. Lockridge, James A. Henretta—usually framed them in modernization theory. Greene became interested in "the pre-conditions of Revolution." Historians interested in "the causal pattern of revolution," he claimed in 1973, sidestepping Bernard Bailyn, "now give as much attention to social strain as to political and ideological conflict; to social dysfunction, frustration, anomie, and their indices as to weaknesses and tensions within the political system." He postulated two hypotheses, first, "that colonial society underwent a dramatic erosion of internal social cohesion over the period from 1690 to 1760, and second, that the social structure was becoming more and more rigid and social strain correspondingly more intense." But Greene was dubious about a "direct causal relationship" between such social strains and the Revolution, arguing that the "broader social revolution" of "modernization" was "in many respects far more crucial to an understanding of the first two

[192] Rowland Berthoff and John M. Murrin, "Feudalism, Communalism, and the Yeoman Freeholder: The American Revolution Considered as a Social Accident," in Kurtz and Hutson, eds., *Essays on the American Revolution*, 256–88, quotations at 264, 267, 272, 281.

centuries of American life and far more worthy of scholarly attention than the American Revolution" because it "would have been completed with or without the American Revolution."[193]

Kenneth A. Lockridge, like Nash and unlike Greene, tried to find links between long-range social change and the Revolution. He was the author of an influential demographic study of Dedham, Massachusetts, in transition in its first hundred years from a communal utopia to a "modern" town, and of a pioneering study of the rise of literacy in New England. He revisited the Dedham of the late eighteenth century and found that New England was becoming "seriously overcrowded" and "more and more an old world society." He summed up the major trends of the half century before the Revolution as "increasing population density, pressure on land supply, migration, concentration of wealth, social differentiation and commercial dependency." He then asked, "How might men have reacted to these changes? How might their various reactions have entered into the debates of those who sought to give political definition to the new nation?" He concluded there was a "sharpened concern over the concentration of wealth and the decline of social equality" that provided the "reality" for the "rhetoric" examined by Gordon Wood in the intense conflict of 1776 to 1787 between "democracy" and "aristocracy."[194]

James Henretta's extended "interdisciplinary" essay in 1973 was in many ways a summa of the point at which a scholar steeped in modernization theory with an ear attuned to issues raised by the New Left had arrived in the early 1970s. The Revolution took place in the context of an evolution of long-range social trends. There was a "crisis of American colonial society." "For nearly a generation a succession of religious struggles, economic disturbances, and armed conflicts had shaken the foundations of social stability, creating a tense social environment conducive to an aggressive, even violent reaction to new and unexpected pressures" from the imperial relationship. Unlike most scholars of social change, he allowed for agency. "By destroying the established system of government and authority, the

[193] Jack P. Greene, "The Social Origins of the American Revolution: An Evaluation and an Interpretation," *Political Science Quarterly* 88 (1973): 1–2, 22.

[194] Kenneth A. Lockridge, *A New England Town, the First Hundred Years: Dedham, Massachusetts, 1636–1736* (New York, 1970); Lockridge, *Literacy in Colonial New England: An Enquiry into the Social Context of Literacy in the Early Modern West* (New York, 1974); Lockridge, "Social Change and the Meaning of the American Revolution," *Journal of Social History* 6 (1973): 403–39, quotations at 414, 405, 417; Lockridge, "Land, Population, and the Evolution of New England Society, 1630–1790," *Past and Present* 39 (1968): 62–80.

quest for home rule had made it possible for previously powerless groups to raise the question of who should rule at home."[195]

But as Henretta measured the "parameters of change" after the Revolution, he found only a "modicum of social mobility" and an uneven democratization of the political process. "Except for the disruptions produced by the war itself and by Loyalist emigration . . . most of the changes that took place during these years represented the culmination of previous trends." The "acceleration of the historical process had followed *linear* lines of development." In effect this repudiated Jameson. Turning to blacks and women, Henretta struck a harsh judgment. While "some previously disadvantaged groups, like the militant farmers of the interior and urban artisans, had also been sufficiently prepared by past events that they were able to seize the historical moment and realize some of their goals through purposeful political and social action, . . . other deprived groups were not." The abolition of slavery "did not touch the overwhelming majority of the black population," and the new ideology of republicanism was little applied to women. "The liberation of blacks and of women was intimately connected," Henretta argued with uncommon boldness, "because both occupied the same type of structural position within the American social order. Both were members of a caste, one racial, and the other sexual, . . . [both] were the legal chattels of the white male section of the population. . . . They joined those who were white and male, but also poor and propertyless as members of the hidden and oppressed *majority*."[196]

For Henretta, therefore, the American in comparison to other revolutions, was not a "total" revolution but "rather a movement for home rule led, managed, and ultimately controlled by those groups who occupied privileged positions in the society." By 1815 the end of two centuries of social evolution was "urban middle class capitalism" in the North and "a rural landed aristocracy" in the South. Those who expressed optimism about the performance of these societies "were as a rule neither red, nor black, nor poor, nor female."[197] The first wave of new social history thus beckoned to scholars who would focus on the groups still missing the transforming benefits of either the Revolution or the new social history.

[195] James A. Henretta, *The Evolution of American Society, 1700–1815: An Interdisciplinary Analysis* (Lexington, MA, 1973), 158.

[196] Ibid., 169, 173.

[197] Ibid., 225; see also Richard D. Brown, *Modernization: The Transformation of American Life, 1600–1865* (New York, 1976).

10. Explorations: New Left, New Social, New Progressive

A collection of essays I edited in 1976, *The American Revolution: Explorations in the History of American Radicalism*, became in time something of a benchmark, a point at which to measure the challenge to reigning interpretations. Edmund Morgan considered it "the most important book on the Revolution yet produced by historians of the New Left." "It would be impossible to do justice to the range of interpretive insights offered in this book," he wrote. "It gives a new lease on historiographical life to the contest over who should rule at home." The collection made its way in the field fairly rapidly, suggesting that it filled a need for those groping for an alternative vision of the Revolution. Richard Morris cited six essays in his presidential address to the AHA in 1976 as evidence of the ways in which "ordinary people gave a distinct cast" to the era, making it "a people's revolution." In 1982 Robert Shalhope, reviewing the state of the "republican synthesis" he had found pervasive in 1972, analyzed the essays as embodying the central themes of the "fragmentation" of the ideological school. It was "no longer possible to see a single monolithic political ideology characterizing American thought on the American Revolution."[198]

"New Left" hardly conveyed the range of politics and historiographic traditions of the eleven essayists and myself as editor. I thought of it as a mix of new social, old Progressive, New Left, new feminist, and other histories that fit no categorization. I was looking for scholars who, like myself, were trying to open old themes in new ways. I had begun my exploration of the Revolution in the grim 1950s with a study of the Democratic-Republicans of New York from 1763 to 1797 that early had convinced me of the role of the Revolution in democratizing American political culture. I assumed politics was defined in a world of parties, associations, and elections as conveyed by newspapers, pamphlets, and broadsides, an assumption which probably owed something to my experience in the Old Left. When I set out to explore mechanics more intensively, I was impressed by the power of the scholarship by Lynd and Lemisch, who became fellow explorers. And by the late 1960s and early 1970s I was inspired by Rudé and Thompson, who showed that it was possible to recover the "crowd" and the value systems of artisans, and by the example of my friend Herbert G.

[198] Edmund S. Morgan, "The American Revolution: Who Were 'the People'?" *New York Review of Books*, Aug. 5, 1976; Morris, "We the People"; Shalhope, "Republicanism and Early American Historiography"; Kammen, *Season of Youth*, 40; Alfred F. Young, ed., *The American Revolution: Explorations in the History of American Radicalism* (1976; 7th printing, DeKalb, IL, 1993).

Gutman in recovering the workplace and community culture of American preindustrial classes in the nineteenth century. I was going down various paths to get at the laboring classes in Boston—the ritual of Pope's Day, popular culture conveyed by graphic arts, the life history of a shoemaker.[199]

I chose historians who were involved in major research touching on the theme of radicalism in the Revolution and who, as it happens, were at unusually productive points in their careers. Some had recently published books (Ira Berlin, Ronald Hoffman, Joseph Ernst, Francis Jennings) and others were close to completing books (Gary Nash, Dirk Hoerder, Eric Foner, Edward Countryman, Rhys Isaac) which have since won recognition as standard works of synthesis. Joan Hoff Wilson's essay won the distinction of the Berkshire Prize in women's history.

I did not know the politics of most of the scholars I invited until they handed in autobiographical prefaces for their essays. I was partial to "outsiders" who might bring a fresh perspective, which meant to non-Americans (Isaac and Hoerder), to an American long abroad (Countryman), or to scholars drawn to the Revolution to cope with some long-range analytical issue (Berlin, Jennings, Wilson). Two were students of Merrill Jensen (Hoffman, Ernst); a number were practitioners of the new social history, like Nash, engaged in quantifying an analysis of urban social structures, or Wilson, drawing on demography and family reconstitution to analyze the status of women, or Isaac, reading "body language" to decode evangelical and gentry ways of life in Virginia.

The essays registered a perceptible shift of attention in the phase of the Revolution under study. Six of the eleven focused on the time of origins

[199] Alfred F. Young, *The Democratic Republicans of New York: The Origins, 1763–1797* (Chapel Hill, NC, 1967). I had edited *Dissent: Explorations in the History of American Radicalism*; the opening essays in that book were by Lynd and Lemisch, who were both invited to take part in the 1976 volume. I had also served with Leonard W. Levy as one of the two general editors of the American Heritage Series (45 vols.; Indianapolis, 1965–75), whose contributors to the early history ranged across the spectrum (Morgan, Perry Miller and Alan Heimert, Jensen, Cecilia Kenyon, Lynd), and which included the first volumes of modern sources on slavery (Willie Lee Rose), women's history (Gerda Lerner), and the black experience (August Meier, Elliott Rudwick, and John Bracey); for my scholarship: Young, "Pope's Day, Tar and Feathers, and Coronet George Joyce, Jun.: From Ritual to Rebellion in Boston" (paper presented at the Anglo-American Scholars Conference, New Brunswick, NJ, 1973); Young, "English Plebeian Culture and Eighteenth-Century American Radicalism," in Margaret Jacob and James Jacob, eds., *The Origins of Anglo-American Radicalism* (London, 1984), 185–213; Young, "George Robert Twelves Hewes (1742–1840): A Boston Shoemaker and the Memory of the American Revolution," *William and Mary Quarterly*, 3d ser. 38 (1981), reprinted in *In Search of Early America*, 234–88, and in Young, *The Shoemaker and the Tea Party: Memory and the American Revolution* (Boston, 1999).

to 1776, but one took Thomas Paine, the quintessential radical of the era, through the Revolution, one dealt with the war and the resistance of "the disaffected" to the gentry, and three dealt with results for women, free blacks, and American Indians—groups then on the edge of the historiography of the Revolution. Although no one was inspired by Jameson, the essays and the expanded scholarship in the authors' books had major implications for the study of the internal transformations in the Revolution in at least four ways.

They revealed, first, the agency of the common people in shaping events. The crowd, both urban and rural, took on new life. In the major cities the growing class stratification and the long tradition of popular movements against elites revealed by Gary Nash provided a context for crowd action during the political crisis with Britain. Crowds in the most "mobbish" town, Boston, as mapped by Dirk Hoerder, fit no single pattern; some were self-led, some whig-led; some were consensual; others struggled for their own identity. In the countryside Edward Countryman showed a long history of popular struggles over land for New Jersey, the Hudson Valley, and what became Vermont, while Marvin L. Michael Kay portrayed the Regulators of backcountry North Carolina as engaged in a class conflict against their local elites rather than in a sectional conflict.[200]

Class conflict, in general, was neither scanty nor sporadic, nor was it muted by the war. Wherever there was a prior history of intense class antagonism in the countryside, and patriot leadership was from the elite, there was a wartime pattern of loyalism or "disaffection" among the "lower" orders. Ronald Hoffman traced this with acuity for Maryland, Delaware, and the southern interior. Wartime inflation and profiteering could produce intense conflicts in the cities over price control, dividing artisans.[201]

Second, the essays suggested the kinds of ideologies scholars were likely to encounter—in political economy, evangelical religion, and democratic

[200] Gary B. Nash, "Social Change and the Growth of Prerevolutionary Urban Radicalism," in Young, ed., *American Revolution*, 3–36; Nash, *The Urban Crucible: Social Change, Political Consciousness, and the Origins of the American Revolution* (Cambridge, MA, 1979); Dirk Hoerder, "Boston Leaders and Boston Crowds," in Young, ed., *American Revolution*, 233–72; Hoerder, *Crowd Action in Revolutionary Massachusetts, 1765–1780* (New York, 1977); Edward Countryman, "Out of the Bounds of Law: Northern Land Rioters in the Eighteenth Century," in Young, ed., *American Revolution*, 37–70; Countryman, *A People in Revolution: The American Revolution and Political Society in New York, 1760–1790* (Baltimore, 1981); Marvin L. Michael Kay, "The North Carolina Regulation, 1766–1776: A Class Conflict," in Young, ed., *American Revolution*, 71–124.

[201] Ronald Hoffman, "The 'Disaffected' in the Revolutionary South," in Young, ed., *American Revolution*, 273–318; Hoffman, *Spirit of Dissension*.

thought—if free from the assumption of a uniform consensual ideology. There was a political economy implicit in the whig ideology of elites revealed by Ernst and the possibility of a distinct political economy among farmers. There were also clear signs of the "moral economy" Thompson had identified in eighteenth-century English crowds in Countryman's land rioters. Evangelical religion in Virginia as explored by Isaac armed Baptists and Methodists to challenge not only the Anglican religious establishment but the entire value system of the planter elite. Paine's success in Foner's analysis revealed the immense popularity of a strain of English thought—democratic and egalitarian—lying beneath the Commonwealthman ideology as well as a commitment to the tenets of capitalism. All these were strands of a popular ideology. They did not permit, I thought, a claim for a distinct ideology among those below, but neither did they permit scholars to continue on the bland assumption of a consensus behind a single patriot ideology descended from a single English tradition.[202]

Third, in dealing with consequences of the Revolution the authors pushed the subject into dark terrain not in keeping in 1976 with the celebratory fife and drum tones of the Bicentennial. The Revolution was not fought to free the slaves, but Berlin portrayed a revolution in black life. African Americans, who achieved freedom by their own efforts or by acts of individual manumission in the South or of state governments in the North, forged the first free black communities. Jennings saw American Indians who fought against the Americans on the side of the British, their traditional protectors, as engaged in effect in a series of peasant wars fought against the barons who resisted the king; after the disaster of the American victory they continued to resist the new United States. Through the eyes of women Wilson perceived only the illusion of change; their legal status, economic position, and social condition, she argued, were probably worse after than before the Revolution.[203]

[202] Joseph A. Ernst, "Ideology and an Economic Interpretation of the Revolution," in Young, ed., *American Revolution*, 159–86; Ernst, *Money and Politics in America*; Rhys Isaac, "Preachers and Patriots: Popular Culture and the Revolution in Virginia," in Young, ed., *American Revolution*, 125–56; Isaac, *The Transformation of Virginia, 1740–1790* (Chapel Hill, NC, 1982); Eric Foner, "Tom Paine's Republic: Radical Ideology and Social Change," in Young, ed., *American Revolution*, 187–232; Foner, *Tom Paine and Revolutionary America* (New York, 1976).

[203] Ira Berlin, "The Revolution in Black Life," in Young, ed., *American Revolution*, 349–82; Berlin, *Slaves without Masters: The Free Negro in the Antebellum South* (New York, 1974); Berlin, "Time, Space, and the Evolution of Afro-American Society in British Mainland North America," *American Historical Review* 85 (1980): 44–78; Francis Jennings, "The Indians' Revolution," in Young, ed., *American Revolution*, 319–48; Jennings, *The Invasion of America* (Chapel Hill, NC,

Fourth, this cluster of scholarship suggested to me a new way of measuring the success of radical movements—by their capacity to influence those in power. There was a process by which the pressures of internal radicalism and the sheer need of elites to mobilize popular support during a long war forced the creation of a new type of sophisticated conservatism. The Revolution led to upheavals that the gentry struggled to control, whether it was crowds in Boston before the war or, during the war, price-control rioters in Philadelphia, poor Maryland farmers disaffected from the effort to conscript them, or evangelical farmers in Virginia in search of religious liberty. Authors showed would-be ruling classes learning, as had New York's aristocratic patriot Robert R. Livingston, "to yield to the torrent if they hoped to direct its course." They accommodated artisans and farmers but bent relatively little to outsiders to the political system: African Americans, American Indians, or women (or so it seemed to me in 1976).[204]

The essays stimulated criticism from many points on the historical spectrum. Edmund Morgan thought that they "succeeded in demonstrating a large amount of class antagonism" but that "the content of this popular ideology remains elusive and seems to consist more in attitude than in general ideas which can be differentiated from those of the Whig ideology." Jesse Lemisch, on the other hand, did not think several scholars drew out enough consciousness; he criticized Hoerder for deducing the consciousness of crowds from behavior or Wilson for relying on quantitative data to measure changes in consciousness among women, a criticism implicit in later books on women in the Revolution by Linda Kerber and Mary Beth Norton. A scholar of the Wisconsin school thought the essayists (as well as Lynd, Lemisch, and Young) who searched for popular ideology were wrong to accept the premise of the importance of ideology, while an intellectual historian considered the collection "Beard-dominated" in its orientation around interests and its skepticism about the importance of ideas. Such disparate reactions I thought reflected the mix in the book and the fact

1975); Joan Hoff Wilson, "The Illusion of Change: Women and the American Revolution," in Young, ed., *American Revolution*, 338–446.

[204] Robert R. Livingston to William Duer, June 12, 1777, Robert R. Livingston Papers, New-York Historical Society; Young, afterword to *The American Revolution*, 449–62; Young, "Conservatives, the Constitution, and the 'Spirit of Accommodation,'" in Robert A. Goldwin and William A. Schambra, eds., *How Democratic Is the Constitution?* (Washington, DC, 1980), 117–47, and, in a revised version, "The Framers of the Constitution and the 'Genius of the People,'" in *Radical History Review* 42 (1988): 7–47, with commentary by Barbara Clark Smith, Linda K. Kerber, Michael Merrill, Peter Dimock, William Forbath, and James A. Henretta.

that scholars were puzzling out pieces of the puzzle in search of a new overview.[205]

The collection as a whole pointed to new possibilities for the study of transformation in the Revolution. If the emphasis on the agency of the common people was valid, then forces came into being that might transform the society. Paine could no longer be put down as "the Peter Pan of the Revolution" or as a "bizarre" figure of "marginal" influence, nor could evangelical enthusiasts and radical crowds be dismissed as paranoid foes of intellectualism. Rural rebellion, while sporadic, seemed to be a recurring constant before and after the Revolution. And in light of Revolutionary ideals, the real "losers" were redefined as African Americans, Native Americans, and American women, people who could no longer be shunted aside historiographically as passive victims. If, as Morgan generously wrote, the book "gave a new lease on historiographical life to the contest over who shall rule at home," Becker's political formulation, it also took out leases on houses on the landscape of social history that historians were only beginning to enter for the first time. It helped to shift the axis of inquiry among scholars who were redefining the questions in the transformation debate.

IV. Synthesis

11. The Transformation of Early American History

In 1949, when I started to prepare for my Ph.D. exam at Northwestern University, I began a loose-leaf notebook, devoting a page to each important scholar in early American history I assumed I was responsible for: Henry Adams, Andrews, Bancroft, Becker, Beer, Beard, through Gipson, Jameson, Perry Miller, Morison, Parkman, Parrington, down to Turner and Thomas Jefferson Wertenbaker. I had a few pages on subjects ("mercantilism as a cause") and a page for "Negro history" (Ulrich B. Phillips, Aptheker, and John Hope Franklin), with many more titles from a course I had taken with Melville Herskovits in anthropology ("African Retentions in the New World") because no one in history taught "Negro history." I had no page for American Indians; presumably Francis Parkman sufficed.

[205] Morgan, "The American Revolution: Who Were 'the People?'"; Jesse Lemisch, review of *The American Revolution*, ed. Young, *American Historical Review* 82 (1977): 737–39; Gordon, "Crafting a Usable Past," 691–95; Rodgers, "Republicanism," 24–27.

Early in the 1950s, as a young instructor at Wesleyan, I remember traveling up to Boston to join my former classmate Bill Towner at a conference of the Colonial Society of Massachusetts at Parkman's restored mansion on Beacon Hill. I was not only in the presence of Perry Miller and Samuel Eliot Morison, who were on my list, but over sherry I could chat with what seemed like all the rising young men in colonial history. I remember Miller telling good naturedly how vexed he was with some moviemaker he was advising who could not grasp that the Puritans did not wear black clothing. What passion went into breaking stereotypes at Harvard when it came to the Puritans. After the lobster à la Newberg, we all climbed the stairs to the attic to tour Parkman's restored study, where a metal grid frame that the partially blind historian used to guide his handwriting lay on his desk.

Today a graduate student might still compose a list of the "greats" (a much shorter list), but he or she is more likely to consult the Institute of Early American History and Culture's guidebook, *Books about Early America*, subtitled *2001 Titles*, to focus on several subjects in more than fifty categories, and to plead for a concentration on a few themes. Today all the capable young men and women in early American history could not fit into a large auditorium in Williamsburg, let alone Parkman's second-floor living room, and most would not be inclined to make a pilgrimage to the shrine of a blatantly racist historian who saw American Indians, blacks, Catholics, and the "lesser breeds" thronging America through the vision of a very WASP Boston Brahmin.[206]

In turning from the historiography of the first thirty years after the Second World War to the outpouring of scholarship on the Revolution in the twenty years that followed, several qualities are striking—its sheer volume and diversity, the way the issue of transformation has moved to a central place, the attention scholars have given to groups left out by almost all previous schools, and the new syntheses that are emerging. If few young scholars now read J. Franklin Jameson, many take it for granted that they should consider the American Revolution as a social movement. The Revolution that is emerging is more many-sided and more perplexing, at once more radical and more conservative than anything Jameson or his critics envisioned.

[206] William R. Taylor, "Francis Parkman," in Marcus Cunliffe and Robin W. Winks, eds., *Pastmasters: Some Essays on American Historians* (New York, 1969), 1–38; Francis Jennings, "Francis Parkman: A Brahmin among Untouchables," *William and Mary Quarterly*, 3d ser. 42 (1985): 305–28.

The volume and diversity of the scholarship: It is not only that the Institute's "selected bibliography" of books about early America, which in 1970 had about 650 titles, had more than tripled by 1989. Both listings embraced the colonial era as well as the Revolution, yet in the second list an even larger proportion of the titles would be relevant to a scholar seeking to understand the social dimensions of the Revolution. It took fourteen scholars to write the bibliographic essays for a volume covering colonial social and economic history, and by choice they only went up to but did not include the Revolution. Bibliographic essays, once the stock in trade of the profession, cannot keep up with the pace of scholarship about the Revolution. But if the field is daunting, it is also exhilarating.[207]

The diversity is most apparent in the new fields that have come into being. Historians have been doing so many "new" histories that one wonders how they dealt with the majority of the people before. There is the new African American history, which studies unfree slaves and free blacks, who on the eve of the Revolution numbered five hundred thousand in a population of 2.5 million; the new labor history, which deals with artisans in the skilled trades (masters, journeymen, and apprentices, all told the most numerous group of workers in the cities), seamen (the largest group of wageworkers in colonial times), and indentured servants (the largest group of immigrants); the new agrarian history, which encompasses farmers of all conditions (slaveholding planters, yeomen, tenants, and the rural landless); the new women's history, which attempts to embrace women in all classes; and a new American Indian history, which deals with Native Americans (more than 150,000 of whom lived east of the Mississippi) and the complex interactions of a multitude of diverse tribal societies with Anglo-Americans.

Diversity is also apparent in the geographic areas of the country now receiving scholarly energies. It is not only that Chesapeake-area studies

[207] Institute of Early American History and Culture, *Books about Early America: A Selected Bibliography*, 4th ed. (Williamsburg, VA, 1970); compare to Ammerman and Morgan, comps., *Books about Early America: 2001 Titles*; Greene and Pole, eds., *Colonial British America*, in which the following essays are germane: Richard S. Dunn (labor); T. H. Breen (peoples and cultures); Gary B. Nash (social development); James A. Henretta (wealth and social structure); Joyce Oldham Appleby (value and society); Richard L. Bushman (vernacular cultures); Ronald L. Gephart, comp., *Revolutionary America, 1763–1789: A Bibliography*, 2 vols. (Washington, DC, 1984), has 14,810 entries of books, articles, and primary sources, many with multiple titles; for the best recent bibliographic essays, see James A. Henretta and Gregory H. Nobles, *Evolution and Revolution: American Society, 1600–1820* (Lexington, MA, 1987), and Edward Countryman, *The American Revolution* (New York, 1985).

may be overtaking New England, but historians are going back to the frontier, off to the West Indies, and even outside Anglo-America. Ethnicity is under scrutiny, as are the variations in the culture of English migrants.[208] Diversity is also apparent in the kinds of history being done. Intellectual history, which once flaunted its divorce from social history, may be cohabiting with its old mate. There is a "new" political history as well, probing political culture. The shelves of biographies and "papers" of the Founding Fathers, groaning ever since the 1950s, are now joined by studies of Founding Mothers and unknown and lesser-known men and women, based on long-neglected diaries, memoirs, and letters.[209] And most important, there is no longer one dominant interpretation—if there ever was—but many competing points of view and among younger scholars a wariness of overarching interpretations that try to squeeze this bulging diversity into the confines of a single container.

This diversity owes much, in the first place, to the explosion of American higher education that began in the 1960s. There were more universities granting the doctorate in history (some 132 in 1972) and more doctorates granted in history (one thousand a year through the 1970s, six hundred or so in the 1980s). And there were more jobs for historians, especially as early American history—pronounced "a neglected field" in 1947 by Carl Bridenbaugh, the first director of the Institute of Early American History and Culture (1945–50)—came into its own, in part due to the efforts of the Institute in promoting scholarship. The circulation of the *William and Mary Quarterly*, published by the Institute, went from 777 in 1947 to 2,469 in 1965 to 3,589 in 1985. Jameson's "convivium historicum" could not survive the polycentrism of a profession with many graduate departments, multiple research centers, the geographic decentralization of source materials

[208] Jack P. Greene, "Interpretive Frameworks: The Quest for Intellectual Order in Early American History," *William and Mary Quarterly*, 3d ser. 48 (1991): 515–30; Bernard Bailyn, *The Peopling of British North America: An Introduction* (New York, 1986); Bailyn and Philip D. Morgan, eds., *Strangers within the Realm: Cultural Margins of the First British Empire* (Chapel Hill, NC, 1991); David Hackett Fischer, *Albion's Seed: Four British Folkways in America* (New York, 1989); Jack P. Greene, *Pursuits of Happiness: The Social Development of Early Modern British Colonies and the Formation of American Culture* (Chapel Hill, NC, 1988).

[209] Laurel Thatcher Ulrich, *A Midwife's Tale: The Life of Martha Ballard, Based on Her Diary, 1785–1812* (New York, 1990); Barbara Clark Smith, *After the Revolution: The Smithsonian History of Everyday Life in the Eighteenth Century* (New York, 1985); Barbara E. Lacey, "The World of Hannah Heaton: The Autobiography of an Eighteenth-Century Connecticut Farm Woman," *William and Mary Quarterly*, 3d ser. 45 (1988): 280–304; Joy Day Buel and Richard Buel Jr., *The Way of Duty: A Woman and Her Family in Revolutionary America* (New York, 1984); Young, "George Robert Twelves Hewes."

made possible by new technologies, and the expanded outlets for publication in university presses and new specialized journals. As a consequence, historians can now analyze the decline of deference, their perennial subject of inquiry in early American history, among themselves.[210]

Expansion changed the social composition of the profession, Carl Bridenbaugh's worst dreams come true. In his presidential address to the AHA in 1962, he complained of the "environmental deficiency" of the rising generation of historians: "urban bred" and "products of lower middle-class or foreign origins," they lacked the "understanding . . . vouchsafed to historians who were raised in the countryside or in the small town." "Their emotions," said Bridenbaugh, "not infrequently get in the way of their historical reconstructions. They find themselves in a very real sense outsiders on our past and feel themselves shut out." Soon the "environmental deficiencies" included gender; in 1980 one in four new history doctorates was a woman, in 1990 one in three. And had Parkman's ghost visited the D'Arcy McNickle Center for the Study of the American Indian at the Newberry Library, it might have encountered scholars of Native American descent as well as outsiders of many stripes.[211]

The political coloring of early American historians also changed. There was something to Edmund Morgan's observation that "there is a sort of self-selecting process" in which "politically oriented" students were not drawn to early American history. But his retort to his interviewer in 1985 —"colonial history, seventeenth- and eighteenth-century history is pretty safe (*laughs*). People may be drawn to it as a safe subject"—might not have been echoed in New York, Princeton, Philadelphia, Washington, Williamsburg, Durham, Chicago, Madison, Berkeley, or Los Angeles, or any number

[210] For recent statistics, see Nell Irvin Painter, "The Academic Marketplace and Affirmative Action," *Perspectives* 31 (1993): 7–11, tables 2 and 3; for the changes in technology, see Lawrence W. Towner, *Past Imperfect: Essays on History, Libraries, and the Humanities*, ed. Robert W. Karrow and Alfred F. Young (Chicago, 1993); for the overall social changes, see Novick, *That Noble Dream*, chaps. 8 and 9; for the changes in the field, see Joyce Oldham Appleby, "A Different Kind of Independence: The Postwar Restructuring of the Historical Study of Early America," *William and Mary Quarterly*, 3d ser. 50 (1993): 245–67; for the Institute, see Fredrika J. Teute, "A Conversation with Thad Tate," *William and Mary Quarterly*, 3d ser. 50 (1993): 268–97; statistics on the circulation of the *Quarterly* provided by Ronald Hoffman, director of the Institute of Early American History and Culture.

[211] Carl Bridenbaugh, "The Great Mutation," *American Historical Review* 68 (1973): 322–23, 328; see also the entries under anti-Semitism and anti-Catholicism in the index to Novick, *That Noble Dream*, 633; for the changing character of scholars awarded fellowships by the Institute, see the essays by former Fellows of the Institute in "Forum: The Future of Early American History," *William and Mary Quarterly*, 3d ser. 50 (1993): 299–424.

of places where, as Linda Kerber of the University of Iowa has put it, "a new generation of historians" was helping to "restore *rebellion*" to the histories of the Revolution. Anathemas against "present-mindedness," in any case, had lost the power of excommunication; there were too many churches. Anticommunism lost its sting, what with Bailyn saying "we are all Marxists" and Morgan admitting that he "admires immensely" the writings of E. P. Thompson, a "sophisticated" Marxist.[212]

Transformation as a central concern: Scholars have been giving more and more attention to the results of the Revolution. We have long known about North America "before" (at least along the eastern seaboard); we are learning much more about North America "after" the Revolution. This shift can be measured in a number of ways—in the themes addressed from a wide range of views in the annual conferences on the Revolution sponsored by the United States Capitol Historical Society under the direction of Ronald Hoffman: the economy, internal civil wars, African Americans, women, religion, American Indians, the Jameson thesis;[213] in the focus of scholars exploring radicalism in the 1993 successor to my 1976 volume of essays;[214] in the scholarship about the Revolutionary War, long neglected for its social and political dimensions;[215] in the burst of books on the internal history of American Indian societies and the subject of Indian-"white" relations, which shows promise of breaking into the consciousness of nonspecialists.[216]

[212] Courtwright, "Interview with Morgan," 355; Bailyn, "Challenge of Modern Historiography," 6.

[213] The following volumes are in the series Perspectives on the American Revolution: Ira Berlin and Ronald Hoffman, eds., *Slavery and Freedom in the Age of the American Revolution* (Charlottesville, VA, 1983); Ronald Hoffman, John J. McCusker, Russell M. Menard, and Peter J. Albert, eds., *The Economy of Early America: The Revolutionary Period, 1763–1790* (Charlottesville, VA, 1988); Hoffman and Albert, eds., *Women in the Age of the American Revolution* (Charlottesville, VA, 1989); Hoffman and Albert, eds., *Religion in a Revolutionary Age* (Charlottesville, VA, 1994); Hoffman and Albert, eds., *Transforming Hand of Revolution*; Frederick E. Hoxie, Hoffman, and Albert, eds., *Native Americans and the Early Republic* (Charlottesville, VA, 1999).

[214] Alfred F. Young, ed., *Beyond the American Revolution: Explorations in the History of American Radicalism* (DeKalb, IL, 1993).

[215] Ronald Hoffman and Peter J. Albert, eds., *Arms and Independence: The Military Character of the American Revolution* (Charlottesville, VA, 1984); Don C. Higginbotham, "The Early American Way of War: Reconnaissance and Appraisal," *William and Mary Quarterly*, 3d ser. 44 (1987): 230–73; Charles Royster, *A Revolutionary People at War: The Continental Army and American Character, 1775–1783* (Chapel Hill, NC, 1979).

[216] For surveys of the literature, see James Axtell, "The Ethnohistory of Early America: A Review Essay," *William and Mary Quarterly*, 3d ser. 35 (1978): 110–44; and T. H. Breen, "Creative Adaptations: Peoples and Cultures," in Greene and Pole, eds., *Colonial British America*, 195–232.

Why this shift of scholarly attention? It may be part of a worldwide trend among scholars of revolutions who have responded to what Hobsbawm calls "the neglected problem of how and when revolutions finished," poignant even before the collapse of communism and the unforeseen paths of victorious colonial revolutions.[217] In part it is the influence of the *Annales* school, in part the stimulus of scholars of the new social history working in the nineteenth century and inspiring inquiries into the eighteenth. In good part it stems from asking what is the significance of the Revolution to African Americans and women, a question that can only be measured at the point of outcomes. Without being conscious of it, scholars are overcoming the occupational fallacy that a major historical event can be explained only by its "causes."

The centrality of transformation is apparent in books on single subjects and in the shifting themes of area studies, long the staple of the field. Take, for example, two recent books dealing with land and religion, issues central to Jameson. Lee Soltow's unassuming monograph, *The Distribution of Wealth and Income in the United States in 1798*, tests Jameson's hypotheses head on. Analyzing the little-used returns from the federal direct tax of 1798 on dwellings and buildings, coupled with the census of 1800, Soltow calculated 433,000 owners of land in a country with 877,000 adult white males. Comparing this to data assembled by Alice Hanson Jones for 1774, Soltow concluded that inequality may have decreased but that Jameson's claims for the impact of the forfeiture of loyalist estates, the ending of entail and primogeniture, and the opening of the West are difficult to measure. The thrust of his argument is that "inequality has been found to be substantial in 1798. It was not as extreme as in Europe, nor was it as egalitarian perhaps as Tocqueville suggested. But it was considerable."[218]

Nathan Hatch, in his prize-winning study of "the wave of popular religious movements that broke upon the United States in the half century after Independence" between 1780 and 1830, posited that the American Revolution was "the most crucial event in American history" because it

For a critique of the failure to integrate Indian history, see James Merrell, "Some Thoughts on Colonial Historians and American Indians," *William and Mary Quarterly*, 3d ser. 46 (1989): 94–119; and Daniel K. Richter, "Whose Indian History?" *William and Mary Quarterly*, 3d ser. 50 (1993): 379–93.

[217] Eric Hobsbawm, "Revolution," in Roy Porter and Mikulas Teich, eds., *Revolution in History* (Cambridge, UK, 1986), 6–46, quotation at 6. This essay is based on a report Hobsbawm gave in 1975.

[218] Lee Soltow, *The Distribution of Wealth and Income in the United States in 1798* (Pittsburgh, 1989), 252; for Jameson, see ibid., 141, 145, 148, 240.

"dramatically expanded the circle of people who considered themselves capable of thinking for themselves about issues of freedom, equality, sovereignty, and representation." His study of the Methodists, Baptists, black churches, and Mormons reversed the negative value judgments of the Second Great Awakening and religious populism in general, put down in fear by Richard Hofstadter in the era of McCarthyite anti-intellectualism. To Hatch religious populism, "leadership that is deliberate in championing the interests of the common people against professional expertise and elite institutions," has been "a residual agent of change in America over the last two centuries."[219]

Transformation has also been the theme of area studies, which have moved from the unit of the New England town before the Revolution to larger units before and after the Revolution. This trend is exemplified by four much-honored books by Edward Countryman, Rhys Isaac, Allan Kulikoff, and John Brooke.

Countryman's study of New York and Isaac's study of Virginia make transformation central in the Revolutionary era per se. "How different was New York in 1790 from 1760?" is Countryman's question. Organizing his study around the concept of "political society," he is interested in "the changes that took place . . . between power wielders and people affected by power." He finds "an explosion of political participation" by new groups, especially mechanics, farmers, and "expectant small capitalists," all of whom made gains as a defensive ruling class accommodated them. On the other hand, "neither blacks, Indians, nor women took part as a group in the revolutionary coalition, and none of them got much that they wanted out of its radicalism." The Revolution was successful in "laying the foundations of a liberal bourgeois society."[220]

Isaac attempted to portray "half a century of religious and political revolution" in Virginia between 1740 and 1790, which he called a "double revolution." He offered a series of tableaux interpreting physical landscapes —the great plantation house and the Anglican church—and the symbolic rituals of court day, militia muster, the horse race, and cockfight that bound together a consensual society. In the Revolution the ruling slaveholding gentry were confronted by the challenges of an evangelical upsurge of Baptists and the popular mobilization the war required. In this framework the successful disestablishment of the Anglican Church—an old Jameson

[219] Nathan Hatch, *The Democratization of American Christianity* (New Haven, CT, 1989).
[220] Countryman, *People in Revolution*, xv–xix, 292–96.

theme—became a major result, leaving a landscape of "broken down" Anglican churches amid the "rude and unadorned chapels" of the Baptists and Methodists. The gentry also had to confront republicanism as "a vehicle of popular assertion among the yeomanry" and "the consolidation of a communal pattern" among slaves—in all, "a polarized world."[221]

By contrast, the two more recent books, Kulikoff's study of the Chesapeake region from 1680 to 1800 and Brooke's study of Worcester County, Massachusetts, between 1712 and 1861, were framed over the *longue durée*, Kulikoff aspiring to "a grand thesis in the French style" and Brooke to a kind of "total history." Yet unlike eventless modernization history, both assigned a role to the Revolution as a transforming event and to what Brooke calls "political insurgencies." Kulikoff's goal was to describe and explain the "processes of class formation" that emerged in Virginia and Maryland on the basis of a political economy of tobacco. In place of Isaac's graphics and tableaux he offered proof via maps, figures, and tables in an uncommon effort to synthesize the historians' findings of demographic and family patterns with the findings of Isaac, Hoffman, and Morgan on political and cultural developments. During the Revolution, according to Kulikoff, the gentry class that held political power in the 1760s confronted a triple crisis—a popular movement that transformed politics, the dissenters who threatened the Anglican establishment, and the surge for freedom among slaves. In Virginia large planters consolidated their rule by accommodating yeomen with land and a voice in government, dissenters with religious liberty, and African Americans for a short time with manumission and over a longer time with space for the development of their own institutions and culture within the confines of slavery. This new history thus located in time the origins of the antebellum Old South.[222]

Brooke set the Revolution geographically in Worcester County, a vast domain in central Massachusetts, and conceptually in the framework of an inquiry into the competing "worldviews" of republican and liberal ideologies. His effort "to bridge the gap between social experience and intellectual discourse" presented the committee that bestowed on it the Merle Curti Award with the happy dilemma of deciding whether the book was intellectual or social history. Unlike other studies in which ideology appeared as an independent variable, Brooke placed his conflict of ideologies

[221] Isaac, *Transformation of Virginia.*

[222] Allan Kulikoff, *Tobacco and Slaves: The Development of Southern Cultures in the Chesapeake, 1680–1800* (Chapel Hill, NC, 1986).

in the context of "rapid economic change [which] spawned a dramatic and unique concentration of political insurgencies between the 1730's and the 1850's." A new social order led by "the Popular Whig gentry" evolved during and after the war amid the struggle of Baptists for religious liberty, Shays's regulation, which divided farmer loyalties, and a deep populist fear that the Constitution of 1787 would, as the Worcester farmer Amos Singletary put it, permit "the moneyed men" to "swallow up all us little folks." Through these conflicts alternate visions of Lockean liberalism and Harringtonian republicanism competed.[223]

Attention given to groups left out: The outsider historians—and a good many insiders—are doing the history of the outsiders. It is remarkable how much the new histories—of the laboring classes, farmers, African Americans, and women—has not only made transformation central but is forcing historians to reconsider the Revolution as a whole. These new histories have some traits in common. Some take the new social history's path of quantitative measurement of condition, but more take paths opened by the New Left to deal with agency and consciousness; some risk both. They are generally less subject to the strictures about "history with the politics left out" leveled earlier against Schlesinger's old social history, echoed in the mid-1970s against the new social history by the Marxists Eugene Genovese and Elizabeth Fox-Genovese.[224]

The new history of the laboring classes, for example, has recovered the agency of mechanics in the making of the Revolution and the shaping of institutions, especially in the seaboard cities, Philadelphia, New York, and

[223] John L. Brooke, *The Heart of the Commonwealth: Society and Political Culture in Worcester County, Massachusetts, 1713–1861* (Amherst, MA, 1989); for other regional studies dealing with transformation, see Richard R. Beeman, *The Evolution of the Southern Backcountry: A Case Study of Lunenburg County, Virginia, 1746–1832* (Philadelphia, 1984); Gregory H. Nobles, *Divisions throughout the Whole: Politics and Society in Hampshire County, Massachusetts, 1740–1775* (New York, 1983); Nobles, "'Yet the Old Republicans Still Persevere': Samuel Adams, John Hancock, and the Crisis of Popular Leadership in Revolutionary Massachusetts, 1775–1790," in Hoffman and Albert, eds., *Transforming Hand of Revolution*, 258–85; Rachel N. Klein, *Unification of a Slave State: The Rise of the Planter Class in the South Carolina Backcountry, 1760–1808* (Chapel Hill, NC, 1993); Jean B. Lee, "Lessons in Humility: The Revolutionary Transformation of the Governing Elite of Charles County, Maryland," in Hoffman and Albert, eds., *Transforming Hand of Revolution*, 90–117.

[224] Elizabeth Fox-Genovese and Eugene D. Genovese, "The Political Crisis of Social History: A Marxian Perspective," *Journal of Social History* 10 (1976): 205–20, reprinted in Fox-Genovese and Genovese, *Fruits of Merchant Capital: Slavery and Bourgeois Property in the Rise and Expansion of Capitalism* (New York, 1983), chap. 7.

Boston. The urban crowd is being placed in historical perspective. From the mid-eighteenth through the early nineteenth century, there is a sense of an artisan presence as well as of a conflict emerging between journeymen and masters and apprentices and masters.[225] Lemisch's seamen have been taken out to sea in an earlier era by Marcus Rediker and then back to land, where they are a source of transatlantic radicalism. In the quantitative tradition other scholars have provided vivid portraits of "the lower sort" of tradesmen, of indentured servants, and of the vast prewar migration of the poor from the British Isles.[226]

The pattern in the new agrarian history is similar. Scholars in the *Annales* tradition have described a wide array of rural communities and opened a fruitful debate about agrarian "*mentalité*" that others pursue as "moral economy" or "vernacular culture." We are getting a sense of the fear of debt and dependency and of the importance of acquiring and keeping land as the underpinning of the agrarian response to politics.[227] To the long history of agrarian insurrections in the late colonial period, recent studies of Shays's regulation of the 1780s, the Whiskey Rebellion of the 1790s, and agrarian protest in northern New England in the 1800s and

[225] For surveys of the literature, see Sean Wilentz, "The Rise of the American Working Class, 1776–1877," in J. Carroll Moody and Alice Kessler-Harris, eds., *Perspectives on American Labor History: The Problem of Synthesis* (DeKalb, IL, 1989), 83–90; and Gary J. Kornblith, "The Artisanal Response to Capitalist Transformation," *Journal of the Early Republic* 10 (1990): 315–21. For a synthesis, the titles by Nash are cited in notes 248ff. For the early nineteenth century, see Wilentz, *Chants Democratic: New York City and the Rise of the American Working Class, 1788–1850* (New York, 1984); and Christopher L. Tomlins, *Law, Labor, and Ideology in the Early American Republic* (Cambridge, UK, 1993).

[226] Marcus Rediker, *Between the Devil and the Deep Blue Sea: Merchant Seamen, Pirates, and the Anglo-American Maritime World, 1700–1750* (New York, 1987); Rediker, "A Motley Crew of Rebels: Sailors, Slaves, and the Coming of the American Revolution," in Hoffman and Albert, eds., *Transforming Hand of Revolution*, 155–98; Daniel Vickers, "Beyond Jack Tar," *William and Mary Quarterly*, 3d ser. 50 (1993): 418–24; Sharon V. Salinger, *"To Serve Well and Faithfully": Labor and Indentured Servants in Pennsylvania, 1682–1800* (Cambridge, UK, 1987); Billy G. Smith, *The "Lower Sort": Philadelphia's Laboring People, 1750–1800* (Ithaca, NY, 1990); Bernard Bailyn, *Voyagers to the West: A Passage in the Peopling of America on the Eve of the Revolution* (New York, 1986); Jean B. Russo, "Chesapeake Artisans in the Aftermath of the Revolution," in Hoffman and Albert, eds., *Transforming Hand of Revolution*, 118–54.

[227] James A. Henretta, "Families and Farms: *Mentalité* in Pre-Industrial America," *William and Mary Quarterly*, 3d ser. 35 (1978): 3–22; Allan Kulikoff, *The Agrarian Origins of American Capitalism* (Charlottesville, VA, 1992), chap. 1, sums up the debate; Richard L. Bushman, *King and People in Provincial Massachusetts* (Chapel Hill, NC, 1985), chap. 5; Barbara Clark Smith, "Social Visions of the American Resistance Movement," in Hoffman and Albert, eds., *Transforming Hand of Revolution*, 27–55.

other backcountries suggest a pattern of continuing and widespread rural protest.[228] We are also rediscovering plebeian agrarian thinkers such as William Manning, the radical millennialist Herman Husband, and religious dissenters who often led agrarian movements.[229]

The new history of African Americans in the Revolution is the culmination of the rediscovery that slaves had a history in the years before the "antebellum" period from 1830 to 1860, which has long dominated the modern study of slavery. As recently as 1976, Herbert Gutman wrote that "most slave communities had their start in the eighteenth century but no aspect of African-American history has received so little attention as the eighteenth-century social and cultural processes by which enslaved Africans became Afro-American slaves." For the second half of the eighteenth century, historians have begun to recover the slave family, slave religion, the slave community, and the retention of African culture and its influence on Anglo-American culture.[230] And for the Revolution they have located the agency of slaves in the wave of insurrection that peaked in 1775, in the triangular struggle during the war among slaves, whig patriots, and the British, in the pressures by slaves for greater autonomy in the labor system, and in the rebellions that erupted in 1800–1802.[231] Postwar eman-

[228] David P. Szatmary, *Shays' Rebellion: The Making of an Agrarian Insurrection* (Amherst, MA, 1980); Thomas P. Slaughter, *The Whiskey Rebellion: Frontier Epilogue to the American Revolution* (New York, 1986); Robert A. Gross, ed., *In Debt to Shays: The Bicentennial of an Agrarian Rebellion* (Charlottesville, VA, 1993); Gross, "White Hats and Hemlocks: Daniel Shays and the Legacy of Revolution," in Hoffman and Albert, eds., *Transforming Hand of Revolution*, 286–345; Alan Taylor, *Liberty Men and Great Proprietors: The Revolutionary Settlement on the Maine Frontier, 1760–1820* (Chapel Hill, NC, 1990); Taylor, "'To Man Their Rights': The Frontier Revolution," in Hoffman and Albert, eds., *Transforming Hand of Revolution*, 231–57; Michael A. Bellesiles, *Revolutionary Outlaws: Ethan Allen and the Struggle for Independence on the Early American Frontier* (Charlottesville, VA, 1993).

[229] Michael Merrill and Sean Wilentz, eds., *The Key of Liberty: The Life and Democratic Writings of William Manning, "A Laborer," 1747–1814* (Cambridge, MA, 1993); Ruth H. Bloch, *Visionary Republic: Millennial Themes in American Thought, 1756–1800* (Cambridge, UK, 1985); Mark Jones, "Herman Husband: Millenarian, Carolina Regulator, and Whiskey Rebel," Ph.D. diss., Northern Illinois University, 1983.

[230] Herbert G. Gutman, *The Black Family in Slavery and Freedom, 1750–1925* (New York, 1976), 327; for surveys of the scholarship, see Wood, "I Did the Best I Could," 185–225; Peter H. Wood, *Black Majority: Negroes in Colonial South Carolina from 1670 through the Stono Rebellion* (New York, 1974); Berlin and Hoffman, eds., *Slavery and Freedom*; Mechal Sobel, *The World They Made Together: Black and White Values in Eighteenth-Century Virginia* (Princeton, NJ, 1987).

[231] Peter H. Wood, "'Liberty Is Sweet': African-American Freedom Struggles in the Years before White Independence," in Young, ed., *Beyond the American Revolution*, 149–84; Sylvia R. Frey, *Water from the Rock: Black Resistance in a Revolutionary Age* (Princeton, NJ, 1991); Philip D.

cipation studies show how blacks shaped their own emancipation and their own communities. Meanwhile, the scholarship of slavery as an issue in national affairs continues to draw attention to the incompleteness of the Revolution.[232]

The modern historical study of women in the era of the Revolution is even more recent than African American history. "Until the mid-1970s, historians of the American Revolution largely ignored women," Mary Beth Norton writes, "and historians of women largely ignored the Revolution." Joan Hoff Wilson's argument in 1976, based on modernization analysis, that the Revolution produced only the "illusion of change," has been challenged since 1980 by the pathbreaking books by Norton and Linda K. Kerber that emphasized changes in women's consciousness, especially as a result of their experiences during the war and the opening of postwar educational opportunity. These contributed to the accommodations of "matrimonial republicanism" and what Kerber has called "Republican Motherhood."[233] Since then one line of scholarship has reinforced a picture of changing consciousness expressed, for example, in rising literacy, the creation of a women's reading public, and the rise of the American novel, while another has stressed the institutional conservatism of the Revolution, measured by laws on inheritance and women's property rights, and demographic patterns.[234] Still other scholars are stitching together patterns of women's exercise of

Morgan, "Black Society in the Low Country, 1760–1810," in Berlin and Hoffman, eds., *Slavery and Freedom*, 83–142; Douglas R. Edgerton, *Gabriel's Rebellion: The Virginia Slave Conspiracies of 1800 and 1802* (Chapel Hill, NC, 1993); Billy G. Smith, "Runaway Slaves in the Mid-Atlantic Region during the Revolutionary Era," in Hoffman and Albert, eds., *Transforming Hand of Revolution*, 199–230.

232 For a summary of the literature, see Shane White, *Somewhat More Independent: The End of Slavery in New York City, 1770–1810* (Athens, GA, 1991), 211–14.

233 Mary Beth Norton, "Reflections on Women in the Age of the American Revolution," in Hoffman and Albert, eds., *Women in the Age of the American Revolution*, 479–93; Wilson, "Illusion of Change"; Norton, *Liberty's Daughters: The Revolutionary Experience of American Women, 1750–1800* (Boston, 1980); Linda K. Kerber, *Women of the Republic: Intellect and Ideology in Revolutionary America* (Chapel Hill, NC, 1980).

234 For analyses of the scholarship, see Mary Beth Norton, "The Evolution of White Women's Experience in Early America," *American Historical Review* 89 (1984): 593–619; and Linda K. Kerber, "Separate Spheres, Female Worlds, Woman's Place: The Rhetoric of Women's History," *Journal of American History* 75 (1988): 9–39; Cathy Davidson, *Revolution and the Word: The Rise of the Novel in America* (New York, 1986); William J. Gilmore, *Reading Becomes a Necessity of Life: Material and Cultural Life in Rural New England, 1780–1835* (Knoxville, TN, 1989). For the limitations of reform, see the essays by Daniel Scott Smith, Carole Shammas, and Marylynn Salmon in Hoffman and Albert, eds., *Women in the Age of the American Revolution*.

citizenship.[235] Synthesizing essays proffer long lists of unstudied subjects, especially of non-middle-class, nonwhite women, while the appearance of biographical studies of women offers some prospect of resolving competing claims.

12. Toward a New Synthesis?

The recovery of all the new histories has been both a major challenge and a stumbling block to synthesis from any point of view. The old political question about "who shall rule at home" posed by Becker and refined by Jensen has been more or less resolved for all but the first generation of counter-Progressives. There were two concurrent struggles; whether one was more important than the other is a red herring; how to fit them together remains problematic. As to the outcome of the internal conflict, Robert R. Palmer's analysis of the American Revolution as both radical and conservative has more resonance now than before. There seems to be a consensus that a republican system emerged with strong democratic currents. On the other hand the new social histories have forced a reformulation of the question of the Revolution as a social movement offered with such artful vagueness by Jameson. The question no longer is *whether* there was social change but *how much* change occurred and especially how much in the direction of equality. And the corollary question—because we know there were such disparities—is how do we explain the so-called contradictions in the results of the Revolution?

Wherever one turns to examine social consequences of the Revolution, one finds scholars struggling to make sense of opposites. By 1820 the number of free blacks had grown to almost 250,000, and the number of slaves, to 1.5 million. The Revolution, in Ira Berlin's words, "was not only a stride forward in the expansion of black liberty, [but it] strengthened the plantation regime and slavery grew as never before, spreading across a continent. Thus if the Revolution marked a new birth of freedom, it also launched a great expansion of slavery." When and if "a new narrative" of

[235] Alfred F. Young, "The Women of Boston: 'Persons of Consequence' in the Making of the Revolution," and Linda K. Kerber, "I Have Don . . . Much to Carrey on the Warr': Women and the Shaping of Republican Ideology after the American Revolution," in Harriet B. Applewhite and Darlene G. Levy, eds., *Women and Politics in the Age of the Democratic Revolution* (Ann Arbor, MI, 1990), 181–259; Elaine Forman Crane, ed., *The Diary of Elizabeth Drinker*, 3 vols. (Boston, 1991); Susan Branson, "Politics and Gender: The Political Consciousness of Philadelphia Women in the 1790s," Ph.D. diss., Northern Illinois University, 1992.

the Revolution integrates gender, Linda Kerber writes, it "will be understood to be more deeply radical than we have hitherto perceived it because its shock reached into the deepest and most private human relations." But it will also be understood to be "more deeply conservative, . . . purchasing political stability at the price of backing away from the implications of the sexual politics implied in its own manifestos." For free white men the contrasts in the achievement of personal independence present similar dilemmas. Soltow's finding that in 1800 less than half the adult white males were property holders, even when adjusted for variations in the life cycle, raises the question of whether the glass was half full or half empty. Sean Wilentz's analysis of artisans in the 1790s and early 1800s reveals contrasts between prospering entrepreneurial masters threatened by merchant capitalists and impoverished journeymen shoemakers driven to strikes. The new Indian histories churn up even greater challenges of irreconcilable opposites between Anglo-Americans and Native Americans as well as within tribal societies divided over how to resist.[236]

To understand these "contradictions" historians have moved toward analyses in which inequalities and exploitation were inherent either in the social system or in the ideologies. "The American colonists were not trapped in an accidental contradiction between slavery and freedom," David Brion Davis writes. As they emerged from the Revolution, "slavery was of central importance to both the southern and national economies and thus to the viability of 'the American system.'" The continuing subordination of women seems implicit in the values of republicanism, if not in the exploitation of the labor of women in a patriarchal system. Personal independence, the goal of every Tom, Dick, and Harry, whether farmer, mechanic, or merchant, was defined by the dependence of his wife and children. Independence, Joan Gunderson writes, "was a condition arrived at by exclusion, by not being dependent or enslaved." The decline of the independent artisan was a concomitant of a developing commercial capitalism. The displacement and disruption of American Indian tribal societies was a consequence of a system of landed expansion that met the needs of would-be settlers, land speculators, southern slaveholders, and the suppositions of ethnocentrism, racism, and an ideology of expansion that

[236] Berlin and Hoffman, introduction to Berlin and Hoffman, eds., *Slavery and Freedom*, xv; Linda K. Kerber, "'History Can Do It No Justice': Women and the Reinterpretation of the American Revolution," in Hoffman and Albert, eds., *Women in the Age of the American Revolution*, 10; Wilentz, *Chants Democratic*; Hoxie, Hoffman, and Albert, eds., *Native Americans and the Early Republic* (Charlottesville, VA, 1999), brings together major trends in the new scholarship.

envisioned, among the most benevolent expansionists, in Jefferson's words, an "empire for liberty."[237]

I have suggested that the concept of conflict, negotiation, and accommodation may help us to reconcile the seemingly contradictory results in the multiple facets of the Revolution. In my own efforts at synthesis I have attempted to draw attention to the impact of popular movements on elites. There were many radicalisms in the Revolutionary era: a radicalism born of hope encapsulated by Thomas Paine's *Common Sense*, whose millennialist plea that the "birthday of a new world is at hand" was appropriated by unequals in the society; a radicalism born of experience during the war among soldiers, seamen, and slaves who learned how to cast off deference; and a radicalism born of frustration, especially in the 1780s and 1790s, of promises unfulfilled.

Such radicalisms constantly shaped elites, would-be ruling classes trying to create or stabilize a system. Some turned to coercion, some to accommodation, learning how to "yield to the torrent if they hoped to direct its course," as Robert R. Livingston put it; some did both. At a crisis in the "political system" in 1787, Madison led elites at the Constitutional Convention to shape a government "intended for the ages" that would conform to "the genius of the people," including the Shaysite farmers and Paineite mechanics who were a presence even if they were not present.[238]

In 1976, in my afterword to the collection of essays on radicalism in the era, I thought that while farmers and artisans were a force to be reckoned with, the outsiders—African Americans, women, American Indians—had little effect in pressuring elites. As I reflect on the new social histories, it is apparent that scholars are now working out similar processes of negotiation with the so-called outsiders. This is a hallmark of recent scholarship on slavery—the processes of negotiation by which slaves won "space" for themselves within an oppressive system. After the Revolution, as slavery grew and expanded, Ira Berlin finds central "continued renegotiations of

[237] Davis, *Problem of Slavery*, 256, 259, 262; Joan B. Gunderson, "Independence, Citizenship, and the American Revolution," *Signs* 13 (1987): 59–77; see also Ruth H. Bloch, "The Gendered Meanings of Virtue in Revolutionary America," *Signs* 13 (1987): 37–58; James Merrell, "Declarations of Independence: Indian-White Relations in the New Nation," in J. Greene, ed., *American Revolution*, 197–223.

[238] Young, "Conservatives"; Young, "Framers of the Constitution"; Young, afterword to Young, ed., *American Revolution*; Young, "How Radical Was the American Revolution?" in Young, ed., *Beyond the American Revolution*; Young and Terry Fife with Mary Janzen, *We the People: Voices and Images of the New Nation* (Philadelphia, 1993).

the terms under which slaves worked for their masters." "We are ready to ask," Linda Kerber writes, "whether and how the social relations of the sexes were renegotiated in the crucible of the Revolution." James Merrell portrays Anglo-American elites oscillating between coercion and accommodation of Indians. The alternatives Americans offered to Indians —"civilization or extinction," as Merrell writes—were "alternative routes to obliteration," but they were in response to resistance by tribal societies.[239]

How do historians attempting syntheses of the Revolution deal with these opposites? The deans of the counter-Progressive school, Edmund S. Morgan and Bernard Bailyn, judging by the most recent editions of their books, stand pat with their earlier interpretations. James A. Henretta, who in 1973 presented a new social history synthesis in the framework of modernization, in a recent revision in collaboration with Gregory H. Nobles, puts more emphasis on the "actions of thousands of 'unheeded' and obscure men and women" and on the "contradictions" in the results posed by the inequality of blacks and women and the displacement of the Indians. The framework, however, remains modernization, with stress on the "transition to capitalism," a theme that is drawing the attention of many scholars.[240]

The first New Left synthesis has a different emphasis. In 1985 Edward Countryman drew together the new history that has "explored the experience, the consciousness, and the purposes of artisans, farmers, militiamen, blacks, and women." For Countryman the Revolutionary movement was a complex "series of coalitions that formed, dissolved, and re-formed as people considered what they needed and what they believed." They lived through "a massive, disruptive, immensely confusing but popular Revolution" in which there was a "grand transformation that bound together many separate changes." Ordinary people, if they did not find equality, "found their own voices." "But change did begin. Like artisans and farmers

[239] Ira Berlin, "Rethinking Afro-American Slavery in Mainland North America" (paper presented at the Southern Historical Association, Ft. Worth, TX, Nov. 1991); Kerber, "History Can Do It No Justice," 10; Merrell, "Declarations of Independence," 197–223.

[240] Henretta and Nobles, *Evolution and Revolution*, chap. 10; Henretta, "The Transition to Capitalism in America," in Henretta, Kammen, and Katz eds., *Transformation of Early American History*, 218–38, and Henretta, "The War for Independence and American Economic Development," in Hoffman et al., eds. *Economy of Early America*, 45–87, both reprinted in Henretta, *The Origins of American Capitalism: Collected Essays* (Boston, 1992); Joyce Oldham Appleby, *Capitalism and a New Social Order: The Republican Vision of the 1790s* (New York, 1984); for reflections on this theme, see Allan Kulikoff, "Was the American Revolution a Bourgeois Revolution?" in Hoffman and Albert, eds., *Transforming Hand of Revolution*, 58–89.

of the revolutionary era, women and blacks would have to go through a long painful struggle to win their freedom."[241]

The contrast in interpretations of transformation in the Revolution is best represented in the work of two senior scholars, Gary B. Nash and Gordon S. Wood. Nash has produced the largest and most multifaceted body of scholarship on the era of the Revolution of any scholar in the new social history. Wood, identified with the republican ideological interpretation and the new intellectual history, has produced the first synthesis embracing the Revolution as a whole. The two stand at opposite poles of the current debate on the Revolution.

That Gary Nash (1933—) has been perceived differently is a sign that over the past quarter of a century he has crossed boundaries within as well as among schools. "I am sometimes called a 'neo-Progressive,'" he wrote in 1986, "a label that pleases me because I hope my work has some utility in the wrestling with the awesome problems of contemporary American life." He was happy to give the first Merrill Jensen lectures at Wisconsin. When his multicultural textbook for the elementary schools was the object of public hearings in California, he found himself the target of attack by ethnic nationalists who accused him of tokenism and Eurocentrism. He found this odd because, he said, "I spent my whole career trying to get rid of Eurocentric teaching and catching it from conservatives at the university level who think my work is too left-of-center." He is most comfortable defining himself as a social historian; he is unique in attempting to bring together the two traditions of social history analyzed by James Henretta that stem from the *Annales* school and English revisionist Marxism and adding to it a third, ethnohistory of American Indians and African Americans.[242]

The evolution of Nash's interests and methods suggests the way his own ideas are rooted in experience—a theme of his scholarship. As a senior at Princeton in 1954, to Richard S. Dunn, then a teaching assistant, Nash was a "a sandy-haired, clean cut youth who wore his snappy Naval ROTC

[241] Countryman, *American Revolution*; Countryman, "'To Secure the Blessings of Liberty': Language, the Revolution, and American Capitalism," in Young, ed., *Beyond the American Revolution*, 123–48. For a variant synthesis, see American Social History Project, *Who Built America? Working People and the Nation's Economy, Politics, Culture, and Society*, 2 vols. (New York, 1989); Alfred F. Young and Eric Foner were the consulting editors for volume 1, for which the first drafts of the early American history chapters were written by Dorothy Fennell, and the revisions, by Edward Countryman and Marcus Rediker.

[242] Gary B. Nash, preface to *Race, Class, and Politics: Essays on American Colonial and Revolutionary Society* (Urbana, IL, 1986), xix; David L. Kirp, "The Battle of the Books," *San Francisco Examiner Sunday Image*, Feb. 24, 1991, 17–25, Nash quotation at 19.

uniform to class and seemed from my jaundiced graduate school perspective to be designed by God for a military career." After three years on a destroyer in the Mediterranean, he returned to Princeton, where he was an assistant to the dean of the graduate school and then a student. He did a thesis under Wesley Frank Craven on the divisions among elites in early eighteenth-century Pennsylvania politics. In 1966, when he moved from teaching at Princeton to UCLA, he "became deeply involved in the Civil Rights movement," and "at the same time," he writes, "I found that my students were far more diverse than in the East—diverse in terms of race, class, sex, age, and cultural background. My course in the history of colonial and revolutionary America began to change under this dual influence." In this environment his scholarship turned in two new directions—to the triracial character of colonial society, encapsulated in the title of the book that evolved from his teaching, *Red, White, and Black: The Peoples of Early America*, and to the study of social stratification, which made him one of the pioneers we have discussed in the first wave of the new social history.[243]

In the mid-1960s this trajectory from political history of elites to quantitative social history from the bottom up was not unique for scholars in Nash's cohort. What was unusual was that he was interested in social class as the matrix for understanding the politics of the origins of the Revolution. He collected his essays from 1963 to 1983 under the title *Race, Class, and Politics*. In focusing on the common people, he was as much interested in their agency, for which he reexamined traditional literary sources, as in analyzing their underlying life conditions, for which he quantified aggregates of mute sources. That he could carry on this research in California (with research trips to the East) is testimony to the decentralization of primary sources made possible by the microform revolution.[244] *The Urban Crucible* (1979) brought together the two methods. Later, when he moved from the origins to the results of the Revolution, as did other scholars, he focused on the experiences of African Americans. His efforts at synthesis came after he had worked on results as well as origins and with a sense a

[243] Richard S. Dunn, foreword to Nash, *Race, Class, and Politics*, xiii; Meier and Rudwick, *Black History*, 198–99; Nash, *Red, White, and Black* (1974; 2d ed., 1982; 3d ed., 1991); Nash, *Quakers and Politics: Pennsylvania, 1681–1726* (Princeton, NJ, 1968).

[244] Nash and Lemon, "Distribution of Wealth"; Nash, *Class and Society*; Nash, *Red, White, and Black*; Nash, "Up from the Bottom"; Nash, "Urban Wealth and Poverty." For Nash's analysis of this scholarship, see his "Social Development," in Greene and Pole, eds., *Colonial British America*, 233–61; for a response to a critic, see Nash, Billy G. Smith, and Dirk Hoerder, "Laboring Americans and the American Revolution," *Labor History* 24 (1983): 414–39.

triracial society in his mind. His synthesis appeared in works intended for a general audience—a college text, a series of elementary school texts, a museum exhibit on the history of Philadelphia, and a project to establish national standards in the teaching of history from kindergarten through high school. In this concern for reaching a larger public the "new" social history is akin to the "new" history of Beard, Becker, and Merle Curti in the interwar years.[245]

Nash revealed the assumptions that guide his study of subordinate classes in *Red, White, and Black*. He was concerned with rescuing groups blotted out by American "historical amnesia" but not in portraying them as victims of exploitation or aggression. His focus was "the dynamic process of interaction" that shaped the history of American Indians, Europeans, and Africans in North America, a history that included cultural exchange and the mixing of peoples as well as conflict and conquest. He rejected both the Gramscian notion of hegemonic domination of subordinate classes and the celebration of the masses. In introducing a collection of biographies of obscure individuals among colonial Spanish Americans, American Indians, and Anglo-Americans, Nash (and his coeditor, David Sweet) wanted to avoid "Horatio Alger stories about individuals triumphing against adversity" as well as "Howard Fast stories about people triumphing against oppression." Nash has used biography of unknown and lesser-known figures to explore both agency and ideology.[246]

The Urban Crucible, his magnum opus, rooted politics in the "social morphology" of the cities (in the *Annales* tradition) and in the interrelations among classes, defining class (as did E. P. Thompson) as the product

[245] For the permanent exhibit "Finding Philadelphia's Past: Visions and Revisions" at the Historical Society of Philadelphia, see Nash, "Behind the Velvet Curtain: Academic History, Historical Societies, and the Presentation of the Past," *Pennsylvania Magazine of History and Biography* 114 (1990): 3–26. The texts are known as the "Houghton Mifflin Social Studies" series, 10 vols. (Boston, 1991), each volume with a different title; *America Will Be* goes through the Civil War; for the controversy over adoption of the texts, see Robert Reinhold, "Class Struggle, California's Textbook Debate," *New York Times Magazine*, Sept. 29, 1991, 26–29, 46–47, 53. Nash and Charlotte Crabtree were cochairs of the National History Standards Project task force; the report is in Crabtree and Nash, *National Standards for United States History* (Los Angeles, 1994); see also Nash, "History for a Democratic Society: The Work of All People," in Paul Gagnon, ed., *Historical Literacy: The Case for History in American Education* (New York, 1989), 234–48.

[246] Nash, *Red, White, and Black*; Nash and David Sweet, introduction to Nash and Sweet, eds., *Struggle and Survival in Colonial America* (Berkeley, CA, 1981), 1–13, quotations at 5; for biographies, see Nash, "Thomas Peters: Millwright and Deliverer," in Nash and Sweet, eds., *Struggle and Survival*, 69–85, and Nash, "'To Arise Out of the Dust': Absalom Jones and the African Church of Philadelphia, 1785–95," in Nash, *Race, Class, and Politics*, 323–55.

of conflict. Portraying the three major seaboard cities, Boston, New York, and Philadelphia, on a broad canvas from 1690 to 1775, it was the richest single book to set the Revolution in the context of social change and prior internal conflicts. Nash placed his social analysis in the framework of a political narrative that integrated changing patterns of economic growth and the concentration of wealth with the Great Awakening, colonial wars, and factional conflict, building the variations among the three cities into his story. His theme is that from the 1760s to 1776 the Revolution "was accompanied by a profound social upheaval" but no "social revolution." The agency was clear: the Revolution "could not have unfolded when or in the manner it did without the self-conscious action of laboring people, both those at the bottom and those in the middle." Ideology was more problematic. Nash saw a division between "two broad ideologies"—whigs, whom he divided between conservatives and liberals, both of whom "embraced the bourgeois spirit of commercial life," and evangelicals, who "clung to traditional ideals of moral economy" and an "egalitarian and communalistic ethos." There was "no perfect crystallization of class or class consciousness" and clearly "no unified ideology among the laboring classes."[247]

Nash has explored the transformations of the Revolution for artisans and African Americans in the cities and around the national issue of race. For artisans the decades from the close of the Revolution to the 1820s were a time of "momentous transformation" that "created permanent fissures in the structure of the mechanical arts." While mechanics became a political force in urban politics, masters and journeymen were in increasing conflict. The longstanding tension among artisans saw a "capitalistic mentality" winning out over the "older communalistic ethos."[248]

For African Americans in the northern cities, Nash portrayed a dual theme of "triumph and tragedy." In his book on African Americans in post-Revolutionary Philadelphia, the fullest study of the "inner history" of one of the first free black communities, the tragedy lay in the relatively harmonious race relations of the postwar years turning into growing discrimination and blatant racism; the triumph lay in blacks forging their

[247] Nash, *Urban Crucible*, 339–84, 340–41 (ideologies).

[248] Gary B. Nash, "Artisans and Politics in Eighteenth-Century Philadelphia," in Jacob and Jacob, eds., *Origins of Anglo-American Radicalism*, 162–82; Nash, "A Historical Perspective on Early American Artisans," in Michael Conforti and William Puig, eds., *The American Craftsman and the European Tradition, 1620–1820* (Amherst, MA, 1989), 1–16; Nash, "The Social Evolution of Preindustrial American Cities, 1700–1820: Reflections on New Directions," *Journal of Urban History* 13 (1987): 115–45.

own churches, societies, and fraternal orders. Analyzing ideology, Nash found evidence for W. E. B. Du Bois's "two warring ideals" between African and American identities. The alternative institutions cultivated by the first generation of free blacks, especially the autonomous African American churches, enabled them to maintain "the dialectical existence" of this "double consciousness."[249]

In his analysis of race as an issue in the post-Revolutionary era, he focused on the failure of abolitionism, a question raised in the late 1960s by Lynd, Jordan, and Davis. He attributed this not to the intransigence of the lower South and the political fragility of the national union but to white northerners who "lost the abolitionist fire in their bellies." They failed to respond to liberal southern plans for compensated emancipation and succumbed to "a rampaging white racism." Examining how slavery ended in Pennsylvania, Nash found "a tug of war between ideological commitment and economic interests."[250]

In Nash's way of thinking, ideology is rooted in experience. "All Americans could agree on many elements of the republican ideology," but "continuing debate over the meaning of republicanism lay at the center of the Revolutionary experience." Skeptical of the pervasiveness of a single ideology, he has variously portrayed alternative ideologies among white laboring people as "evangelical" or as a "small producer" ideology centering on equality. He sees this outlook as "more traditional than modern," which "does not fit comfortably within the bounds of classical republican thought" posited by Gordon Wood or the liberalism posited by Joyce Appleby. And among the "outsiders," he finds evidence for ways of thinking that hardly fit into any frames.[251]

Nash's vision of transformation in the Revolution stresses the agency of the common people and their conflicts with their betters. "In the course of resisting English policy" from 1765 to 1776, "many previously inactive

[249] Gary B. Nash, *Forging Freedom: The Formation of Philadelphia's Black Community, 1720–1840* (Cambridge, MA, 1988), 6–7; Nash, *Race and Revolution*, 72; Nash, "Forging Freedom: The Emancipation Experience in the Northern Seaport Cities, 1775–1820," in Berlin and Hoffman, eds., *Slavery and Freedom*, 3–48; Nash, "The Forgotten Experience: Indians, Blacks, and the American Revolution," in William F. Fowler, ed., *The American Revolution: Changing Perspectives* (Boston, 1981), 27–46.

[250] Nash, *Race and Revolution*, chaps. 1–2, quotations at 35, 49; Nash and Jean R. Soderlund, *Freedom by Degrees: Emancipation in Pennsylvania and Its Aftermath* (New York, 1991), introduction.

[251] For Nash's approach to ideology, see his "Also There at the Creation: Going beyond Gordon Wood," *William and Mary Quarterly*, 3d ser. 44 (1987): 602–11.

groups entered public life to challenge gentry control of political affairs. Often occupying the most radical ground in the opposition to England, they simultaneously challenged the concentration of economic and political power in their own communities." Then, ordinary people "elbowing their way into a political system in which they had never been centrally involved . . . shaped the Revolutionary process in vital ways." The war "transformed the lives of all Americans" but had "different consequences for men than for women, for black slaves than for white masters, for Native Americans than for frontier settlers, for overseas merchants than for urban workers." "Outsiders," defined as black slaves, Native Americans, and white loyalists, "suffered the effects but reaped few of its rewards." American Indians suffered "both betrayal and defeat"; when peace came, "the Indians' interests were totally ignored." The Revolution "changed many aspects of American life," but "changes did not come easily" as "people struggled with each other for political power and the ability to influence what government did."[252]

Criticism of Nash's work spans a range. Gordon Wood, characterizing Nash as someone who "has devoted his career to writing about the weak and dispossessed," expresses a debt to him "for uncovering the experience of these neglected groups." But Wood argues that Nash "sentimentalizes" the traditionalism and moral economy of popular majorities; small producers, he insists, were "entrepreneurial minded." Among social historians Nash receives the kind of criticism often directed to scholars who open up a field: incompleteness. At a panel devoted to race and class in his work, Nash pleaded guilty to Jean Soderlund's charge that he subordinated gender analysis to race and class. "Historians can do double axels quite gracefully these days," he quipped, and perhaps they will catch up with Olympic figure skaters and be able to do triple axels without falling." Accepting Allan Kulikoff's criticism that his work lacks "a systematic theoretical analysis of class relations," Nash suggests this may be a possible advantage. He is intensely aware of the problem of establishing unifying themes in ethnohistory to avoid the pitfalls of "cameo" history. After several years on the combat lines synthesizing the new histories in fifth-, eighth-, and eleventh-grade textbooks, and drawing up national standards, Nash expects to return to the challenge of synthesis in the era of the Revolution

[252] Gary B. Nash, Julie Roy Jeffrey, et al., *The American People: Creating a Nation and a Society*, 2 vols. (New York, 1990), 1: chaps. 5–7, quotations at 159, 164, 188, 191, 196, 200, 205, 211, 228. Several chapters in this section of the book were written in collaboration with John R. Howe.

by exploring American Indians and taking *Red, White, and Black* through the Revolution, which will enable him to attempt a general social history of the Revolution.[253]

Gordon Wood, in his work of synthesis, *The Radicalism of the American Revolution*, entered the door he left open to the Jameson thesis at the conclusion of his first book, *The Creation of the Republic, 1776–1787*, in 1969. Indeed, in the 1990s he rattled Jameson's dry bones with such provocative and often extravagant claims that one wonders whether the cautious Jameson, his predecessor at Brown University in the 1890s, might ask, "Has Gordon Wood *over*considered the American Revolution as a social movement?"

Wood's formulations are nothing if not bold. "Measured by the amount of social change that actually took place—by transformations in the relationships that bound people to each other," he writes, the Revolution was "not conservative at all; on the contrary: it was as radical and as revolutionary as any in history," and it was "as radical and social as any revolution in history." "It was the Revolution, more than any other single event, that made America into the most liberal, democratic, and modern nation in the world." "The idea of equality, . . . the most radical and most powerful ideological force, [was] let loose in the Revolution. Once invoked, the idea of equality could not be stopped." Wood speaks of the "social transformation" and the "social radicalism" of the Revolution.[254]

The Radicalism of the American Revolution is a very different book from *The Creation of the American Republic*, and the changes reflect Wood's response in the intervening years to changes in the landscape of scholarship. Wood (1933—) was born in West Acton, near Concord, where, an interviewer reports, "his family had a chicken farm. His voice still carries traces of a blue-collar Massachusetts accent." He received an undergraduate degree from nearby Tufts and, after three years as a lieutenant in the Air Force (1955–58), did his Ph.D. at Harvard, where, if it needs to be said, as a student of Bernard Bailyn he became an unexpected enthusiast of early

[253] Gary B. Nash, "Response to Commentaries," at a panel entitled "Race and Class in the Work of Gary B. Nash" (Annual Meeting of the Organization of American Historians, Chicago, Apr. 1992). The commentators were Jean R. Soderlund, Richard White, and Allan Kulikoff; for Gordon S. Wood's criticism, see his "Ideology and the Origins of Liberal America," *William and Mary Quarterly*, 3d ser. 44 (1987): 635–40.

[254] Gordon S. Wood, *The Radicalism of the American Revolution* (New York, 1992), introduction, 3–8, quotations at 5, 7, 232 ("idea of equality"). "An early version of the book was presented in 1986 as the Anson G. Phelps lectures at New York University" (ibid., ix).

American history. He completed *Creation of the American Republic* on a fellowship at the Institute of Early American History and Culture (1964–66), taught at Harvard and the University of Michigan, and has been at Brown University since 1969.

Wood has never been accused of being a popularizer. *Creation* was a meticulously argued, very long book that my graduate students made me feel I inflicted on them. Wood has published articles for fellow historians and reviews for intellectuals in the *New York Review of Books* and the *New Republic* and has given invited lectures in academic settings. The text he coauthored with Bailyn, David B. Davis, and three other distinguished historians in its first edition proved too intellectual and too sophisticated for its college audience. He has also never been accused of political partisanship. He takes pride in what his interviewer called his refusal to pick sides. "People have said to me," he said, "I never knew whether you're for the federalists or for the anti-federalists. Are you for the elites, or are you for the common people? I think I would have been one of those people on the fence, the mugwump, I guess."[255]

This seeming diffidence notwithstanding, in his later book there is a passion of a crusader which takes on meaning in the context of the critical reaction to his own scholarship and the republican "school" (with which he feels he is overidentified) and of what he has called a "crisis" in the field of intellectual history. From the publication of his first article in 1966 challenging his mentor to deal with the reality that underlay the rhetoric, through his 1969 book devoted to conflict rather than consensus, to his festschrift essay of 1991 interpreting Bailyn as a social historian who had for a time lost his way, Wood has established his independence of judgment. In the parlance of eighteenth-century artisans who passed from apprentice to journeyman to master, Gordon Wood became "a man on his own." But, by staking out a middle position between a so-called idealist or intellectual approach on the one hand and the so-called realists or materialists on the other, it was inevitable that he should be criticized by both and leave others bewildered. Bailyn was criticized by eminent intellectual historians because he "tend[ed] to exaggerate the autonomous power of ideas" (David B. Davis) or because he "elevated ideology to causal preeminence" (Joyce Appleby). I, for one, never thought this was true of the *Creation of the Republic*, a book I welcomed at the time as an exploration of the ideology of the

[255] Missy Daniel, "A Radical History," *Brown Alumni Monthly* 93 (1993): 23–27; Gordon S. Wood's curriculum vitae, kindly provided by Wood.

debate over the Constitution that restored conflict to the era, rather than as an ideological interpretation.[256]

Over the years Wood has staked out his own position. He has disassociated his interpretation from Bailyn's "aversion" to anything that smacks of a social analysis and from those who saw in the belief in conspiracy a paranoid psychological interpretation of history; such a belief, Wood argues, was quite rational in the eighteenth century. He has also separated himself from "the so-called republican synthesis" of the 1970s and 1980s, which became "something of a monster that has threatened to devour us all." And he explored the terrain of "interests" in the 1780s that he had bypassed earlier. Focusing, for example, on William Findley, an Irish-born former weaver and self-made politician in western Pennsylvania, he concluded that the Antifederalists were spokesmen for "middling aspirations, middling achievements, and middling resentments."[257]

For all the recognition *Creation of the Republic* received, twenty years after its publication Wood was put on the defensive about it. It is the only book the *William and Mary Quarterly* honored as a "modern classic," with a symposium in 1987 in which a dozen historians participated. Wood had to reply to a wide range of critics. On the one hand were those who faulted him for an "overly intellectual approach" to ideology (Jack N. Rakove) or for neglecting other ideologies such as liberalism or evangelical religion (Ruth H. Bloch, John Howe) or the seminal role of Thomas Paine (Pauline Maier). On the other he had to reply to historians who deal with the nitty-gritty of politics, such as Jackson Turner Main, or the role of capitalism, such as Edward Countryman, or the agency of popular movements, such as Gary Nash. Nash, not surprisingly, finds Wood's version of the period 1776 to 1787 "too homogeneous, too static, and too shallowly rooted in the soil of social experience."[258]

[256] Wood, "Rhetoric and Reality"; idem, *Creation of the American Republic;* idem, "Democratization of the Mind"; idem, "Creative Imagination"; Davis, *The Problem of Slavery in the Age of Revolution*, 274n (his reference is to Jordan and Bailyn); Appleby, "A Different Kind of Independence," 261; Alfred F. Young, review of Wood, *Creation of the American Republic, New-York Historical Society Quarterly* 55 (1971): 391–92.

[257] Gordon S. Wood, "Conspiracy and the Paranoid Style: Causality and Deceit in the Eighteenth Century," *William and Mary Quarterly*, 3d ser. 39 (1982): 401–41; Wood, postscript to "Rhetoric and Reality," in *In Search of Early America*, 76–77 ("something of a monster"); Wood, "Interests and Disinterestedness in the Making of the Constitution," in Beeman, Botein, and Carter, eds., *Beyond Confederation*, 69–109.

[258] "*The Creation of the American Republic, 1776–1787*: A Symposium of Views and Reviews," *William and Mary Quarterly*, 3d ser. 44 (1987): 550–627, including Wood's rejoinder, 628–40.

Wood secondly has confronted the impasse of intellectual history as a field. In the post–World War II years, young historians who had entered the field at Harvard under Perry Miller or at Wisconsin under Merle Curti felt intellectual history was their crusade. "I taught, wrote, and believed in intellectual history," writes Henry F. May, at Harvard in the late 1930s. "When I came to Berkeley [after the war], intellectual history was a satisfying radical cause," and then in the 1950s "my kind of history became for a short and heady few years, the rising fashion." The 1960s, of course, started the era of the new social history. By 1977, when Wood, like Bailyn an admirer of Perry Miller, spoke to his fellow scholars at a conference called by John Higham, Curti's student, to address the crisis in the field, he felt the need to save intellectual history from being relegated to "the backwaters of the historical profession." "We have not made many people believe that ideas can 'cause' something like a revolution," he said. Speaking to the fear among historians of ideas that the new social history would once again reduce ideas to being simply the consequences of behavior, he pleaded with them to address "the larger cultural world, the system of values and conventions, in which historical actors lived—what historians have called 'traditions,' 'climates of opinion,' or 'habits of thought,'" especially if they wished to recover the mind of ordinary people.[259]

This is what Wood has tried to do in *The Radicalism of the American Revolution*. The spirit of J. Franklin Jameson hovers over the book. Jameson, Wood writes, "was at least right about one thing: 'the stream of revolution once started, could not be confined within narrow banks, but spread abroad upon the land.'" Wood's metaphor trumped Jameson's: "The revolution resembled the breaking of a dam, releasing thousands upon thousands of pent-up pressures." He found proof for Jameson's claims about the importance of the displacement of the loyalists and the destruction of feudal land forms, but these were minor matters. Regardless of his intention, Wood expanded the argument in all four Jameson lectures—the status of persons, the land, commerce, and thought and feeling. But in his claims

[259] Henry F. May, *Coming to Terms: A Study in Memory and History* (Berkeley, 1987), 307, 231–32 (Miller)—May was at Harvard in the late 1930s and got his Ph.D. in 1947; Gordon S. Wood, "Intellectual History and the Social Sciences," in John Higham and Paul K. Conklin, eds., *New Directions in American Intellectual History* (Baltimore, 1979), 27–41—the paper was given at the Wingspread Conference, 1977, Racine, Wisconsin, in honor of Merle Curti, in the year of his eightieth birthday; Higham, introduction to Higham and Conklin, eds., *New Directions*, xi–xix; for the state of the field, see Higham, *Writing American History*, chaps. 1–3, and Robert Darnton, "Intellectual and Cultural History," in Michael G. Kammen, ed., *The Past Before Us: Contemporary Historical Writing in the United States* (Ithaca, NY, 1980), 327–53.

for the "social radicalism" of the Revolution, Wood makes Jameson look like a piker.[260]

Wood continues to write history in which a central idea—"the spirit of equality"—is the principal engine of change and is "the single most powerful and radical ideological force in all of American history."[261] He has organized his book under three rubrics—"Monarchy," which gives way to "Republicanism," which gives way to "Democracy"—in which he explores the impact of ideas thematically; one will search in vain for familiar events of the Revolution. And he continues, in the consensus mode, to generalize frequently about what "all Americans," "the colonists," or "the revolutionary generation" thought, as if equality made its way with the agreement of Virginia slaveholding planters, Hudson Valley estate holders, Philadelphia merchant princes, and wealthy land proprietors on the frontiers.

But his causal framework is more complex. He recognizes that "a broader revolution," modernization, was under way but argues that it and the American Revolution were "inextricably bound together." "Perhaps the social transformation would have happened 'in any case,' but we will never know. It was in fact linked to the Revolution; they occurred together." He sees a third dynamic factor in migration into the interior: "This demographic explosion, this gigantic movement of people, was the most basic and most liberating force working on American society during the latter half of the eighteenth century."[262] And in capitalism he finds a fourth dynamic. America in the early republic "may have been still largely rural, still largely agricultural, but now it was also largely commercial, perhaps the most thoroughly commercialized nation in the world." By 1812 Benjamin Rush thought "we are indeed a bebanked, bewhiskied, and a bedollared nation," and Wood agrees.[263] And if these four dynamics—the idea of equality, modernization, westward explosion, and capitalism—are not enough, Wood finds another in "the rise of popular evangelical Christianity. . . . As the Republic became democratized, it became evangelized."[264] Together these transformed American society after the war. "By every measure there was a sudden bursting forth, an explosion—not only of

[260] Wood, *Radicalism of the Revolution*, 5–6 (Jameson), 230 ("dam"), 175–76 (loyalists), and chap. 10, "Revolution."

[261] Ibid., 200.

[262] Ibid., 7., 133, 306–7, chap. 8, "Loosening the Bands of Society," and chap. 17, "A World Within."

[263] Ibid., 309–10, 364 (Rush), and chap. 18, "The Celebration of Commerce."

[264] Ibid., 331.

geographical movement, but of entrepreneurial energy, of religious passion, and of pecuniary desires."[265] As Wood describes changes as late as the 1820s and 1830s, puzzled readers are left to their own devices to disentangle the effects of the Revolution from the effects of these five dynamic factors. What Wood seemingly has done is to absorb under the umbrella of the ideological force of equality the rival historical interpretations stressing either modernization, the alternative ideology of liberalism, the development of capitalism, and (is it possible?) Frederick Jackson Turner's frontier thesis.[266]

Wood has also introduced agency, but his notion of agency is highly selective. Ordinary people challenge deference, and in the cities there is an urban artisan presence. We hear much of "a new breed of popular leader[s]" risen from below asserting their "interestedness" and of acquisitive capitalists (often the same men). We hear the strong democratic voices of William Findley, Matthew Lyon, Abraham Bishop, Abraham Clark, and William Manning lambasting aristocracy, voices we did not hear in *Creation*.[267] Yet Wood writes a history of radicalism in which one often has to search for familiar radicals. There is equality but not the egalitarian Thomas Paine of *Common Sense*, millennialism but no Herman Husband, religious dissent but no Isaac Backus. And while there is an explosion of population onto numerous frontiers, there are no explosions of Regulators, Shaysites, Whiskey Rebels, Green Mountain men, or Maine's Liberty Boys.

Wood's world is built around binary opposites: dependence/independence, inequality/equality. Yet it is a world free from paradoxes or contradictions. The book is remarkable for the scholarship of the preceding twenty years it does not synthesize. The unequals at the bottom of white male society are silent. There seem to be no seamen, apprentices, indentured servants, landless farmers, or angry impoverished war veterans. Nor are the outsiders a presence. Slavery is important chiefly as a concept defining utter dependence that everyone wanted to avoid. Well aware that the Revolution did not bring freedom for blacks or equality for women, Wood argues, as did Bailyn and Morgan before him, that the Revolution "made possible the anti-slavery and women's rights movement of the nineteenth century and in fact all our current egalitarian thinking." He claims that "in effect [it] set in motion ideological forces that doomed the institution of slavery in the

265 Ibid., 230; see also 356, 366.

266 Ibid., 308.

267 Ibid., chap. 14, "Interests," and chap. 15, "The Assault on Aristocracy," an outstanding chapter.

North and led inexorably to the Civil War."[268] This is whig history, evading the historian's responsibility to explain by pointing to later progress; one could just as easily argue that the failure of the Revolutionary generation to destroy slavery made the Civil War inevitable. Understandably, therefore, the voices of African Americans who sought liberty or the free blacks who sought equality in their own day, Phillis Wheatley, Thomas Allan, Absalom Jones, Prince Hall, James Forten, Paul Cuffe, Gabriel Prosser, Denmark Vesey—all, by the way, the subject of recent scholarship—are missing. One would have thought that an examination of the failure to achieve racial equality in the era—a theme that has occupied some of the best minds in the profession—would have illuminated the character of equality.

Wood recognizes that women who were subordinated in the colonial era (perhaps, Laurel Thatcher Ulrich might say, less than he thinks) gained after the war when the family was "republicanized" (perhaps much less than Linda Kerber might claim). But in a book with so many new male voices, it is puzzling that the voices of women are missing. John Adams writes to Abigail Adams, but strangely we never hear Abigail reply, and in a book heavy with New Englanders, we do not hear Mercy Otis Warren, Sarah Osborn, or Judith Sargent Murray speak to the inequality of their sex, much less from other women who speak only in the privacy of their diaries or letters.[269]

Perhaps more striking for a narrative in which "it is impossible to exaggerate the significance of the westward movement," there are no American Indians, not even for their impact on frontiersmen, which might come as a surprise to the generals who acquired fame in the early republic as Indian fighters, Andrew Jackson and William Henry Harrison. We do not hear the voices of Neolin or Pontiac, Joseph Brant or Alexander McGillivray, Tecumseh or The Prophet; but, then again, we do not hear them in the pages of most historians.[270]

Wood's book is resonant of Alexis de Tocqueville's. Indeed, he projects the themes of the French traveler of the 1830s back on to the half century before. Wood's book has the sweep, insights, and enthusiasm of de Tocqueville. It also shares many of his blind spots. It is a synthesis so protective of the achievements of equality that it seems unwilling to come to grips with inequality. It is as if to allow all these voices to speak at the table would spoil the celebration.

[268] Ibid., 7–8 ("made possible"), 186 ("set in motion").

[269] Ibid., 147, 182–83, 354–55, 357–58.

[270] Ibid., 355, about efforts to "civilize" the Creeks and Cherokees.

Wood's book has been bepraised, beprized, and beleaguered. To those who can still follow the cast of historians in this essay's benumbing account of the past century of scholarship, the critical response to Wood's book may even augur a redrawing of the lines of debate over the Revolution. Edmund Morgan, the consistent holdout against social transformation, despite his reservations about Wood's "exaggerations" and "the overstatement of his case," finds "that case convincing." But Pauline Maier, Wood's fellow shaper of the republican interpretation, after warm praise, chides him for failing to do justice to the radical political implications of republicanism, wondering whether he has fallen into "a time-bound assumption —the modern conviction that real revolutions are fundamentally social."[271] Joyce S. Appleby, the most trenchant critic of the failure of the republican interpretation to integrate economic liberalism, is dismayed at Wood's "reducing democratic values to crass material striving and competitive individualism." She thinks the book reifies the radicalism of the Revolution "so that it could have been written by George Bancroft—if he had only read Clifford Geertz." On the left some historians have welcomed the book, as has Sean Wilentz, as a "powerful repudiation of the Revolution as a consensual, conservative legalistic event" or, as has Edward Countryman, for describing what amounts to "a bourgeois revolution." But they and others along a wide spectrum have been skeptical for reasons my analysis anticipated: the utter failure of Wood's celebration of capitalism and hosannah to American equality to come to grips with inequality. I suspect many historians will agree with Michael Zuckerman's criticism that the book "denies class at every turn. It disregards race, gender, and ethnicity almost entirely. It is oblivious to region." Wood "has shrunk America to a country without slaves, women, families, or the South." "Whether the book has clarified the streams overflowing J. Franklin Jameson's banks or muddied the waters remains to be seen."[272]

[271] Morgan, "Second American Revolution," 23–24; Pauline Maier, "It Was Never the Same after Them," *New York Times Book Review*, Mar. 1, 1992, 34; see also Drew R. McCoy, review of *Radicalism of the Revolution*, *Journal of American History* 79 (1993): 1563–65.

[272] Joyce Appleby, "The Radical Recreation of the American Republic," *William and Mary Quarterly*, 3d ser. 51 (1994): 679–83; Barbara Clark Smith, "The Adequate Revolution," in ibid., 684–92; Michael Zuckerman, "Rhetoric, Reality, and the Revolution: The Genteel Radicalism of Gordon Wood," in ibid., 693–702; Gordon S. Wood, "Equality and Social Conflict in the American Revolution," in ibid., 703–16; Sean Wilentz, "The Power of the Powerless," *New Republic*, Dec. 23 and 30, 1991, 32–40; Edward Countryman, "Revolution, Radicalism, and the American Way," *Reviews in American History* 20 (1992): 480–85. Wood's book won the Pulitzer Prize in History and the Ralph Waldo Emerson Award of Phi Beta Kappa.

Is there a future to considering the American Revolution as a social movement? Yes, I would argue, as long as Americans seek to fulfill the promise of the Declaration of Independence, the Constitution, and the Bill of Rights. And yes, as along as young scholars have the skepticism to challenge received wisdom and a passion about what they discover.

They do, judging, for example, by the fellows of the Institute of Early American History and Culture who responded in 1993 to the Institute's plea on its fiftieth anniversary "to look forward to the next half century and project lines of vision and revision for the field."[273] I do not wish to homogenize the views of these diverse, individualistic scholars (and I am very likely reading my own biases into their essays). But their responses are encouraging. Those for whom the Revolutionary era is central to their research confront issues of transformation, whether the dawn of the penitentiary or the "plebeian populism" of the anti-Federalists.[274] And others whose fields are African American, Native American, and women's history call for rewriting the "master narrative" of American history. To a scholar of African American history "it is not simply a matter of fitting non-European voices into an existing narrative as another stitch in the fabric while the fabric retains its basic pattern." To a scholar of Native American history the prime need is to overcome the "cameo theory of history" and notions of "victimization" and explore the "middle ground" between cultures. Kathleen M. Brown asks not merely that we continue to add women's lives but that we confront "the centrality of gender history."[275] A scholar of maritime history asks that we go "beyond Jack Tar" in the spirit of Jesse Lemisch. A scholar of agrarian history struggles with the transformations among the yeomanry, the vast Anglo-American majority. A scholar of ideas calls for a "materialist intellectual history" to understand "the thinking class."[276] Given such passions, as these scholars confront the American Revolution,

[273] "Forum: The Future of Early American History," *William and Mary Quarterly*, 3d ser. 50 (1993): 298–424, quotation at 298.

[274] Michael Meranze, "Even the Dead Will Not Be Safe: An Ethics of Early American History," *William and Mary Quarterly*, 3d ser. 50 (1993): 367–78; and Saul Cornell, "Early American History in a Postmodern Age," in ibid., 329–41.

[275] Jon F. Sensbach, "Charting a Course in Early African-American History," *William and Mary Quarterly*, 3d ser. 50 (1993): 394–405; Richter, "Whose Indian History?" in ibid., 379–93; and Kathleen M. Brown, "Brave New Worlds: Women's and Gender History," in ibid., 311–28.

[276] Vickers, "Beyond Jack Tar," *William and Mary Quarterly*, 3d ser. 50 (1993): 418–24; Allan Kulikoff, "Households and Markets: Toward a New Synthesis of American Agrarian History," in ibid., 342–55; and Darren Marcus Staloff, "Intellectual History Naturalized: Materialism and the 'Thinking Class,'" in ibid., 406–17.

most would probably share Michael Meranze's tough-minded vision that "the accomplishments of the Revolution and of liberal society are inseparable from its repressions and exclusions."[277]

Shaking the scarecrow of "presentism" at these scholars will not deter them. Most of them would take for granted the observation of Thad Tate after his long tenure at the Institute: "I am unabashed in believing that historians choose to do their work in terms of what's going on around them."[278] Many I suspect would heed Meranze's plea for "a new presentism that blocks false identification with the past but still disrupts the security of the present," a plea for "a critical socially engaged historiography."[279] Thus, there are good grounds to anticipate that this new generation of scholars will consider the social dimensions of the Revolution but in their own ways, ways that we cannot yet imagine.

[277] Meranze, "Even the Dead Will Not Be Safe," 378.
[278] Teute, "Conversation with Thad Tate," 273.
[279] Meranze, "Even the Dead Will Not Be Safe," 372.

Historians Extend the Reach of the American Revolution

Gregory H. Nobles

Introduction

Could the study of the American Revolution ever be over? It may have seemed that way to some historians attending the annual meeting of the Organization of American Historians—held, quite appropriately, in Boston—on a late Friday afternoon in March 2004. After sitting in a hotel meeting room for over an hour and listening to several presentations surveying "The State of the Field: The American Revolution," a few people expressed their persistent suspicion that the field had become rather sparse in recent days, that the history of the American Revolution had already been essentially written, that all the good work had been done, and done some time ago. One member of the audience even admitted to his colleagues that in making up his syllabus for a course on the Revolution, he found himself assigning books published three decades ago. In reporting a few months later on this historian's professional confession, Pauline Maier humorously suggested that the professor assign her own thirty-something-year-old book, but she also admitted that he might have had a point. "Scholarship on the Revolution between 1960 and 1980 was so intense," she observed, "that it was perhaps destined to go into a certain eclipse." She added a hopeful note that "there's no doubt that it will become a more active field," but she also noted the somewhat darker conclusions of other colleagues in the profession. A junior scholar, she said, had complained that "the literature of the founding period is . . . approaching saturation," and a more senior scholar had declared that "all the big questions have been answered."[1]

Any estimation of eclipse or saturation in a scholarly field depends, of course, on what questions get asked. In surveying the historical literature on the American Revolution in the years surrounding the turn of the twenty-first century—that is, the period that picks up past the coverage in the first essay in this volume—my own reading of the scholarly record is that fresh questions keep coming up and that the study of the Revolution remains as intellectually exciting a field as it ever was. When J. Franklin Jameson wrote that "the stream of revolution, once started, could not be confined within narrow banks," he could just as well have been talking about the scholarship of the Revolution. Today, historians do not typically look back to Jameson as a specific frame of reference, but they do continue to underscore his observation that the Revolution cannot be seen as "solely a series of political or military events." Modern scholars offer us an increasingly inclusive view of American society, bringing a larger and more diverse ensemble of historical figures into view—prominent men in positions of political and military leadership, to be sure, along with men and women in the middling or lower rungs of Euro-American society, but also African Americans, both enslaved and free, and Native Americans, some of them quite far away from the immediate battlegrounds contested by Great Britain and the American colonies. This more expansive approach now challenges us to extend not only the societal reach of the Revolution but also its temporal bounds; it is becoming increasingly common to look beyond the traditional time frame of 1763–89 and talk of the "long" Revolution that lasted well past the framing of the Constitution and had much wider implications beyond the creation of an independent nation.

One of the big questions that remains, then, is "Whose American Revolution was it?" My approach to answering it in the pages that follow is not to describe a vast scholarly divide between studying the experiences of people at the top of society as opposed to those at the bottom, nor is

[1] Pauline Maier reported on the OAH session in her keynote address "Teaching the Nation's History," delivered to the National Endowment for the Humanities "We the People" Forum (2004), published in *Humanities* 25 (July–Aug. 2004) and available online at http://www.neh.gov/news/humanities/2004-07/nationshistory.html (accessed July 30, 2010). Maier's older book, to which she referred, is *From Resistance to Revolution: Colonial Radicals and the Development of American Opposition to Britain, 1765–1776* (New York, 1972). Among Maier's more recent contributions to keeping the field active are two books on the nation's founding documents: *American Scripture: Making the Declaration of Independence* (New York, 1997) and *Ratification: The People Debate the Constitution, 1787–1788* (New York, 2010).

it to insist on stretching the traditional limits of the Revolutionary era to fit a longer time frame. I want to argue, ultimately, that these different perspectives on the past can do much to inform each other and that the best historical works do indeed bridge this apparent gap: by bringing both prominent leaders and ordinary people together in the same view, they help us see them as they doubtless sometimes saw each other, as fellow participants in an unfolding historical process that had sometimes uncertain boundaries. To ask "Whose American Revolution was it?" asks us to rethink both terms, "American" and "Revolution," and in doing so, to appreciate the ways that serious scholarship continues to refresh the field. To ask that question, in fact, makes us realize that the Revolution encompassed essentially everyone on the scene at the time. As scholars continue to explore their stories, its history will never fall into eclipse.

I. Refocusing on the Founders

1. Twenty-first-Century "Founders Chic"

Some the most familiar faces have found renewed life in the new century, and they now invite careful scrutiny in the context of the times, both their own and ours. One compelling indication of the continuing interest in the Revolution is an outburst of biographical studies of the Founders, quite a few of which became sudden best-sellers that far surpassed the market for typical academic offerings. To be sure, biography has always been an active area of historical writing, and studies of the leading figures of the Revolution have long been popular with the reading public, reaching back to Parson Weems's didactic and largely fictitious biography of George Washington. But the turn of the twenty-first century brought a remarkable upsurge of interest in the Founders—what *Newsweek* dubbed "Founders Chic"—that seemed striking even for so familiar a historical genre.[2] Rightly anticipating a rapidly emerging market in the most famous men of the Revolutionary era, trade presses soon found accommodating authors, both academics and others, who got into the biographical act.

[2] Evan Thomas, "Founders Chic: Live from Philadelphia," *Newsweek*, July 9, 2001, 48. After originating in the popular press, the term later made its way into scholarly publications. See, for instance, David Waldstreicher, "Founders Chic as Culture Wars," *Radical History Review* 84 (2002): 185–94; and Jeffrey Pasley, Andrew W. Robertson, and David Waldstreicher, eds., *Beyond the Founders: New Approaches to the Political History of the Early American Republic* (Chapel Hill, NC, 2004).

The big news in the publishing industry, at least as far as historical writing on the American Revolution was concerned, had a bold headline: the twenty-first century started with a biographical bang. The bang, however, echoed with important reverberations, causing scholars and other observers to try to assess the meaning of what it all meant.

No book became more immediately emblematic of the sudden-seeming fascination with the Founders than David McCullough's best-selling biography of John Adams, which set the publishing world afire when it first hit the stores in early summer of 2001: it quickly went on to sales of several million hardcover and paperback copies and, in 2008, a made-for-TV miniseries.[3] McCullough was by no means the only author to focus on Adams in recent years—John Ferling and Joseph Ellis had both published substantial studies of Adams in the 1990s—but he was undoubtedly the best known: a gifted writer of a sizable string of big but readable books, he had also become familiar to the public as the lead narrator for Ken Burns's epic public-television documentary series *The Civil War* (1990), providing an authoritative but still avuncular voice that resonated with a reassuring, matter-of-fact gravitas.[4] McCullough's treatment of John Adams did nothing to break new scholarly ground, but that was not his purpose; rather, it was to give readers a pleasing, even uplifting portrait of a man McCullough felt had been too often dismissed as difficult, irascible, and perhaps overintellectual to a fault. In McCullough's own estimation, the most significant common thread that tied his biography of Adams to his previous work was a consistent concern with another sort of quality—heroism. "All my books are about courage and what makes civilization," he told a reporter for CNN. "I'm interested in the creators." Given that emphasis, his study of John Adams seemed to him a logical fit. "The man who emerges is truly heroic," McCullough explained.[5]

[3] David McCullough, *John Adams* (New York, 2001). The HBO series *John Adams*, which was based on McCullough's book, first appeared on the screen in March 2008.

[4] John Ferling, *John Adams: A Life* (Knoxville, TN, 1992); Joseph Ellis, *Passionate Sage: The Character and Legacy of John Adams* (New York, 1993). Before McCullough wrote the John Adams book, he had written three works dealing with people facing the challenges of water—*The Johnstown Flood* (New York, 1968), *The Great Bridge: The Epic Story of the Building of the Brooklyn Bridge* (New York, 1972), and *The Path Between the Seas: The Creation of the Panama Canal, 1870–1914* (New York, 1977)—and two books on American presidents: *Mornings on Horseback: The Story of an Extraordinary Family, a Vanished Way of Life and the Unique Child Who Became Theodore Roosevelt* (New York, 1981) and *Truman* (New York, 1992).

[5] "David McCullough Brings 'John Adams' to Life," CNN.com, June 7, 2001, http://archives.cnn.com/2001/SHOWBIZ/books/06/07/david.mccullough/index.html (accessed July 30, 2010).

The question of heroism, or at least personal character, figured prominently in the subsequent discussion of the Founders phenomenon. The author of the *Newsweek* article suggested that in a modern era of "media-obsessed, poll-driven politicians . . . many Americans are nostalgic for an earlier era of genuine statesmen."[6] Indeed, the immediate comparison may well have been to Bill Clinton, the president who left office under a cloud of controversy in January 2001, less than six months before McCullough's biography of Adams first appeared in print the following June. In the wake of Clinton's extramarital exploits, Adams's affectionate and enduring marriage to Abigail made him seem like a model of moral propriety. "Clearly," Edith Gelles wrote in a review of McCullough's book, "it's an appealing portrait of a political figure in an era when there's not a great deal to admire in the stature of our politicians." Writing in November 2001, Gelles also reflected on the book's impact in light of the 9/11 crisis: "Perhaps because our times are so complex and out of our control, it is nice to recall as well that there were dangerous times in our past, more dangerous probably, where great people were needed and rose to the occasion."[7]

Other academic reviewers, however, seemed comparatively wary of McCullough's emphasis on Adams's allegedly heroic character, especially to the extent that character analysis overshadowed a more acute intellectual analysis of Adams's political stance. Writing in the *New Republic*, Sean Wilentz observed that "when he gets to Adams's enormous intellect, McCullough looks lost." Wilentz portrayed Adams as a political leader who became lost himself, who never quite adjusted to the democratizing spirit of the revolution he helped make, but who "who fell out of touch with the country that he loved and that he served so diligently and often so well." Despite McCullough's graceful and gentle treatment of his subject, Wilentz concluded, Adams "is not the hero we need now, if a hero is what we need."[8] Jeffrey Pasley suggested that even a yearning for heroes might be too lofty an explanation for the popularity of McCullough's book: "As little sense as it seems to make," he grumbled in the online journal *Common-Place*, "the origins of the Adams craze are not mysterious. It is a by-product of the celebrity culture that is coming to dominate

[6] Thomas, "Founders Chic," 48.

[7] Edith Gelles, review of *John Adams*, by David McCullough, H-SHEAR, Nov. 6, 2001, http://www.h-net.org/reviews/showrev.php?id=5623 (accessed July 30, 2010).

[8] Sean Wilentz, "America Made Easy: McCullough, Adams, and the Decline of Popular History," *New Republic*, July 2, 2001, 35–40.

American history publishing as thoroughly as it does most other aspects of our society."[9]

The larger issue inherent in these observations went far beyond McCullough's book on John Adams alone: it spoke, rather, to the question of how historians—and *which* historians—could successfully reach the reading public and what message should get conveyed about the connection between the past and present. For years, academic historians had been complaining that they felt increasingly ignored by that most elusive audience, the educated general reader. They could look back, as Wilentz did, to a time in the middle decades of the twentieth century when a number of prominent scholars had been able to engage, perhaps even influence, a reasonably wide readership on serious historical issues—not just political history as traditionally defined but also slavery, race relations, women's rights, and other socially contentious issues. "Critical analysis was in the saddle," Wilentz argued, and "American history was meant to rattle its readers, not to confirm them in their received myths and platitudes about America." Somewhere in the latter part of the century, though, academic historians seemed to lose touch with the reading public, particularly as American political life shifted to the right in the Reagan era and, as some critics argued, scholarly writing became intellectually arcane and increasingly unintelligible to the general reader. "And into the breach," Wilentz observed, "stepped a new breed of popular historians, led by David McCullough and an assortment of journalists, novelists, PBS film-makers, plus the odd crossover professor."[10]

Some of those "crossover professors," in fact, were not so odd at all, or certainly not found on the fringes of the profession. A handful of scholars at some of the most prominent colleges and universities in the country joined in feeding the Founder phenomenon, publishing generally appreciative books that tended to portray the leading figures of the Revolutionary era as individual actors within an enclosed circle of political insiders, all seemingly isolated from the social and political turmoil outside the doors of their parlors and meeting rooms. Joseph Ellis, for instance, in writing about the men he called "Founding Brothers," put his focus squarely on the "relatively small number of leaders who knew each other, who collaborated and collided with one another" in a face-to-face political world where character mattered and personal relationships ruled the day. In this socially

[9] Jeffery L. Pasley, "Federalist Chic," *Common-Place* 2 (2002), http://www.common-place.org/publick/200202.shtml (accessed July 30, 2010).

[10] Wilentz, "America Made Easy," 36.

exclusive context, ordinary people, "the marginal or peripheral people, whose lives are more typical," seemed to have no place on the stage.[11]

In itself, this emphasis on individual character and political connections may not seem especially surprising or problematic: it is, after all, one basic approach of biography. But several of the scholarly studies of the Founders that emerged at the beginning of the twenty-first century did raise significant questions about the portrayals they presented to the reading public.

First, what price popularization? In a series of reviews in the *New Republic*, Alan Taylor assessed several of the Founder-focused works that had come from his fellow academic historians, and he concluded that the books tended to be intellectually lightweight, not by any means an author's best effort. He typified H. W. Brands's "clear and sprightly" biography of Benjamin Franklin, which came out about the same time as McCullough's book on Adams, as "popular history: light on analysis but rich in the description of settings, personalities, and action." Edmund Morgan, also publishing a biography of Franklin in 2003, could "count on the revived cult of the Founding Fathers," Taylor noted, but he failed to make the most of the opportunity. Morgan "has surprisingly little to say about Franklin that is new or challenging," Taylor observed, and has even given us "the impossible: a superficial Franklin." Bernard Bailyn's collection of essays on the Founders was, according to Taylor, "a set of five easy pieces," an "amiable" but underanalytical portrayal of the Revolution reflective of an old, consensus-based paradigm—"a revolution initiated and controlled at the top, by learned colonists writing on behalf of an apparently prosperous and homogeneous American people." In the end, Taylor could only conclude that these accessible and "amiable" books about the Founders might still do some good by engaging readers and encouraging them to undertake a more extensive consideration of the Revolutionary era, one that looks beyond the Founders themselves to the more complicated process of change that swept all levels of American society.[12]

2. The Elite Critique of Social History

That hopeful, even rather charitable notion of a Founder-based beginning for further study would quickly have been dashed, however, by a

[11] Joseph Ellis, *Founding Brothers: The Revolutionary Generation* (New York, 2001), 13, 17.

[12] The *New Republic* reviews of these books have been collected in Alan Taylor, *Writing Early American History* (Philadelphia, 2005), 165–74 (Brands), 225–36 (Morgan), 215–24 (Bailyn).

second and more serious aspect of the emphasis on the elite leadership of the Revolution. It seemed insufficient for some authors of the Founders studies to concentrate almost solely on the famous figures under their scrutiny. They apparently also found it necessary to shake some of the old scholarly scarecrows, to preface their works with a sharp, at times even scathing denunciation of the new (or by now perhaps not-so-new) social history. The practitioners of history "from the bottom up," so the claim went, had toppled the Founders from the pillars of respect and left them belittled and embattled victims of an inversion of historical emphasis. In a review of McCullough's biography of John Adams, for instance, Robert Middlekauff lamented that "grand manner history" and its "first cousin, grand manner biography," had both become "an old form largely disavowed by professional historians on university faculties."[13] John Ferling took an even more strident stance, accusing recent historians of the Revolution of being so "[c]ommitted to social history, and shaped by political correctness and multiculturalism," that during the previous quarter century they had "by and large . . . neglected the role played by leaders in important events."[14] Gordon Wood echoed the charge, arguing that while the Founders had always been subject to scholarly criticism, "there does seem to be something new and different about the present-day academic vilification. . . . Academic historians over the past forty years have tended to focus on issues of race, class, and gender in the early Republic and to shun issues of politics and political leadership."[15] Joseph Ellis became the most consistent scourge of social history, elevating his attack to a near conspiracy theory. The historical profession's emphasis on "the concerted effort to recover the lost voices of the revolutionary generation," he claimed, had led scholars to ignore, even drown out, the voices of the prominent leaders of the Revolution and the political ideas they promoted. "This trend is so pronounced," he concluded, "that any budding historian who announces that he or she wishes to focus on the political history of the early republic and its most prominent practitioners is generally regarded as having inadvertently confessed a form of intellectual bankruptcy." So it went in subsequent publications, with Ellis later recycling his reference to "intellectual bankruptcy"

[13] Robert Middlekauff, review of *John Adams*, by David McCullough, *New England Quarterly* 75 (2002): 139.

[14] John Ferling, *Setting the World Ablaze: Washington, Adams, Jefferson, and the American Revolution* (Oxford, UK, 2000), ix–x.

[15] Gordon Wood, *Revolutionary Characters: What Made the Founders Different* (New York, 2006), 7–8.

and excoriating the "currently hegemonic narrative within the groves of academe" and "reigning orthodoxy in the academy" for allegedly putting the Founders beyond the political pale of scholarship.[16]

This increasingly shrill, almost cartoonish caricature of social history's place in writing about the Revolution raised the stakes in historical scholarship. Given the gratuitously negative portrayal of the profession by Ellis and others, the renewed emphasis on the lives and characters of the Founders cannot be easily dismissed as an intellectually neutral issue, merely a matter of individual authorial choice of one topic or approach over another. Neither can it be considered simply a consumer-driven commercial outcome, an attempt to cash in on a faddish fascination with eighteenth-century celebrities. Rather, it also speaks directly to central questions about the writing of the Revolution: What story gets told? And whose? And for what purpose? The answers to those questions depend on our fundamental understanding of the Revolution and the success of scholars in communicating that to an educated reading public, both within and beyond the academy.

It would be fatuous, of course, to suggest that the Founders do not count, and no serious scholar would argue that. Certainly no ordinary person living in the Revolutionary era—Indian, artisan, farm woman, soldier, or slave—could ignore the power of such prominent people. By the same token, it seems equally unrealistic to limit one's focus on the Founders to a collective assessment of a supposedly enclosed group of political demigods, great men locked in splendid social or intellectual isolation, whose enduring significance stemmed primarily from the force of their words, much less the measure of their character. As T. H. Breen has sensibly observed, "Without tens of thousands of ordinary people willing to set aside their work, homes, and families to take up arms in expectation of killing

[16] Ellis, *Founding Brothers*, 12; for his subsequent use of the "intellectual bankruptcy" passage, see Ellis, *His Excellency: George Washington* (New York, 2004), xii. As late as 2006, in fact, Ellis again voiced a similar complaint that "the agenda of the academy remains resolutely focused elsewhere, on the inarticulate rather than the articulate. As a general rule, the founders are either studiously ignored or contemptuously condemned as the deadest, whitest males in American history." See Ellis, foreword to *Something That Will Surprise the World: The Essential Writings of the Founding Fathers*, ed. Susan Dunn (New York, 2006), vii–ix, quotation at viii. During the time Ellis was leveling this attack at academic history, he had become embroiled in another academic battle of his own making, this one having to do with his repeated misrepresentation of his military record to students in his Mt. Holyoke College classes on the Vietnam War; for an account of that controversy, see Peter Charles Hoffer, *Past Imperfect: Facts, Fictions, and Frauds in the Writing of American History* (New York, 2004), 208–29.

and possibly being killed, a handful of elite gentlemen arguing about political theory makes for a debating society, not a revolution."[17] Instead of taking an individual or socially internal perspective on these prominent figures, a more historically realistic approach to the Revolutionary elite is to show them as political figures connected to—even accountable to—the many peoples of America who exerted a power of their own, who made the American Revolution truly a social movement in the broadest possible terms, and who thus help reveal the ultimate meaning of the struggle they all experienced.

II. Redefining Freedom in the Revolution

3. The Contradiction of Slavery

John Hope Franklin, in a 2006 ceremony at the Library of Congress honoring his long and distinguished career as a pioneering scholar of African American history, spoke of his personal confrontation with a fundamental issue that lies at the heart of the American Revolution: "I have struggled to understand how it is that we could fight for independence and, at the very same time, use that newly won independence to enslave many who had joined in the fight for independence. As a student of history, I have attempted to explain it historically, but that explanation has not been all that satisfactory."[18] While pointing to the obvious problem, the contradiction of maintaining human bondage in a movement that proclaimed human liberty, Franklin also noted an important additional dimension, the role of black people "who had joined in the fight for independence." African Americans, enslaved and free, were not simply passive spectators sitting on the sidelines of the larger contest; they were active participants in the struggle for liberty, for themselves as well as for white Americans. Indeed, Franklin had made that point almost sixty years earlier, in his much-admired and long-enduring study *From Slavery to Freedom* (1947), in which he noted that around five thousand African Americans fought for

[17] T. H. Breen, *American Insurgents, American Patriots: The Revolution of the People* (New York, 2010), 4.

[18] John Hope Franklin died in 2009, at the age of ninety-four, and the passage quoted appeared in his obituary in the *New York Times*, Mar. 26, 2009. His remarks at the Library of Congress came in response to his receiving the John W. Kluge Prize in the Human Sciences in 2006, which he shared with fellow historian Yu Ying-shih. The full text of his address is available online at http://www.loc.gov/loc/kluge/docs/franklin_kluge_2006.pdf (accessed July 30, 2010).

the patriot side: "Hardly a military action between 1775 and 1781 was without some Negro participants." Their contribution to the cause of freedom cast a harsh light on the perpetuation of slavery, providing a compelling measure of the much-compromised meaning of the American Revolution as a social movement. "Ironically enough," Franklin concluded, "America's freedom was the means of giving slavery itself a longer life than it was to have in the British Empire."[19]

The contradiction of slavery in the independence movement is an issue as old as the Revolution itself. In 1775, Samuel Johnson, the English lexicographer, famously tweaked American patriots by asking "how is it that we hear the loudest yelps for liberty among the drivers of negroes?" In the same year, the radical pamphleteer Thomas Paine raised a similar point, asking how Americans could "complain so loudly of attempts to enslave them, while they hold so many hundreds of thousands in slavery?"[20] The situation became even more striking in the ensuing years: from 1775 to 1825 the number of slaves in the United States tripled, and as Seymour Drescher has observed, "Slavery was more secure in the South when Thomas Jefferson died on July 4, 1826, than it had been on the day when his Declaration of Independence was proclaimed fifty years earlier."[21]

David Brion Davis, who has spent essentially his entire scholarly career on the problem of slavery, locates the contradiction of American slavery within a larger comparative context. Slavery had been an accepted fixture in Western society since the ancient era, he reminds us, and "neither the Bible nor any other known ancient sources contain a clear denunciation or repudiation of slavery, coupled with a call for even its gradual abolition." Still, he argues, "Western Judeo-Christian culture transmitted a deep tension or unease over slavery, a fairly common belief that the institution could be justified only by an appeal to our sinful nature, that it could not

[19] John Hope Franklin, *From Slavery to Freedom: A History of American Negroes* (New York, 1947), 89–90, 135, 143. Over time, the book's subtitle has changed to reflect changing usage, from *A History of American Negroes* to *A History of Negro Americans* (1967) to *A History of African Americans* (1994), but the book has remained a landmark of scholarship throughout the second half of the twentieth century and on into the twenty-first. It has been translated into six languages and was in its eighth edition at the time of Franklin's death; a ninth edition came into print in 2010.

[20] Samuel Johnson, *Taxation No Tyranny: An Answer to the Resolutions and Address of the American Congress* (1775), in *The Works of Samuel Johnson*, vol. 14 (Troy, NY, 1913), 93–144; Thomas Paine, "African Slavery in America," in Philip Foner, ed., *The Complete Writings of Thomas Paine*, vol. 12 (New York, 1945), 15–19. For similar examples, see also David Brion Davis, *The Problem of Slavery in the Age of Revolution* (Ithaca, NY, 1975), 398–400.

[21] Seymour Drescher, "History's Engines: British Mobilization in the Age of Revolution," *William and Mary Quarterly*, 3d ser. 66 (2009): 737–56; quotation at 753.

be tolerated in a truly perfect or ideal world." By the eve of the American Revolution, even as slavery remained geographically widespread and economically viable, that "unease" had increased, as antislavery sentiment had begun emerging more visibly and vocally in the Atlantic world over the course of the eighteenth century. The implications of that antislavery impulse became suddenly evident in Revolutionary America, as thousands of slaves gained their freedom through escape or emancipation, and the states in the North provided at least for gradual abolition of the institution of slavery. In the South, however, the prospects for freedom steadily diminished, so that by the 1830s, Davis writes, "the moral doubts of the Revolutionary generation were giving way . . . to strong religious, economic, and racial arguments that defended slavery as a 'positive good.'" Thus the result of the American Revolution presents us, he concludes, with "the paradox of a revolution that seemed to challenge slavery but in fact entrenched and strengthened it."[22]

The point is not simply to expose the paradox, however. Rather, Franklin, Davis, and other historians have sought to explore the ways people of the Revolutionary era, both white and black, dealt with the disturbingly stark contrast between liberty and slavery, using it both as a politically charged rhetorical device and as a source of direct political action. From the ancient Mediterranean to the Americas, slave resistance had as long a history as slavery itself, but as Davis observes, those revolts "were not so far as we know directed against slavery in *principle*."[23] That began to change in the eighteenth century, and the language of liberty gained increasing salience among slaves in the years preceding the American Revolution. In the British-American colonies, both on the North American mainland and in the West Indies, slave revolts repeatedly punctuated the pre-Revolutionary period. Peter Wood's now classic study of the Stono Rebellion in South Carolina in 1739 or Jill Lepore's more recent book on the interracial conspiracies in New York in 1741 represent two important case

[22] David Brion Davis, "Re-examining the Problem of Slavery in Western Culture," *Proceedings of the American Antiquarian Society* 118, part 2 (2009): 247–66, quotations at 254–55, 265. Davis, *Inhuman Bondage: The Rise and Fall of Slavery in the New World* (Oxford, UK, 2006), 143, 145. Davis's earlier works on slavery include *The Problem of Slavery in Western Culture* (Oxford, UK, 1966), *The Problem of Slavery in the Age of Revolution, 1770–1823* (Oxford, UK, 1975), and *Slavery and Human Progress* (Oxford, UK, 1984).

[23] Davis, *Inhuman Bondage*, 144. Philip Morgan makes a similar point, noting that up to the time of the American Revolution, "never before had slaves challenged slavery on the grounds of human rights." See Philip Morgan, *Slave Counterpoint: Black Culture in the Eighteenth-Century Chesapeake and Lowcountry* (Chapel Hill, NC, 1998), 667.

studies of slave unrest a generation or so before the outbreak of the Revolution. Directing our attention to the West Indies, Christopher Brown points to similar rebellions and plots in Barbados (1692), Antigua (1739), and Jamaica (1760 and 1776). Indeed, Peter Linebaugh and Marcus Rediker locate all those incidents within a much larger series of multiracial uprisings in the Atlantic world in the era preceding the American Revolution, a "furious barrage of plots, revolts, and war [that] ripped through colonial Atlantic societies like a hurricane" from the 1730s up to the 1770s.[24] The spread of radical ideology during the era of the American Revolution, Davis argues, sharpened the focus of revolt, bringing "a wholly new perspective to blacks whose ears—and whose understanding of contradictions—were at least as sensitive as those of their masters." Whether they took up arms or the pen, slaves began to claim the same humanity and therefore the same basic human rights as whites, thus demonstrating, as Davis aptly puts it, that "the idea of natural rights could not be monopolized by white Americans."[25]

Ira Berlin extends the geographical and chronological context to the post-Revolutionary era: "The war and the libertarian ideology that accompanied it extended beyond the boundaries of the newly established United States," fueling revolutionary fervor in France, of course, but also in French colonial possessions in Saint Domingue and in the lower Mississippi Valley and the Gulf region. To be sure, Berlin notes, "the impact of the Age of Revolution was anything but uniform," and his point is not to offer a simple, much less single, picture of the relationship between slave resistance and revolution in the Atlantic world.[26] It is, rather, to direct our attention to the significance of the American Revolution as a heightened ideological movement for black people as well as white, and for people in the Atlantic world as well as in the original British-American mainland colonies.

[24] Peter Wood, *Black Majority: Negroes in Colonial South Carolina from 1670 through the Stono Rebellion* (New York, 1974); Jill Lepore, *New York Burning: Liberty, Slavery, and Conspiracy in Eighteenth-Century Manhattan* (New York, 2005); Christopher Leslie Brown, *Moral Capital: Foundations of British Abolitionism* (Chapel Hill, NC, 2006), quotation at 76; and Peter Linebaugh and Marcus Rediker, *The Many-Headed Hydra: Sailors, Slaves, Commoners, and the Hidden History of the Revolutionary Atlantic* (Boston, 2000), quotation at 193.

[25] Davis, *Inhuman Bondage*, 144.

[26] Ira Berlin, *Many Thousands Gone: The First Two Centuries of Slavery in North America* (Cambridge, MA, 1998), 219–23, 11. Berlin's *Generations of Captivity: A History of African American Slaves* (Cambridge, MA, 2002) further explores the slave experience, and *The Making of African America: The Four Great Migrations* (New York, 2010) sets the migrations of the colonial and Revolutionary era in a larger perspective.

4. The Revolution of the Enslaved

In the immediate context of the Revolutionary War itself, the widespread struggle for liberty gave enslaved people both the impetus and the opportunity to seek freedom where they could find it, whether with the British or the patriot side. Black people's political commitment in the Revolution, Benjamin Quarles explained almost a half century ago, "was not to a place nor to a people but to a principle. . . . Whoever invoked the image of liberty, be he American or British, could count on a ready response from the blacks."[27] Following Quarles's lead, more recent historians have explored the impact of the African Americans' struggle within a struggle. They especially underscore the extent to which the widespread upsurge of agency among black people created a heightened sense of urgency among white officials, both British and patriot, forcing policymakers on both sides to take closer account of the ways African Americans could contribute to or disrupt their respective war efforts.

The patriot side came to include thousands of soldiers of African descent, even though that had not been the original plan of American policymakers. In July 1775, when George Washington assumed command of the ragged army assembled in Cambridge, Massachusetts, he was dismayed to find a force that already included black soldiers. In the short time since the first shots at Lexington and Concord, black volunteers had, as John Wood Sweet observes, "discreetly slipped into service." Henry Wiencek notes that "left to itself, the army had integrated spontaneously," leaving "no record of a popular outcry against the black presence, no record of fights or disciplinary problems caused by racial integration." Caroline Cox likewise finds "little evidence . . . of racial anxiety from white soldiers who served alongside blacks," at least in the enlisted ranks.[28] Still, no matter how spontaneous and successful this initial enlistment of black patriots,

[27] Franklin, *From Slavery to Freedom*, 89, 90; Benjamin Quarles, *The Negro in the American Revolution* (Chapel Hill, NC, 1961), x–xi. See also Quarles, "The Revolutionary War as a Black Declaration of Independence," in Ira Berlin and Ronald Hoffman, eds., *Slavery and Freedom in the Age of the American Revolution* (Charlottesville, VA, 1983), 283–304.

[28] John Wood Sweet, *Bodies Politic: Negotiating Race in the American North, 1730–1830* (Philadelphia, 2007), 200; Henry Wiencek, *An Imperfect God: George Washington, His Slaves, and the Creation of America* (New York, 2003), 199, 201; Caroline Cox, *A Proper Sense of Honor: Service and Sacrifice in George Washington's Army* (Chapel Hill, NC, 2004), 17–18; Cox does make an exception for white soldiers in the lower South, particularly South Carolina, where longstanding anxiety about racial unrest among the black majority made whites especially wary about arming either slaves or free blacks.

Washington took steps to undo it, issuing a general order barring all blacks from military service no matter what their status, free or slave.

Despite this racially motivated rebuff, people of color persisted in their efforts to enlist in the American cause, and their willingness to fight soon stood in contrast to the waning commitment of many whites. In Washington's own Virginia, Michael McDonnell writes, "Enough black Virginians, free and unfree, showed a willingness to serve that recruiting officers were more than happy to take them on." Moreover, enough white men "were also more than willing to send enslaved Virginians to the army as substitutes" that the number of black soldiers reached at least five hundred, and probably more.[29] In the North, especially as the Continental army settled into the grim Pennsylvania winter of 1777–78, black enlistment became even more common. "Indeed, Valley Forge deserves a place in the history of emancipation," Wiencek writes, because it was there that Washington finally approved a plan from Rhode Island to recruit a regiment of black soldiers, some of whom were slaves who were offered freedom for fighting for the American side. The larger interpretive point is that the army became integrated not so much because of the decisions of Washington or the rest of the Revolutionary leadership but because of black people's insistence that they play a role in making the Revolution a war for freedom on all fronts. "Emancipation," Wiencek notes, "which had been heretofore an incidental side effect of black enlistment, was gaining momentum as a goal in itself."[30]

The refusal of the Revolution's leaders to make the most of that momentum underscores the limits of liberty available on the patriot side, a point that black people perceived only too well at the time and that historians emphasize now. Runaway slaves took part in a massive movement away from patriot control, fleeing to the British lines for better prospects of freedom. How many slaves ran away? How many eventually gained their freedom? Both are important questions that have not yielded easy answers. Taking into account the whole wartime experience, David Brion Davis concludes that "the British invasion, occupation, and final withdrawal from the Southern states led to an estimated net loss of eighty thousand to one hundred thousand black slaves."[31] Cassandra Pybus provides a more conservative count, suggesting that around twenty thousand slaves made

[29] Michael A. McDonnell, *The Politics of War: Race, Class, and Conflict in Revolutionary Virginia* (Chapel Hill, NC, 2007), 417, 486–87.

[30] Wiencek, *Imperfect God*, 231. See also Cox, *Proper Sense of Honor*, 16–17.

[31] Davis, *Inhuman Bondage*, 150.

their way to British lines between 1775 and 1782. Not all of them found freedom. In Virginia, for instance, she estimates that perhaps half of the runaway slaves in that period succumbed to smallpox and other diseases, and another fifth were recaptured and sent back into slavery. Still, she points to the larger importance of the eventual evacuation of runaway slaves: by 1783, the total number of black evacuees accompanying the British forces leaving northern and southern ports stood somewhere between eight and ten thousand.[32] Although the numbers may be difficult to calculate, the overall meaning of this massive freedom movement is not: the diaspora of the once-enslaved now commands our attention as a striking outcome of the Revolution.

For one thing, this Revolutionary-era exodus provides a reversal of historical perspective on white people, giving a new cast to the commonly unflattering portrayal of the Revolution's most unpopular players—British officers and pro-British Americans—as comparatively progressive partners in a parallel freedom movement. Scholars point first to the military and political importance of Governor Dunmore's proclamation in November 1775, which called on Virginia's slaves to gain their freedom by fighting on the British side. Several thousand slaves answered by escaping to Dunmore's lines—not only men but women and children as well, some of them fleeing as complete family units. The political impact of the slaves' escape was immediate. The reciprocal relationship between the much-despised Dunmore and the insurgent slaves seemed especially perfidious in the eyes of angry patriots: "This attachment to personal liberty was not something Patriots appreciated in their chattel," Pybus wryly observes. From the former slaves' point of view, the opinion of slaveholders had long ceased to matter.[33] Escaped slaves also played a significant part in a broader British military strategy. British generals in the southern campaign, including Henry Clinton and Lord Cornwallis, increased white anxiety by following Dunmore's lead and enlisting African American fighting men and,

[32] Cassandra Pybus, "Jefferson's Faulty Math: The Question of Slave Defections in the American Revolution," *William and Mary Quarterly*, 3d. ser. 62 (2005): 258–64; Pybus, *Epic Journeys of Freedom: Runaway Slaves of the American Revolution and Their Global Quest for Liberty* (Boston, 2006), 71. Wiencek provides a slightly higher estimate, between thirteen thousand and fourteen thousand; see *Imperfect God*, 258. He also notes that some of the evacuees, the slaves of British officers and loyalists, were not free upon leaving, and some others even lost their freedom, being later sold as slaves in East Florida and the West Indies. See also Gary B. Nash, *The Forgotten Fifth: African Americans in the Age of Revolution* (Cambridge, MA, 2006), 36–39; Berlin, *Many Thousands Gone*, 258–60.

[33] Pybus, *Epic Journeys of Freedom*, 12, 63.

with them, women and children who played a variety of support roles. In late 1778, the British succeeded in taking Savannah, Georgia, the patriots' southernmost port and a significant strategic stronghold, with the critical assistance of organized black troops, spies, and guides, some of them slaves of white masters in Savannah. By offering refuge to thousands of slaves, Sylvia Frey observes, "the British army had thus made the revolutionary war in Georgia a war about slavery."[34]

This British embrace of the slaves rushing to their lines may be misleading, however, giving Dunmore and his fellow officers perhaps too much credit for instigating such widespread escape. As McDonnell points out, many enslaved Virginians had already anticipated the opportunity to forge an alliance with the British, some of them even meeting a year earlier, in November 1774, and choosing their own leader, as they put it, "to conduct them when the English Troops should arrive." Dunmore's Proclamation did not provide the all-embracing emancipation they had hoped for, but it gave them the opening they needed, and they took it. McDonnell and other scholars thus underscore the agency of restive slaves, who pushed Dunmore to act and, in doing so, pushed white patriots closer to the eventual break with Great Britain: "By drawing the last royal governor into an alliance with them," Woody Holton argues, "freedom-seeking Afro-Virginians helped estrange white Virginians from the royal government and prepare them for Independence."[35] Indeed, in Gary Nash's interpretation, the widespread flight of runaway slaves in the British southern campaign "marked the height of the greatest slave rebellion in American history."[36]

Looking beyond the South, other historians have explored the impact of runaway slaves who took refuge wherever the Crown provided protection. Some runaways, especially skilled slaves who made their way to cities in the North, changed their names and succeeded in creating a new life of freedom in a less oppressive part of America. Many of them, men and women alike, were able to pursue a host of skilled and semiskilled occupations

[34] Sylvia Frey, *Water from the Rock: Black Resistance in a Revolutionary Age* (Princeton, NJ, 1991), 107. For the experiences of escaped slaves in the South, see also Pybus, *Epic Journeys of Freedom*, 37–38; Simon Schama, *Rough Crossings: Britain, the Slaves, and the American Revolution* (New York, 2006), 93–94; and Betty Wood, "Southern Women of Color and the American Revolution, 1775–1783," in S. Jay Kleinborg, Eileen Boris, and Vicki L. Ruiz, eds., *The Practice of U.S. Women's History: Narratives, Intersections, and Dialogues* (New Brunswick, NJ, 2007), 67–81.

[35] McDonnell, *Politics of War*, 47; Woody Holton, *Forced Founders: Indians, Debtors, Slaves, and the Making of the American Revolution in Virginia* (Chapel Hill, NC, 1999), 160, xx; see also Sweet, *Bodies Politic*, 188, 194.

[36] Nash, *Forgotten Fifth*, 39.

and make a decent living during wartime.[37] Above all, Pybus's painstaking success in tracing former slaves to places far beyond the site of their former bondage gives us a wide-ranging and revealing picture of the post-Revolutionary result. Some escaped slaves found freedom far away from the new nation, in England and Sierra Leone; still others found themselves transported to Great Britain's new colony in New South Wales, where they shared the experience of living in squalor and near bondage with the poor whites sent there. The differing fates of the escaped slaves, however, should not distract us from Pybus's larger point about "the experience of people who emancipated themselves from enslavement and struggled tenaciously to make the rhetoric of liberty a reality in their own lives."[38] It was the effort as much as the outcome that defined their common bond.

On the whole, the ex-slaves' struggle for liberty, along with that of other African Americans, both enslaved and free, who remained in post-Revolutionary America, invites us to take a longer view of the outcome of the War for Independence. "From this perspective," Nash concludes, "the African Americans' Revolution had only begun as the white patriots' Revolution ended in victory after eight years of war."[39] The first stages of this struggle had become evident from the early stirrings of protest in the 1770s, but the post-Revolutionary revolution spread far beyond the United States and lasted at least until the Civil War, even far beyond that.

5. Emancipation's Fate in the Revolutionary Era

The ultimate measure of slavery's significance in the meaning of the Revolution concerns not only the thousands of slaves who gained their

[37] On escaped slaves in British-controlled communities in the North, see Pybus, *Epic Journeys of Freedom*, 25–35; Gary B. Nash, *Forging Freedom: The Formation of Philadelphia's Black Community, 1720–1790* (Cambridge, MA, 1988); Gary Nash and Jean R. Soderlund, *Freedom by Degrees: Emancipation in Pennsylvania and Its Aftermath* (Oxford, UK, 1991); Shane White, *Somewhat More Independent: The End of Slavery in New York City* (Athens, GA, 1991); Graham Russell Hodges, *Root and Branch: African Americans in New York and East Jersey, 1613–1863* (Chapel Hill, NC, 1999); Hodges, *"Pretends to Be Free": Fugitive Slave Advertisements from Colonial and Revolutionary New York and New Jersey* (New York, 1994); Billy G. Smith and Richard Wojtowicz, *Blacks Who Stole Themselves: Advertisements for Runaways in the Pennsylvania Gazette* (Philadelphia, 1989); and Billy G. Smith, "Runaway Slaves in the Mid-Atlantic Region during the Revolutionary Era," in Ronald Hoffman and Peter J. Albert, eds., *The Transforming Hand of Revolution: Reconsidering the American Revolution as a Social Movement* (Charlottesville, VA, 1995), 199–230.

[38] Indeed, the major part of Pybus's *Epic Journeys of Freedom*, 75–205, deals with the fate of escaped slaves far beyond the shores of North America; quotation at xvii.

[39] Nash, *Forgotten Fifth*, 67.

freedom during the era but the very issue of freedom itself. What was the Revolution's impact on the institution of slavery, both in the new United States and in the broader Atlantic world? What did the era of the Revolution mean in either promoting or postponing the abolition of slavery? Here historians offer a necessarily mixed view, describing both the acceleration of antislavery sentiment and the solidifying defense of slavery in the wake of the Revolution. They also show us that the two processes did not define a stark and straightforward choice between only two options. Rather, several works explore the murky area in between, the reformist, yet subtly discriminatory stance among some opponents of slavery on one side and the ameliorationist, almost apologetic arguments of some uneasy supporters of slavery on the other. Taken together, the range of post-Revolutionary positions on the future of slavery in the Atlantic world gives us a better awareness of the enduring power of the racial restrictions the Revolution did not eradicate and therefore of the obvious failure of the Revolution to resolve its most glaring contradiction.

The contradiction of slavery was by no means an American monopoly. Studies of the emerging antislavery movement in the eighteenth-century Atlantic world focus much more on Great Britain, where voices of opposition to slavery faced considerable political and social obstacles. To be sure, Christopher Brown reminds us, there was nothing altogether new about opposition to slavery in eighteenth-century Britain: taking a cue from earlier Catholic critics in Portugal and Spain, some British writers at the time echoed the complaint about the cruelty and abuse that accompanied the traffic in human beings. Neither was there any shortage of reasons to find slavery to be a baneful, even dangerous, institution. Leaving aside its deadly effect on slaves themselves (which some people seemed able to do all too easily), British critics pointed to the possible problems slavery could create for white people as well as black: it inhibited the spread of Christianity, while it promoted sin and debauchery; it debased labor and led to laziness; it elevated a class of nouveau-riche slaveholders and created a mass of resentful, potentially rebellious slaves; it undermined the rule of law and instituted a regime of violence.[40] Even one of the country's leading critics of slavery, Granville Sharp, could become uneasy when slavery—or more to the point, black slaves—came into sight. In 1768, Sharp worried that the number of slaves in England had become "already much too numerous," and he advised that "the public good seems to require some restraints

[40] Brown, *Moral Capital*, 38–39.

on the unnatural increase of black subjects." Sharp and other opponents of slavery in Britain warned that if slavery (and slaves) became common in the country, its presence would displace liberty and institute tyranny for all.[41]

For all that, however, slavery tended to remain out of sight and out of mind for most Britons, who could generally enjoy their status as free citizens yet still enjoy the benefits of being part of an empire enriched by slave labor. They seemed quite able to maintain a stance of self-serving separation between themselves, free people who lived in the British Isles, and the slaves (and slaveholders) who inhabited their nation's West Indian and North American possessions and enriched the empire from a distance. Indeed, Davis notes, eighteenth-century Britain did not seem likely to become a society poised to promote the abolition of slavery and the slave trade: "For British leaders the very ideal of equality was abhorrent," he observes.[42] The British voices that did raise questions about slavery and the slave trade tended to be people who were "largely excluded from political power," Robin Blackburn explains, "writers rather than those with direct power or responsibility," or as Christopher Brown puts it, "isolated moralists" and members of the Protestant clergy, men and women who meant well enough but whose numbers were few and whose actions were feckless. Far more vocal and politically effective were their proslavery opponents, particularly the West Indian planters and slave traders who managed to gain the ear of British officials and lobby successfully for supporting the ongoing interests of the slave system.[43]

But the run-up to the American Revolution began to change all that. Beginning in the wake of the Seven Years' War, both sides of the conflict over the colonies claimed to be the last bastion of liberty while blaming each other for promoting slavery at the expense of liberty. The result, as Brown observes, was that the "conflict offered up identifiable villains:

[41] Ibid., 93–97, quotation at 94. On Sharp, see also Robin Blackburn, *The Overthrow of Colonial Slavery, 1776–1848* (London, 1988), 98–100; Davis, *Problem of Slavery*, 386 ff.; and Schama, *Rough Crossings*.

[42] Davis, *Inhuman Bondage*, 232–33.

[43] Blackburn, *Overthrow of Colonial Slavery*, 58, 78. Like Davis, Blackburn has written extensively on slavery in the Atlantic world; see also *The Making of New World Slavery: From the Baroque to the Modern, 1492–1800* (London, 1998) and, for a condensed summary of his work on slavery, *The Rise and Fall of Slavery in the Americas: Slavery, Emancipation and Human Rights* (London, 2007). Brown, *Moral Capital*, 40–55; see also Brown, "The Politics of Slavery," in David Armitage and Michael J. Braddick, eds., *The British-Atlantic World, 1500–1800* (Houndmills, UK, 2002), 214–32.

colonials who cried out for liberty but denied freedom to their slaves, British statesmen who honored the interests of African traders and prevented colonials from curtailing slave imports."[44] Radical American writers expressed fears about the eventual enslavement of the colonial people, white as well as black, at the hands of an oppressive empire. Jefferson's famous attempt to insert into the Declaration of Independence an attack on the British responsibility for American slavery only reflected a more pervasive, albeit self-serving, sentiment of victimization. In turn, British authors and officials came to paint the North American colonies as a slave society, not just as a society with slaves, much less a cultural extension of Great Britain itself. Many Britons had begun to see slave owning as a defining feature of the colonial American character, the source of the unruly hypocrisy that enabled Americans to claim special protection from the empire even as they challenged its authority. In the end, the main good that came from the terms of the debate was that ideologues on both sides increasingly came to define slavery as a vice and opposition to slavery as a virtue.

How important, then, was the American Revolution in contributing to the rise of antislavery sentiment? Brown argues that "the history of antislavery in Britain would have been very different without the American Revolution"—different in its timing, different in its scope, and different even in its very definition of the evils of slavery. The Revolution caused a rift that underscored the difference between Great Britain and the new United States, unifying British opponents of slavery and giving their agenda a new energy and a sense of national identity, transforming "the political and cultural significance of antislavery organizing." British abolitionists were not selfless altruists, nor was their movement a logical, almost inevitable result of ideological trends of Enlightenment thinking. Brown argues that they gained a certain personal benefit from their position, and the emergence of their movement depended more on a larger context of contingent events than on mere human decency and force of will. Still, the British antislavery movement does provide an important point for American comparison, because it gave shape and, in a sense, moral support to similar movements that soon sprang up elsewhere in the Atlantic world—including, of course, the United States.[45]

Turning the question around to the American side, the issue of slavery assumes an inescapable place in the discussion of the prospects for

[44] Brown, *Moral Capital*, 114–53, quotation at 153.
[45] Ibid., 451–61, quotation at 451.

abolition in a post-Revolutionary Atlantic world. If its contribution to the spread of the language of liberty on this side of the Atlantic were the main measure, then the American Revolution would have to be considered a progressive success. On a more immediate level, if we could peer into the hearts and minds of many individual Americans, we would see an emerging emancipationist sentiment taking root in ways that affected the lives of thousands of people, masters and slaves alike. Evangelical religion encouraged spiritually minded masters to set their slaves free or at least to soften the terms of their servitude. Economic considerations—a shift from tobacco to wheat production, the growth of towns and their attendant trades—likewise led to a loosening of the colonial-era restrictions on manumission in the upper South, as some masters found it more beneficial to hire free blacks as laborers when they needed them rather than house and feed them year-round. As Ira Berlin reminds us, "the terms of manumission were set by slaveholders, for the benefit of slaveholders," and we should not be deceived by illusions of enlightenment or altruism. Still, if we add to the mix some significant steps toward general, albeit gradual, emancipation in several of the individual American states, then the antislavery trajectory of the new nation might seem at least modestly promising.[46] But taking all that into consideration, if we ask why the American Revolution—and above all, the leaders of the Revolution, the men who became enshrined as the Founders—did not go even further, did not do more to eradicate slavery altogether in the new nation, we confront a series of awkward-seeming explanations, even excuses, that leave us looking at the debilitating political limits of the era set in stark contrast with its more progressive political possibilities.

6. The Founders' Failures on Slavery

"Americans tend to think of the Virginia gentry, the colonial elite that gave us Thomas Jefferson and George Washington, as a proud and optimistic

[46] On the effect of evangelical religion on slavery in the Revolutionary-era South, see especially Morgan, *Slave Counterpoint*, 420–37, and Berlin, *Many Thousands Gone*, 272–73. On the various factors contributing to emancipationist changes in the Revolutionary-era North and upper South, see Berlin, *Many Thousands Gone*, 228–89, quotation at 331–32. For other works dealing with emancipation in the North, see T. H. Breen, "Making History: The Force of Public Opinion and the Last Years of Slavery in Revolutionary Massachusetts," in Ronald Hoffman, Mechal Sobel, and Fredrika Teute, eds., *Through a Glass Darkly: Reflections on Personal Identity in Early America* (Chapel Hill, NC, 1997), 67–95; and Robert E. Desrochers Jr., "Slave-for-Sale Advertisements and Slavery in Massachusetts, 1704–1781," *William and Mary Quarterly*, 3d ser. 59 (2002): 623–64.

ruling class," Woody Holton has observed. But beneath that confident image, he argues, lay a tangle of anxieties stemming from their relationships with those below them on the social scale—Indians and poorer whites, to be sure, but also slaves, who lived in the most immediate proximity on the plantation. Those anxieties, as much as anger about British policy, helped shape prominent patriots' responses to the revolutionary crisis in the 1770s and beyond. Holton's notion of Jefferson, Washington, and their counterparts as "forced founders"—that is, men who eventually took the most visible steps in the movement for independence "partly because they were feeling pressure from below"—offers us a more complex but ultimately compelling way of looking at the Founders' role in the Revolution.[47] Tempting though it might be to some scholars to portray the southern Founders primarily as members of a colonial elite engaged in a lofty level of political discourse about independence, more socially rooted studies remind us that we cannot take the Founder-slave relationship for granted. Even the most politically prominent planters not only depended on slavery for their economic and social standing but associated with slaves on a daily basis. That close association had its consequences. It affected the way the masters defined their position in a slaveholding society, and it accentuated the way they defended the slave system in an emerging republican society. Thus it reshapes our understanding of them as politically engaged individuals and as members of a socially powerful class.

Two books on less celebrated figures among the Revolutionary-era gentry give us especially valuable insights into the ways of plantation patriarchs. In these works, we see Chesapeake planters who were different in tone and temperament but who struggled in their respective ways to balance their commitment to the independence movement with their control of dependent people. Ronald Hoffman and Sally Mason offer a joint portrait of Maryland's two Charles Carrolls—the father, Charles Carroll of Annapolis (or "Papa"), and son, Charles Carroll of Carrollton—that emphasizes the general stability of the plantations and the emotional restraint of the planters. Like all large slaveholders, the Carrolls took careful note of the daily details of life and labor on the plantation, paying special attention to the health and work habits of their slaves and trying to correct deficiencies in both when need be. But for the most part, they did not become closely involved in the personal or spiritual lives of their slaves, and they exhibited a "distant, almost dehumanized, attitude" toward their slaves' deaths. Indeed,

[47] Holton, *Forced Founders*, xiii.

they kept their emotional distance not only from their slaves but also from the institution of slavery itself. Hoffman and Mason find "no evidence that Charles Carroll of Annapolis ever questioned the morality of slaveholding or that he felt any guilt about its practice . . . or that it ever occurred to him to care what [his slaves] thought of him."[48] On the whole, the picture Hoffman and Mason draw is of two slave owners who were more economically calculating than excessively cruel, masters who looked on their human property primarily as a valuable investment that needed to be kept in decent condition for productive labor. In some ways, the Carrolls' chilly restraint makes them seem all the more disturbing.

There was nothing restrained about Landon Carter, the subject of Rhys Isaac's striking study of the "deep-dyed patriarchal monarchist" whose own "uneasy kingdom" of Sabine Hall seemed a constant scene of apprehension, if not paranoia, in the Revolutionary era. Drawing on Carter's diary, Isaac intersperses the slave owner's own words throughout his narrative to create a revealing portrait of a patriarch facing the prospect of revolution both in his own province and on his own plantation. Always lurking near the core of Carter's anxiety was his uncertain hold on his slaves. Isaac opens the book with Carter's account of the escape of a group of male slaves in late June 1776, and more than anything else that upset the old patriarch's sense of stability, the impact of his slaves' rebelliousness brought home the significance of the larger social transformation taking place in his "uneasy kingdom." The flight of the runaways haunted Carter's days, even his dreams, ever after. He refused to assume he bore any responsibility for their leaving ("*I have no kind of Severity in the least to accuse myself of to one of them*"), and he could only wonder how the work of the plantation could continue without their labor. Yet even by raising the prospect of a plantation without slaves, Isaac observes, Carter "was already getting caught up in the imagined new order that the Revolution was evoking."[49]

The "imagined new order" of the Revolution seemed menacing indeed to both Papa Carroll and Landon Carter as elder statesmen of the

[48] Ronald Hoffman and Sally Mason, *Princes of Ireland, Planters of Maryland: A Carroll Saga, 1500–1782* (Chapel Hill, NC, 2000), 256, 253. For a collection of the Carroll correspondence, see also Ronald Hoffman, Sally Mason, and Eleanor S. Darcy, eds., *Dear Papa, Dear Charley: The Peregrinations of a Revolutionary Aristocrat, as Told by Charles Carroll of Carrollton and His Father, Charles Carroll of Annapolis, with Sundry Observations on Bastardy, Child-Rearing, Romance, Matrimony, Commerce, Tobacco, Slavery, and the Politics of Revolutionary America* (Chapel Hill, NC, 2001).

[49] Rhys Isaac, *Landon Carter's Uneasy Kingdom: Revolution and Rebellion in a Virginia Plantation* (Oxford, UK, 2004), 14, 308.

plantation. The policies of the Crown and Parliament led both to accept the need for a break with the old regime, but they did so guardedly, anxious about the implications of the changes that were coming into play. Landon Carter denounced what he saw as the miscues and excesses of the radicals, ranging from the widespread embrace of Thomas Paine's *Common Sense* (based on "*the most absurd Arguments in the world*," Carter wrote) to the confused conduct of the county militia ("*because everything in the shape of a soldier must be now raw and undisciplined*"). By 1776, Carter had become increasingly torn by the tension between his roles as patriarch and patriot. He acknowledged the need for the broader resistance movement even as he tried to stem the various rebellions in his personal world, from the democratic challenges of lesser landowners in the region to the subversive behavior of the slaves on his plantation to the sullen insolence of own children. Landon Carter had always grumbled about his son, Robert Wormeley Carter, for his dissolute self-indulgence in alcohol and cards, but he expressed especially harsh disdain for Robert's emerging role in the Revolution as a would-be leader who spouted the latest democratic principles and pandered shamelessly—and even worse, unsuccessfully—to the local electorate ("*My son has merely kissed the arses of the people and very servilely accommodated himself to others—and yet he has been shamefully turned out*").[50]

Papa Carroll's son had considerably more electoral success, but Charley too had to face his father's displeasure about his political posture in the Revolution. Chosen as a member of Maryland's delegation to the Continental Congress, Charley was the only Roman Catholic to sign the Declaration of Independence—an act, Hoffman and Mason point out, that suggests "a powerful metaphor for a personal and emotional transition of which he was as yet only dimly aware." By joining with other men in leading a revolutionary movement, he was declaring a sort of independence of his own, going beyond "the shadows of ancient prejudices" in Papa's Irish past and making "a place for his lineage in the sun of a new nation." In his new role in that new nation, Charley was no radical democrat, to be sure,

[50] Ibid., 290–301, quotations at 293, 299, 300. For other studies of tumultuous relations on Virginia plantations, see Kathleen M. Brown, *Good Wives, Nasty Wenches, and Anxious Patriarchs: Gender, Race, and Power in Colonial Virginia* (Chapel Hill, NC, 1996); Kenneth Lockridge, *The Diary and Life of William Byrd II of Virginia, 1674–1744* (Chapel Hill, NC, 1991); and Kevin Berland, Jan Kirsten Gilliam, and Kenneth Lockridge, eds., *On the Sources of Patriarchal Rage: The Commonplace Books of William Byrd and Thomas Jefferson and the Gendering of Power in the Eighteenth Century* (Chapel Hill, NC, 2001).

and perhaps an even greater elitist than his father; he did, however, come to understand better than his father ever had the need for compromise in the name of common cause, meeting some popular demands even while trying to maintain control of a politically tumultuous process. In this new political environment, Charley realized, conservatives had to make concessions to preserve their positions. But like Landon Carter, the elder Carroll would have none of his son's apparent temporizing, and Papa chastised him for pandering to "the rabble" for political popularity.[51] And like Isaac's exploration of Carter's "uneasy kingdom," Hoffman and Mason's study of the Carrolls' saga does much more than assess the strains in father-son relationships occasioned by the Revolution. It also gives us an insightful lesson in patriarchal style, contrasting the chilly, unyielding stance of the elder Carroll with the more pragmatic approach of his more conciliatory-seeming son. Indeed, both books give us compelling pictures of how two families of fundamentally conservative men, fathers and sons alike, confronted the suddenly precarious-seeming condition of their accustomed authority, whether in their plantation households or in society as a whole.

Neither the Carters nor the Carrolls stood anywhere near as close to the center of the Revolutionary movement—or Revolutionary memory—as the more powerful slaveholder-statesmen of the era, Thomas Jefferson and George Washington. Both have become all but emblematic of the Revolution's critical contradiction, as leaders of a struggle for liberty that extended the life of slavery. Both have also become the subjects of new scholarly scrutiny that assesses the issue of slavery more centrally in their lives and, perhaps most important, diminishes the distinction between their roles on the plantation and in politics.

Certainly, the biggest historical news about Jefferson in recent years has centered on the two-centuries-old controversy over his sexual connection to Sally Hemings, a long-divisive issue that was revived in the latter part of the twentieth century and has continued to capture considerable attention in the twenty-first. The suggestion that Jefferson had an illicit liaison with a young slave woman had in fact first made the rounds of political gossip around the turn of the nineteenth century, most notably when James Callendar, a disgruntled former supporter, spread the story to smear the new president. The rumor never fully disappeared during the nineteenth century, but it tended to be dismissed or buried in footnotes until 1974, when Fawn Brodie addressed it directly in her book about the romantic side of

[51] Hoffman and Mason, *Princes of Ireland*, 303–33, quotations at 310, 323.

the Jefferson-Hemings relationship.[52] Brodie's book gained a good deal of notoriety in the reading public, but the scholarly protectors of the Jefferson legacy gave it little currency. In 1997, Joseph Ellis added a brief, five-page appendix, "A Note on the Sally Hemings Scandal," to his Jefferson biography, *American Sphinx*. He acknowledged that Dumas Malone's multivolume biography of Jefferson inadvertently contributed some circumstantial credibility to the story: by documenting Jefferson's presence at Monticello nine months before the births of Hemings's children, Malone made it plausible to suspect Jefferson's paternity. Still, Ellis concluded, unless there were some scientific way to support the veracity of the story—he suggested DNA testing—"it leaves the matter a mystery about which advocates on either side can freely speculate, and surely will." Ellis's own position at the time was that "within the community of Jefferson specialists, there seems to be a clear consensus that the story is almost certainly not true."[53]

If such a consensus truly existed, it quickly collapsed soon after Ellis published his opinion, and a newer community of Jefferson specialists would now agree that the story is indeed almost certainly true. In 1997, Annette Gordon-Reed's lawyerly investigation of the evidence took into consideration not only the standard documentary sources available in archival repositories but also the oral traditions embedded in the African American community. Although Gordon-Reed did not claim to put forth positive proof about the Jefferson-Hemings link, she challenged historians to revisit the evidence and, above all, to be more inclusive in their investigation of sources.[54] Then, in 1998, science silenced all but Jefferson's most diehard defenders when, indeed, DNA analysis indicated a perfect match on Y-chromosome markers that linked Jefferson and Sally Hemings's youngest

[52] Fawn M. Brodie, *Thomas Jefferson: An Intimate Portrait* (New York, 1974). A few years earlier, Winthrop D. Jordan had discussed the Jefferson-Hemings relationship in *White over Black: American Attitudes toward the Negro, 1550–1812* (Chapel Hill, NC, 1968), 461–69, but he concluded that the "question of Jefferson's miscegenation . . . is of limited interest and usefulness even if it could be satisfactorily answered" (467).

[53] Joseph Ellis, *American Sphinx* (New York, 1997), 302–7, quotation at 305. Ellis noted that the three final volumes of Malone's six-volume biography of Jefferson, *Jefferson and His Time* (Boston, 1948–1961), provided the chronological connection between Jefferson's time at Monticello and Sally Hemings's pregnancies, but he later noted that it was Winthrop Jordan who "deserves credit for being the first historian to notice this conjunction." See Ellis, "Jefferson: Post-DNA," *William and Mary Quarterly*, 3rd ser. 57 (2000): 125–38, quotation at 129n. 5.

[54] Annette Gordon-Reed, *Thomas Jefferson and Sally Hemings: An American Controversy* (Charlottesville, VA, 1997). Gordon-Reed subsequently placed the Jefferson-Hemings relationship in the context of Sally's family in *The Hemingses of Monticello: An American Family* (New York, 2008).

son, Eston.[55] At that point, the question for historians was no longer "Did he or didn't he?" but "What difference does it make?"

In 2000, a forum in the *William and Mary Quarterly* gave seven Jefferson specialists an opportunity to consider that latter question in light of the then-new DNA evidence.[56] For the still-skeptical Ellis, who now admitted that the post-DNA proof of Jefferson's paternity seemed "*pretty* convincing," the answer to the question of its significance was still "not much at all." Whatever one might make of outcome or meaning of the Jefferson-Hemings relationship, he argued, Jefferson remains such a multifaceted figure in American history that no single factor, even flaw, in his personal character could undo the significance of his political achievements: "Jefferson's place in American history is secured by multiple guidewires," Ellis observed, and in his estimation the master of Monticello would continue to stand as he always had, an elusively paradoxical but undeniably prominent embodiment of the Revolutionary generation's greatness.[57]

On the other hand, two other contributors, Peter Onuf and Andrew Burstein, made a case that the Hemings relationship does indeed matter, and not only to decry the most obvious evidence of his personal hypocrisy. Their larger point was to draw a connection between Jefferson's private and public lives, especially the extent to which his relationship with his own slaves, and with Sally Hemings in particular, was reflected in his larger approach to race and slavery. Where some might see in Jefferson's behavior and beliefs a contradiction, Burstein saw compartmentalization, an ability to isolate and even to ignore paradoxical issues by identifying with the cultural standards of manhood current in his day: "he rationalized without feeling guilt," Burstein concluded, "because his society provided him with the means to do so."[58] Onuf moved in the other direction by arguing that Jefferson's ability, even need, to separate the reality of his black family from

[55] Eugene A. Foster, M. A. Jobling, P. G. Taylor, P. Donnelly, P. De Knijff, Rene Mieremet, T. Zerjal, and C. Tyler-Smith, "Jefferson Fathered Slave's Last Child," *Nature* 396 (1998): 27–28.

[56] *William and Mary Quarterly*, 3rd ser. 57 (2000): 121–210. Two of the contributors to this forum, Jan Lewis and Peter Onuf, also co-edited a collection of scholarly essays titled *Sally Hemings and Thomas Jefferson: History, Memory, and Civic Culture* (Charlottesville, VA, 1999), the published results of a conference held in Charlottesville, Virginia, just over four months after the DNA story appeared in *Nature*. For the sake of considering the most up-to-date discussion of the controversy, I focus here on the *WMQ* forum, from which the works cited in the following paragraphs originate.

[57] Ellis, "Jefferson: Post-DNA," 125, 127–28.

[58] Andrew Burstein, "Jefferson's Rationalizations," *William and Mary Quarterly*, 3rd ser. 57 (2000): 183–97, quotation at 196.

"the myth of his white family's perfect happiness" helped inform his life-long embrace of colonization for slaves—that is, the plan to rid America of slavery by ridding it of African American slaves themselves, who would be exported to Africa or elsewhere. Only by removing the sexual temptation posed by slaves, Onuf explained, could Jefferson expect white Virginians to be able to exercise the personal virtue they would need to fashion a virtuous republican society; by the same token, only by removing black people from white society could Americans hope to preserve the racial purity—and power—that Jefferson deemed necessary for the long-term success of white society.[59]

To the extent that these authors could reach a new consensus on Jefferson, it was that he will probably always remain a perplexing, paradoxical, and problematic figure, someone who embodies both the Revolutionary era's brightest promise of equality and its most dismal denial. Whether democratic icon or racist hypocrite or sphinxlike enigma, Jefferson cannot escape his association with slavery, and that makes it unwise to try to pin one persona onto him, much less tie him to a single position on the meaning of freedom. On this score, Gordon-Reed has offered an insightful perspective drawn from the long-term perceptions of African Americans: "The contradictions that make Jefferson seem problematic and frustrating . . . to whites," she argues, "make him more accessible to blacks, who find his conflicted nature a perfect reflection of the America they know: a place where high-minded ideals clash with the reality of racial ambivalence."[60] Thus she invites scholars in the present to take a cue from slaves in the past, including Sally Hemings, and see Jefferson not only as an unsettling contradiction as an individual but as an essential symbol of the conflicted origins of the American republic.

Yet for all the focus on Jefferson, which generally addresses the later years of his life, Henry Wiencek's study of George Washington gives us a fresher perspective on a famous slave-owning Founder throughout the era of the Revolution. Washington, of course, is most commonly remembered for his role as military leader and not so much for his involvement with slavery. Yet the core of Wiencek's argument is that nothing stood closer to the center of Washington's identity than the institution of slavery. In this

[59] Peter S. Onuf, "Every Generation Is an 'Independant Nation': Colonization, Miscegenation, and the Fate of Jefferson's Children," *William and Mary Quarterly*, 3rd ser. 57 (2000): 153–70, quotation at 170.

[60] Annette Gordon-Reed, "Engaging Jefferson: Blacks and the Founding Father," *William and Mary Quarterly*, 3rd ser. 57 (2000): 171–82, quotation at 172–73.

sense, Wiencek makes Washington a more complicated-seeming character than the staid, stiff figure still familiar in historical memory.

Like Jefferson, Washington embodied the contradiction of his seemingly competing roles, as "the slaveholder who led the war for liberty," but Wiencek does much more than merely posit the obvious paradox.[61] He looks at Washington critically yet sympathetically and, above all, locates Washington's life squarely within the "interlocking network of public and private systems" that tied together political, personal, and property considerations.[62] Washington, who acquired most of his slaves through his marriage to Martha Custis, had to develop the practices of plantation management that the elder Charles Carroll had apparently mastered so well, coming to place a similar emphasis on tranquility, profitability, and personal authority, even at the cost of "the profound psychological dislocation" that came with keeping fellow human beings, including offspring of one's own family, as property.[63] He found it perplexing when slaves failed to follow his instructions or to see the wisdom of his ways, and he found it especially unsettling when slaves and free whites engaged in sexual relations that produced mixed-race people, "blurring the definitions upon which the labor and social systems depended." But then, as Wiencek observes, "women and blacks represented the irrational" in Washington's world, and "the slaves and he did not occupy the same logical universe."[64]

It is Washington's moral universe that Wiencek explores most effectively. Like other members of the slaveholding class, Washington "became personally engaged in a mode of slavery that required certain evasions, denials, and psychological cruelties," and he apparently accepted all these as the price one had to pay for prominence in his society.[65] But Washington's own experience with buying and selling slaves—and in the process, breaking up slave families—caused him to reach a "moral nadir" on the eve of the Revolution.[66]

The necessities of war soon caused him to change his behavior, if not completely his beliefs. Despite his initial attempt to keep black men out of the Continental army, he quickly realized he needed them. He remained adamant about excluding enslaved blacks from his forces, however, and

[61] Wiencek, *Imperfect God*, 191.

[62] Ibid., 78.

[63] Ibid., 86.

[64] Ibid., 130, 40

[65] Ibid., 86.

[66] Ibid., 188.

unlike his British counterparts, he certainly had no inclination to make an open announcement of emancipation for slaves who became soldiers: Washington was still too much identified with his slaveholding roots to undermine other men's property rights. Nonetheless, Wiencek credits him with taking a significant step by making a distinction between slaves and free blacks, accepting the latter into the army: Washington thus "removed race as the defining element" in military mobilization. In the end, Wiencek gives Washington reasonably good marks for eventually responding positively to the bottom-up push, not to mention military need, for enlisting black soldiers, particularly since he did so without the support of his fellow southerners or, indeed, many northerners: "At the start of the war this Southern plantation master wanted no blacks in his army, but he changed. Under his leadership, the Continental Army became integrated."[67]

It was not until late in the Revolutionary era that Washington reached a more progressive position, when he famously emancipated his slaves in his will. While some people might reasonably argue that this posthumous emancipation was a concession that did far too little far too late, Wiencek gives Washington more moral credit than that. To be sure, in evaluating Washington's long life as a slaveholder, he does not use this final testament as evidence of any exceptional enlightenment on Washington's part. He does see it, however, as Washington's ultimate "indictment of the laws, the country, and the people that enacted events that, to him, had the feeling of death."[68] In that regard, Washington's will becomes a point of departure for entering, as Wiencek puts it, "a dangerous and, some would say, 'unhealthful' realm of questioning" that addresses one basic issue for the revolutionary era: "*Could* the founders have ended slavery then and there? Washington freed his slaves. He did not think emancipation was impossible. Why did the others not follow? Why not judge Washington's peers by Washington's standards?"[69]

Why not, indeed? Most historians remain reluctant to judge the leading men of the Revolution by strict emancipationist standards on slavery, and Wiencek admits as much.[70] Slavery was pervasive, virtually ubiquitous, in the eighteenth-century Atlantic world—not only in the British-American colonies but also in the French, Dutch, Spanish, and Portuguese possessions, from one end of the Western Hemisphere to the other; while some

[67] Ibid., 205, 220.
[68] Ibid., 188.
[69] Ibid., 174.
[70] Ibid., 135, 218–19.

people found slavery to be execrable, no one could think it at all exceptional. The vast majority of white people, no matter what their political and moral persuasions, took slavery for granted as one of many forms of inequality in society. Gordon Wood argues further that any modern-day emphasis on the failure of the American Revolution to abolish slavery "is to miss the great significance of what it did accomplish," particularly putting into place the ideological and social foundations for the eventual abolition of slavery.[71] Similarly, Edward Countryman calls it "wrong-headed" to challenge the radical nature of the Revolution because it did not abolish slavery in the immediate era, noting instead that the "long global destruction of slavery . . . began in revolutionary America." Indeed, George Washington was not the only Revolutionary-era southerner to free his slaves, Countryman adds, and "there were far more slave owners, including Thomas Jefferson, who worried a great deal while doing relatively little."[72] Still, the question remains: Could they have done relatively more?

Gary Nash pushes the point most emphatically. Having engaged the issue of slavery in early America throughout his scholarly career, Nash has brought the question to a head in a brief but provocatively argued essay, asking "Could Slavery Have Been Abolished?" Nash says yes—but only, he argues, if the most prominent men in power had indeed done more to bring about its demise. In challenging the failures of the Founders, he also very pointedly takes to task the tendency of historians to concede the impossibility of Revolutionary-era abolition too easily: "The argument that slavery could *not* have been abolished reeks of the dangerous, indeed odious, concept of historical inevitability," a notion Nash calls a "winner's weapon" held in the hands of those who would excuse the unjust mistakes of the powerful as a predictable, albeit perhaps unfortunate, product of their time.[73] Unwilling to let the leaders of the Revolution off the historical hook, Nash offers an impassioned antidote to indulgent concessions commonly granted them by some of their more admiring modern biographers.

Looking at the political context of the immediate post-Revolutionary era, Nash addresses the main explanation generally advanced to argue against the abolition of slavery—that the new nation was simply too frail to endure the convulsions that might come with such a dramatic step. True, he admits, political leaders from South Carolina and Georgia, the states

[71] Gordon Wood, *The Radicalism of the American Revolution* (New York, 1991), 7, 186–87.
[72] Edward Countryman, *The American Revolution* (New York, 1985; rev. ed., 2003), xix–xx.
[73] Nash, *Forgotten Fifth*, 69–122, quotation at 70.

most committed to the slave system, repeatedly blustered about separating themselves from the other states if the existence of slavery were threatened, thus breaking up the fragile federation before it had even had a chance to cohere. And true, political leaders in the other states often seemed quite willing to accommodate their southernmost neighbors, making concessions to them for the sake of forming the new federal government and taking only gradual, sometimes grudging steps toward the abolition of slavery in their own environs. But Nash argues in the first case that the Deep South bluster might have been little more than that: at the end of the Revolution, Georgia and South Carolina were themselves so militarily and economically weakened, and so exposed to the attacks of both European and Native American enemies, that they "needed a strong federal government far more than the rest of the states needed them."[74] And in the rest of the states, he notes, repeated questions about the viability and morality of slavery never seemed to quiet down, nor did the advocates of abolition completely cede the debate to those who would more willingly see the issue deferred or dismissed altogether. Indeed, despite all the obvious odds against the eradication of slavery in the immediate post-Revolutionary period, Nash sees the era as a time that could have been reasonably propitious for abolition—but only if the right people had done the right thing.

As a longtime proponent of seeing history from the bottom up, Nash is among the last to engage in any celebration of the Founders as exemplars of leadership. He does, however, underscore the importance of power at the top, noting that "in cases where a fundamental change has been accomplished against heavy odds, inspired leadership has been critically important." In that regard, he offers his own standards for measuring character. Providing enlightened leadership in the face of a reluctant public could be not only politically unpopular but personally draining, requiring embattled leaders to "sacrifice amiability, politeness, and even friendship in order to achieve a goal dictated by conscience." In the end, those dictates of conscience could exact a stiff price, leaving a leader with little more than a legacy of historical courage, of "facing political ruin with honor."[75] Set against that standard, Nash argues, the Founders failed to meet the leadership challenge of courageously embracing the controversy of slavery and promoting humane change. Considering one of the most prominent political figures in the North, Nash challenges David McCullough's claims that

[74] Ibid., 80.
[75] Ibid., 91.

John Adams was "utterly opposed to slavery and the slave trade." It was Abigail Adams who took a strong stance against slavery, Nash points out, while John "did his best to keep slavery *off* the patriot reform agenda" and "did nothing to hurry slavery to extinction" after the Revolution.[76] Nash notes that in the South, the leading national figures in the Virginia gentry —Washington, Jefferson, and James Madison—all "professed a hatred of slavery and a fervent desire to see it ended in their own time," as did several of their most prominent planter counterparts, who could have been extremely useful allies in a southern antislavery movement. That being the case, Nash faults these three Founders for failing to spend the necessary political and moral capital in the public realm to see their antislavery sentiments through to a political conclusion.[77]

Nash's own conclusion—that the three leading Virginians, and especially Washington and Jefferson, could have taken the most successful steps against slavery *precisely because* they occupied such lofty positions in the slaveholding class *and* in the national arena—relies on a significant series of "ifs," probably more than most other historians would be willing to accommodate. Still, his provocative position represents more than historical second-guessing or counterfactual speculation. It poses a question not only about the Founders themselves but also about the scholars who study them: Why not confront the seemingly unthinkable possibility of a very different historical outcome based on very different personal leadership? Why not ask the question seriously rather than simply consign it to the all-too-charitable category of its admittedly difficult historical context? The point is not to pass moral judgment and hold the Founders personally responsible for slavery. Rather, it is to see them as men of considerable influence who could have done more to make a difference. In an odd, certainly inadvertent, way, holding the Founders to a higher antislavery standard gives them greater credit for their political prominence and leadership—or leadership *potential*—than do some of the more generous-seeming studies: by giving the Founders an apparent pass on the issue, sympathetic scholars have failed to take the full measure of the men whose characters they might otherwise seek to celebrate.

The truest test of the Founders' failure may rest with the case of the one man among them who seemed to be the most progressive on the issue of slavery: Benjamin Franklin. Printer, inventor, politician, diplomat,

[76] Ibid., 93–94.
[77] Ibid., 95.

self-made man, and ladies' man, Franklin remains probably the most intellectually engaging of the Founders and arguably the most personally enjoyable.[78] That seemed especially evident with the emergence of "Founders chic," when Franklin was the subject of five scholarly studies in five years, 2000–2004. It is Franklin, Gordon Wood observes, "who seems to have the most common touch" of the great men of his generation. As Walter Isaacson notes mischievously, "Benjamin Franklin is the founding father who winks at us."[79]

On the question of slavery, several of Franklin's recent biographers have been willing to wink back, treating his involvement with slavery in somewhat the same way as his dalliance with women: it was not quite right, but it was common among many other men; and in the end, after all, Franklin came out seeming reasonably virtuous on the issue. In his early years, "Franklin's conscience apparently pained him little on the subject," H. W. Brands notes, and Isaacson observes that Franklin's eventual uneasiness about slavery came "mainly from an economic perspective rather than a moral one."[80] Edmund Morgan concurs, arguing that Franklin lived "pretty comfortably with slavery" for most of his many years, and "not until late in life did it begin to trouble his conscience."[81] Wood locates Franklin within the larger context of colonial American culture: "While we today can scarcely conceive of one person holding another in bondage," he writes, "most eighteenth-century white Americans, living in a hierarchical society composed of ranks of dependency and unfreedom, accepted black slavery as a matter of course. Franklin was no exception."[82]

Focusing on Franklin through this glass of historical, if not moral, relativism on the issue of slavery gives us one clear view of this multifaceted Founder, but it obscures, even hides, another. It makes sense on one level, of course, because it does define the dominant sentiment of his era, when, as Wood rightly points out, white people tended to take slavery more or less for granted. But it is precisely the deeply embedded nature of slavery

[78] The Franklin studies that came into print in the first few years of the twenty-first century are H. W. Brands, *The First American: The Life and Times of Benjamin Franklin* (New York, 2000); Edmund S. Morgan, *Benjamin Franklin* (New Haven, CT, 2003); Walter Isaacson, *Benjamin Franklin: An American Life* (New York, 2003); Gordon Wood, *The Americanization of Benjamin Franklin* (New York, 2004); and David Waldstreicher, *Runaway America: Benjamin Franklin, Slavery, and the American Revolution* (New York, 2004).

[79] Wood, *Americanization of Benjamin Franklin*, 2; Isaacson, *Benjamin Franklin*, 2.

[80] Brands, *First American*, 118; Isaacson, *Benjamin Franklin*, 464.

[81] Morgan, *Benjamin Franklin*, 106.

[82] Wood, *Americanization of Benjamin Franklin*, 226.

in colonial society that makes it stand out all the more dramatically, and its widespread acceptance provides a way to reflect on the Founders in ways that cannot, in fact, be taken for granted by historians. For Franklin, as indeed for all the Founders, the issue of slavery remains an important measure by which we understand them more fully as representative men, much less as enlightened leaders, of the Revolutionary era. One of the more positive parts of Franklin's posthumous reputation depends on his involvement in the abolitionist movement in Pennsylvania. In 1787, Franklin became the president of the Society for Promoting the Abolition of Slavery and the Relief of Negroes Unlawfully Held in Bondage, and in 1790 he put his name to a memorial sent to Congress calling for the abolition of slavery in the new nation. "This was a very different Franklin from the earlier pragmatic Franklin," Wood concludes.[83] Franklin died just two months after presenting that antislavery petition, an elder statesman of eighty-four with a long life of public service brought to completion finally, perhaps fittingly, by a late-in-life embrace of abolition. Nothing could better provide an opportunity for apotheosis.

By contrast, David Waldstreicher's study of Franklin, *Runaway America*, takes a different approach by making slavery a central and by no means incidental issue running throughout Franklin's life, much less a late-breaking source of enlightenment. Indeed, Waldstreicher's title reminds us of Franklin's own escape from servitude early in life, when as a seventeen-year-old he ran away from what he later described as the "harsh and tyrannical treatment" he received as an apprentice to his brother, James, who, Franklin said, "considered himself as my Master."[84] This act of self-liberation gave Franklin the opportunity to become the self-made man of legend, but it also eventually gave him the power to make other men unfree. In Philadelphia, Franklin entered a social milieu in which the reliance on unfree labor had become commonplace, and indentured servants and slaves had become essentially interchangeable elements in the labor supply—a system, Waldstreicher explains, that was "predicated upon the continued flow of unfree labor and the master's ease in switching between one supply and the other." In such a context, it seems hardly surprising that a man on the make like Franklin would demonstrate his success by purchasing slaves for his household, which he did in the mid-1730s. "Seen this way," Waldstreicher

[83] Ibid., 227.

[84] Benjamin Franklin, *The Autobiography of Benjamin Franklin*, ed. Leonard W. Labaree et al. (New Haven, CT, 1964), 68, quoted in Waldstreicher, *Runaway America*, 4.

observes, "Franklin's investment in and ownership of slaves becomes an unthinking and late decision," and his "involvement with slavery was quite typical of Pennsylvanians."[85]

But what makes Waldstreicher's view of Franklin less than typical is the extent to which he explores Franklin's thoughts about servitude and slavery and, in the process, the question of race. Although Franklin gave antislavery Quakers a print venue for protest in the pages of his *Pennsylvania Gazette*, he adopted a broader, liberal-seeming position: relying on principles of religious pluralism and the freedom of the press, he committed himself to no single stance. Doing so enabled Franklin to stay "a sympathetic distance from antislavery," Waldstreicher observes. "He brought it to the marketplace of ideas only to leave it there."[86] His own ideas began to focus on the implications of unfree labor as a critical commodity in a developing colonial economy, obviously valuable but to Franklin potentially troublesome in the larger context of colonial stability. Unfree laborers, white or black, could not be trusted, or they could only be trusted to try to run away (as he himself had done)—and in the worst of cases, sometimes to become a subversive force by running away to the enemy in times of war. But even in times of peace, slavery especially seemed an unsettling threat to the welfare of the colonies. Not only did slaves undermine the frugality and industry of their masters, but they created what Waldstreicher calls a "bad bargain" as cheap labor, "taking up spaces that could be occupied by white immigrants who would in the long run add more wealth to an expanding empire."[87]

Slavery became emblematic of the larger imperial issues that Franklin and his colonial colleagues were beginning to confront in the 1760s. The existence and expansion of slavery did much more than merely block opportunities for white immigrants to the American colonies; it raised questions about what rights white people already in the colonies could reasonably espouse, much less hope to preserve. To the extent that slavery thus posed a problem for the freedoms of white Americans as well as African American slaves, Waldstreicher argues, Franklin's eventual solution was to make an increasing distinction between the North America colonies' place in the empire and the larger imperial policy agenda being created in England. "Ultimately Franklin projected the blame for slavery onto England and the West Indies," he argues, and in doing so Franklin began to

[85] Waldstreicher, *Runaway America*, 20, 25.

[86] Ibid., 82–83.

[87] Ibid., 137.

define the connection between the colonies' racial identity and revolutionary independence. The answer to the question of slavery in the colonies, Waldstreicher suggests, came in a question: "Why not simultaneously reform both colonial relations and that subset of colonial relations known as African slavery?"[88] It comes as no surprise that Franklin and his fellow Founders failed to accomplish both. Even in Franklin's post-Revolutionary embrace of antislavery, Waldstreicher concludes, he seemed hardly ahead of the rest: "His antislavery, like that of the American Revolution, was a runaway's antislavery: compromised, and compromising."[89]

The strength of Waldstreicher's book does not depend on his estimation of the strength of Franklin's character or the timing and depth of Franklin's commitment to antislavery. Rather, it stems from his convincing insistence that the question of slavery, far from being a late-breaking result of revolutionary strategy or ideology, "was present at the creation." Franklin's own journey from runaway to revolutionary took him down "the path from British to American nationhood, a path that . . . would be traced not only around, but also directly through, the problem of slavery."[90]

Franklin did not walk alone. How other Founders navigated the same path through the problem of slavery becomes, then, a similarly critical question to ask of all the prominent men in the Revolution's upper reaches. No student of the Founders can now responsibly turn away from that path and, without careful investigation and explanation, dismiss it simply as the road not taken.

III. Facing the Revolution from Indian Country

7. Native American Perspectives on Euro-American Struggles

At the beginning of the twenty-first century, Daniel Richter challenged early American historians to do what he and other scholars of Native Americans had been doing for years: to look at the colonial and Revolutionary eras by "facing east from Indian country." Making that simple-seeming shift in perspective had important implications. First, it meant turning around from the Eurocentric viewpoint of the determined conquest of the continent (or "the invasion of America," as Francis Jennings called it a gen-

[88] Ibid., 181, 186.

[89] Ibid., 244.

[90] Ibid., 177, 144. Waldstreicher expands his interpretation of the Founders in *Slavery's Constitution: From Revolution to Ratification* (New York, 2002).

eration ago) and the traditional east-to-west, colony-to-nation narrative of early American history.[91] Instead, taking the view from Indian country helps us understand Native people's perspectives on what they saw. Seeking the perspective of Indian people *on* history, in fact, means seeing Indians *in* history, not only as people who made an appearance on the margins of the American narrative but as people central to the story, who made a critical contribution to the long-term transformation of early America. The long-enduring tendency among earlier historians to portray Indians as stereotypical savages turned them into subhuman obstacles, ominously blocking the path of progress until swept aside by modernity or, more often, by the military. The more patronizing but equally dehumanizing tendency to see them as nature's natives turned them into saccharine symbols, frozen in tradition and suspended on the sidelines of history.[92] As an alternative, taking the view from Indian country now gives us a better understanding of Native peoples as active participants in a past they helped shape.

Second, this alternative perspective of "facing east" also sets forth new geographical and conceptual boundaries for framing early American history, up to the American Revolution—and beyond. Facing east (or, better to accommodate other perspectives that come into play, outward, in all directions) from Indian country re-centers the narrative away from the coastal colonies and takes us deeper into the interior regions of the continent, where Native Americans, no less than Euro-Americans, pursued their own diplomatic and military strategies to secure their own interests. Indeed, the very terms "Native American" and "Euro-American" lose much

[91] Daniel Richter, *Facing East from Indian Country: A Native History of Early America* (Cambridge, MA, 2001). Francis Jennings's pathbreaking book, *The Invasion of America: Indians, Colonists, and the Cant of Conquest* (Chapel Hill, NC, 1975), was one of the first works to offer scholars an alternative perspective on the implications of the European entry into North America, and the subsequent emergence of the so-called "new Indian history" discussed in this essay owes a great debt to this provocative approach. For the more immediate era of the American Revolution, see Jennings's essay "The Indians' Revolution," in Alfred F. Young, ed., *The American Revolution: Explorations in the History of American Radicalism* (DeKalb, IL, 1976), 319–48. For an overview of Jennings's impact on the field, see Kirsten Fischer, "In Retrospect: The Career of Francis Jennings," *Reviews in American History* 30 (2002): 517–29. The most comprehensive single study of Indians in the Revolutionary era, with a primary focus on the years 1775–83, is Colin Calloway, *The American Revolution in Indian Country: Crisis and Diversity in Native American Communities* (Cambridge, UK, 1995). I have chosen to highlight Richter's work at the outset, however, to locate the Revolution within a longer history of Native American and Euro-American affairs.

[92] For valuable perspectives on Native Americans as historical actors, see Richard White, "Using the Past: History and Native American Studies," in Russell Thornton, ed., *Studying Native America: Problems and Prospects* (Madison WI, 1998), 217–43; and Shepard Krech III, *The Ecological Indian: Myth and History* (New York, 1999), 15–28.

of their meaning: there are no monoliths in this picture, no culturally cohesive forces that can even be labeled "French" or "British" or "Iroquois" or "Algonquian," no consistent strategy or approach that could constitute a coherent policy on anyone's part. Throughout the first two-thirds of the eighteenth century, the various periods of war and peace that have typically been defined by the fractious and always fragile relationships among the major contestants on the European continent—Queen Anne's War, the War of Jenkins's Ear, King George's War, the Seven Years' War—were not at all solely European in origin. They were also "indigenously *North American*," Richter notes, in the sense that they emerged from the welter of long-standing alliances and rivalries that had existed for years among Native peoples. These enduring but often unstable relationships provided inviting ground for the intervention of European powers, with their unwieldy armies and unruly colonists. Once Euro-Americans ventured away from the colonial strongholds along the coastal regions, however, they entered an interior that had long been hotly contested terrain; the newcomers then found themselves playing a dangerous game in which they could not dictate the terms of engagement or even determine the identity of the enemy.

In many instances, Native people knew better how to play the game to their own advantage; those who did so most successfully and consistently, Richter explains, were those who best "capitalized on their geographic position, their economic and military value to European governors, and their decentralized political systems to keep their options open, to maintain connections with more than one imperial power, and thus to maintain their cultural and political autonomy."[93] Indeed, Richter argues, "coexistence in the imperial world remained possible because the interests of at least *some* groups in the British, French, and Spanish colonies coincided with those of at least *some* Indians *some* of the time."[94] The repeated use of "some" in that sentence underscores the specificity, contingency, and impermanence of the intra- and intercultural relationships. On the whole, the picture that emerges is one in which no single entity, Native American or Euro-American, could define the course of events, much less assert control or gain a complete victory.

[93] Richter, *Facing East*, 164.

[94] Ibid., 182; emphasis added. For a brief but broad-reaching survey of all the imperial players in North America, see Gregory Evans Dowd, "Wag the Imperial Dog: Indians and Overseas Empires in North America, 1650–1776," in Philip Joseph Deloria and Neal Salisbury, eds., *A Companion to American Indian History* (London, 2004), 46–67.

That notion of uncertain or incomplete victory posits a third important point, particularly for the purposes of this essay: taking the view from Indian country also redefines the timeline to locate the American War for Independence along a more extensive continuum of inter- and intracultural conflicts, some of which can rightly be called Indian independence movements. In fact, we can begin to see that the American Revolution was not as much a sharply defined watershed in Native American history as it was in Anglo-American history. Rather, it could be called the beginning of a "Twenty Years' War," as Colin Calloway has put it, running forward at least as far as the Treaty of Grenville in 1795, or, to take the even more extensive frame of reference some other scholars have suggested, the continuation of a "Long War" that began in the middle of the eighteenth century and ran well into the early decades of the nineteenth.[95] We can hardly understand the significance of the Revolution in Indian country—much less the significance of Indians to the Revolution's outcome—without looking at the decades before and after the competing British and American forces first fired on each other at Lexington and Concord.

In the process of offering a useful way of looking at history, *Facing East from Indian Country* also offers a valuable perspective on important developments in writing Native American history. Richter's book is a cogent and coherent synthesis of the "new Indian history," an approach that first gained scholarly attention in the 1970s and then generated a burst of important work in the 1980s and '90s.[96] The impact of that scholarship was

[95] Calloway, *American Revolution in Indian Country*, 288–89. For examples of the "Long War" perspective, see John J. Bukowczyk, Nora Faires, David R. Smith, and Randy William Widdis, *Permeable Border: The Great Lakes Basin as Transnational Region, 1650–1990* (Pittsburgh, 2005), 23–28, in which Bukowczyk defines the period from 1763 to 1815 as the "Long War" for the interior. Francois Furstenberg likewise writes of the "Long War for the West" in "The Significance of the Trans-Appalachian Frontier in Atlantic History," *American Historical Review* 113 (2008): 647–77.

[96] In addition to the works by Francis Jennings, cited in note 91, significant early works in the "new Indian history" include Neal Salisbury, *Manitou and Providence: Indians, Europeans, and the Making of New England, 1500–1663* (Oxford, UK, 1982), and several books by James Axtell: *The European and the Indian: Essays in the Ethnohistory of Colonial North America* (Oxford, UK, 1981), *The Invasion Within: The Contest of Cultures in Colonial North America* (Oxford, UK, 1985), *After Columbus: Essays in the Ethnohistory of Colonial North America* (Oxford, UK, 1988), *Beyond 1492: Encounters in Colonial North America* (Oxford, UK, 1992), *The Indians' New South: Cultural Change in the Colonial Southeast* (Baton Rouge, LA, 1997), and *Natives and Newcomers: The Cultural Origins of North America* (Oxford, UK, 2001). Other books that helped define the "new Indian history" in the 1980s and '90s are, in addition to the works cited in notes 97 and 98, Ramon Gutierrez, *When Jesus Came, the Corn Mothers Went Away: Marriage, Sexuality, and Power in New Mexico, 1500–1846* (Stanford, CA, 1991); Gregory Evans Dowd, *A Spirited Resistance: The North*

becoming clear a decade before Richter's book came into print. In 1990, one of the profession's most prominent awards, the Bancroft Prize, went to James Merrell for his first book, *The Indians' New World*. For over forty years, since the Bancroft Prize had first been awarded in 1948, no book on Native American history had previously been accorded such recognition. Between 1990 and 2009, six other books dealing with Indians in early America received the Bancroft Prize.[97] At the same time, Cambridge University Press began a new series under the co-editorship of Frederick Hoxie and Neal Salisbury, the Cambridge Studies in North American Indian History, which has produced several significant books that address the period encompassing the American Revolution.[98] Indeed, the study of the Revolution now encompasses a much larger collection of players and places, and the history of the new nation has to include many of the nations in Indian country.

No volume of the Cambridge Studies has had a more dramatic impact than the first in the series, Richard White's *The Middle Ground*, a powerful book that has become a scholarly landmark since its publication in 1991. Looking specifically at the broad region of the Great Lakes, what the French called the *pays d'en haut*, White explores the strategies of accommodation developed by the various peoples who lived there in the eighteenth century

---

American Indian Struggle for Unity (Baltimore, 1991); and Michael McConnell, *A Country Between: The Upper Ohio Valley and Its Peoples, 1724–1744* (Lincoln, NE, 1992). Two important anthologies offer a valuable overview of the field: Daniel K. Richter and James H. Merrell, eds., *Beyond the Covenant Chain: The Iroquois and Their Neighbors in Indian North America, 1600–1800* (Syracuse, NY, 1987); and Peter C. Mancall and James Hart Merrell, eds., *American Encounters: Natives and Newcomers from European Contact to Indian Removal, 1500–1850* (New York, 2000).

[97] The Bancroft-winning books are, in chronological order, James H. Merrell, *The Indians' New World: Catawbas and Their Neighbors from European Contact through the Era of Removal* (Chapel Hill, NC, 1989); Jill Lepore, *The Name of War: King Philip's War and the Origins of American Identity* (New York, 1998); James H. Merrell, *Into the American Woods: Negotiators on the American Frontier* (New York, 1999); James F. Brooks, *Captives and Cousins: Slavery, Kinship, and Community in the Southwest Borderlands* (Chapel Hill, 2001); Alan Gallay, *The Indian Slave Trade: The Rise of English Empire in the American South, 1670–1717* (New Haven, CT, 2001); Peter Silver, *Our Savage Neighbors: How Indian War Transformed Early America* (New York, 2007); and Pekka Hämäläinen, *The Comanche Empire* (New Haven, CT, 2008).

[98] The Cambridge Studies in North American Indian History began in 1991 with the publication of Richard White's *The Middle Ground: Indians, Empires, and Republics in the Great Lakes Region, 1650–1815* (Cambridge, UK, 1991), which is discussed in the next pages. Other books in the Cambridge series relevant to the Revolutionary era include Calloway's *The American Revolution in Indian Country*, cited in note 91; Eric Hinderaker, *Elusive Empires: Constructing Colonialism in the Ohio Valley, 1673–1800* (1997); Claudio Saunt, *A New Order of Things: Property, Power, and the Transformation of Creek Indians, 1733–1816* (1999); and John P. Bowes, *Exiles and Pioneers: Eastern Indians in the Trans-Mississippi West* (2007).

—most significantly Algonquian-speaking Indians and French-speaking Europeans, along with several Iroquoian- and English-speaking groups as well—and, equally important, the ambiguities that often enveloped them all. "The middle ground," White explains, "is the place in between: in between cultures, peoples, and in between empires and a nonstate world of villages, . . . a place where many of the North American subjects and allies of empires lived." As much as people in the *pays d'en haut* searched for the common meaning that would make mutual understanding possible, they also engaged in what White calls a "process of creative, and often expedient, misunderstandings" of the other culture, seeking to "justify their own actions in what they perceived to be their partner's cultural premises." By acknowledging the needs of others, even in an attempt to turn them to their own advantage, the many players in the eighteenth-century *pays d'en haut* created innovative modes of mutual understanding, "the shared meanings and practices of the middle ground."[99]

That is not to say that accommodation obviated, much less eradicated, violence. The middle ground became a very bloody ground at times, a scene not only of mass ambush, attack, and battle but of individual murder, rape, and retribution. Still, White's emphasis draws our attention to less fearsome forms of interaction: economic exchange, diplomatic concession, and subtle shifts of position made it possible for people of different cultures to communicate, cooperate, and coexist—at least in periods of comparative peace that separated the more deadly dramas of frontier warfare. Instead of portraying the eighteenth-century Great Lakes region as a violently contested territory inhabited by winners and losers, *The Middle Ground* offers an alternative means of measuring success, much more in terms of compromise, reciprocity, and survival.

White's book made an immediate impression on the academic community. Richter rated it one of those rarest of books, a work that "articulates a vision toward which scholars have been struggling and defines a framework for future research . . . and give[s] names to phenomena that otherwise remain amorphous."[100] Indeed, the name it gave to the phenomenon of accommodation, "middle ground," quickly became a byword in the profession. Colin Calloway also predicted that the term would "surely remain part of the lexicon of interethnic relations," and he was right. Seldom has

[99] White, *Middle Ground*, x, 52.

[100] Daniel Richter, review of *The Middle Ground*, by Richard White, *William and Mary Quarterly*, 3d ser. 49 (1992): 715–17, quotation at 715.

one book—indeed, one book title—had such widespread success in establishing a simple shorthand expression for a very complicated situation.[101]

Shorthand, of course, can often lead to imprecision, and "middle ground" has run the risk of lending itself to loose interpretation and facile application to too many situations. Richter warned of "the possibility that future scholars, less subtle and careful than White, may become so enamored of the middle ground and its possibilities for accommodation between natives and invaders that they lose track of the underlying power relationships and conflict that made the ground so fragile."[102] Other historians have in fact become careful to make scholarly distinctions, even disclaimers and dissents, as they have made a bow to the middle ground. Gregory Evans Dowd has noted that not every zone of intercultural contact gave evidence of the kind of accommodation that White found in the *pays d'en haut*. "Middle grounds," he argues, may have been the exceptions, "unusual, isolated, and fleeting in eastern North America."[103] Alan Taylor, while expressing a respectful debt to White's notion of the middle ground, notes that scholars need to take into consideration "variations in geographic and temporal emphasis." In his book on upstate New York in the post-Revolutionary era, he adopts the term "divided ground" to indicate that the practice of mutual accommodation had passed in that region, and the best remaining tactic of the Native people was to "cope with an invasion of settlers, coming in great and growing numbers to divide the land into farms, reservations, and nations."[104] On the other hand, Kathleen DuVal cautions against assuming too easily that "Native Americans *wanted* to construct middle grounds with Europeans. In reality, only relatively weak people desired the kind of compromises inherent in the middle ground." Stronger Indian groups—such as the ones she studies, the Osage, Quapaw, and other Indian groups of the Arkansas Valley—did not concern themselves so much with developing diplomatic relations with Europeans for the sake of those relationships alone; rather, they used their connections

[101] Colin G. Calloway, "Native American History and the Search for Common Ground," *Reviews in American History* 20 (1992): 447–52. As Andrew Cayton and Fredrika Teute have pointed out, White's "conceptual framework became one of the most widely imitated in early American history." See "Introduction: On the Connection of Frontiers," in Cayton and Teute, eds., *Contact Points*, 1–15, quotation at 9.

[102] Richter, review of *Middle Ground*, 716.

[103] Gregory Evans Dowd, "'Insidious Friends': Gift Giving and the Cherokee-British Alliance in the Seven Years' War," in Cayton and Teute, *Contact Points*, 114–50, quotation at 118n. 3.

[104] Alan Taylor, *The Divided Ground: Indians, Settlers, and the Northern Borderland of the American Revolution* (New York, 2006), 11.

with Europeans "to gain an advantage in their more pressing foreign relations, those with other powerful native peoples." Indeed, by emphasizing the primacy of relations between Native groups and downplaying the focus on the Euro-American role, DuVal leads us to understand that in many cases, the middle ground could better be seen as "Native ground."[105]

In 2006, the *William and Mary Quarterly* published a forum titled "The Middle Ground Revisited," a clear indication of the continuing scholarly impact of White's book fifteen years after its original publication, but also an opportunity for further scholarly refinement of the notion of the "middle ground."[106] Several contributors to the *WMQ* forum raised challenges to the wider applicability of the middle-ground approach to other regions, and even to its specific application to the *pays d'en haut* itself, but White declined to defend the broad applicability of the concept. Instead, he reminded the *Quarterly*'s readers that he was only the author of the book, not the arbiter of its interpretation by others. Since its publication, *The Middle Ground* had "taken on something of a life of its own," he observed, and had generated perhaps as many "creative misunderstandings" among modern scholars as among the people of the *pays d'en haut* in the eighteenth century. "So, do I think that the middle ground as a process is replicable in other places and other times?" White asked rhetorically. "Yes, I do. Is every instance where academics find this process at work the equivalent of the Upper Country? No, but sometimes other academics might think so." In the end, White took a sensible position: "I have absolutely no desire to become chief judge in the court of the middle ground."[107]

Still, whatever the misuse and misgivings one might find in the work of those "other academics," there is no denying the power of the "middle ground" as an intellectually innovative notion. It redirected historians' approach away from what had so long and so easily been defined as "colonial" history, with its thinly covered assumption that the presence and persistence and power of the eighteenth-century Europeans colonizers established the longer teleological trajectory of American (or, more specifically, United States) history. Considering early American history from the vantage point of the middle ground does not change the eventual outcome, of course, but it does challenge historians to appreciate the complexity of

[105] Kathleen DuVal, *The Native Ground: Indians and Colonists in the Heart of the Continent* (Philadelphia, 2006), 5, 183.

[106] "The Middle Ground Revisited," *William and Mary Quarterly*, 3d. ser. 63 (2006): 3–96.

[107] Richard White, "Creative Misunderstandings and New Understandings," *William and Mary Quarterly*, 3d. ser. 63 (2006): 9–14, quotation at 10.

its unfolding.[108] Where the standard story pointed toward the inevitability of westward-moving nation-making, the notion of the middle ground has complicated that aspect of the master narrative: by underscoring the importance of context and contingency, and suggesting the possibility of alternative intercultural arrangements, it gave greater attention to temporally specific, locally focused relationships rather than to linear-seeming, long-term results.

The emphasis on the local has become especially evocative in several studies of Indian-European diplomacy, in which scholars have directed our attention to the nuance of negotiation, the rituals of diplomatic discourse, the necessity of concessions to cross-cultural custom, and even the subtle suggestions of dress and self-decoration.[109] No matter what the grand designs of longer-term strategy, neither side could dictate, much less dominate, the treaty-making process. Coming together on a rough woodland meeting ground rather than around a conference table in an elegant hall of state, representatives of competing peoples met face to face, exchanging gifts, making speeches, sharing food and drink, and generally creating a visual, auditory, and olfactory experience that had as much to do with theater as with diplomacy.

To make sense of it all—and of each other—the participants often relied on intercultural intermediaries, of whom James Merrell's portrait of the *métis* Andrew Montour provides an instructive case study. Montour, "a multilingual man from a mixed family of Iroquois and French folk," became a notable negotiator on the Pennsylvania frontier in the early 1740s and played a prominent go-between role for three decades. Wearing an eclectic combination of European clothing and Indian tattoos and jewelry, demonstrating familiarity with rituals and religious rites on both sides of the cultural divide, and fashioning an individual identity between the two, he "sent out mixed signals," Merrell observes, but he also proved to be a "very useful Person" in diplomatic councils. To a degree, that cultural

[108] Cayton and Teute, "Introduction," 9.

[109] See especially Merrell, *Into the American Woods* and "'The Cast of His Countenance': Reading Andrew Montour," in Hoffman, Sobel, and Teute, eds., *Through a Glass Darkly*, 13–39; Timothy J. Shannon, *Indians and Colonists at the Crossroads of Empire: The Albany Congress of 1754* (Ithaca, NY, 2000) and "Dressing for Success on the Mohawk Frontier: Hendrick, William Johnson, and the Indian Fashion," *William and Mary Quarterly*, 3d ser. 53 (1996): 13–42; Jane T. Merritt, *At the Crossroads: Indians and Empires on a Mid-Atlantic Frontier, 1700–1763* (Chapel Hill, NC, 2003) and "Metaphor, Meaning, and Misunderstanding: Language and Power on the Pennsylvania Frontier," in Cayton and Teute, eds., *Contact Points*, 60–87.

confusion enhanced Montour's status as an intermediary, enabling him to understand the men speaking for both sides, to translate the talk between them, and sometimes even to put words into their mouths. Yet this elusive, elastic, and ambiguous identity turned out to be as much a curse as a blessing, Merrell concludes, making Montour not only a middleman but an odd man out: "Trying to be both Indian and European, Montour ended up being neither." In that sense, he represents not so much a human manifestation of the middle ground as the embodiment of the "deep fissure between Indian and colonial worlds." Instead of pointing toward a hopeful future of intercultural cooperation, Montour and other intermediaries like him can sometimes stand as symbols of the failure, even refusal, of Indians and Europeans to turn treaties into lasting peace.[110]

8. Eighteenth-Century American Empires

As much as the focus on the middle ground has helped us understand the nuances of negotiation at the local level, it has also sharpened our perception of intercultural diplomacy at the loftier plane of imperial policy. The European negotiators who met their Indian counterparts face to face on the treaty ground also represented unseen officials in distant places, policymakers whose task it was to make the map of the North American continent fit their respective national interests and vision. In that regard, historians of pre-Revolutionary treaty negotiations find the most consistent, and ultimately most significant, failure of vision to have been on the Anglo-American side. Indeed, one of the tragic ironies of eighteenth-century American history is that the imperial powers that ultimately proved most successful in exerting control over the continent—first Great Britain, then its post-Revolutionary successor, the new United States—also proved to be the least skilled when it came to making the most of the middle ground and the possibilities it offered.

To put in context the clumsiness of Anglo-American missteps, scholars frequently note the comparative diplomatic perspicacity of the French. Throughout the first six decades of the eighteenth century, the various French functionaries in the North American interior—missionaries, military men, merchants, and fur traders—had generally been able to establish a decent working relationship with Indians. On a very basic level, they had

[110] Merrell, "Cast of His Countenance," 19, 26, 39; Merrell, *Into the American Woods*, 294.

to. The French did not come in large numbers to occupy territory and establish permanent settler colonies, and by midcentury, they had only seventy thousand inhabitants scattered widely throughout the North American interior, compared to some 1.5 million British-American colonists concentrated along the eastern seaboard. Lacking colonists, the French made concessions to necessity.[111] They certainly seemed better able to appreciate the literal give-and-take of Indian affairs, the expectations of exchange, both verbal and material, that undergirded diplomacy.

The picture that emerges of the British, on the other hand, makes them appear much less accommodating and therefore much less accomplished in their diplomatic approach. When their victory in the Seven Years' War sharply decreased the French weight in the European balance of power, the British victors took a more aggressive stance that seemed to change the rules of the North American interior. Their sizable population was poised to pour into the trans-Appalachian region, and no one on the ground seemed especially concerned about protecting Indian interests. "With the French expelled from North America," Jane Merritt explains, "Indians could no longer use the competition between nations to extract favorable terms from treaties. Forced to fight or negotiate with the British alone, Indians gave up the flexibility and accommodation formerly possible on a loosely structured and ungoverned frontier."[112]

General Jeffrey Amherst, the main British military commander who sought to impose a British structure on the frontier, could hardly be said to have brought flexibility to his negotiating approach. Operating, as Fred Anderson explains, "in the name of rationality and economy," Amherst rapidly reversed longstanding traditions of frontier reciprocity, frustrating and infuriating Indians with his inflexible restrictions on trade and gift-giving. Anderson seeks to explain Amherst's approach as "no more an act of caprice than it was an expression of arrogance." Rather, he argues, Amherst acted as "a conscientious European soldier" who, "for reasons perfectly understandable in terms of his own culture, . . . sought to reform Indian relations without fully understanding why they functioned as they did."[113] Other scholars are considerably less charitable. Amherst suffered from the "imperial delusion," as Taylor puts it, that he could somehow

[111] Alan Taylor, *American Colonies* (New York, 2002) 425–28; Fred Anderson, *Crucible of War: The Seven Years' War and the Fate of Empire in British North America, 1754–1766* (New York, 2000), 454.

[112] Merritt, *At the Crossroads*, 304.

[113] Anderson, *Crucible of War*, 455.

suddenly exert military control over the complex patterns of coexistence in Indian country.[114] White portrays Amherst as an unbending general who rejected conciliation in favor of a foolish confidence in the prospect that British conquest would render the Indians mere subjects of the Crown. Forsaking the practice of reciprocity for a position of racial superiority, he immediately curtailed the customs of mutual respect that had formerly accompanied diplomatic relations and symbolized accommodation. "It was a view," White concludes, "that abolished the middle ground."[115]

Yet for all the errors inherent in Amherst's judgment, British policy cannot be reduced to the single simplistic position he embodied. Concerned officials in the British Board of Trade, to their credit, began to see the problems inherent in Amherst's arrogance, and to their dismay, they also realized that their military resources would be far too sparse to assert authority over so vast a region. Thus they tried to restore more equitable relations with the Indians in the interior, hoping to revive some of the middle-ground diplomatic practices that had seemed to work for the French earlier in the century. Particularly in light of the pan-Indian uprising that swept the *pays d'en haut* in 1763 (commonly, but erroneously, called Pontiac's Rebellion), British policymakers suddenly understood the wisdom and necessity of accommodating Native interests—and thereby, they hoped, protecting their own.[116]

Patrick Griffin has provided a fresh interpretation of the way that accommodationist approach first and most famously manifested itself in the Proclamation Line of 1763, the flawed and futile attempt to stop colonial expansion by mapping a cultural boundary along the Appalachian range. This ultimately ineffective measure still deserves serious consideration, not so much for its regulatory effect as for its cultural assumptions. As Griffin explains in *American Leviathan*, a book about late eighteenth-century struggles along the Appalachian frontier, the Proclamation Line represented an expression of "stadial theory," which was gaining influence among some British officials in the 1760s. As put forth by the Scottish Enlightenment thinker Francis Hutcheson, stadial theory posited that all human beings—even apparent "savages" in Ireland, the West Indies, or North America—had the innate moral sense that could allow them to rise through stages of development and become decently civilized, or enough

[114] Taylor, *American Colonies*, 434.

[115] White, *Middle Ground*, 256–57.

[116] For a comprehensive study of this conflict, see Gregory Evans Dowd, *War under Heaven: Pontiac, the Indian Nations, and the British Empire* (Baltimore, 2002).

so, at least, to coexist with the British. The assumptions underlying this sort of thinking were certainly ethnocentric, defining the stages of civilization in terms that led to eighteenth-century England, but at least they could accommodate non-British peoples in a long-term cultural climb. In the short term for North America, however, particularly in the immediate aftermath of the Seven Years' War, the adherents of this approach argued that any hope for future coexistence would depend, at least for the time being, on a separate existence between Native Americans and Euro-Americans. Thus they insisted that the two groups of supposed subjects should live on opposite sides of the Appalachians. Setting aside the trans-Appalachian region for Indians also enabled imperial policymakers to set aside the hostile-seeming assumptions of men such as Amherst and take a more patient and peaceful approach toward the Native peoples in the interior. Moreover, trying to keep aggressive settlers east of the Proclamation Line enabled them to maintain some hope of holding on to their newly won territories in the interior, giving them what Griffin calls "a conceptual fig leaf for peace" that could cover up their paltry power.[117]

Given the vicious hostility that had already come to permeate the erstwhile middle ground, this feeble-seeming attempt on the part of the British government to replace the French "Father" with their own paternal protection may have seemed far too little and much too late. The Proclamation Line never really worked, of course, creating only disdain on the part of white settlers and doubt among Indians. As aggressive Euro-American intruders ignored the Proclamation Line and pushed across the mountains seemingly without restraint, they did not by any means come into the region to share a middle ground with Native peoples. Facing east at this unwanted surge of newcomers, Indians were not at all willing to welcome them. On the other hand, as Taylor points out, the British at least looked better in Indian eyes than their colonial counterparts, and the British took a more positive view of Indians as well. Recognizing the unfettered resistance of land-hungry settlers to the feckless restraints of British authority, the more enlightened British officials began to understand that they might in fact find better allies among the Indians. To be sure, with such a late start and with such a dubious background, the British would never be especially skilled or successful in their dealings with Native peoples, but their attempts to recognize Indian interests did give them a credible

[117] Patrick Griffin, *American Leviathan: Empire, Nation, and Revolutionary Frontier* (New York, 2007), 19–45, quotation at 45.

advantage over their own colonists. When they faced those colonists in war, their standing with Indians became a significant factor in their ability to withstand the challenge of their former Anglo-American allies.[118] Thus the *inter*cultural considerations of Indian engagement help clarify the *intra*cultural implications of the growing division between the British government and its American colonists. In that regard, the "new Indian history" has created an important context for understanding the diplomatic history of the American Revolution.

The question, though, is how the American Revolution contributes to understanding Native American diplomatic history. Facing east to the Revolution, we first have to acknowledge how little the ideological and political issues that came to divide those erstwhile Anglo-American allies mattered to the inhabitants of Indian country. Native people had no need for the nuances of whig ideology: they did not become caught up in the radical colonists' contrast of tyranny and liberty, nor were they moved much by the British claims to constitutional legitimacy or assertions of royal authority. What mattered most to them was the continuing and apparently increasing presence of aggressive antagonists in their homelands and, above all, the devastation it commonly brought to their villages. No less than British-Americans, Native Americans valued both autonomy and community, and for that reason historians now direct our attention to an Indian war for independence within the context of—and largely as a consequence of—the American War for Independence.[119]

When the British-American people brought this new war into the interior, Indians faced an old choice, to make an alliance with the lesser of the two evils, whichever side that may be. For most Native peoples this time, that appeared to be the British—even if, in the long run, not by much.[120] In fact, no matter which side Indians allied with, they received little reward for their efforts. The American War for Independence again gave some Indian groups some ability to exercise some measure of independence of their own in choosing between neutrality and engagement, but in almost all parts of the interior touched by the war, the struggle between white people brought death and devastation to Indian people. Colin Calloway has aptly summarized the consequences in one comprehensive

[118] Taylor, *American Colonies*, 437.

[119] Gregory H. Nobles, *American Frontiers: Cultural Encounters and Continental Conquest* (New York, 1997), 89; Calloway, *American Revolution in Indian Country*, 288–89; and Richter, *Facing East*, 216–35.

[120] Calloway, *American Revolution in Indian Country*, xiv–xv.

sentence: "Burned villages and crops, murdered chiefs, divided councils and civil wars, migrations, towns and forts choked with refugees, economic disruption, breaking of ancient traditions, losses in battle and to disease and hunger, betrayal to their enemies, all made the American Revolution one of the darkest periods in American Indian history."[121] Then, when the Euro-Americans' war was over and Great Britain and the United States signed the Treaty of Paris in 1783, the British backed away from the few alliances they had managed to forge, and the newly independent Americans assumed the stance General Amherst had taken two decades earlier, setting aside the delicate gestures of diplomacy in favor of high-handed estimations about their own power: the surrender of the British, they assumed, should likewise assure them of Indian surrender of the interior.[122] Writing about American-Iroquois relations in the Revolutionary era, Timothy Shannon observes that "the federal government followed the example set by the British Crown, administering Indian affairs through centralized offices rather than local, autonomous agents" and directing these administrative efforts not so much at diplomacy as at dispossession.[123] Alan Taylor concludes his survey of early American history by putting an important twist on Jefferson's hopeful-sounding term: the new "empire of liberty," he writes, would be "by and for the white citizenry."[124]

This reference to the "white citizenry" of the new American empire cannot be too easily taken for granted; indeed, it draws our attention to an increasingly important element in the diplomatic mix, the definition of "whiteness" and the larger question of race, an issue that is coming more sharply into focus in the study of the Revolution in Indian country. Scholars have long challenged the notion that the creation of racial categories and an ideology of racial superiority could be accepted as more or less inherent, much less "natural," responses to perceptions of difference between peoples. Instead, they more commonly consider ideas of race to be a form of social and political construction, a set of definitions that one group develops to distinguish itself from another. Nancy Shoemaker writes, for instance, of the ways Native Americans and Euro-Americans both "experimented with biological difference in an attempt to develop methods for discerning individual alliances." Of all the biological differences (not to

[121] Ibid., 272.

[122] On the Amherst-like arrogance of American negotiators, see Stephen Aron, *American Confluence: The Missouri Frontier from Borderland to Border State* (Bloomington, IN, 2006), 75.

[123] Shannon, *Indians and Colonists at the Crossroads of Empire*, 239.

[124] Taylor, *American Colonies*, 443.

mention similarities) Indians and Europeans could observe in each other, skin color increasingly came to be the most important—but only gradually so. "At the start of the eighteenth century," Shoemaker explains, "Indians and Europeans rarely mentioned the color of each other's skin. By mid-century, remarks about skin color and the categorization of peoples by simple color-coded labels (red, white, black) had become commonplace."[125] Shoemaker's emphasis on change over time reminds us that the growing practice of skin-color categorization was a historical process, and "discerning individual alliances" did not immediately lead to denigrating or discriminating against the other color. It is difficult to date with any precision, of course, the emergence of racism as a coherent category of belief, although most scholars would now point to the nineteenth century as the time when racist thought gained the most social currency. For that reason, argues Peter Silver, it can be intellectually lazy to apply the term "racist" to Euro-American attitudes toward Indians throughout most of the eighteenth century.[126]

The Revolutionary era, however, began to reveal what Silver defines as "a new rhetoric for decrying Indians that was genuinely worth calling racist."[127] He and other scholars point especially to the cultural effects of frontier warfare, in which vicious fighting and a sense of victimization generated among white settlers a growing tendency to see all Indians as the bogeymen who bore the responsibility for the worst depredations. Indeed, James Merrell finds the appearance of such sentiment fairly early in the century, in the late 1720s, with the tendency of some Pennsylvania colonists "to lump all Delawares, Iroquois, Shawnees, and the rest into one menacing mass." By midcentury, the white response to violence had become more pronounced, undermining the role of treaty negotiators: "Tales of Indian cruelty, spread by word of mouth and by provincial newspapers, made it harder to think kindly of natives," Merrell writes, and harder still to think optimistically about diplomacy and peace.[128] Patrick Griffin sees a similar escalation of racist sentiment in Revolutionary-era Pennsylvania, when frontier settlers discarded the last shreds of civility and attacked Indians with an intense vengeance, "killing women and scalping children."

[125] Nancy Shoemaker, *A Strange Likeness: Becoming Red and White in Eighteenth-Century North America* (Oxford, UK, 2004), 129, 139. See also Shoemaker, "How Indians Got to Be Red," *American Historical Review* 102 (1997): 624–44.

[126] Silver, *Our Savage Neighbors*, xxi.

[127] Ibid.

[128] Merrell, *Into the American Woods*, 167, 282.

"In 1763," he observes, "the slaughter of innocents at least raised eyebrows in the West. By 1783, it did not. . . . Racist violence, in other words, was becoming the new basis of society in the West."[129] John Grenier likewise underscores the vicious nature of warfare on the Revolutionary-era frontier and its implications for the future, noting that as the War for Independence was coming to an end in the East, "participants in the frontiersman-Indian struggle in the West made it clear that they still had scores to settle."[130] Gregory Knouff identifies an increasingly racist sentiment inherent in the unrestrained brutality of this war of no quarter: the more scalping, mutilation, and torture became common practices, the more patriots begin to equate "whiteness" with "Americanness." In the process, they also began to drop the linguistic distinction that separated, for instance, Mohawk from Shawnee and increasingly categorized Native peoples simply—"and ominously," he adds—as "Indians," undifferentiated from each other but clearly identified as nonwhite "Others," and decidedly not "Americans."[131]

Thus the incipient sense of a national identity depended, at least in part, on an enhanced sense of racial identity that gained salience, if not complete coherence, during the Revolutionary era. Some historians have even begun to draw a modern-day analogy to the term made infamous in the Balkans in the 1990s, "ethnic cleansing."[132] Seen in those terms, then, the notion of a "white citizenry" emerging from the Revolution carries much more meaning—and menace—than might first appear in passing.

With the emergence of that new American empire, Native peoples struggled to make sense of the new scenario. In the Ohio valley, Indians who faced the double disappointments of the recent war—the betrayal by the British, the arrogance of the Americans—formed new confederacies with former Indian enemies, making it clear that they would not easily cede the region to accommodate the territorial claims of the new nation. "No more than in the 1760s," Stephen Aron explains, "did Ohio valley Indians in the 1780s see themselves as having been conquered." Other Indian groups in the region chose to move away, usually west toward the Mississippi and

[129] Griffin, *American Leviathan*, 154.

[130] John Grenier, *The First Way of War: American War Making on the Frontier, 1607–1814* (Cambridge, UK, 2005), 161.

[131] Gregory T. Knouff, *The Soldiers' Revolution: Pennsylvanians in Arms and the Forging of Early American Identity* (University Park, PA, 2004), 162, 178–79.

[132] For the use of the term "ethnic cleansing," see Richter, *Facing East*, 190; and John Mack Faragher, "'More Motley than Mackinaw': From Ethnic Mixing to Ethnic Cleansing on the Lower Missouri, 1783–1833," in Cayton and Teute, eds., *Contact Points*, 304–26.

south of the Ohio River, hoping to find more peaceful environs without the presence of so many white settlers. Writing about what he calls the "confluence region" of the Ohio, Mississippi, and Missouri rivers, Aron has pointed to the "remapping" that took place in the wake of the Revolution, creating a need for continuing the patterns of intercultural accommodations and reconciliations that had earlier marked the middle ground to the north.[133] Beginning in the 1770s, the disruptions of war brought thousands of newcomers to the region, both Indians from the Ohio valley and Euro-Americans from the United States—along with, in an increasing number of cases, their African American slaves—adding new constituencies to an already complicated and conflicted area.

Yet migration did not constitute surrender of Indians' independent status or diplomatic skills. The old diplomatic possibilities of the pre-Revolutionary era may have become comparatively limited, but they did not by any means cease to exist. In some cases, in fact, they became even more delicate and diverse. Focusing attention on the Arkansas valley, an area just to the south of Aron's "confluence region," Kathleen DuVal describes how the increasing immigration of Chickasaws, Choctaws, and Cherokees in the 1770s and 1780s, followed by the arrival of Delawares, Shawnees, Miamis, Abenakis, and some Illinois, significantly altered the political landscape for the main Native groups that had long been dominant there, the Osages and Quapaws. The presence of people of European origin—not just unruly newcomers from the United States but remaining Spanish and French colonists and officials and even some still-lingering British traders—further complicated the mix, creating a multiplicity of possible political alliances.

For the most part, the Quapaws exercised considerable diplomatic skill in this multicultural environment, using their relationships with the Spanish, the Chickasaws, and other Indian allies to counter the power of their Osage enemies: "The Quapaws shaped new Indians' and Europeans' impressions of the region and persuaded them that Quapaw approval and methods were essential to peace." DuVal's emphasis on shaping impressions and persuading potential allies underscores Indian agency in making these arrangements in their native ground, and not only on the part of the Quapaws: "Between 1763 and 1780," she writes, "the Quapaws and the Osages instructed Spanish officials in Indian expectations and power." She uses similar language to explain a later situation, when in 1803 the United

[133] Aron, *American Confluence*, 69–70, 75.

States presumed to purchase the larger Louisiana Territory from France, which had only recently acquired it from Spain: "As Jefferson determined to teach [Indians] how to live differently, the Osages and Quapaws set out to teach the United States that Indians held the power and would determine how their new friend would act."[134] Whatever the depth of mutual affection among these "new friends," DuVal's notion of the Indian instruction of Euro-American powers offers an important perspective on the intercultural outcome of the American Revolution, particularly in parts of Indian country that had not been immediately involved in the military intensity of the war. The real authority still resided with the longstanding Indian inhabitants of those regions, and any assertion of possession, much less of control, could be little more than a political conceit on the part of the new United States.

Writing about the "Comanche Empire" in Texas, for instance, Pekka Hämäläinen describes how this seemingly distant Indian power "profoundly shaped the history of European colonialism along the Mississippi valley" in the eighteenth century by forming "a daunting barrier against westward expansion—not of European colonial powers but of Osages, the most dominant Native people of the eastern Great Plains."[135] Indeed, although not directly involved in the American Revolution, the Comanches launched their own raids against Spanish outposts in Texas in the late 1770s and early 1780s and thus "deprived Texas of a major source of imports just as Spain's involvement in the American Revolution began to generate material shortages throughout the empire."[136] In general, Comanches not only promoted their own interests over other Indians but also had an impact on the ability of the Euro-American powers—including, by the turn of the nineteenth century, the United States—to assert their imperial will in the region. The point applies not only to the immediate case of Comancheria but to the larger picture of intercultural competition on a larger geographical scale. By looking at Indians as well as Euro-Americans as "full-fledged historical actors who played a role in the making of early America," Hämäläinen observes, "the colonization of the Americas is now seen as a dialectic process that created new worlds for all involved."[137]

[134] DuVal, *Native Ground*, 183. On the intercultural impact of the Louisiana Purchase, see also Peter J. Kastor, *The Nation's Crucible: The Louisiana Purchase and the Creation of America* (New Haven, CT, 2004), 32–34.

[135] Hämäläinen, *Comanche Empire*, 357.

[136] Ibid., 98–99.

[137] Ibid., 6.

The point here is not to try to explain, much less untangle, all the intricate (and typically impermanent) intra- and intercultural relationships in the regions far beyond the more familiar geographical context of the American Revolution. Clearly, scholars of the "new Indian history" have already done that well enough in a number of specific studies, and the number seems quite likely to increase, especially given an increasing emphasis on regions west of the Mississippi in the eighteenth and early nineteenth centuries.[138] The American Revolution was much more than a political process or war or even a social movement that concerned only people living in the thirteen British-American colonies. It had a dramatic impact on a much larger, much more diverse, and much more widespread population in North America.

Where, then, does facing east from Indian country leave us? It leaves us looking in all directions, in fact, opening the Revolution up in terms of space to see the changing world from the perspective (or perspectives, plural) of Native peoples. We can now discern new ways to conceptualize different parts of the North American map, from the Atlantic coast to the "middle ground" of the Old Northwest, down to the "confluence region" of the rivers that flowed into the Mississippi River and eventually to the Gulf of Mexico, then westward into regions on the far side of the Mississippi, certainly as far as the Comanche empire. It leaves us looking at a more complex picture of the many peoples who defined the issues and dictated the action. We have to consider not just the putative policymakers on both sides of the cultural divide—the chiefs and military officers and political officials—but also the people allegedly under their authority—young warriors on the Indian side, for instance, or traders, soldiers, and settlers on the Euro-American side—who often preferred conflict over peace and occasionally took significant steps on their own initiative.[139] Finally, it leaves us looking much farther back and ahead in time, extending the traditional chronological periodization beyond the bounds of 1763, 1775, or 1776 at one end and 1781, 1783, or 1789 at the other. The drama of the "long war,"

[138] In addition to Hämäläinen's *Comanche Empire*, other books that deal with Native Americans west of the Mississippi include Bowes, *Exiles and Pioneers*; Brooks, *Captives and Cousins*; and Juliana Barr, *Peace Came in the Form of a Woman: Indians and Spaniards in the Texas Borderlands* (Chapel Hill, NC, 2007).

[139] On the role of "unruly young men" in ignoring the authority of—and sometimes forcing the hands of—their more diplomatically minded leaders, see David Andrew Nichols, *Red Gentlemen and White Savages: Indians, Federalists, and the Search for Order on the American Frontier* (Charlottesville, VA, 2008); and John Craig Hammond, *Slavery, Freedom, and Expansion in the Early American West* (Charlottesville, VA, 2007).

of which the American Revolution was only a part, puts before us not only a larger ensemble of actors but also broader notions of some fundamental issues, including independence and the very meaning of liberty.

Within this expanded view of the larger period of conflict, the American victory in the Revolution clearly put the United States into the mix as a new imperial player. This self-celebratory "empire of liberty" also became an empire of property—and an empire in which the acquisition of land depended on a selective sense of liberty and a restrictive sense of race. From the first years of its existence, the United States began to chart a path of territorial growth that relied on an increasingly clear racial agenda, promoting the extension of slavery for African Americans and the exclusion, even ethnic cleansing, of Native Americans. Facing ahead into the nineteenth century from the end of the eighteenth, Daniel Richter offers a useful last word on the results of the Revolution: "It would take more than fifty years for White Americans to win, and Indian Americans to lose, their respective wars for independence, for events on the battlefield, in the conference hall, and on the treaty ground to recast eastern North America conclusively as a White rather than Indian country."[140]

IV. Reconsidering Class in the American Revolution

9. The Roots and Resurgence of Class Analysis

To talk about "White Americans" as the winning side raises another question about historical perspective, this one largely internal to white society itself. The near-monolithic identity implicit in the term might well make sense when we consider, as Native Americans and African Americans no doubt did, aggressive assertions of racial solidarity on the part of Euro-Americans, but it begins to break apart when we explore the conflicted relations among those white Americans themselves. If we see them as they saw each other, they seem anything but unified. Throughout the extended era of the Revolution—that is, essentially the second half of the eighteenth century—the history of Euro-American society reveals important patterns of underlying tension and recurring conflict, none more widespread and more far-reaching than that defined by class.

To talk about class conflict in the Revolutionary era, however, takes us immediately into an area of scholarly conflict in the modern era, in which

[140] Richter, *Facing East*, 191.

the nature, extent, and even existence of class consciousness in early America have been dissected, debated, and even denied. Class analysis had an especially difficult history in the middle of the twentieth century, when the reluctance of many American historians to talk in terms of class became common in the academic culture of the Cold War. Part of the reason had to do with a longstanding pragmatic tradition in American historical writing, which tended to value empiricism over theory, but it also reflected the larger political climate of the postwar era, which celebrated social consensus and American exceptionalism as an alternative to class conflict and socialism. The reigning historical orthodoxy reinforced an image of early America as an essentially classless, socially harmonious society, in which internal conflict was portrayed as muted and the notion of class consciousness all but meaningless.[141]

Yet it was not simply the culture or outcome of the Cold War that put class analysis on uncertain scholarly footing. Class, no less than capitalism, can be a much-contested term, and the very notion of class does not by any means assume a uniform understanding of, much less a scholarly prescription for, the importance of class analysis. Some scholars who do take class seriously as a category of analysis nonetheless remain reluctant to talk explicitly about class for an era that precedes the rise of industrial capitalism. Others have come to criticize class from an altogether different perspective, questioning it as a culturally skewed category that could obscure other equally important divisions in society. Historians of gender and race have often been critical of the existing studies of class because of the overemphasis on the experience of white, working-class men. Some have borrowed from postmodernist literary theory to challenge the significance of verbal contests about class, portraying them as a set of "discursive encounters" between different groups of white men: in that sense, so the argument goes, the language of class says more about the uses of language than about the true depth of class inequality.[142] In general, given the various sources

[141] For discussions of the postwar context of American historiography, see James A. Henretta, "Social History as Lived and Written," *American Historical Review* 84 (1979): 1293–1322, esp. 1306–8; Ronald Schultz, "A Class Society? The Nature of Inequality in Early America," in Carla Gardina Pestana and Sharon V. Salinger, eds., *Inequality in Early America* (Hanover, NH, 1999), 203–21; Greg Nobles, "Class," in Daniel Vickers, ed., *A Companion to Colonial America* (London, 2003), 259–87; Simon Middleton and Billy G. Smith, introduction to Middleton and Smith, eds., *Class Matters: Early North American and the Atlantic World* (Philadelphia, 2008), 1–15; and Gary Kornblith, "Introduction to the Symposium on Class in the Early Republic," *Journal of the Early Republic* 25 (2005): 523–26.

[142] Nobles, "Class," 262–63; Middleton and Smith, introduction to *Class Matters*, 5–8.

of uneasiness about the notion of class that became evident in both the political and the scholarly contexts of the past half century, it might seem surprising that class analysis still has any purchase in the profession, at least among scholars of early America.

But it does. As Simon Middleton and Billy Smith have put it, "class analysis of early North America and the Atlantic world is recovering from its wilted stage and is now enjoying a period of renewed growth."[143] Indeed, Middleton and Smith themselves have been active agents of that resurgence. First, they offered scholars of early American history an important opportunity for reinvigorating class analysis in 2003, when they organized a conference called "Class and Class Struggles in North America and the Atlantic World, 1500–1820," a gathering whose participants ranged from younger historians in the early stages of their careers to midcareer colleagues to a few longtime students of class. Meeting in an unlikely seeming location—a guest ranch in western Montana, about as far away as one could be from the sites of class struggles of the Revolutionary era—the scholars covered a remarkably wide range of topics, from slavery to sex to language to manners to middle-class formation, with the formal papers punctuated by powerful personal narratives from some of the senior scholars present. Almost all the papers presented at the conference found their way into print, either in a collection of essays edited by Middleton and Smith or in several prominent scholarly journals.[144] In fact, the quantity and quality of the work presented at the Montana conference was itself an indication that the study of class, however "wilted" it may have seemed at times, never really disappeared from the scholarly scene. Its apparent resurgence in the early years of the twenty-first century stemmed from work that had been going on in the latter part of the twentieth century, when scholars were not the only ones to notice that the culture of continuing economic expansion could not hide or diminish the deep social and economic inequalities inherent in American life.[145] As Gary Kornblith has noted, "even at the

[143] Middleton and Smith, introduction to *Class Matters*, 1–2.

[144] In addition to the essays that appeared in Middleton and Smith, eds., *Class Matters*, works from the Montana conference also appeared in special issues of *Labor: Studies in Working-Class History of the Americas* 1 (2004), *Early American Studies* 3 (2005), and *William and Mary Quarterly*, 3d ser. 63 (2006).

[145] The earlier work of one of the most senior participants in the conference, Staughton Lynd, has experienced a resurgence of its own, with the republication of two of his most influential books, his 1967 *Class Conflict, Slavery, and the United States Constitution*, with a foreword by Robin Einhorn (Cambridge, UK, 2009), and his 1968 *Intellectual Origins of American Radicalism*, with a foreword by David Waldstreicher (Cambridge, UK, 2009).

peak of American prosperity in the 1990s, critics warned that globalization benefited the few at the expense of the many. Once the New Economy bubble burst, class regained saliency as an analytical category both inside and outside the academy."[146]

Inside the academy, the current study of class in early American history still stands to a large degree on the foundation established by the emergence of the "new social history" in the late 1960s and early 1970s, with its creative innovations in looking at history on the local level and from the bottom up. The new social history had no single theory or methodology, James Henretta observed some years ago, "no single handbook or work of scholarship [that] decisively shaped its development." It did, however, draw on two approaches developed by scholars on the far side of the Atlantic in the middle of the twentieth century, the French *Annales* school and the English Marxists. With an increasing reliance on quantitative methods, the *Annalistes* sought to analyze not so much specific events but long-term trends, paying special attention to the overarching structural and chronological contexts that shaped people's lives. On the other hand, the English Marxist tradition—best embodied in the work of Christopher Hill, Eric Hobsbawm, George Rudé, and Edward Thompson—sought to emphasize human consciousness and behavior, especially as people in the lower classes challenged those above them in struggles over property and power. Both approaches have exerted considerable influence on the writing of early American history in the United States, first evident in an upsurge of quantitative studies of economic and social conditions at the local level and then with a growing emphasis on the agency of ordinary people, particularly in times of conflict—including, but by no means limited to, the era of the "long" American Revolution.[147]

Looking at that era from the perspective of the early twenty-first century, Seth Rockman has offered a valuable approach to thinking about class, particularly in light of some of the scholarly challenges it faced in the late twentieth century. The study of class in the early republic need not

[146] Kornblith, "Introduction to the Symposium on Class in the Early Republic," 524.

[147] Henretta, "Social History as Lived and Written," 1296–1306; see also Schultz, "A Class Society?" 205–6 ; Alfred F. Young, "How Radical Was the American Revolution?" in *Liberty Tree: Ordinary People and the American Revolution* (New York, 2006), 227–29. For a brief but broad view of the place of social history in American historiography, see Gary J. Kornblith and Carol Lasser, "More than Great White Men: A Century of Scholarship on American Social History," *OAH Magazine of History* 21 (2007): 8–13; this essay has also been published in James Banner, ed., *A Century of American Historiography* (New York, 2010).

depend on the existence of a fully developed factory system, because most people in the period, free and enslaved alike, worked in a wide variety of other ways. Neither does the study of class depend on obvious evidence of the agency on the part of people engaging in conscious collective action, much less defining themselves according to their class status over other forms of identity, including gender and race. The critical issue, rather, is the development of American capitalism, whose emergence enmeshed ordinary people of all sorts in "an economy whose currents flowed from overlapping systems of inequality and created different vulnerabilities and possibilities for people of different racial status, sex, age, ethnicity, and legal condition."[148]

10. The Urban Context of Class

Not surprisingly, the significance of class has become especially evident in early American cities, where the comparatively large and diverse populations offer scholars the most obvious opportunities for exploring the emergence of economic inequality and class identity. A critical step in the study of urban social structure came in a pair of *William and Mary Quarterly* articles, one by James Henretta in 1965 and the other by Allan Kulikoff in 1971, that offered a sustained quantitative measure of the economic structure in Boston throughout the colonial era and on into the years after the Revolution. Together, both essays made a compelling case for increasing inequality in Boston over the course of the eighteenth century, resulting in the emergence of an unmistakable class structure that seemed even more pronounced at the end of the Revolutionary era. "Rich and poor were divided by wealth, ascribed status, and segregated living patterns," Kulikoff concluded, and a "class system based primarily on economic divisions slowly developed." The widespread embrace of democratic rhetoric in the wake of the Revolution might mitigate but it could not conceal the growing sense of class identity—and enmity—that was to come forth more fully in the nineteenth century.[149]

[148] Seth Rockman, "Class and the History of Working People in the Early Republic," *Journal of the Early Republic* 25 (2005): 527–35, quotation at 535. Rockman has put this approach to class analysis skillfully into play in *Scraping By: Wage Labor, Slavery, and Survival in Early Baltimore* (Baltimore, 2009).

[149] James A. Henretta, "Economic Development and Social Structure in Colonial Boston," *William and Mary Quarterly*, 3d ser. 22 (1965): 75–92; Allan Kulikoff, "The Progress of Inequality in Revolutionary Boston," *William and Mary Quarterly*, 3d ser. 28 (1971): 375–412, quotation at 411.

Then, in 1979, Gary Nash's monumental study *The Urban Crucible* gained near-classic status almost as soon as it came into print, and it still remains one of the most important comparative works on urban America in the Revolutionary era.[150] As an appreciative scholar observed some twenty-five years after the book came into print, "Based on my listening to conference papers and reading articles over the years, my sense is that if Nash were to update *Urban Crucible* now his footnotes would balloon in length to almost comical proportions, but he would not have to correct too much of what he wrote over a quarter century ago."[151] The impact of Nash's book stemmed not just from its broad reach—parallel analyses of Boston, New York, and Philadelphia based on tax lists, inventories, and other sorts of evidence Henretta and Kulikoff had employed—but also from the depth of its inquiry into the political implications of social inequality of those cities, particularly the emerging manifestations of class tensions. People in the lower classes, in the process of living their lives in a context of recurring economic privation, "formed a picture of the social arrangements by which they lived," a picture, Nash concludes, that gave them a new and much less respectful perspective on the more powerful people at the top.[152]

Nash never inflated his claims for class identity in the cities. Indeed, he talked about the "laboring classes" in the plural, taking into account the social gradations that distinguished different sorts of working people—slaves and indentured servants at the bottom of the social ladder, mariners and other poorly paid laborers just above them, and different sorts of craftsmen, ranging from shoemakers and weavers in the lower ranks to more prosperous silversmiths and cabinetmakers near the top of the artisanal hierarchy. "There was, in short, no unified laboring class at any point in the period under study," he admitted at the outset. Still, he added, "that does not mean that class formation and the shaping of class consciousness was not happening in the era culminating with the American Revolution."[153] The self-conscious use of that double negative spoke to the necessary care with which Nash addressed the question of class in the cities, and he thus gave subsequent scholars a sensible basis for following his lead.

[150] Gary B. Nash, *The Urban Crucible: Social Change, Political Consciousness, and the Origins of the American Revolution* (Cambridge, MA, 1979).

[151] Shane White, "Founding Others," *Common-Place* 3 (2003), http://www.common-place.org/vol-03/no-04/reviews/white.shtml (accessed July 30, 2010).

[152] Nash, *Urban Crucible*, 384.

[153] Ibid., xii.

In the period that followed the publication of Nash's *Urban Crucible*, the scholarly literature on economic inequality and class relations in Revolutionary-era American cities has expanded our view of class relations in urban society, from artisans' shops to the waterfront and even out to sea. We now have a better understanding of the diversity of workers who constituted the laboring classes and, above all, the variability of their economic conditions. Taking the measure of economic inequality is not the same as taking the pulse of class-conscious activity, of course: poverty and politics can indeed be connected, but the connection is not always explicit, much less automatic. By the same token, talking about the "lower sort" or the "laboring classes" is not at all the same as talking about a, much less *the*, working class: the heterogeneous nature of the trades in eighteenth-century cities defies categorizing such different people in a such a generic group. Still, historians do acknowledge the ways the changing economic and political conditions surrounding the American Revolution heightened ordinary people's perceptions of their place in society, disrupting the status quo and requiring them to rethink their relationships with the elite leaders who governed the urban scene—and, to a significant degree, governed their lives. Members of the laboring classes developed a sense of themselves as interested and engaged participants in the radical political activity taking place in the cities, and during the Revolutionary era they emerged as an increasingly discernable force in shaping the nation's founding.

Coming over thirty years after Nash's *Urban Crucible*, Benjamin Carp's multi-city study of the urban scene in Revolutionary America, *Rebels Rising*, provided both an ambitious bookend to Nash's earlier book and a useful point of reflection on the scholarship that came between the two. With a focus on the coming of the Revolution and the mobilization of city dwellers in the incipient struggle, Carp argues that cities were "the places that made the Revolution possible." Looking at critical public spaces—the waterfront in Boston, churches in Newport, taverns in New York, the patriarchal household in Charleston, and the State House in Philadelphia—he posits two views of the social and political relationships in the five cities he studies. First, given the limited physical space, modest populations, and face-to-face familiarity common to colonial cities, he underscores the interdependence inherent in urban life. "Connected economically and politically, city dwellers had always depended on one another for their livelihoods," he points out, and over time, they had developed a sense of "civic consciousness, civic responsibility, and civic power." In the years leading up to the Revolution, the growing external threat posed by British imperial policy brought the "cities' panoply of interdependent groups" even closer together out of necessity, and "revolutionaries could harness this civic awareness in the service of resistance and revolt." Second, however, Carp notes that this civic interdependence had its limits, particularly in barriers defined largely by class. In one sense, those barriers were physical, the "walls, locked doors, and restricted areas" of certain churches, public houses, and political meeting places that kept the elite leadership of the cities insulated from ordinary folk, who inhabited the "shadow landscape" of the streets and other less refined spaces. But those barriers were social as well, defined by the inherent inequalities of gender, race, and class that not only left the majority of urbanites on the periphery of civic power but also gave them grievances of their own that they voiced over and above the Patriots' protests against imperial power. "The revolutionary movement was therefore both inclusive and exclusive," Carp argues: it created opportunities for some city dwellers, primarily poor and middling white men, to claim a place in the political limelight, even as "the propertied white men who led the Revolution were content to leave certain segments of society in the shadows."[154]

Nowhere in the shadows of the cities did the various manifestations of class identity become more politically apparent than in the taverns that occupied almost every corner, particularly in New York but in other cities as well. "There were more taverns in a colonial city than any other type of building besides houses," Carp notes, and as he and other scholars have repeatedly pointed out, the patrons of those public houses consumed prodigious amounts of rum and other potables, often becoming predictably rowdy as a result.[155] But drunkenness and disorderly behavior are not the main reasons that historians have begun to look into tavern culture in the cities. Instead, they have become attentive to the ways taverns played a role in providing a public space where men (and some, but comparatively few, women) could come together for conversation and debate. In the era leading up to the Revolution, the urban drinking establishment served as an important source of cross-class sociability and a locus of incipient protest.

[154] Benjamin Carp, *Rebels Rising: Cities and the American Revolution* (Oxford, UK, 2007), 3–22, quotations at 224, 4, 14–16.

[155] Ibid., 63–65. A much earlier work that explores alcohol consumption in early America is W. J. Rorabaugh, *The Alcoholic Republic: An American Tradition* (Oxford, UK, 1979). More recent works on tavern culture, all of which contribute to Carp's account, are David W. Conroy, *In Public Houses: Drink and the Revolution of Authority in Colonial Massachusetts* (Chapel Hill, NC, 1995); Peter Thompson, *Rum Punch and Revolution: Taverngoing and Public Life in Eighteenth-Century Philadelphia* (Philadelphia, 1999); and Sharon V. Salinger, *Taverns and Drinking in Early America* (Baltimore, 2002).

Members of different social classes, meeting in an indoor venue with much looser rules than they would find in the formal institutions of politics, spoke openly on the issues of the day, not just *with* each other but also *to* each other, engaging in a face-to-face exchange that challenged the conventions of socially acceptable speech. As Peter Thompson has put it, "tavern talk" represented a form of discourse that could be decidedly direct and undeferential, a socially looser form of speech that gave ordinary people a language to engage their alleged betters. In this more politically unfettered tavern environment, David Conroy observes, "republican concepts gripped men's imaginations and unleashed new levels of participation."[156] In that sense, it seems hardly surprising that taverns became significant nodes in the network of protest reaching across the colonies. Samuel Adams and other radical organizers in colonial cities and towns became "leaders who knew how to mobilize tipplers and taverngoers," Carp concludes, and they often located their committees of correspondence in public houses, where an increasingly politically literate clientele defined a critical connection to the larger community. Alcohol may have been the original main attraction of the tavern, but the personal associations also available there gave its patrons, organizers and ordinary people alike, the cross-class sociability that seemed much like solidarity on the eve of the Revolution.[157]

Yet these studies also suggest that the democratizing culture of the public house may already have peaked at that point. Once the galvanizing period of protest had passed, tavern culture began to lose some of its custom of social mixing, and the class segregation of such establishments became increasingly pronounced. Despite the democratic rhetoric of the Revolution, different types of drinking establishments began to attract different sorts of people, increasingly revealing a hierarchy of a socially defined clientele, from refined coffee-house customers at the top to a broader mix of mechanics and other taverngoing workers in the middle to the sailors, slaves, and other impoverished grog-shop drinkers at the lower end of society. Some upscale public houses served essentially as voluntary associa-

[156] Thompson, *Rum Punch and Revolution*, 75–110; Conroy, *In Public Houses*, 254. Looking beyond taverns to Philadelphia society in general, Nicole Eustace has suggested that the years preceding the Revolution saw a new and increasingly emotional sort of language forming a "spirit of liberty" that cut across classes and provided a rhetorical opening for greater equality, at least among white men; see Eustace, *Passion Is the Gale: Emotion, Power, and the Coming of the American Revolution* (Chapel Hill, NC, 2008), esp. 385–437. On the sociability of Revolutionary-era men, see Sarah Knott, "Sensibility and the American War for Independence," *American Historical Review* 109 (2004): 19–40.

[157] Carp, *Rebels Rising*, 98.

tions, self-consciously enclosed male spaces where successful and socially aspiring men could practice polite behavior and thus seek to promote personal as well as civic improvement. Other taverns operated as much more raucous refuges where poorer patrons could let off social steam, often giving vent to bitter resentment at the injustices of their economically constrained situation and expressing disdain for those in superior positions who built their wealth on the backs of those below them.[158] Some port-city pubs, as Peter Linebaugh and Marcus Rediker have pointed out, also played a role as vital, albeit illegal, "linchpins of the waterfront economy," in which tavern keepers served as fences for stolen goods appropriated by soldiers, sailors, servants, and slaves who needed to "pad their meager or nonexistent wages."[159]

Though the poorest of the city-dwelling people were sometimes spurned by their elite neighbors in the urban environment, they have increasingly gained the attention of modern scholars. Billy G. Smith's detailed study of everyday life among Philadelphia's "lower sort" in the second half of the eighteenth century gives us an important point of departure. In an era when the overall economy of the city as a whole showed steady growth and considerable prosperity, Smith shows that the hopeful upward mobility that had defined Benjamin Franklin's more prosperous path in life could hardly be considered the norm. The benefits did not trickle down to those in the bottom rungs of society, and by almost every measure of misery—economic depression, epidemic disease, early death—the lives of working people appeared limited and grim, and the only certainty seemed to be insecurity.[160] Simon Newman has underscored Smith's description by focusing closely on the physical appearance of Philadelphia's poor, finding evidence of the implications of poverty in the "undernourished, undersized, and poorly clad bodies, which were far more likely to be scarred by disease and accidents than were the bodies of the well-to-do." To take just one example, the bodies of the prosperous might have a small mark from a smallpox inoculation, a medical procedure, Newman notes, that "was expensive and required a quarantine of as long as two weeks, which

[158] On the social distinctions inherent in some urban taverns, see Carp, *Rebels Rising*, 66–67, 97; Thompson, *Rum Punch and Revolution*, 111–43; and Steven Rosswurm, *Arms, Country, and Class: The Philadelphia Militia and the "Lower Sort" during the American Revolution* (New Brunswick, NJ, 1987), 35.

[159] Linebaugh and Rediker, *Many-Headed Hydra*, 181.

[160] Billy G. Smith, *The "Lower Sort": Philadelphia's Laboring People, 1750–1800* (Ithaca, NY, 1999).

workingmen and their families could ill afford." The bodies of the poor, by contrast, often revealed the ravages of the disease, which not only scarred their skin but underscored their status as well. In general, in an urban milieu where the more prosperous members had developed a discourse about the various "sorts" in their society—the "better," the "middling," and the "lower"—people who inhabited that latter category often carried seemingly indelible marks of class clearly in their physical appearance, making it evident to everyone what "sort" they were and where they stood in the city's social structure.[161]

Some of those embodied marks, however, were tattoos put there on purpose by the poor themselves. In an imaginative investigation of the bodies of sailors, some of the poorest and most physically scarred people in Philadelphia or any other seaport city in the Atlantic world, Newman shows how tattoos could serve as signs of personal, even professional, identity and pride. With an appearance that set them apart from everyone else, even other urban workers, "these men took some control of their image by writing their own stories in their own fashion on their own skin." On a very basic level, a tattoo of one's initials or perhaps some religious symbol might help a mariner get a decent burial should he face death in some faraway spot, but these marks also bespoke a seaman's broader social connections to life ashore. In the era of the Revolution, a man with 1776, an American flag, a liberty tree, or some other such patriotic symbol tattooed on his arm essentially wore his heart beneath his sleeve, and he declared his individual independence even as he embraced a larger cause. "Their tattoos enabled them to articulate everything from religious faith to political principles to loving relationships," Newman says of ordinary sailors, "and we can employ the designs to learn more about the *mentalité* of those who worked at sea."[162]

The mariners' *mentalité* has been the subject of significant scholarship at least since Jesse Lemisch's classic study "Jack Tar in the Streets," and Newman's book builds on that and the body of subsequent work that has come into print since. No one is a more direct heir to Lemisch than Marcus Rediker, who has become the most prolific and outspoken student of the social and political implications of the mariner's life, both on board ship and ashore. Like Lemisch, Rediker has consistently taken seamen seriously

[161] Simon Newman, *Embodied History: The Lives of the Poor in Early Philadelphia* (Philadelphia, 2003), 2–5, 112.

[162] Newman, *Embodied History*, 123, 113. See also Newman, "Reading the Bodies of Early American Seafarers," *William and Mary Quarterly*, 3d. ser. 55 (1998): 59–82.

for their sense of political agency, portraying them as men motivated by ship-born standards of egalitarian social justice who developed an "oppositional culture" in the face of autocratic authority. In his 1987 investigation of maritime life in the first half of the eighteenth century, *Between the Devil and the Deep Blue Sea*, Rediker writes pointedly of the "class relationship between the seaman who provided the labor power and the captain who directed that labor power within a productive, profit-oriented enterprise." Seamen were not just hapless victims of that class relationship, he argues, but workers with a collective identity who engaged in conflict against, or at least negotiation with, the authority of their officers.[163]

The standards of egalitarian struggle and antiauthoritarian resistance seamen developed on board ship did not desert them on dry land. "Jack Tar participated in almost every port-city riot in England and America in the early modern period," Rediker notes, and nowhere was that protest more potent than in the cities of pre-Revolutionary America.[164] "The American Revolution began on the waterfront," Paul Gilje likewise reminds us: "Maritime workers not only provided many of the shock troops for the mobs that underpinned the resistance movement of the 1760s and 1770s; they also helped propel the resistance movement toward greater social change and gave voice to a call for equality." In a hierarchical society such as that of British America, the "rough egalitarianism" of sailor society represented an alternative challenge to the status quo, Gilje suggests, "that some historians identify as class conflict."[165]

If Gilje does not directly declare himself to be one of those historians, Rediker and his co-author, Peter Linebaugh, decidedly do. In a sweeping survey of the late eighteenth-century Atlantic world, Linebaugh and Rediker focus more closely on the multiethnic "motley crew" of sailors, slaves, and other workers in the waterfront proletariat who injected so much energy and urgency into the urban protest movements. Their willingness to take action against Tories and other suspect targets sometimes served the interests of the Sons of Liberty, but their sense of self-direction

[163] Marcus Rediker, *Between the Devil and the Deep Blue Sea: Merchant Seamen, Pirates, and the Anglo-American Maritime World, 1700–1750* (Cambridge, UK, 1987), quotation at 212. Rediker wrote the foreword to the reprint of Jesse Lemisch's 1962 Yale doctoral dissertation, "Jack Tar vs. John Bull: The Role of New York's Seamen in Precipitating the Revolution" (New York, 1997). Rediker's most recent study of social and class relations in life at sea is *The Slave Ship: A Human History* (New York, 2007), which was winner of the George Washington Book Prize.

[164] Rediker, *Between the Devil and the Deep Blue Sea*, 249.

[165] Paul Gilje, *Liberty on the Waterfront: American Maritime Culture in the Age of Revolution* (Philadelphia, 2004), 99–106, quotations at 99, 105, 106.

did not easily lend itself to control from above. The militant members of the urban underclass, Linebaugh and Rediker argue, "provided an image of revolution from below that proved terrifying to Tories and moderate patriots alike."[166]

The "motley crew" did not have a monopoly on making revolution from below, however. Despite the longstanding tradition of deference toward their social "betters," whether truly felt or artfully feigned, other urban workers engaged in "the casting off of deference" and began to assert greater political agency in the Revolutionary era.[167] They often made class alliances with the "respectable" radicals at the head of the revolutionary movement, but they also discovered their own energy and interests in the process of protest and thus developed a clearer class identity that they carried through the Revolutionary era. As Alfred Young has observed, "It is hard not to exaggerate the influence of urban mechanics" in creating the upheaval that helped initiate the Revolution: from 1765 to 1776, from Boston to Charleston, mechanics and members of the laboring classes "came alive politically for reasons they shared with other classes as well as for reasons of their own." To be sure, the term "mechanics" does not define a single, coherent category of urban worker, and historians have taken great pains to note the varieties of trades and economic gradations inherent in the description. Artisans in trades that required a high degree of skill or capitalization—jewelry, cabinetry, instrument making, and baking, for instance—tended to form a craft elite, assuming a social status slightly above other producers in "lesser" pursuits, such as cordwainers and tailors. The internal organization of the artisan's shop, with its hierarchy of master, journeyman, and apprentice, likewise spoke to divisions within each trade.[168]

Looking beyond the shop and into the streets, recent scholarship indicates that those differences among urban workers became manifest in political alliance and activity. Some joined sailors and other members of

[166] Linebaugh and Rediker, *Many-Headed Hydra*, 23; see also Marcus Rediker, "A Motley Crew of Rebels: Sailors, Slaves, and the Coming of the American Revolution," in Hoffman and Albert, eds., *Transforming Hand of Revolution*, 155–98.

[167] Alfred Young provides a classic case of an individual worker's departure from deferential behavior in his study of George Robert Twelves Hewes, *The Shoemaker and the Tea Party: Memory and the American Revolution* (Boston, 1999), quotation at 4. I have discussed the broader cultural complications of deference, feigned or otherwise, in Gregory Nobles, "A Class Act: Redefining Deference in Early American History," *Early American Studies* 3 (2005): 286–302.

[168] Alfred Young, "The Mechanics of the Revolution," in *Liberty Tree: Ordinary People and the American Revolution* (New York, 2006), 46–52; on the distinctions among the various crafts, see also Rosswurm, *Arms, Country, and Class*, 18–24.

the "lower sort" in occasionally spontaneous and frequently raucous multi-class crowd actions; others worked more closely in concert with prominent political leaders to promote moderation and to try to control the crowd. There was, in short, no universal or unified form of mechanic behavior in pre-Revolutionary protest in the cities, Young notes, except increased involvement overall. The exact nature of that involvement often depended, however, largely on local conditions, often reflecting the relative degrees of radicalism displayed by merchants and other elite leaders. In Boston, for instance, the Sons of Liberty embraced both merchants and mechanics in its membership, providing one all-purpose political movement that made separate organizations essentially superfluous. In Philadelphia, by comparison, the laggard leadership of the ruling elite gave the mechanic community both the opportunity and the need to fill the political void with its own self-directed agenda.[169]

The difference proved to be dramatic. Steven Rosswurm's study of the war years in Philadelphia offers a revealing illustration of the increasingly complicated and eventually conflicted class relations between the middling and lower sorts of urban workers in the Revolutionary movement. Members of the city's laboring classes worked more or less in concert with the whig leadership in the immediate pre-Revolutionary period, helping to topple the city's proprietary elite in 1776 and, more broadly, exerting a democratizing influence in the creation of Pennsylvania's constitution. They began to assert themselves more independently during the War for Independence, however, not only mobilizing a local militia but also shaping it to the interests of working people. The Committee of Privates, whose leadership "generally had organic ties to Philadelphia's lower sort and artisan communities," espoused equality alongside patriotism. "The militia transformed the laboring poor," Rosswurm writes, and "the laboring poor transformed the militia," using the social cohesion of a military organization as a means to promote policies beneficial to the city's lower sort.[170] Their insistence on such issues, most notably a more inclusive political system and more protective price controls, led them into open opposition to Philadelphia's patriot leadership, which they considered insufficiently responsive. In the early autumn of 1779, recurring demonstrations of militia-led

[169] Young, "Mechanics of the Revolution," 51. Mechanic action in New York and Charleston, he suggests, fell somewhere in between. For the rifts among mechanics, see Young, "Liberty Tree: Made in America, Lost in America," in *Liberty Tree*, 327–46; for changing mechanic consciousness, see Young, "How Radical Was the American Revolution?" in *Liberty Tree*, 227–31.

[170] Rosswurm, *Arms, Country, and Class*, 69, 75.

protest within the city culminated in the Fort Wilson Riot of October 4. This seemingly unplanned attack on the house of James Wilson, a moderate patriot, resulted in an armed confrontation between the militia and the city's elite light-horse troop, in which several people were killed, wounded, or arrested. The action of the Philadelphia militia represented a clear case of an emerging class-consciousness among the impoverished poor, but it also deepened the mutual suspicion that had come to exist between the middling sort and the lower sort in Philadelphia's Revolutionary movement. The fallout from the Fort Wilson affair eventually led once-friendly radicals in the middle to reconsider their own interests and identify more with those at the top, Rosswurm concludes, and "shattered the coalition that had undergirded the popular movement since 1775."[171]

The collapse of the laboring classes' coalition may have been most notable in Philadelphia, but the war years resulted in a recalibration of political alliances in other American cities as well. "The inequities of the war, the profiteering of merchants, and the failure of price controls increased class antagonisms," Young notes, "but also pitted mechanics against one another."[172] For all that, though, urban workers had discovered a greater sense of themselves as a legitimate political force during the Revolution, and their influence endured throughout the war years and contributed to the process of constitution-making at both the state and federal levels. "In general," Young observes, "in the states with the large cities, the greater the mechanics' influence within the patriot alliance, the more democratic the state constitution." Pennsylvania's was the most striking case in point, of course, but the Massachusetts and New York constitutions also reflected the democratizing effect of working people. And in the drafting of the federal Constitution, Young adds, "mechanics were a presence even if they were not present in the convention." They made themselves heard outside the enclosed confines of the Pennsylvania State House, taking part in the print debate that appeared in newspapers and broadsides, and they also expressed their position in pro-ratification parades in major American cities.[173] On the whole, mechanics formed an important part of a new politi-

[171] Ibid., 205–27, quotation at 226. See also Ronald Schultz, *The Republic of Labor: Philadelphia Artisans and the Politics of Class, 1720–1830* (New York, 1993).

[172] Young, "Mechanics of the Revolution," 54–55.

[173] Ibid., 61. On the participation of working people in post-Revolutionary parades and other forms of public political display, see David Waldstreicher, *In the Midst of Perpetual Fetes: The Making of American Nationalism, 1776–1820* (Chapel Hill, NC, 1997); Simon P. Newman, *Parades and the Politics of the Street: Festive Culture in the Early American Republic* (Philadelphia, 1999); and

cal coalition with urban merchants, the often uneasy alliance that Sean Wilentz has described as "city democracy." Mechanics saw the future success of the new nation—and certainly that of the seaport cities and, therefore, their own—tied to transatlantic trade, tariffs, and a far-reaching financial policy promoted by an energetic national government.[174] In doing so, though, they did not define themselves solely as city dwellers, with interests that depended on or reflected those of the urban merchants; rather, they demonstrated an increasingly acute awareness of their own interests as working people within a larger urban context, and in that regard they began to define the outlines of a more coherent class identity that was to become unmistakably manifest in the century to come.

By the end of the Revolutionary era, however, the significance of the urban scene had begun to fade, Benjamin Carp argues. Military considerations had dictated that the focus of the Revolutionary movement shift to the countryside, and in the aftermath of the war, rural regions had gained an aura of moral superiority to the cities: "Americans of the early republic observed the rioting, labor actions, fires, filth, diseases, crimes, irreligion, ethnic mixing, and vice that plagued the cities and saw ample proof of their prejudices."[175] The most famous expression of that antiurban bias came from Thomas Jefferson, of course, who warned his fellow citizens against the corruptions of the city and celebrated common farmers as "the chosen people of God." To be sure, when it became politically useful to do so, Jefferson expanded his view of virtuous Americans to embrace those urban workers who had gravitated away from the Federalists to his own Democratic-Republican faction, calling them the "yeomanry of the city."[176] Yet his use of that agrarian term invites us to turn our attention away from the urban context and explore the implications of class relations in the countryside,

---

William Pencak, Matthew Dennis, and Simon P. Newman, eds., *Riot and Revelry in Early America* (University Park, PA, 2002); and Young, "Liberty Tree: Made in America, Lost in America."

[174] Sean Wilentz, *The Rise of American Democracy: Jefferson to Lincoln* (New York: Norton, 2005), 20–27, 35–37; Wilentz made an important earlier contribution to the study of urban working people with *Chants Democratic: New York City and the Rise of the American Working Class, 1788–1850* (Oxford, UK, 1984). For a valuable survey of mechanics in the politics of the new nation, see also Gary J. Kornblith, "Artisan Federalism: New England Mechanics and the Political Economy of the 1790s," in Ronald Hoffman and Peter J. Albert, eds., *Launching the "Extended Republic": The Federalist Era* (Charlottesville, VA, 1996), 249–72.

[175] Carp, *Rebels Rising*, 213–24, quotation at 219.

[176] Jefferson's famous reference to farmers as "the chosen people of God," comes from his *Notes on the State of Virginia* (London, 1787; reprint ed., New York, 1954). He used the phrase "yeomanry of the city" in letters to James Monroe and Thomas Randolph, both in 1793; see John P. Foley, ed., *The Jefferson Cyclopedia* (New York, 1900; reprint New York, 1967), 297, 354.

where the mass of Americans lived and likewise struggled, both against the British and against each other, throughout the era of the Revolution.

11. Class in the Countryside

"*Yeoman* is a class term," Allan Kulikoff has argued, "relating to farmers who owned the means of production and participated in commodity markets in order to sustain familial autonomy." With that straightforward sentence, Kulikoff brought the question of class squarely to bear on rural society as clearly as a scholar could, and he has devoted over two decades of his career to a consistent pursuit of that analysis. Ranging from the seventeenth to the nineteenth centuries, he has taken on the task of investigating the economic and cultural conditions of common farmers, always being explicit about bringing class analysis to the countryside and exploring, as the title of one of his books puts it, *The Agrarian Origins of American Capitalism*.[177]

Kulikoff is not by any means the first scholar to consider the question of class in the early American countryside, and his work builds on important studies from the 1960s and '70s. The upsurge of community studies that began to dot the intellectual landscape at the time also brought issues of inequality into closer focus, and that provided a significant first step. Taking the town as a unit of analysis gave scholars the opportunity to provide quantitative measurements of local economic conditions, especially the distribution of property, and in many cases increasing economic stratification over the course of the eighteenth century. More to the point, these town studies often revealed long-simmering internal tensions that suddenly erupted in conflict, tearing the mask off the image of communal consensus and personal deference. Not all of the "peaceable kingdoms" of

[177] Allan Kulikoff, "The Rise and Demise of the American Yeoman Classes," in *The Agrarian Origins of American Capitalism* (Charlottesville, VA, 1992), 34–59, quotation at 34. This collection of essays, some of them previously published, is bracketed by Kulikoff's two other books dealing with agrarian society: *Tobacco and Slaves: The Development of Southern Culture in the Chesapeake* (Chapel Hill, NC, 1986) and *From British Peasants to Colonial American Farmers* (Chapel Hill, NC, 2000). Kulikoff's scholarly articles on class formation in the countryside include "The Transition to Capitalism in Rural America," *William and Mary Quarterly*, 3d ser. 46 (1989): 120–44; "Households and Markets: Toward a New Synthesis of American Agrarian History," *William and Mary Quarterly*, 3d ser. 50 (1993): 340–55; "The American Revolution and the Making of the American Yeoman Classes," in Alfred F. Young, ed., *Beyond the American Revolution: Further Explorations in the History of American Radicalism* (DeKalb, IL, 1993), 80–119; and "Was the American Revolution a Bourgeois Revolution?" in Hoffman and Albert, eds., *Transforming Hand of Revolution*, 58–89.

early America reflected the calm and equality that the classic image of rural society might suggest. Yet for all the attention that these closely focused community studies drew to the prevalence of inequality at the local level, they did not, in and of themselves, create a coherent case for a broader class-based analysis of rural society in the Revolutionary era. Indeed, sometimes the inward-looking investigation of the individual community, not to mention the often intense emphasis on the intricacies of social science methodology, took precedence over the consideration of larger historical questions raised by the local results.[178]

Building on those local studies, Kulikoff joined other scholars in making the leap from the immediate community to a broader view of the rural landscape, better explicating the economic and political connections that tied small farmers in small communities to the larger Atlantic world. In the late 1970s, the exploration of an emerging eighteenth-century rural *mentalité*—a safety-first, family-centered approach to agricultural production that put the interests of the household ahead of those of the market—offered important insights into understanding rural society in terms of class. "Yeomen were embedded in capitalist world markets and yet alienated from capitalist social and economic relations," Kulikoff explains, and they became skeptical, if not openly resistant, to the economic and political interests, both in the cities and in the countryside, who threatened to exert control over their lives. Yeomen did not have a coherent class consciousness as such, but they did have clear interests in defending their economic autonomy as propertied producers, their familial authority as patriarchal figures, and their political participation in the public sphere as citizens.[179]

[178] Nobles, "Class," 270–74.

[179] Kulikoff addresses the question of rural *mentalité* throughout much of *Agrarian Origins of American Capitalism*; quotation at 36. The scholarly exploration of the issue stems from a triad of much-cited essays in the 1970s: Michael Merrill, "Cash Is Good to Eat: Self-Sufficiency and Exchange in the Rural Economy of the United States," *Radical History Review* 4 (1977): 42–71; James Henretta, "Families and Farms: Mentalité in Pre-Industrial America," *William and Mary Quarterly*, 3d ser. 35 (1978): 3–32; and Christopher Clark, "The Household Economy, Market Exchange, and the Rise of Capitalism in the Connecticut Valley, 1800–1860," *Journal of Social History* 13 (1979): 169–90. Significant contributions to the debate in the 1980s included Bettye Hobbs Pruitt, "Self-Sufficiency and the Agricultural Economy of Eighteenth-Century Massachusetts," *William and Mary Quarterly*, 3d ser. 41 (1984): 333–64; Winifred Rothenberg, "The Market and Massachusetts Farmers 1750–1855," *Journal of Economic History* 41 (1981): 283–314; and "The Emergence of Farm Labor Markets and the Transformation of the Rural Economy," *Journal of Economic History* 45 (1985): 547–66. The discussion reached a culmination, if not a conclusion, in Daniel Vickers, "Competency and Competition: Economic Culture in Early America," *William and Mary Quarterly*, 3d ser. 47 (1990): 3–29.

The Revolution put all that in jeopardy. The most obvious and overarching danger, of course, came from the threat of British assaults on their land and liberty. At the same time, the defense against that external threat created internal concerns as well. The constriction of wartime economy, with the disruption of traditional distribution patterns and the decline in available labor, "turned the lives of farmers . . . upside down," Kulikoff argues. At the same time, the demands and depredations of the Continental army, with its constant calls for recruits and aggressive requisition of food and other scarce supplies, caused what Kulikoff has described as "civil war" in response to the perceptions of theft on the part of the Revolutionary leadership.[180] On the whole, we can now see a better connection between the conditions of life in the countryside and the conscious—indeed, class-conscious—response of American yeomen to the wartime exigencies of the Revolution.

The case of Virginia has become a particularly evocative example of the internal class tensions that became exposed during the Revolution. Once the authority of the British had been generally rejected by white Virginians in 1775, members of the gentry had to be sensitive to gaining the assent of lesser landowners in order to make wartime policy. In this sense, the "forced founders" of whom Woody Holton writes not only had to respond to the unrest among Indians and slaves, but they also had to worry about the "well over 200,000 people in the yeomanry" who first felt the full impact of the war. Those "smallholders" put forth "an agrarian response that, in complex ways, contributed to the gentry's decision to make a formal declaration of Independence."[181] And as Michael McDonnell has observed, different groups in Virginia "defined Independence very differently." Indeed, he carries the analysis of internal conflict forward through the war years, bringing the divided loyalties among whites to the foreground and putting class at the center of the story: "There was no force, not even the constellation of fears and issues of race that often animated this slaveholding society, that was strong enough to overcome class interests and forge unity among Virginia's white population."[182]

The class-based fissures in rural society have become readily evident in

[180] Kulikoff, "The Farmers' War and Its Aftermath," in *From British Peasants to Colonial American Farmers*, 255–88, quotations at 261, 271.

[181] Holton, *Forced Founders*, xx–xxi.

[182] McDonnell, *Politics of War*, 213, 13; see also McDonnell, "Class War? Class Struggles during the American Revolution in Virginia," *William and Mary Quarterly*, 3d. ser. 63 (2006): 305–44.

the analysis of the complicated relations that surrounded the issue of military service. The "embattled farmers" that Emerson so famously celebrated in his "Concord Hymn" may still be perceived in popular lore as the backbone of the patriot army, but modern scholars have shown how yeomen and other rural folk often became embattled with the patriot leadership over the implications of military service, both as soldiers and as civilian supporters of the common cause. By the same token, the "summer soldier" of whom Thomas Paine complained has received a better explanation, if not a complete justification, in studies of the internal struggles of the Revolution. John Shy's provocative essay on "Long Bill" Scott and his fellow citizen-soldiers in Peterborough, New Hampshire, pointed the way in the 1970s, underscoring the importance of economic position in understanding American military service in the Revolution. Farmers of middling means typically entered the military only for short periods of time, and usually only when the fighting came close enough to threaten their immediate community. Longer terms of service tended to be the lot of the less prosperous and less settled members of the community, "an unusually poor, obscure group of men," who did most of the fighting and dying—"a very old story," he concludes.[183]

It is indeed a very old story, but one that has subsequently been told on a larger scale and one that has drawn us deeper into the complexities of class relations in rural society. The case of Peterborough offers an instructive departure point. Following Shy's lead, Charles Neimeyer has argued that few of the men who went to war from Peterborough "could be termed 'yeomen soldiers'"—nor, for that matter, could most soldiers from the other locales he studies. Instead, he portrays the majority of Revolutionary recruits as members of the lower classes, lured into the military by the promise of pay and turned into "military workers," oppressed by their officers and sent into battle to promote the interests of a less-than-grateful society.[184] John Resch, on the other hand, looks at the soldiers of Peterborough and sees a much more representative cross section of rural society, men who might well be considered "embattled farmers" at the beginning of the war and who subsequently became honored as "suffering soldiers" in

[183] John Shy, "Hearts and Minds in the American Revolution: The Case of 'Long Bill' Scott and Peterborough, New Hampshire," in *A People Numerous and Armed: Reflections on the Military Struggle for American Independence* (Ann Arbor, MI, 1990), 163–80, quotation at 173.

[184] Charles Patrick Neimeyer, *America Goes to War: A Social History of the Continental Army* (New York, 1996); on military recruitment in Peterborough, see 15, 19, 25.

the post-Revolutionary period.[185] Peterborough itself may not be the most representative community in Revolutionary America, but it has certainly been one of the most studied, and historians have clearly staked out the terms of the debate about the implications of class and military service.

Kulikoff offers a sharper and more subtle class analysis of military service by focusing on yeomen and their middle position in Revolutionary Virginia, between the planters and merchant-capitalists above them on the economic ladder and the poorer and propertyless people, including slaves, below. Seen in the light of that social context, the comparatively selective and short-term service of the members of the yeoman class raises fresh questions not just about their military motivation but about their political position as well. Whereas some of the yeomen's upper-class contemporaries might have been inclined to dismiss them as shirkers and deserters of the common cause, Kulikoff and other scholars now offer us a different approach that gives a better appreciation of the social and economic implications of military service. On the one hand, Kulikoff points out, about half of all white men over sixteen performed some measure of military service in Virginia, a "remarkably high proportion" compared to other states. On the other hand, he adds, "the Revolution was a young man's war," in which men with little or no property did military duty for a longer duration, some of them serving as substitutes for better-off farmers—including, in some cases, their own fathers.[186] Although the state's legislators attempted to devise recruitment policies that would, in the republican spirit of the times, encourage both voluntarism and equity, they had to accede to the realities of the social order. Yeomen successfully pressured members of the gentry to keep the burden of military service on the poor and landless men who constituted the lowest stratum of whites, the common people deemed most fit for service as common soldiers.

We might well understand the motivation of those poorer men, who saw military service as a means of social mobility, or perhaps simply as the best available way of getting by in difficult times. As McDonnell points out in his study of military service in Virginia, those lower-class soldiers

[185] John Resch, *Suffering Soldiers: Revolutionary War Veterans, Moral Sentiment, and Political Culture in the Early Republic* (Amherst, MA, 1999), esp. 9–10, where Resch challenges Neimeyer's view.

[186] Kulikoff has addressed the question most directly in "The Political Economy of Military Service in Revolutionary Virginia," in *Agrarian Origins of American Capitalism*, 152–80, quotation at 163.

had a sense of their own interests, too, and they increasingly "demanded a high price for their services"—enlistment bounties for volunteers and higher compensation for substitutes. In doing so, though, they ultimately, if grudgingly, accepted a role that reinforced the social structure, not only doing the military will of the political elite but also allowing the more established yeomen to maintain their patriarchal roles over family and farm.[187] In the end, the larger picture of the Revolutionary period in Virginia is one not of martial solidarity but of internal tensions over military service that festered throughout the war, finding expression in various forms of protest, from petitions to outright resistance.

Beyond the immediate emphasis on military service, the important point is that as yeomen expressed themselves politically during the Revolution, they gained greater political recognition, both in the eyes of the elite leadership and, equally important, in their own eyes. "Between 1776 and 1781 the yeomanry made a revolution for themselves," Kulikoff writes, making their own choices about their role in the Revolution and gaining a greater voice in the larger political conversation taking place in society—a voice that spoke the language of class and one that did not go quiet once the war itself was over.[188] Indeed, by shining new light on rural protest *during* the Revolution, Kulikoff and others have given greater context and coherence to the period of almost unbroken agrarian unrest *before* and *after* the Revolution, running from the 1760s through the 1790s and reaching all along the eastern seaboard, from the backcountry of the lower South to the northernmost reaches of New England. The Revolution itself no longer seems so much a time of internal unity on the patriot side but instead appears as a period of ongoing class struggle located in a larger, decades-long process. The distinction between pre-Revolutionary and post-Revolutionary protest has now dramatically diminished.

In the case of Pennsylvania, for instance, Patrick Griffin and Terry Bouton have shown that the connection between the Paxton Boys' protests of the 1760s and the more widespread unrest of the 1790s runs right through the Revolution and, indeed, far beyond Pennsylvania itself. The Paxton Boys' initial violence against peaceful Indians stemmed from a broader backcountry anxiety about white settlers' vulnerability to more menacing

[187] McDonnell, *Politics of War*, 6. See also McDonnell, "Popular Mobilization and Political Culture in Revolutionary Virginia: The Failure of the Minutemen and the Revolution from Below," *Journal of American History* 85 (1998): 946–81.

[188] Kulikoff, *Agrarian Origins of American Capitalism*, 136.

Indians, but the protesters also expressed hostility toward colonial officials, who they felt imposed burdensome taxes and provided inadequate protection. That second aspect of the protest played into the politics of the period immediately preceding the Revolution. The economic grievances laid against the British contributed to a growing cross-class consensus in favor of greater equality, what Bouton describes as a "political awakening among the lower and middling sorts and a changed world view among much of the gentry . . . that caused them to redefine liberty as reducing wealth inequality and opening the political system." He also notes, however, that this "seismic ideological shift" among the Pennsylvania elite did not come because of genteel self-reflection; echoing Holton, Bouton argues that "members of the gentry were also pushed to transform by those below them."[189]

Even with that push, however, the "forced founders" in Pennsylvania eventually lost their democratic momentum. As the Revolution dragged on and the original leaders who helped design a radical state constitution in 1776 became increasingly frustrated and war weary, they came to be replaced by new men who were much less committed to economic or political equality. Members of this new gentry, Bouton explains, indulged themselves with luxuries and expressed antidemocratic disdain for ordinary people. The fragile class alliance that had taken Pennsylvania into the war gradually fell apart, creating resentment among the poor and retrenchment among the prosperous. The new elite leaders attempted to scale back democracy, or at least redefine it for their own purposes. Prominent Pennsylvanians such as Robert Morris adopted a self-serving "gospel of moneyed men" that called for aligning the interests of the state with their own and turning some public functions over to new private, for-profit corporations under gentry ownership. "By transforming democracy into a concept that encouraged uninhibited wealth accumulation rather than wealth equality," Bouton concludes, "the founding elite (and subsequent generations of elites) tamed what they could not defeat."[190]

Bouton and Griffin point to a different sort of democracy taking shape in the western part of the state, where nothing seemed tame. As members of the Pennsylvania gentry lined their own pockets, western settlers

[189] Terry Bouton, *Taming Democracy: "The People," the Founders, and the Troubled Ending of the American Revolution* (New York, 2007), 32.

[190] Ibid., 62–87, quotation at 263.

continued to live with the same problems that had beset them since the 1760s, particularly friction with Indians and frustration with debt and taxes. As we have seen, Bouton and Griffin do not trivialize the vicious behavior that marked the many instances of violence in the western regions, nor do they minimize the emerging race hatred that motivated white settlers in their attacks against native inhabitants. But these struggling settlers also developed another sort of hatred that faced eastward. They insisted on the protection of their land, not just from Indians but from devious eastern speculators and aggressive government tax collectors as well. People in western Pennsylvania and, indeed, throughout the Ohio River valley region turned their anti-Indian, anti-eastern hostilities into an assertion of local sovereignty, what Griffin calls a "western vision," in which resistance to various external threats became a positive source of political identity, a "blueprint for the creation of commonwealth."[191]

That growing sense of backcountry identity provides an important background for the main political event of 1787, when another group of people in eastern Pennsylvania went to work on another sort of political blueprint, the federal Constitution. Given the upsurge of recent scholarship on agrarian unrest in the Revolutionary era, the relationship between farmers and the Framers now stands in sharper contrast. In *Unruly Americans*, a book that picks up where *Forced Founders* ended and expands its view to Constitution-making, Woody Holton reminds us that in a nation in which nine out of ten free Americans were farmers, there were no yeomen directly involved in the Constitution-making process; the Framers were "demographically speaking, unrepresentative in the extreme."[192] Still, Holton argues, even though formally excluded from the framing process, yeomen did gain an implicit sort of representation among the men who went to Philadelphia in 1787. Agrarian protests had been a consistent force of internal pressure on government, repeatedly pushing state officials for various forms of redress—religious toleration, or at least relief from paying taxes to support a religious establishment; paper money, or at least relief from paying taxes in scarce specie; and greater political representation, or at least relief from the power of entrenched elites. The rural uprising that swept Massachusetts in 1786–87—commonly, but erroneously, called Shays's Rebellion—has become the most historically visible among these

[191] Griffin, *American Leviathan*, 154, 214.

[192] Woody Holton, *Unruly Americans and the Origins of the Constitution* (New York, 2007), 181.

movements, and it still generates a good share of historians' attention.[193] As Holton notes, however, Massachusetts was not the only state to experience unrest in that period: neighboring New England states—New Hampshire, Connecticut, and Rhode Island—also witnessed an upsurge of protest, as did other states down the eastern seaboard, from New Jersey to Virginia to South Carolina.[194] Many elite political leaders looked on with frustration at the concessions rural folk wrung out of their state governments, and part of their purpose in calling for a new national framework of government was to correct the alleged excess of democracy they deplored. "From the Founders' perspective," Holton explains, "the policies adopted by the state legislatures in the 1780s proved that ordinary Americans were not entirely capable of ruling themselves."[195] And yet any attempt to assert greater control over the various state governments still had to take account of the popular protests that had made those states concede to their people. "As the delegates traveled to Philadelphia late in the spring," Holton notes, "they were looking over their shoulders"—fearful, even forced, Framers,

[193] David Szatmary, in *Shays' Rebellion: The Making of an Agrarian Rebellion* (Amherst, MA, 1980), approached the Massachusetts insurrection from the standpoint of the farmers' vulnerable position at the end of a "chain of debt" that originated with British and Boston merchants. Leonard Richards, in *Shays's Rebellion: The American Revolution's Final Battle* (Philadelphia, 2002), focused more on analyzing familial and community connections in what he calls "banner towns" that rose up against the government. The essays in Robert Gross, ed., *In Debt to Shays: The Bicentennial of an Agrarian Rebellion* (Charlottesville, VA, 1993), offer a variety of perspectives, from legal questions to the religious background and social structure of local communities.

Even though these books use "Shays" or "Shays's Rebellion" in their titles, presumably for familiarity's sake, the authors tend to use other terms to denote the participants in the movement. The longstanding label "Shays's Rebellion" is no more than an anachronistic misnomer first invented by the Massachusetts movement's opponents and subsequently used for two centuries by historians, focusing the origins of the protest on a single person and thus diminishing the deeper roots of regional unrest. Daniel Shays always denied being the central leader, much less the conspiratorial instigator, of the rural unrest, and it makes sense to believe him. When he and other rural insurgents spoke of themselves, they commonly used terms such as "the body of the people" or "Regulators," the latter harking back to an identification with the pre-Revolutionary protests in the Carolinas. On the shift from "Shays's Rebellion" to "Regulation," see Ronald Formisano, "Teaching Shays/The Regulation: Historiographical Problems as Tools for Learning," *Uncommon Sense* 106 (1998): 24–35; Robert A. Gross, "A Yankee Rebellion? The Regulators, New England, and the New Nation," *New England Quarterly* 82 (2009): 112–35; and Gregory Nobles, "'Satan, Smith, Shattuck, and Shays': The People's Leaders in the Massachusetts Regulation," in Alfred F. Young, Gary B. Nash, and Ray Raphael, eds., *Revolutionary Founders: Rebels, Radicals, and Reformers in the Making of the Nation* (New York, 2011), chap. 13. Because *Revolutionary Founders* was in press at the time of this writing, this and subsequent references to essays in this volume will be by chapter, not by page numbers.

[194] Holton, *Unruly Americans*, 145–61.

[195] Ibid., 16.

wary of unruly ordinary folk who still seemed less than fully reconciled to the results of the Revolutionary settlement. Even though the Framers enclosed themselves in secret session inside the Pennsylvania State House, "the temper of the times," as Sean Wilentz usefully puts it, "seeped into the room."[196]

That seepage proved to be significant. Historians who focus primarily on the men inside the room at the Constitutional Convention often portray the Framers as an enclosed, if often contentious, intellectual community who, for "all their prejudices, their passions, their errors of opinion, their local interests, and their selfish views," as Franklin so famously put it, still produced a "system approaching so near to perfection as it does." But the debates among the delegates that Madison so carefully recorded were only one part of the convention's controversies. The degree of disagreement among the Framers on the inside seems comparatively pale when compared to the passionate opinions of ordinary people on the outside, who increasingly claimed recognition for the role—and the rights—they had established during the Revolution. No matter how much the men who created the Constitution might have hoped to establish a government that relied on the guidance of a "natural aristocracy"—men such as themselves, for instance—they could not do as they pleased. To "secure domestic tranquility," the architects of the Constitution realized, meant more than designing a central government that could suppress internal insurrection; it also meant, as Holton notes, disguising their antidemocratic intentions: "If the federal convention delegates had not feared that the nation's agrarian majority would reject it, they would have created a considerably more elitist document."[197]

Even so, the document they did create did not receive a free pass from farmers. Richard Beeman, whose *Plain, Honest Men* provides a perceptive, inside-the-State-House analysis of the Framers' debates, also turns his attention beyond Philadelphia to the nature of the subsequent ratification debate in rural regions. In Pennsylvania, he notes, the combination of urban professionals and artisans and tradesmen in Philadelphia along with "surprisingly strong showings in some of the western counties" gave the Federalists a decided edge, but some rural Antifederalists attacked the

[196] Holton, *Unruly Americans*, 181; Wilentz, *Rise of American Democracy*, 32. Holton and Wilentz thus echo Young's observation, quoted earlier, that "mechanics were a presence even if they were not present in the convention."

[197] Holton, *Unruly Americans*, 193, 276–77; see also Kulikoff, *Agrarian Origins of American Capitalism*, 142–46.

elitist-seeming Constitution with "a rhetoric of grassroots populism that was well suited to their backcountry constituencies." In Virginia, voters in the Piedmont and backcountry likewise opposed the new Constitution, as did backcountry inhabitants of North Carolina, where a "hearty distrust of central authority was deeply entrenched, . . . dating at least to the so-called Regulator movements of the 1760s." The more recent Regulation in Massachusetts also weighed on the delegates to that state's ratifying convention, and residual sympathy for the insurgents' grievances remained a factor in the debate, which "turned on issues of social and economic conflict." Although Beeman does not directly engage Charles Beard's economic analysis of the ratification vote—indeed, Beard's name does not appear in the book—he does remind us that resistance to ratification became most prominent in the countryside and that such resistance often spoke "the language of populist democracy" to the power of the new political system.[198]

Rural resistance was not just a flash in the political pan. "Something strange happened in the Pennsylvania countryside in the years following the federal Constitutional Convention of 1787," Bouton reports: "large numbers of farmers closed the main road that led in and out of their communities," and he counts sixty-two such incidents for the next eight years, until 1795. Rural people apparently took such action, he explains, to defend themselves from the encroaching power inherent in two recently ratified constitutions, the federal Constitution of 1787 and the new Pennsylvania Constitution of 1790, a Federalist-sponsored effort to overturn the state's dramatically democratic constitution of 1776. In both cases, farmers feared, the new political systems represented a threatening victory on the part of the financial and political elites, and they closed the roads to try to protect themselves from the external agents of the state, particularly tax collectors, magistrates, and justices. The road closings had a short-term practical effect, slowing the operations of court proceeding and sheriffs' auctions for debt, but they also symbolized a more general retreat from the larger political arena into overly localized isolation. "In this hostile new environment, ordinary folk who wanted to uphold their vision of the Revolution urgently needed to find ways to work together," Bouton observes. Instead,

[198] Richard Beeman, *Plain, Honest Men: The Making of the American Constitution* (New York, 2009), 369–405. A more closely neo-Beardian approach to ratification can be found in Holton, *Unruly Americans*, and in Saul Cornell, *The Other Founders: Anti-Federalism and the Dissenting Tradition in America, 1788–1828* (Chapel Hill, NC, 1999). Pauline Maier's *Ratification: The People Debate the Constitution, 1787–1788*, appeared in print too late for consideration here.

they barricaded roads, a politically feckless step that cut them off from each other and undercut common action.[199]

This pattern of localized yeoman resistance began to take a decidedly different turn in 1794, however, when rural people in Pennsylvania reached beyond their local communities and joined in a more widespread expression of protest that challenged both state and national officials. Like the so-called Shays's Rebellion of the previous decade, the "Whiskey Rebellion" has received fresh scholarly attention, beginning with the implications of the liquid commodity in question. To be sure, whiskey had something to do with the rise of unrest, not just as a commodity of trade and eventual target of taxation but, as Patrick Griffin notes, a symbol of "the sense of alienation, anti-authoritarianism, and violence that permeated many of the poorer settlements."[200] Yet the too-easy use of the label "Whiskey Rebellion," a dismissive term first coined by Alexander Hamilton, tends to limit our view to local events and reinforces Hamilton's original ridicule, leaving a simplistic image of "drunken, gun-wielding hillbillies," Bouton writes, "frightening but too comical to be taken seriously." Taking the resistance quite seriously and, equally important, locating it in the larger political context of the longer Revolutionary era, Bouton and Griffin underscore the chronological and geographical connections to events elsewhere in time and place. Engaging in familiar forms of protest reaching back through the Revolutionary era, "the whiskey men drew upon the lessons learned during their own period of politicization," Griffin explains. To underscore that longer period of political connection, Bouton argues for calling the regional unrest the "Pennsylvania Regulations," adopting a term that links the actions of the western settlers in the 1790s to other recurring attempts of rural people to control or correct the actions of their government officials, from the Carolinas in the pre-Revolutionary years to Massachusetts and other parts of New England in the 1780s. "The 1790s uprisings in Pennsylvania," Bouton argues, "fit seamlessly into this pattern of popular regulation."[201]

[199] Bouton, *Taming Democracy*, 197–215, quotations at 197, 215. See also Bouton, "A Road Closed: Rural Insurgency in Post-Independence Pennsylvania," *Journal of American History* 87 (2000): 855–87.

[200] Griffin, *American Leviathan*, 222–23.

[201] Griffin, *American Leviathan*, 212–39, quotation at 225; Bouton, *Taming Democracy*, 216–43, quotation at 219. Bouton's preference for "Pennsylvania Regulations" (218) over "Whiskey Rebellion" reflects the growing reluctance of other scholars to use the term "Shays's Rebellion" to refer to the earlier movement in New England. In that regard, it makes sense to take note of the appearance of other prominent figures from one protest to the next—Herman Husband in North

Connection across time and region has increasingly become the key to understanding Revolutionary-era agrarian unrest. To be sure, the organizational vision and abilities of eighteenth-century yeomen did not yet reach across regional boundaries, nor did the widespread spirit of opposition constitute a fully articulated political position. Yeoman protests did reflect a pattern of shared concern, however, extending from the familial (a reliance on patriarchal control over the family as a productive unit) to the local (a preference or direct exchange of goods and services rather than market production) to the colonial, state, and national (a fear that political elites were operating a political system that favored the few over the many, undermining the economic independence of small producers). The issues at the core of these rural Regulations came to have an increasingly important impact in the politics of the Revolutionary era, up to and including the creation of a national government. "In state after state," Kulikoff concludes, "the success of the yeomanry in influencing public policy during the war years led yeomen to believe that they, the majority of voters, could actually rule."[202]

In the immediate aftermath of the Revolution, that belief in yeoman rule exceeded political reality, and yeomen could not yet make the most of their majority status. The new federal and state constitutions still kept democracy in check with, as Bouton concludes, "governments designed to impede popular reform," which made even ordinary white men "losers in the scaled-back version of democracy that emerged from the Revolution."[203] On another level, however, the formal political settlement provided by the post-Revolutionary constitution-making provides only one measure of the political outcome of the Revolution in terms of the class relationships. The notion of "influencing public policy" directs us to a more subtle but perhaps more substantial process of negotiation that lay in a larger ensemble of relationships, personal as well as political. Though seldom formal or explicit, the negotiation of the broader meaning of in-

---

Carolina in the 1760s and Pennsylvania in the 1780s, or Samuel Ely in Massachusetts in 1780 and then Maine in the 1790s—to suggest not just an individual but an ideological connection across the countryside. See Marjoleine Kars, *Breaking Loose Together: The Regulator Rebellion in Prerevolutionary North Carolina* (Chapel Hill, 2002); Wythe Holt, "The New Jerusalem: Herman Husband's Egalitarian Alternative to the United States Constitution," in Young, Nash, and Raphael, eds., *Revolutionary Founders*, chap. 15; Holton, *Unruly Americans*, 62–63, 170–72; and Gregory H. Nobles, "Breaking into the Backcountry: New Approaches to the Early American Frontier, 1750–1800," *William and Mary Quarterly*, 3d ser. 46 (1989): 641–70, esp. 666–67.

[202] Kulikoff, *Agrarian Origins of American Capitalism*, 141.

[203] Bouton, *Taming Democracy*, 262–63.

dependence played itself out in place after place, and it commands our attention as yet another form of class interaction throughout the post-Revolutionary period.[204]

To appreciate the nature of that negotiation, we can turn to the work of Alan Taylor, who has made good sense of the nuances of rural class relations in post-Revolutionary America. The great strength of Taylor's approach is that he gives credit—and credibility—to the interests and aspirations of both sides, thus avoiding making a Manichean morality play out of the struggles for a post-Revolutionary settlement. In his first book, *Liberty Men and Great Proprietors*, he defined rural settlers in terms of class—not as a class-conscious proletariat, by any means, but as a group of poor people, "small freeholders engaged in manual labor," whose interests remained quite different from those of the land-speculating elite, "mercantile capitalists living off the land payments levied on the fruits of the yeomanry's labor." Like Kulikoff, he portrays the unfolding struggle over property rights as part of a longer-term national process, the development of capitalism in the early United States. But in the late eighteenth century, still in the early stages of that process, the conflict between small producers and powerful property owners played out in terms that were deeply rooted in rural culture, in which both parties believed in the private ownership of property and the pursuit of personal gain. The main difference between the two groups, Taylor explains, was one of vision: yeomen hoped to maintain their independence and "sustain American capitalism at a simple stage of development," while the prominent proprietors looked forward to a more fully elaborated social and economic system "where property would become concentrated in the hands of the capitalists who best understood how to employ it to create more property."[205]

In the immediate context of the Maine frontier, the impact of those conflicting voices sometimes resulted in violent as well as verbal conflict—not serious bloodshed, by any means, but forceful resistance to local authorities by "Liberty Men" and "White Indians" in the post-Revolutionary era. Like the agrarian rebels of other regions, the unruly settlers of Maine did not seek to overthrow the proprietors altogether. Indeed, Taylor notes,

[204] On the notion of negotiation, see Young, "How Radical Was the American Revolution?" 232–33; and Gregory H. Nobles, "'Yet the Old Republicans Still Persevere': Samuel Adams, John Hancock, and the Crisis of Popular Leadership in Revolutionary Massachusetts, 1775–1790," in Hoffman and Albert, eds., *Transforming Hand of Revolution*, 258–85, esp. 279–83.

[205] Alan Taylor, *Liberty Men and Great Proprietors: The Revolutionary Settlement on the Maine Frontier, 1760–1820* (Chapel Hill, NC, 1990), 7, 8.

they "could not conceive of dispensing with their elite rulers." But if they could not dispense with them, the settlers did seek to restrict their power and "restore the necessary equilibrium between central power and local liberty." Once that had been achieved, he adds, the settlers seemed content enough to go back to their farms and leave the "chastened gentlemen" with the positions of formal power, but also with the knowledge that they risked further turmoil if they exercised that power without due concern for the common people.[206]

Like Holton's "forced founders," Taylor's "chastened gentlemen" form an important focus of his subsequent work. In two prize-winning books, *William Cooper's Town* and *The Divided Ground*, Taylor centered his scrutiny on prominent political leaders in post-Revolutionary New York, looking at policymaking from their perspective but, like the leaders themselves, always keeping an eye on the larger populace that provided the base of their political support—or not, as the case may have been.[207] William Cooper, for instance, represents a classic case of the chastened gentleman. An upstart entrepreneur in upstate Otsego County, Cooper amassed thousands of acres in the 1780s and established himself as a formidable man of means at a time when a flood of new settlers was moving into the region. Like the great proprietors of Maine, Cooper had a vision of directing a profitable process of development that would serve both his own interests and, he believed, that of the region's people as well. He had the good financial sense to be in a position to be able to profit from pent-up land hunger, but he also had the good political sense to try to work with the new settlers as allies in mutual advancement, not simply to gouge them for his own gain.

Cooper's political sense failed him, however, when he sought to enter the upper reaches of New York's emerging partisan organizations, the genteel eastern Federalists and the rougher-hewn Republicans. His decision to identify with the former did him little good in either camp: the leaders of the Federalist faction accepted Cooper but never took the nouveau-riche entrepreneur seriously, and the Republicans dismissed his political associations with their aristocratic rivals as ambitious-seeming social pretension. But Cooper's real error was not just a mistake in picking one political elite

[206] Taylor, *Liberty Men*, 190–207, quotations at 112.

[207] Alan Taylor's *William Cooper's Town: Power and Persuasion on the Frontier of the Early American Republic* (New York, 1995) won the Bancroft Prize and the Pulitzer Prize in 1996; in 2007, *The Divided Ground* won the Cox Book Prize of the Society of the Cincinnati and the Book Prize of the Society for Historians of the Early American Republic (SHEAR).

over the other. In New York, as in other northern states, Taylor argues, the Republican movement did not derive its energy by taking top-down direction from Jefferson, Madison, or other prominent men; rather, it was a bottom-up popular movement that reflected the concerns of common people at the local level. By spurning the Republican "insurgency," Cooper lost contact, credibility, and face with the majority of the Otsego settlers, and the resulting loss of goodwill led to his being toppled by small-farmer opposition and, in the long run, to the loss of his legacy in the region.[208] The narrative attraction of Taylor's portrait of William Cooper comes from its intricate telling of this story of an exceptional individual's rise and fall. The ultimate political point, however, speaks to the underlying importance of broader social relations in the region, defining a context in which the consequences of Cooper's life story offer a larger lesson about the class-inflected nature of post-Revolutionary society.

In that regard, in fact, Taylor's more recent study of post-Revolutionary New York, *The Divided Ground*, rests on essentially the same ground as *William Cooper's Town*. Although the more recent book takes as its primary focus the relations between the Indians of the region and the political leaders of the new state and nation, it also speaks to underlying assumptions about the relationships between those white leaders and their own constituents in post-Revolutionary society. One of the main reasons for dispossessing Indians of their lands, of course, was to encourage the dispersal of white settlers, which could bring both financial and political advantage to New York's elite leaders: "The victor would reap public revenues by selling the land; would collect taxes on the new farms; and would consolidate authority by interesting speculators and settlers in support of the victorious jurisdiction and its land title."[209] Once again, the attempt to promote proprietary profit by making accommodation for common people —common white people, to be sure—reflected a strategy for success that had sometimes eluded the great men of Maine, not to mention one near-great man of New York.

Seen in the light of all three books, the persistence of powerful men in trying to settle the northern frontier with white settlers did not reflect racial solidarity alone; rather, it revealed the way class interests could intersect in the new nation, creating a need for an internally (albeit implicitly) negotiated settlement *within* white society. Federal and local officials could

[208] Taylor, *William Cooper's Town*, 256–57.

[209] Taylor, *Divided Ground*, 9, 142–50, quotation at 143.

not always rely on the use or even the threat of armed power to enforce their authority, as they had tried in Massachusetts and Pennsylvania. In many cases—most notably the ones Taylor has described but not those alone—they had to seek peace through conciliation.[210] But to make the necessary concessions to insistent settlers in the lower reaches of their own society, those leaders in post-Revolutionary America had to insist on property concessions from Indians. Looking ahead from Taylor's territory in the North to the subsequent spread of white settlement at the expense of Native peoples in the nineteenth-century West, we can anticipate the pattern that was to become increasingly clear: the interplay of race and class became an essential element in shaping the future of the new nation.

V. Writing Women into the Revolution

12. Energy and Innovation since 1980

In 2005, a ballroom-full of scholars in Philadelphia at the annual meeting of the Society for Historians of the Early American Republic (SHEAR) turned their attention from discussing events that happened two centuries ago to reflect on a significant phenomenon only a quarter century in the past—the publication, in 1980, of two innovative and imaginative books, Mary Beth Norton's *Liberty's Daughters* and Linda Kerber's *Women of the Republic*.[211] It is never easy to point to a particular moment of emergence in any field of scholarship, but the SHEAR session underscored a scholarly consensus that the appearance of those two books gave the study of women in the Revolutionary era a striking significance it had scarcely known before. Susan Klepp, the chair of the SHEAR program committee that organized the plenary session, opened the proceedings by noting that "no reading list for graduate students in early American history or women's history

[210] For Taylor's briefer but broader view of the post-Revolutionary backcountry, see also "Agrarian Independence: Northern Land Rioters after the Revolution," in Young, ed., *Beyond the American Revolution*, 221–45.

[211] Mary Beth Norton, *Liberty's Daughters: The Revolutionary Experience of American Women, 1750–1800* (Boston, 1980); Linda K. Kerber, *Women of the Republic: Intellect and Ideology in Revolutionary America* (Chapel Hill, NC, 1980). For the papers in the 2005 SHEAR panel, see "Women Making History, 1750–1800, 1980–2005," *Uncommon Sense* 121 (2005), available online at http://oieahc.wm.edu/uncommon/121/women.cfm (accessed July 30, 2010). The online version, which is the most readily accessible, does not include pagination, and the references that follow will be only to the essays themselves.

would be complete without including these often paired monographs." Indeed, as Rosemarie Zagarri, one of the other panelists, later observed, "It is no exaggeration to say these two books defined a research agenda for a whole generation of scholars."[212]

The previous generation of scholars had had no such agenda, primarily because it had precious few women. Throughout most of the post–World War II era, women had been all but invisible in scholarly writing on the Revolution—an invisibility that stemmed, of course, not from the demography of eighteenth-century society, in which women accounted for essentially half the population, but from the demography of the twentieth-century historical profession, in which women had been exceedingly scarce and in which male historians refused to take women seriously as a category worthy of research, whether in the Revolutionary era or any other period. The most significant survey of women in the Revolutionary era before the publication of the Norton and Kerber books was a 1976 essay titled "The Illusion of Change" by Joan Hoff Wilson.[213] Assessing the admittedly scant secondary literature available at the time, Wilson reached the disconcerting conclusion that "the American Revolution produced no significant benefits for American women," particularly in terms of legal and political equality. The Revolutionary era even resulted in a loss of some of the social openness that had existed in the colonial era, creating greater constraints rather

[212] Susan Klepp, "A Quarter Century of Women and the American Revolution," and Rosemarie Zagarri, "On the Twenty-fifth Anniversary of the Publication of *Liberty's Daughters* and *Women of the Republic*," *Uncommon Sense* 121 (2005).

[213] Joan Hoff Wilson, "The Illusion of Change: Women and the American Revolution," in Young, ed., *American Revolution*, 385–431. For over a century up to that time, the most ambitious survey was Ellen F. Ellett, *The Women of the American Revolution*, 2 vols., originally published in 1848. Linda Grant DePauw's *Founding Mothers: Women in America in the Revolutionary Era* (Boston, 1975) aimed primarily at a young audience. DePauw and Conover Hunt also published a richly illustrated book for the Bicentennial, *"Remember the Ladies": Women in America, 1750–1815* (New York, 1976). On the historiography of women in the Revolutionary era, see Linda Kerber, "'History Can Do It No Justice': Women and the Reinterpretation of the American Revolution," in Ronald Hoffman and Peter J. Albert, eds., *Women in the Age of the American Revolution* (Charlottesville, VA, 1989), 3–42; and Mary Beth Norton, "Reflections on Women in the Age of the American Revolution," in ibid., 479–95; Jan Lewis, "A Revolution for Whom? Women in the Era of the American Revolution," in Nancy A. Hewitt. ed., *A Companion to Women's History* (Oxford, UK, 2002), 83–99; and Susan Branson, "From Daughters of Liberty to Women of the Republic: American Women in the Era of the American Revolution," in Kleinborg, Boris, and Ruiz, eds., *The Practice of U.S. Women's History*, 50–66. For a more general observation about the lack of scholarly interest paid to women and their history, see Carol Smith-Rosenberg, *Disorderly Conduct: Visions of Gender in Victorian America* (Oxford, UK, 1985), 20.

than expanding opportunities. For women, she concluded, "the American Revolution was over before it ever began."[214]

But at the time Wilson wrote that, new scholarship on women in the American Revolution was just on the verge of coming into view. The academic world was feeling the early effects of a subtle but certain demographic and intellectual shift, and both the number of women in the historical profession and the study of women in history were slowly starting to grow. To be sure, the comparatively few women doing graduate study in early American history in the late 1960s and early 1970s tended to work "within traditional parameters," Norton has observed, "focusing on politics diplomacy, and intellectual life."[215] Indeed, both Norton and Kerber did their dissertations, which later became their first books, on what were primarily political topics.[216] But Norton also points out that "historians' views of the past are always affected by their experiences in the present," and for Norton, Kerber, and many other women entering graduate school in the 1960s, one of the most dramatic experiences was "the modern feminist movement [that] erupted in that most turbulent decade." Both the movement and the moment "helped to create a revolution in the way history was studied"—including a revolution in the way the Revolution was studied.[217] In the still-early days of the "new social history," the particular case of women in the Revolutionary era seemed, as Norton put it, "on the outer fringes of scholarship," but she and Kerber made the most of the opportunity. Given the dearth of historiography on women in the Revolutionary era, Kerber explained to the SHEAR audience, "We did not have to defend

[214] Wilson, "Illusion of Change," 387, 431. Kathleen M. Brown, in "Brave New World: Women's and Gender History," *William and Mary Quarterly*, 3d ser. 50 (1993): 311–28, notes that "colonial women's history . . . served as a baseline for measuring the declension of women's status in the nineteenth century" (311). More recently, Rosemarie Zagarri has argued, in *Revolutionary Backlash: Women and Politics in the Early American Republic* (Philadelphia, 2007), that women's rights suffered a reversal in the post-Revolutionary era. The political and social upheaval of the late eighteenth century created new opportunities for women, she acknowledges, and for "a few brief decades, a comprehensive transformation in women's right, roles, and responsibilities seemed not only possible but perhaps inevitable." By the Jacksonian era, however, "this atmosphere had dissipated" (8).

[215] Mary Beth Norton and Ruth M. Alexander, preface to Norton and Alexander, eds., *Major Problems in American Women's History: Documents and Essays*, 2d ed. (Lexington, MA, 1996), vi.

[216] Kerber's 1968 Columbia dissertation was published as *Federalists in Dissent: Imagery and Ideology in Jeffersonian America* (Ithaca, NY, 1970); Norton's 1969 Harvard dissertation won the Allan Nevins Prize in 1970 and was published as *The British-Americans: The Loyalist Exiles in England, 1774–1789* (Boston, 1972).

[217] Norton and Alexander, preface to *Major Problems in American Women's History*, vi.

any intervention we made—no one had touched our subjects for twenty or thirty years; we could say anything!"[218]

What they said in 1980 marked quite a departure from the declensionist narrative Wilson had offered a few years before. While acknowledging Wilson's emphasis on the institutional restrictions that limited women in the Revolutionary era, Norton and Kerber also explored the social, intellectual, and political openings that women found—or, indeed, created. In addition to asking the obvious questions—How did women affect the course of the Revolution? How did the Revolution affect the condition of women?—both books opened up an even more fruitful line of inquiry: How did women emerge from the Revolutionary era with a greater sense of shaping social and political change to their own purposes? And therein lay an important challenge these books brought to modern scholarship. They made an intellectual breakthrough by addressing the issue of women's awareness and agency, preparing the ground for subsequent studies that would bring about a creative rethinking of the meaning of women's role in the Revolution, and even the meaning of the Revolution itself.

The 2005 SHEAR session offered a good opportunity not just to celebrate both books but also to assess their impact in shaping subsequent scholarship in the quarter century since their publication. Susan Klepp noted that although neither Norton nor Kerber used the word "gender" in their respective works—the term had not yet come into common usage among American historians in 1980—they did anticipate many of the issues that later came to the fore in the study of gender, providing the basis, she observed, "for much of the subsequent work on femininity, masculinity, republicanism, representation, identity, race, class, the body, and more."[219] Zagarri noted that Kerber and Norton "employed an unusual definition of politics" at the time, focusing not just on the formal processes of political life—voting, officeholding, and policymaking, all of which remained in male hands in the Revolutionary era—but on "all sorts of activities that, while not formally political, had political significance." In that regard, Kerber and Norton anticipated by at least a decade the subsequent discussion of the many varieties of political life in the "public sphere," which became

[218] Mary Beth Norton, "*Liberty's Daughters* at Twenty-five Years," and Linda Kerber, "*Women of the Republic* at Twenty-five," *Uncommon Sense* 121 (2005).

[219] Klepp, "Quarter Century of Women and the American Revolution." Joan W. Scott brought the issue of gender closer to the center of scholarly inquiry in a 1986 essay, "Gender: A Useful Category of Historical Analysis," *American Historical Review* 91 (1986): 1053–75, and Kathleen M. Brown addressed it directly in "Brave New World: Women's and Gender History."

an increasingly significant issue of scholarly debate in the 1990s.[220] Moreover, given the chronological coverage of their books, from the middle of the eighteenth century to the beginning of the nineteenth, they also anticipated the extended temporal emphasis of that debate, locating the very notion of the "Revolutionary era" within a somewhat longer, more elastic framework than had typically been the case. Indeed, much of the subsequent scholarship on women in early America deals not so much with the standard chronology of the Revolution, 1763–89, but with the periods before and after, placing particular emphasis on the years after 1790. To a large degree, the study of women's increasing engagement in the political and cultural changes of the "long" Revolutionary era, which now extends into the early republic, stems directly from the work Kerber and Norton began back in 1980.[221]

As innovative as these two books were at the time, both Kerber and Norton have acknowledged the limits of their original perspectives, pointing to some of the exclusions and omissions that subsequent scholarship has since tried to address, albeit with uneven success. As early as 1986, for instance, Kerber offered an insightful reassessment of a central issue in *Women of the Republic*, the political implications of what she called "Republican Motherhood"—that is, the notion that women could have a positive effect on the politics of the new nation by influencing their husbands and sons to be solid, self-sacrificing citizens, even if mothers and their daughters continued to be denied a formal role in the political process. What might have initially seemed like an innovative role in the immediate emergence of a new republican society, Kerber realized, became increasingly rigid in later years and "could be used to defend the exclusion of women from public life, by emphasizing their domestic obligations." At the SHEAR session, she acknowledged that she had never argued that the emergence of the Republican Mother was a "straightforwardly progressive move," nor did the notion of Republican Motherhood represent all mothers or all women. Moreover, she confessed to being appalled that her original emphasis on

[220] In the United States, the scholarly interest in the public sphere emerged with the English-language publication of Jürgen Habermas's 1962 study *The Structural Transformation of the Public Sphere: An Inquiry into a Category of Bourgeois Society*, trans. Thomas Burger (Cambridge, MA, 1989); the impact of this work on early American historians is discussed later in this essay.

[221] Zagarri, "On the Twenty-fifth Anniversary of the Publication of *Liberty's Daughters* and *Women of the Republic*." On the chronological shift in emphasis to the early Republic, see Branson, "From Daughters of Liberty to Women of the Republic," 59–60.

middle-class white women had led her to overlook considerations of race and class. "Why do I have no chapter on the economy?" she asked. "Why no chapter on race? I came so close."[222]

Norton's book originally came a bit closer—it included private writings from the pens of African American women, both free and enslaved—but she too acknowledged that neither she nor the rest of the profession had done enough to go beyond the study of women from elite families. In the preface to the 1996 paperback edition of *Liberty's Daughters*, she noted her disappointment that subsequent scholarship was still limited by "the lack of emphasis on women's actual experiences," and it had yet to provide a fuller picture of the Revolution's effect on ordinary women, including the enslaved: "With rare exceptions," she wrote, "none of that has happened." By 2005, she reminded the SHEAR audience of the paucity of studies offering a broader and deeper exploration of class and race, concluding that since "no one has yet systematically investigated their female contemporaries from non-elite families, it's not clear whether the patterns I described were class-specific or not."[223]

However much Kerber and Norton might reflect on any omissions in the books they originally published in 1980, the scholarly world is now a very different place because of their pathbreaking work. The avenues of inquiry now run in a wide variety of directions, not just toward the social history of women's lives or toward the political history of women's impact but toward a more complex exploration of the varieties of women's experiences, particularly in light of challenges to the traditional notions of gender that emerged during the era. "All women felt the effects of the new definitions of womanhood that emerged during the Revolution," Joan Gundersen has observed, "but the outcomes were not uniform."[224] Indeed they were not. While scholars can still appreciate the significant connections that cut across race, class, and culture—what Norton called the "universals of female lives, . . . the common experiences of femininity"—historians

[222] Linda Kerber, preface to the 1986 edition of *Women of the Republic*, vi; Kerber, "*Women of the Republic* at Twenty-five."

[223] Norton noted the possible biases of her research at the outset, in fact, in the preface to the original edition of *Liberty's Daughters*, xiv. For the subsequent reflections, see the preface to the Cornell Paperbacks Edition (Ithaca, NY, 1996), xv, and Norton, "*Liberty's Daughters* at Twenty-five Years."

[224] Joan R. Gundersen, *To Be Useful in the World: Women in Revolutionary America, 1740–1790* (New York, 1996), xv.

have increasingly come to take note of the differences as well.[225] Comparative considerations of race remain greatly overshadowed by studies of the experiences of Euro-American women, and the study of the effect of the Revolution on African American and Native American women is still spotty at best. Explorations of class have been somewhat more successful, adding new dimensions to our understanding of women's lives and, equally important, providing new methodological approaches to uncovering the lives of ordinary women.[226] On the whole, however, it is now impossible to ask "Whose Revolution was it?" without taking note of the revolution in scholarly writing about women that dates from 1980. Kerber and Norton helped highlight the need for writing women into the Revolution's narrative, and the result has energized the field, leading to a search for new sources and a rereading of old ones, listening for forgotten voices and looking for once-unseen people, and even taking renewed appreciation of a few of the most familiar faces.

13. New Approaches to Elite Women's Lives

Finding individual faces among the mass of women in Revolutionary America, though, can be difficult once one digs beneath the top layer of Revolutionary society, because the bias inherent in the traditional approach to biographical writing has created an imbalance in both the number and the nature of women's portraits available to us. Above all, as Edith Gelles has observed, women still stand in the biographical shadow of men. Even in a time when scholars give greater attention to the gendered differences between women and men, "biographies of women . . . have characteristically used the same analytic models that have long been standard for biographies of men"—among them the basic definition of the life cycle and the various measures of success in work and public life. This male-centered frame of reference leaves female subjects "reduced to a derivative place as a woman in a man's world" and fails to give equal attention or significance to women's identity within their own female world. The critical first step in

[225] Norton, *Liberty's Daughters*, xvi; Brown, "Brave New World," 312; Gundersen, *To Be Useful in the World*, xv.

[226] See, for instance, Lewis, "Revolution for Whom?" 93–96; Branson, "From Daughters of Liberty to Women of the Republic," 55–59; and two essays in Kleinborg, Boris, and Ruiz, eds., *The Practice of U.S. Women's History*: Gail D. Macleitch, "'Your Women Are of No Small Consequence': Native American Women, Gender, and Early American History," 30–49; and Betty Wood, "Southern Women of Color and the American Revolution, 1775–1783," 67–82.

taking the measure of women on their own terms, Gelles argues, is to understand what it meant for them to say, as Abigail Adams did, "I will take praise to myself." [227]

Abigail Adams leads the biographical pack, of course, and she provides the most compelling case in point. As Gelles has noted, the "Abigail industry" has become an enduring biographical genre of its own, making her the most familiar representative among Revolutionary-era women. Even before the rise of "Founders chic," she had been the subject of several biographies in the 1980s and early 1990s, and the publication of David McCullough's blockbuster biography of husband John brought Abigail back into bookstores at the beginning of the new century.[228] But it is precisely the emphasis on that sort of joint portrait, Gelles argues, that highlights Abigail's political side over her personal concerns and leads some scholars to seek a modern-seeming feminist in an eighteenth-century figure. The tendency to portray Abigail Adams as a woman torn between the revolutionary fervor of her times and the conservative temper of her domestic life creates a seeming contradiction, Gelles argues, that speaks more to the authors' present than to Abigail's past. The point is not to turn Abigail Adams's plea to her husband to "remember the ladies" into a radical call for equality (which it was not), nor, on the other hand, is it to turn her into a political or intellectual inferior to her husband (which she was not); rather, it is to understand her as a woman who best expressed her political and intellectual convictions in her private correspondence, not in public broadsides, and to accept her own private world as a subject worthy of study on its own terms, and not just as an adjunct area to husband John's political prominence.[229]

In that regard, Woody Holton offers a fresh approach to seeing Abigail Adams as a woman standing in her own light, and often standing up to John. In the summer of 1777, Holton tells us, she purchased a government

[227] Edith Gelles, "The Abigail Industry," *William and Mary Quarterly*, 3d ser. 45 (1988): 656–83, quotations at 657, 683.

[228] Gelles's own contribution to book-length studies of Abigail Adams is *Portia: The World of Abigail Adams* (Bloomington, IN, 1992). Charles Akers's *Abigail Adams: An American Woman* (Boston, 1980) was part of a biography series popular for classroom use. Lynn Withey's biography, *Dearest Friend: A Life of Abigail Adams* (New York, 1981), got a new lease on life in 2002, when Simon and Schuster, the parent company of her publisher, the Free Press, and the publisher of McCullough's *John Adams*, brought out a new edition of this two-decades-old book to appear in companionate stacks next to McCullough's, providing matching portraits of the most politically articulate and historically self-conscious couple of the Revolutionary generation.

[229] Gelles, "Abigail Industry," 658, 666–67.

bond, apparently as a hedge against the dramatic decline in the value of paper money, and it was the sort of savvy speculative investment she would make many times over in the ensuing years—usually without the permission, and often much to the frustration, of her more fiscally conservative husband. Abigail Adams invested widely and generally wisely, using, as she said, "money which I call mine" to take economic initiative in a society that kept women under the financial subjugation of their husbands. Her pride in using her own money to make her own decisions, Holton argues, particularly her unabashed denunciation of the doctrine of coverture and traditional assumptions about male-dominated property owning, put her well ahead of the cultural curve in Revolutionary America. Moreover, Holton suggests, Abigail Adams "may not have been the only woman who dragged her husband into the modern era" of financial activity.[230]

Thus Holton's emphasis on Abigail Adams's wartime economic activity does not merely offer a footnote to her family's financial status, nor is it simply another scene from this famous American marriage. Rather, it gives us an engaging insight into one woman's entry into a new sort of financial endeavor in the Revolution, opening wider the door to the larger interior of domestic relations. Abigail Adams may have shared her thoughts on women's equality primarily in the privacy of her voluminous letter writing, both to her husband and to many other men and women, but that does not lessen the seriousness of her sentiments or suggest that they were confined only to her correspondence: "She turned her own household into a laboratory where she imagined what the emancipation of women might look like," Holton concludes, and her example invites further investigation of the innovative domestic roles other women may have played as they pursued new opportunities in the Revolutionary era.[231]

For the sake of biographical comparison, Gelles notes that "Abigail's friend Mercy Otis Warren presents a far better example of a woman who was frustrated by the constraints of her sex" and who more openly put those complaints into public by pursuing a role as a published writer.[232] The same statement could as well apply to Judith Sargent Murray, who,

[230] Woody Holton, "Abigail Adams, Bond Speculator," *William and Mary Quarterly*, 3d ser. 64 (2007): 821–38, quotations at 829, 835. Holton continues his exploration of Abigail Adams's economic activities in a book-length biography, *Abigail Adams* (New York, 2009), and in "The Battle Against Patriarchy That Abigail Adams Won," in Young, Nash, and Raphael, eds., *Revolutionary Founders*, chap. 16.

[231] Holton, *Abigail Adams*, xi.

[232] Gelles, "Abigail Industry," 671.

like Warren, has taken a place beside Abigail Adams on the biographical bookshelf.[233] Both figures now offer an important picture of women's entry into public discourse. In addition to Mercy Otis Warren's own copious correspondence, she also wrote poems, plays, and essays with a pointed political perspective, and she has been called "the secret pen of the American Revolution."[234] She reached a literary pinnacle in 1805 with the publication of her three-volume *History of the Rise, Progress and Termination of the American Revolution*. That book marked her own rise to prominence as America's first female historian, but it also led to the near termination of her friendship with John Adams, who took deep offense at some of her observations, especially those about him.[235] Warren argued with Adams about her right to write history, and she refused to accept the notion that women had no political stake in society. Judith Sargent Murray took an equally assertive stance. In her own three-volume work, *The Gleaner* (1798), she included essays that expressed, as Sheila Skemp has put it, an "abiding concern with expanding economic, social, and even political opportunities for women," the then-radical conviction that "women, like men, should have the ability to make choices about their lives, to claim for themselves the promise set forth in the Declaration of Independence: the right to life, liberty, and the pursuit of happiness." Murray thus staked out a protofeminist position that defined, as Skemp puts it, "the outer limits to which any American woman might have aspired in the postrevolutionary age."[236]

And yet those outer limits still remained reasonably well within the bounds of the larger historical context. Zagarri and Skemp point out that both Warren and Murray, for all their individual outspokenness and intellectual eloquence, nonetheless made concessions to social convention, going only so far in promoting the cause of women. How far they went—or failed to go, as it were—is one of the more revealing results of their recent biographical evaluations. No one seeks to measure either Mercy Otis Warren or Judith Sargent Murray—or Abigail Adams, for that matter—by the

[233] Rosemarie Zagarri, *A Woman's Dilemma: Mercy Otis Warren and the American Revolution* (Wheeling, IL, 1995); Sheila Skemp, *Judith Sargent Murray: A Brief Biography with Documents* (Boston, 1998). Skemp has published a more recent and longer biography of Murray, *First Lady of Letters: Judith Sargent Murray and the Struggle for Female Independence* (Philadelphia, 2009), followed by an essay, "America's Mary Wollstonecraft: Judith Sargent Murray's Case for the Equal Rights for Women," in Young, Nash, and Raphael, eds., *Revolutionary Founders*, chap. 17.

[234] The phrase comes from Nancy Rubin Stuart, *The Muse of the Revolution: The Secret Pen of Mercy Otis Warren and the Founding of a Nation* (Boston, 2008), 5.

[235] Zagarri, *Woman's Dilemma*, xvi–xvii, 162–63; Stuart, *Muse of the Revolution*, 217–19.

[236] Skemp, *Judith Sargent Murray*, 5–6.

standards of modern feminist thought, and their biographers take appropriate pains to warn against reading too much radicalism into the record. These most politically articulate American women of the Revolutionary era continued to identify themselves with the men in their social milieu. Indeed, Zagarri observes that while Warren "transcended the traditional boundaries of womanhood in her private life, she felt unwilling or unable to challenge those limits publicly"—hence the title of Zagarri's biography, *A Woman's Dilemma*.[237] Skemp largely concurs in the case of Judith Sargent Murray: for all Murray's insistence about more egalitarian private relationships between women and men, she ultimately "remained an eighteenth-century woman who operated within the ideological and social constraints of her day."[238]

Those social constraints included class, and neither Warren nor Murray ultimately embraced an altogether inclusive view of who should be allowed to enjoy the benefits of greater equality. Mercy Otis Warren "never called for the expansion of women's political or legal rights," Zagarri writes, and she "had no sense of gender identity and little sense of solidarity with other women."[239] Even though Warren, Murray, and other elite women suffered many of the same social and political disadvantages as children, servants, and slaves, Skemp argues, they still "sought to distance themselves from the lower orders."[240] Class trumped gender, in short, and in the end both Zagarri and Skemp conclude that these two female figures represent, as Zagarri puts it, "both the limits and possibilities of woman's role in revolutionary America."[241]

On a larger level, in fact, these portraits of prominent women point to the limits and possibilities of the biographical study of women in Revolutionary-era America. A small number of well-placed and politically articulate women had the opportunity, even the privilege, of being able to communicate directly with patriot leaders—some of whom were, of course, their husbands—and in doing so, they helped create a place for a larger number of middle-class women in the political discourse of the Revolutionary era. Clearly, these studies of socially prominent women, precisely because they seek to explore the question of women's roles, provide much more than mere companion pieces to the individual portraits of their male

[237] Zagarri, *Woman's Dilemma*, 162.
[238] Skemp, *Judith Sargent Murray*, 109.
[239] Zagarri, *Woman's Dilemma*, 165.
[240] Skemp, *Judith Sargent Murray*, 109.
[241] Zagarri, *Woman's Dilemma*, xvii.

counterparts: even though their subjects shared the social position and the political passion of equally prominent men, their second-class status as women still gives them an additional dimension that speaks to the underlying social inequality in the Revolutionary era. But the political emergence of middle-class women cannot represent the full range of women's roles in the era. Women of lesser social status—certainly the majority of women in America at the time—found other ways to express themselves on the issues facing their country and their communities. To see more of their role in the Revolution, we have to look into some of the less refined areas of American society and consider the activities of other women, particularly those who did not possess the advantages of middle-class status, much less politically prominent husbands.

14. The Historical Recovery of Ordinary Women's Lives

To let the ordinary women of Revolutionary America speak more eloquently for themselves, then, has required imaginative means of listening carefully for those silent-seeming voices and asking important questions of fresh-seeming but often forgotten sources. No one has done more to pioneer that approach than Laurel Thatcher Ulrich, whose 1990 book about Martha Ballard, *A Midwife's Tale*, has reached near-iconic status in historical studies, bringing this mother-wife-midwife in rural post-Revolutionary Maine very much into the mainstream of scholarly analysis.[242] The book itself won a host of impressive awards—including the Joan Kelly and John H. Dunning Prize from the American Historical Association, the Bancroft Prize from Columbia University, and the Pulitzer Prize—and it has also been transformed into other media, including a documentary movie and a website, the latter of which provides primary sources, including a copy of Ballard's diary.[243] Now students, teachers, and other readers can not only read the book and see the movie, but they can see for themselves the same

[242] Laurel Thatcher Ulrich, *A Midwife's Tale: The Life of Martha Ballard, Based on Her Diary, 1785–1812* (New York, 1990).

[243] The film, *A Midwife's Tale*, was part of the American Experience series on PBS, and the PBS website contains links to additional sources: http://www.pbs.org/wgbh/amex/mwt/filmmore/index.html (accessed July 30, 2010). An even more elaborate website containing many more materials relating to the book can be found at http://dohistory.org/sitemap.html (accessed July 30, 2010). Another revealing portrait of a Revolutionary-era woman that has appeared as both a book and a film is Joy Day Buel and Richard Buel Jr., *The Way of Duty: A Woman and Her Family in Revolutionary America* (New York, 1984), which was the source for *Mary Silliman's War*, produced by Heritage Films, 1993.

document that stands at the center of Ulrich's study and then, as she did, explore other sources that enhance the historical context. If earlier historians and antiquarians found Ballard's diary to be "trivial and unimportant" or even sexually embarrassing, Ulrich treats it as a rich historical source.[244] In her hands, it has become both a revealing social and economic document, almost as much an account book as a record of day-to-day events, and a very personal material possession—"Martha Ballard, her diary," the front page says. In both respects, Ulrich helps us see Ballard as an individual woman playing a central role in a much wider world of rural women.

The social and economic investigation involved an intricate counting of the various comings and goings, the many events and activities of daily life, all of them accounted for on detailed data sheets. From that deconstruction of the diary, Ulrich was able to fashion a reconstruction of Ballard's considerable reach within her region. Clearly, Ballard was a busy woman, a "gadder" who got out of the house and into an extensive network of women, producing and exchanging foodstuffs and textiles with other women in the area, enlisting and managing the labor of younger women in the family and community, and, in her most celebrated role as midwife, bringing over eight hundred babies into the world. She also played a role Ulrich had identified in an earlier work, the housewife as "deputy husband," a woman who assumed responsibility for the family and finances while her husband was gone from home and, in the process, sometimes began to think about both herself and the family farm in different ways.[245] Abigail Adams famously assumed the title of "farmeriss," and she and other women began to speak of property in the first-person plural, as "our farming business."[246] In the case of Martha Ballard, Ulrich takes that notion one step further, arguing that "there were really two family economies" in the household of Ephraim and Martha Ballard—his, which centered on the timber trade with male landowners and merchants, and hers, which

[244] Ulrich, *Midwife's Tale*, 8–9.

[245] Laurel Thatcher Ulrich, *Good Wives: Image and Reality in the Lives of Women in Northern New England, 1650–1750* (New York, 1982), 50.

[246] See, for instance, Carol Berkin, *Revolutionary Mothers: Women in the Struggle for America's Independence* (New York, 2005), 39–41; and Susan Branson, *These Fiery Frenchified Dames: Women and Political Culture in Early National Philadelphia* (Philadelphia, 2001), 10–11. Edith Gelles offers the cautionary observation that Abigail Adams "took pleasure in her success as 'farmeress' and entrepreneur, but she looked forward to the time when John would return to function properly as head of the Adams household." See Gelles, "Abigail Industry," 671. The spelling "farmeriss" was Abigail Adams's original term, not "farmeress." I am grateful to Woody Holton for pointing out this distinction.

consisted of creating household income through her wide variety of relationships with women in the region.[247] Even "farmeriss" could hardly begin to describe the complexity of her calling.

Like Abigail Adams, Martha Ballard may have been exceptional in her economic reach, but her example points to a larger process, the engagement of women in a variety of economic enterprises, as both producers and consumers of household goods. In Ulrich's study of Ballard's world, for instance, she takes careful note, as Ballard herself did, of the many instances of women engaged in spinning, which was "a universal female occupation," and even quietly taking over weaving, which had traditionally been a man's trade, making the production and exchange of homespun cloth as a "neighborly trade . . . that assured women a place in economic life."[248] In a subsequent study, *The Age of Homespun*, Ulrich pushes the importance of homespun beyond its neighborhood roots, noting its economic value in a consumer revolution that had begun to transform American society on the eve of the social and political revolution: "The history of rural cloth-making," she writes, "is a story about the wealth that ordinary people created."[249] To tell that story, Ulrich again notes the gendered transition of weaving in the American colonial context, when this mostly male artisanal craft in seventeenth-century England increasingly became a form of female labor in rural eighteenth-century New England, where farm women worked as "domestic manufacturers who borrowed and traded implements with their neighbors, producing primarily for household use." But she also locates this feminization of weaving within a broader pattern of economic change in which women played a vital and increasingly visible role, as both purchasers and producers of household goods: "Far from being in opposition to one another," she argues, "'store-bought' and 'homemade' fabrics developed together."[250]

The upturn in textile consumption represented only part of women's participation in the broader market trends in Revolutionary-era America. In the years before the outbreak of war with Great Britain, people in the middle ranks of American society—the families of urban artisans and

[247] Ulrich, *Midwife's Tale*, 80.

[248] Ibid., 77.

[249] Laurel Thatcher Ulrich, *The Age of Homespun: Objects and Stories in the Creation of an American Myth* (New York, 2001), 38. For another work that incorporates material culture into the study of Revolutionary-era women, see Susan Stabile, *Memory's Daughters: The Material Culture of Remembrance in Eighteenth-Century America* (Ithaca, NY, 2004).

[250] Ulrich, *Age of Homespun*, 37, 4–5.

shopkeepers, to be sure, but also of independent yeomen in the countryside—described a sizable and increasingly successful segment of colonial society that enjoyed considerable comfort, whether measured by better nutrition or more material possessions. While scholars may be careful to argue that the increasing access to consumer goods in the second half of the eighteenth century could scarcely match the material accumulation that was to come in the nineteenth century, they do point to the more readily available array of finer items in the eighteenth-century home. "On the eve of the Revolution," Allan Kulikoff notes, "middling families owned knives and forks, fine ceramics, looking glasses, and high-quality cloth, goods about which their grandparents could only dream."[251] Indeed, Timothy Breen has argued that the dreams of American consumers helped make the American Revolution a reality. The more British imports began to spread (if not truly flood) across the American colonies, the more the colonists found themselves facing a then-remarkable range of consumer choices, so much so that they found themselves fashioning a new social consciousness derived from their material desires. They became consumed by consumerism, so to speak. But then, when the change in British tax policies in the 1760s seemed to pose a threat to their ability to have the material goods they wanted, their commitment to individual choice as consumers became conflated with their commitment to individual rights as citizens, and as Breen argues, the question of consumption, albeit a "bourgeois virtue" on the surface, became the psychological cement of the resistance movement.[252]

Women played two important roles in this consumption crisis. On one hand, they drove the demand for certain sorts of consumer goods, whether utilitarian implements for the kitchen and table or finer textiles and decorative domestic items, and if they did not control the purchasing power of the household, they certainly shaped it. Breen quotes a midcentury Marylander who perceptively, if somewhat derisively, noted "the influence of Wives upon their Husbands," pointing out that once women had fixed their desires on some consumer good, "they must be taken notice of or there will be nothing done with them." On the other hand, they produced homemade

[251] Allan Kulikoff, "Whither the Progress of Inequality?" *William and Mary Quarterly*, 3d ser. 57 (2000): 825–32, quotation at 831; for his more extended discussion of changing consumption patterns in the agrarian economy, see *From British Peasants to Colonial American Farmers*, 220–23, 240–42.

[252] T. H. Breen, *The Marketplace of Revolution: How Consumer Politics Shaped American Independence* (Oxford, UK, 2004).

goods that replaced British imports, first as a form of protest in the cause of nonimportation, then as a fact of necessity in the face of British blockades. From the mid-1760s through the early 1780s, the industry and frugality they practiced became emblematic of Revolutionary virtue, providing an alternative to the imported "baubles" of Britain and the underlying vice of "luxury," and the economic contribution of women to the war effort took on considerable symbolic, even patriotic, significance, which both their contemporaries and later historians came to recognize.[253]

Yet the political symbolism of these baubles and homemade goods is not the only measure of their significance to historians. In arguing for "the value of object-centered research in social history," Ulrich adds a different twist to the importance of material objects, focusing on the possible implications of possession within the gendered context of the household. Just as there were "two economies" in the Ballard household, his and hers, so there were two sorts of property in most American households—his, in "real" property, land; and "hers," in "movable" goods, whether utilitarian objects or decorative items. "In a world where most forms of wealth were controlled by male heads of household," Ulrich writes, "certain objects were in some sense owned by women."[254] Indeed, women often expressed ownership by putting their mark on particular pieces of movable property—quite literally, with their names or initials—thus not only claiming possession of a material object but also linking their identity to its later inheritance.

In the longer run, when viewed from the larger trajectory running from the middle of the eighteenth century to the middle of the nineteenth, the significance of consumption during the years surrounding the Revolution can now be seen as part of a longer-term process of economic transformation—one in which the hitherto invisible hand of women can now also be seen as an increasingly important force. By the early decades of the nineteenth century, Christopher Clark has argued in a case study of the Connecticut River valley, the ever-increasing purchase of household

[253] Ibid., 130. See also T. H. Breen, "'Baubles of Britain': The American and the Consumer Revolutions in the Eighteenth Century," in Cary Carson, Ronald Hoffman, and Peter J. Albert, eds., *Of Consuming Interests: The Style of Life in the Eighteenth Century* (Charlottesville, VA, 1994), 442–82; and Jane Merritt, "Tea Trade, Consumption, and the Republican Paradox in Pre-Revolutionary Philadelphia," *Pennsylvania Magazine of History and Biography* 128 (2004): 117–48.

[254] Laurel Thatcher Ulrich, "Hannah Barnard's Cupboard: Female Property and Identity in Eighteenth-Century New England," in Hoffman, Sobel, and Teute, eds., *Through a Glass Darkly*, 238–73, quotations at 240, 273.

goods, especially machine-made textiles, had begun both to reflect and to facilitate a quiet revolution in the economic and demographic patterns of rural society, providing a foretaste of a larger and more general transition yet to come with the spread of industrial capitalism.[255] At the same time, Ulrich reminds us, the consumption of imported goods and the production of homemade items were not separate processes, nor were the goods themselves mere measures of long-term trends in economic activity. They were that, of course, but they were more than that—material manifestations of symbolic expressions of women's changing place in the household and society as a whole, physical representations of a widespread desire for refinement, and a growing political insistence "that in a republic women might be both manufacturers and ladies."[256]

Long before women could become manufacturers, much less "ladies" in the republic, though, they had to contribute to the creation of that republic, which occasionally meant engaging in other than ladylike behavior. In the tumult of revolutionary times, women almost always appeared on the scene in political demonstrations and riots, sometimes on the sidelines as spectators to major events, sometimes as worshipers or mourners or exhorters, and sometimes as active participants in open protest. That last category, of course, took them beyond the standard patterns of what their society considered "acceptable" political behavior. Barbara Clark Smith argues in her exploration of food riots in Revolutionary America that no matter how much women may have been "politically disabled by their dependent status," they broke the constraints commonly associated with their gender: in dozens of instances they became quite politically active when they took part in, even organized, forceful protests against price-gouging merchants thought to be hoarding food or selling it at an exorbitant cost. Although drawing on political traditions of the "moral economy" and popular regulation that reflected longstanding European precedents, the women who engaged in food riots in Revolutionary America also reacted to the more immediate context of crisis in their communities. Indeed, Smith argues, their "capacity to act within a local, plebeian public arose . . . from embeddedness in a community." Turning on local shopkeepers who seemed to be working against the common good, they identified their own communal

[255] Christopher Clark, *The Roots of Rural Capitalism: Western Massachusetts, 1780–1860* (Ithaca, NY, 1990), esp. 121–91. See also Kulikoff, *Agrarian Origins of American Capitalism*, 49; and Catherine Kelly, "Gender and Class Formations in the Antebellum North," in Hewitt, ed., *Companion to American Women's History*, 100–116.

[256] Ulrich, *Age of Homespun*, 415.

protest as part of the larger Revolutionary cause, claiming that "confronting merchants in their shops was a patriotic action, much like facing redcoats on the battlefield."[257]

Some women actually did face redcoats on the battlefield, and a few even served as soldiers, a subject that is now beginning to get its historical due. The partly factual, partly fictionalized figure of "Molly Pitcher" —a composite portrait "both as real and as legendary as G.I. Joe," Linda Grant DePauw tells us—is by no means the only example of women who took up arms in the struggle, either on an emergency basis or for more extended terms of service.[258] Some women disguised themselves as men and enlisted as soldiers, a practice not at all approved by the military command, of course, but also not altogether uncommon in the earlier history of European armies or, to a lesser degree, in the history of the American army in the Revolution. Indeed, the mythical figure of the "Amazonian" woman warrior became a part of popular culture on both sides of the Atlantic in the late eighteenth century, and the image had an especially useful ideological value in a revolutionary society in which many social and political norms were frequently subject to challenge.[259] Image aside, though, the reality of a woman's assuming the military role of a man did not always sit so well in eighteenth-century society: women who actually dared trespass the boundaries of dress, not to mention gender identity, in service to

[257] Barbara Clark Smith, "Food Rioters and the American Revolution," *William and Mary Quarterly*, 3d ser. 51 (1994): 3–38, quotations at 5, 31, 6. For examples of women engaged in Revolutionary-era public protest, see Alfred F. Young, "'Persons of Consequence': The Women of Boston and the Making of the American Revolution," in *Liberty Tree*, esp. 117–19; and Susan E. Klepp, "Rough Music in Philadelphia, July 4, 1778," in Pencak, Dennis, and Newman, eds., *Riot and Revelry in Early America*, 156–76.

[258] Linda Grant DePauw, "Fortunes of War: New Jersey Women in the American Revolution," *New Jersey's Revolutionary Experience* (New Jersey Historical Commission) 26 (1975): 31. She has also written a book for young readers, *In Search of Molly Pitcher* (Lulu.com, 2007), in which an eighth-grade student searches for evidence about the famous figure, sifting fact from fiction as she engages in a detective-like investigation of the past. For explorations of another quasi-fictive female figure in the Revolution, Betsy Ross, see Ulrich, "How Betsy Ross Became Famous: Oral Tradition, Nationalism, and the Invention of History," *Common-Place* 8 (2007), http://www.common-place.org/vol-08/no-01/ulrich/ (accessed July 30, 2010); and Marla R. Miller, *Betsy Ross and the Making of America* (New York, 2010).

[259] On the Amazonian woman warrior in eighteenth-century European culture, see Julie Wheelwright, *Amazons and Military Maids: Women Who Dressed as Men in Pursuit of Life, Liberty and Happiness* (London, 1990). Two essays in Robert Blair St. George, ed., *Possible Pasts: Becoming Colonial in Early America* (Ithaca, NY, 2000), address American examples: Susan Juster, "'Neither Male nor Female': Jemima Wilkinson and the Politics of Gender in Port-Revolutionary America," 357–79, esp. 377; and Sandra M. Gustafson, "The Genders of Nationalism: Patriotic Violence, Patriotic Sentiment in the Performances of Deborah Sampson Gannett," 380–99, esp. 389–90.

their country often suffered public censure upon exposure. Holly Mayer recounts, for instance, the unfortunate tale of a New Jersey woman who enlisted as a man in 1778 and, when found out, was paraded through her town with what the official record called the "whores march."[260]

The unfair association of women in the military with "whores" has long been even more broadly extended to women who came to be called "camp followers," a category that encompassed a much larger number of women in the Revolution. This slur reflects careless historical forgetting or, even worse, a willful misrepresentation of both gender and class among those "others belonging to the army," as they were known at the time. Mayer and DePauw, the leading historians of women in the Revolutionary-era military, have now given the more complex picture of army life the attention it deserves. They provide a more complex picture of these "others," noting that not only were they not all prostitutes, but they were not even all women. Instead of making a simple distinction between male army and female auxiliaries, Mayer offers a useful notion of a diverse and inclusive "Continental community"—male and female, old and young, white and black, free and slave, married and single—a sometimes stationary, often mobile mix of people in which women played a variety of vital roles in support of the military effort.[261]

This wartime community reflected many of the traditional gender and class distinctions of the more settled prewar communities: most women in military encampments performed familiar domestic tasks—cooking, cleaning, caring for the sick and wounded—and most of the difficult and demanding duties fell to poorer women, particularly the wives of enlisted men, not to the wives of officers. In some respects, in fact, the experience of living in this Continental community may have exacerbated the social distinctions that existed in more stable-seeming times. The comparative paucity of people from the middling classes, Mayer suggests, underscored the distance between the officers' wives and other women. Moreover, the uncertainties of war accentuated a nostalgia for normal life that reinforced

[260] Holly Mayer, *Belonging to the Army: Camp Followers and Community during the American Revolution* (Columbia, SC, 1999).

[261] Ibid., 4 ff. Linda Grant DePauw led the way in earlier work on women in the military; see "Women in Combat: The American Revolutionary War Experience," *Armed Forces and Society* 7 (1981): 209–26; and *Battle Cries and Lullabies: Women in War from Prehistory to the Present* (Norman, OK, 1998), 115–31. See also Dorothy Dennen Volo and James M. Volo, *Daily Life during the American Revolution* (Westport, CT, 2003), 229–54; and Nancy K. Loane, *Following the Drum: Women at the Valley Forge Encampment* (Washington, DC, 2009).

the roles of men and women: "Exposed as they were to the horrors of war and the harshness of life on campaign, the men and women of the army may have clung all the more tenaciously to an image of peaceful domesticity." On the other hand, she argues, precisely because the common domestic tasks had become so necessary to the success, even survival, of the army, women of the Continental community gained—at least in their own minds if not always in the estimation of the general public—a heightened sense of their contribution to the patriot cause.[262]

No single example offers a more engaging exploration of the contributions of women to the cause than that of Deborah Sampson, an ordinary woman whose extraordinary role as a soldier made her a post-Revolutionary celebrity. Her story both fascinated and shocked people in her own time, and it has become the subject of fresh scholarly study in ours. Rather than being dismissed as an uncommon anomaly, Deborah Sampson is now getting serious historical attention.

Born to a poor farm family in Massachusetts in 1760, she spent much of her youth as an indentured servant in another family's household and then worked as a spinner, a weaver, and, for a while, a teacher.[263] When she was in her early twenties, she sought an escape from the constraints of her community by disguising herself as a young man, taking the name Robert Shurtliff, and enlisting in the Massachusetts line of the Continental army in 1782. She served as a common soldier in the light infantry for more than a year, her sex undetected until she became ill and a doctor's examination revealed her to be a woman; still, she stayed in the army long enough to be mustered out with an honorable discharge. After the war, she returned to Massachusetts, married Benjamin Gannett Jr., had three children, and, like other veterans, suffered from the after-effects of her wounds and, above all, from the distresses of the postwar economy; also like other veterans, she applied for financial relief and spent years pursuing a pension. To bolster her case, she enlisted the support of two writers, Herman Mann and Philip Freneau, to tell her story in print; Mann's as-told-to memoir, *The Female Review* (1797), became a modest best-seller, giving Sampson some measure of fame in her region. Beginning in 1802, she began to tell her own story in public, speaking to audiences of middle-class men and women across the Northeast, appearing on stage both in decorous female dress and, in the

[262] Mayer, *Belonging to the Army*, 124.

[263] The biographical sketch that follows is drawn from Alfred F. Young, *Masquerade: The Life and Times of Deborah Sampson, Continental Soldier* (New York, 2004).

second part of her performance, in the uniform of a common soldier. By telling her story in print and performance, Sampson inserted herself into the history of the Revolution, gaining a degree of individual visibility few women of her era—and certainly of her class—could ever hope to achieve.

Telling Deborah Sampson's story to a modern audience, however, has posed more than a few scholarly challenges, because her biographical documentation remains spotty and, in some details, specious. She did not produce a voluminous cache of correspondence, as did Abigail Adams and some of her prominent peers: only two of Sampson's letters are extant, along with several short petitions for pension support. Neither did she keep a detailed diary for a long stretch of time, as did Martha Ballard: only a brief diary/account book for 1802–3 remains. Moreover, as is commonly the case in collaborating with an as-told-to author, some of Deborah Sampson's story got lost or distorted in the telling, and Mann occasionally took liberties with the truth (sometimes based on Deborah Sampson's contrivance or compliance). Given the paucity and questionable veracity of the standard sorts of sources historians typically use, then, writing about someone such as Deborah Sampson requires a different, even detective-like approach that involves a considerable amount of triangulation and imagination. In the case at hand, it involved finding clues by looking into the larger context of Sampson's surroundings—her community, her church, her house—and looking at the few intimate remnants of her personal life, from her wedding dress to her recorded dreams. None of those details, of course, can match the wide and well-marked documentary trail of the most prominent people of the era, but Alfred Young portrays the pursuit of evidence as an important moral to the story: "I was amazed at what you could find," he writes, "if you only looked." In that regard, re-creating the elusive life and times of Deborah Sampson serves as a source of historical encouragement, providing an example of seeking "to piece together the lives of people that scholars too often say are beyond recovery."[264]

The larger question remains, of course, what the recovery of this life story tells us. On one level, the case of Deborah Sampson might be little

[264] Young, *Masquerade*, 12–19, quotation at 18. For other studies of Deborah Sampson's collaboration with Herman Mann, see Judith Hiltner, "'She Bled in Secret': Deborah Sampson, Herman Mann and *The Female Review*," *Early American Literature* 34 (1999): 190–220; and Hiltner, "'The Example of Our Heroine: Deborah Sampson and the Legacy of Herman Mann's *The Female Review*," *American Studies* 41 (2000): 93–113. Mechal Sobel, *Teach Me Dreams: The Search for Self in the Revolutionary Era* (Princeton, NJ, 2002), provides a creative investigation and interpretation of Deborah Sampson's dreams (191–93).

more than just an interesting, even idiosyncratic, account of an extraordinary person who emerged among the ordinary people of the Revolutionary era. But by excavating the various shards of Sampson's life, Young and other scholars have used her story to expose several deep-seated fissures in the foundation of cultural assumptions about gender and class that underlay late eighteenth-century society. Sampson gives us an especially evocative view, for instance, of the ways gender identity could become more variable, or at least not so inviolable, as some students of early America might assume. As a woman who put on men's clothing to take on a new persona in public, first playing a soldier's role in the war and then performing that role on the stage, Sampson surely stretched the traditional standards of dress and decorum that helped distinguish male and female identity in her society.[265] But she employed costume as a means of disguising her identity for her immediate purposes, not of defining it on a permanent basis. In Sampson's era, gender identity did not carry the sexual essentialism that it later came to have in more "modern" times. Like a few other eighteenth-century female figures who likewise gained celebrity in men's clothes—Hannah Snell, the "Female Soldier" in the midcentury British army, or Jemima Wilkinson, the messianic evangelist of late eighteenth-century America—Deborah Sampson used male costume to fulfill, ultimately, a female role. Sampson and the others, Susan Juster argues, "dressed in men's clothes not because they believed themselves to be men but because male attire afforded them greater freedom and flexibility in pursuing their goals—goals that their contemporaries almost always accepted as consistent with proper gender norms."[266]

And in the end, Young explains, being consistent with proper gender norms forms a central part of Deborah Sampson's story. As much as she struggled against the constraints of her culture as a young woman in her early twenties, she used her soldier's costume to elicit sympathy, not shock, from her audience as a wife and mother in her early forties. On the stage,

[265] For a valuable analysis of the challenges to gender identity in Deborah Sampson's performances, see Sandra M. Gustafson, *Eloquence Is Power: Oratory and Performance in Early America* (Chapel Hill, NC, 2000), 246–55. Borrowing a term from Martin Duberman, Young refers to Deborah Sampson as a "gender nonconformist." See Young, *Masquerade*, 304.

[266] Juster, "'Neither Male nor Female,'" 374. This essay represents Juster's most thorough treatment of Jemima Wilkinson to date, but Wilkinson has also been a recurring figure in Juster's earlier work: see, for instance, Juster, *Disorderly Women: Sexual Politics and Evangelicalism in Revolutionary New England* (Ithaca, NY, 1994), 165; and "To Slay the Beast: Visionary Women in the Early Republic," in Susan Juster and Lisa Macfarlane, eds., *A Mighty Baptism: Race, Gender, and the Creation of American Protestantism* (Ithaca, NY, 1996), 28.

she performed her soldier's role to help secure a soldier's pension, replaying a part for a belated benefit that would allow her to give up her public appearances and return home to her family. Indeed, she struggled to gain social acceptance *as a woman*, to be sure that "anyone who looked at her could have known that this was the lady who once upon a time was a Continental soldier." Being seen as a "lady" mattered to her, especially when she performed before "respectable" women of polite society, whose class status she did not share but whose approval she nonetheless sought, as Sandra Gustafson notes, with a "concluding celebration of republican womanhood and separate spheres."[267]

In that sense, Deborah Sampson presents modern scholars, no less than her contemporary audiences, with a set of contrasts, even contradictions. She employed sexual ambiguity to pursue social ambition, challenging convention to secure a conventional goal. She performed in public to gain income, but when she addressed her audience, she did not speak out openly for greater social freedom, much less full equality, for women in general. She embodied—quite literally, sometimes, in her physical appearance—the push and pull of gender identity in her society. She pushed against the boundaries of dress and decorum, but she responded to the pull of home and family, and she certainly pulled back from the brink of becoming a champion for women's rights. And yet looking at Deborah Sampson in her own time still invites us to imagine what her presence on stage might have meant to other women who saw her perform and invites us to appreciate, as Young puts it, "how remarkable it was that she was there before them to be seen and heard."[268]

15. Women in the Post-Revolutionary Public Sphere

The ability of women to be seen and heard in the public arena can hardly be taken for granted, and the ways Revolutionary-era women struggled to achieve a greater political presence has become a significant focus of scholarship. American women did not openly seek suffrage, nor did they receive it as a result of the Revolution (but for one brief exception, in New Jersey, from 1777 to 1807). Indeed, Rosemary Zagarri notes that the expansion of the electorate in the post-Revolutionary era actually defined the

[267] Young, *Masquerade*, 319; Gustafson, "Genders of Nationalism," 374; see also Gustafson, *Eloquence Is Power*, 255–57.
[268] Young, *Masquerade*, 224.

"darker side of the democratic process," in which "the broadening of political opportunities for white males meant the increasing exclusion of white females." Yet voting, much less officeholding, can hardly define the political implications of women's place in post-Revolutionary society. Women may have been confined to the sidelines of formal political activity, but they were by no means "political ciphers," as Zagarri puts it, nor were they indifferent to the implications of public affairs: they still exercised some rights of citizenship and, on some occasions, intervened directly in the political world dominated by men.[269] The notion of the Republican Mother's effect on her family, much less the traditional distinction between the public and the private as separate and gendered realms, has by no means disappeared, but both have been subjected to a critical rethinking, emphasizing the forms of women's agency that defined alternative sources of female influence in the broader political world. Making a place in that society involved a new emphasis on education, mutual support, self-improvement, and above all, self-expression in the world of political discourse. Building on the initial insights of Norton and Kerber, subsequent scholarship has turned increasing attention to the ways women, through their own reading, writing, and talking with other women (and with some men), not only engaged political ideas and issues but developed their own voices and began to speak as people educated to play a role in public life beyond the household.

The emphasis on education and self-improvement has received its most comprehensive treatment in Mary Kelley's *Learning to Stand and Speak.* The title aptly expresses the first stage of the process for young women: learning took place in female academies, where lessons in standing (proper posture, gesture, and self-presentation) and speaking (polite conversation, oratory, and elocution) gave young women the confidence and ability to assert themselves gracefully and effectively in society.[270] But Kelley, like other scholars, also pays attention to women's education beyond the formal institution of the female academy, looking at the more informal circles of female society and the process of lifelong learning that began with reading. Indeed, the history of the book, the impact of print culture, and particularly the significance of reading have become particularly prominent

[269] Zagarri provides a very useful and succinct discussion of the gendered implications of the expansion of suffrage in the introduction to *Revolutionary Backlash*, 1–10, quotations at 10, 44. See also Alexander Keyssar, *The Right to Vote: The Contested History of Democracy in the United States* (New York, 2000), 20, 54.

[270] Mary Kelley, *Learning to Stand and Speak: Women, Education, and Public Life in America's Republic* (Chapel Hill, NC, 2006).

fields since the 1980s, especially in scholarly approaches to the social and political roles of Revolutionary-era women.[271] Books and periodicals gave politically literate women an entrée to what Elaine Crane has called a "literary playground," where they could engage men on an intellectually level field. Often drawing directly on the contemporary trans-Atlantic classics—works by Swift, Locke, Molière, Goldsmith, Trenchard, Gordon, and a host of other authors—well-read women could become adept at expressing themselves by appropriating ideas and language through "artistic adaptation," Crane explains, turning to their own rhetorical purposes a set of literary references "replete with hidden meanings, text out of context, and allusions to more progressive writers of [the] time."[272]

More to the point, the recent scholarship on print culture has reshaped our understanding of the very nature of reading, casting new light on what once might have seemed an essentially solitary and comparatively passive activity. We now understand the ways many women made reading a shared experience, not only exchanging volumes that circulated among what Crane calls "informal female book-trading networks" but also exchanging ideas in the conversations that took place in the women's reading circles of which

[271] Since at least the early 1980s, the American Antiquarian Society has become an important center of promoting print history, and Kelley and a growing number of American historians working in concert with the AAS—Cathy Davidson, David D. Hall, Ronald Zboray, and Mary Saraceno Zboray, to name some of the most prominent—have helped make the history of reading a lively field for the study of early America. AAS has also sponsored an ongoing lecture series, the James Russell Wiggins Lectures in the History of the Book in American Culture, and a five-volume series, *A History of the Book in America*, the first two volumes of which have special applicability to the discussion at hand: see Hugh Amory and David D. Hall, eds., *The Colonial Book in the Atlantic World* (Cambridge, UK, 1999); and Robert A. Gross and Mary Kelley, eds., *An Extensive Republic: Print, Culture, and Society in the New Nation, 1790–1840* (Chapel Hill, NC, 2009).

A truly pathbreaking book in the field was Cathy N. Davidson, *Revolution and the Word: The Rise of the Novel in America* (Oxford, UK, 1986; reprint 2002); see also Davidson, "The Novel as Subversive Activity: Women Reading, Women Writing," in Young, ed., *Beyond the American Revolution*, 283–316. Other works on reading and writing in early America include David S. Shields, *Civil Tongues and Polite Letters in British America* (Chapel Hill, NC, 1997); Catherine E. Kelly, *In the New England Fashion: Reshaping Women's Lives in the Nineteenth Century* (Ithaca, NY, 1999); Heidi Brayman Hackel and Catherine E. Kelly, eds., *Reading Women: Literacy, Authorship, and Culture in the Atlantic World, 1500–1800* (Philadelphia, 2009); Eve Tavor Bannett, *Empire of Letters: Letter Manuals and Transatlantic Correspondence, 1620–1820* (Cambridge, UK, 2005); Konstantin Dierks, *In My Power: Letter Writing and Communications in Early America* (Philadelphia, 2009); Carolyn Eastman, *A Nation of Speechifiers: Making an American Public after the Revolution* (Chicago, 2009); and Sarah M. S. Pearsall, *Atlantic Families: Lives and Letters in the Later Eighteenth Century* (Oxford, UK, 2009).

[272] Elaine Forman Crane, "Political Dialogue and the Spring of Abigail's Discontent," *William and Mary Quarterly*, 3d. ser. 56 (1999): 745–74, quotation at 745.

Kelley writes. In fact, Kelley underscores the significance of understanding women's reading not just as a private, individual act but as a collaborative and "profoundly social activity"—and social in two significant ways. First, as women read and discussed books together, they engaged in a process of mutual self-improvement. "In and through their collaborations," Kelley argues, "they sanctioned and supported intellectual productivity. Simultaneously, they fostered in each other the self-confidence that was crucial to their next step—the making of public opinion in civil society." Second, to the extent that women took that next step, from reading together to shaping public opinion, they entered a much larger social and political arena. By reading, writing, and "learning to stand and speak," women did not just gain greater comfort in talking among themselves, Kelley argues. They gave expression to an expanded notion of political participation and laid the groundwork for a greater appreciation of the varieties of citizenship in a new republican society.[273] Defining the various points of entry into the larger political arena suggests subtle but significant shifts in scholarly thinking that now occupy a prominent place in the discussion of women's role in the Revolutionary and post-Revolutionary eras.

Taking up the pen to petition the government represents an important point of entry. Susan Branson argues that a woman's assertion of her rights in a petition to her government could represent "her self-conception as an engaged political individual."[274] Petitioning was, of course, a common political practice that, as Cynthia Kierner puts it, "came to America with its English colonizers," but not one traditionally identified with women. In a study of women in the Revolutionary-era South, Kierner has brought to light several hundred petitions women wrote to their respective state assemblies between 1776 and 1800, documents addressing a wide range of issues, from individual appeals for pension benefits to broader political issues, including emancipation. But when women took up the pen to petition political officials, she adds, "they ventured into an alien and overwhelmingly masculine environment." She does not overstate the boldness of this venture: the women's petitions necessarily expressed deference to male authority, not defiance of it. Still, she argues, the very act of putting their appeals on paper indicates "that women in the revolutionary era did not regard themselves as utterly ignorant and ineffectual."[275]

[273] Kelley, *Learning to Stand and Speak*, 117.

[274] Branson, *These Fiery Frenchified Dames*, 10–11.

[275] Cynthia A. Kierner, *Southern Women in Revolution, 1776–1800: Personal and Political Narratives* (Columbia, SC, 1998), xx, xiv, xxi.

Whether deferential or defiant in tone, the petitions provide an insight into a process of political emergence, when the writings of women reflect the political product of thought, discussion, and debate—a process, in short, of women engaging in the same sort of political activity as many of their male counterparts.

Branson and Catherine Allgor have offered even more extensive studies of women and politics in the immediate post-Revolutionary era, both focusing on the national capitals of the new nation, Philadelphia in the 1780s and 1790s in Branson's case and Washington City in the first three decades of the nineteenth century in Allgor's.[276] Both books look beyond the basic forms of political engagement, such as voting and even petitioning, to explore a variety of women's activities with a political edge—again reading and writing but also taking part in public ceremonies, performances, and productions and, for elite women at least, engaging in pointed political conversation in the class-restricted intimacy of levees and salons. Branson notes, for instance, that unlike contemporary salon culture in France, where politics and politesse did not commonly mix well, "American salons were an arena for national political society." If the elite women of the capital cities did not participate in the political process in a formal way, they nonetheless fashioned their own political parties of a sort, social gatherings that created an alternative arena of political discourse that involved men as invited guests, where both style and substance mattered, and so did the opinions of women. Politically connected women became accustomed to talking to men about political issues, and men increasingly (albeit in many cases grudgingly) likewise became accustomed to the conversation. The impact of politically articulate women on politically powerful men emerges as one of the more subtle results of the Revolution: it was not so much that women suddenly began to talk politics—they had always done so, Branson reminds us, "at the tea table, in the bedchamber, at dancing assemblies"—but that they used the new institution of the salon to "help

[276] Branson, *These Fiery Frenchified Dames*; Catherine Allgor, *Parlor Politics: In Which the Ladies of Washington Help Build a City and a Government* (Charlottesville, VA, 2000). For other studies dealing with middle-class women in the political life of post-Revolutionary capitals, see also Allgor, *Dolley Madison and the Creation of the American Nation* (New York, 2006); and two essays in Donald R. Kennon, ed., *A Republic for the Ages: The United States Capitol and the Political Culture of the Early Republic* (Charlottesville, VA, 1999): Fredrika Teute, "Roman Matron on the Banks of Tiber Creek: Margaret Bayard Smith and the Politicization of Spheres in the Nation's Capital," 89–121, and Jan Lewis, "Politics and the Ambivalence of the Private Sphere: Women in Early Washington, D.C.," 122–51.

create a public political space for women which had not previously existed in America."[277]

The use of the phrase "public political space" speaks to an issue that entered American historical discourse with increasing frequency since the 1990s—the notion of the public sphere. The 1989 translation of the German philosopher Jürgen Habermas's original 1962 work, *The Structural Transformation of the Public Sphere*, offered Anglophone readers a challenging analysis of the emergence of an intellectual arena that defined "a sphere between civil society and the state," as his translator put it, "in which critical public discussion of matters of general interest was institutionally guaranteed."[278] Indeed, so the argument goes, the rise of rational discourse about important social and political issues gave middle-class people—primarily men, in Habermas's estimation—a means of offsetting, even opposing, the power of an absolutist state.

But whereas Habermas was ultimately concerned with what he saw as the eventual disintegration of the public sphere in the twentieth century, early American historians took more immediate notice of his emphasis on its emergence in the latter part of the eighteenth century.[279] In the particular case of the Revolutionary era in the United States, the notion of the public sphere has given historians a way of better explaining the political implications of different varieties of involvement in republican society. John Brooke, one of the leading early Americanists in exploring the applicability of Habermas's study for post-Revolutionary society, has observed that "the concept of a 'public sphere of civil society' is particularly useful in the context of the early republic, suggesting new ways we can link perspectives on society, culture, and politics."[280] What was particularly useful about it was its emphasis on the expanding and increasingly open arena

[277] Branson, *These Fiery Frenchified Dames*, 138, 140–41.

[278] Thomas Burger, "Translator's Note," in Habermas, *The Structural Transformation of the Public Sphere*, xi.

[279] See especially "Forum: Alternative Histories of the Public Sphere," *William and Mary Quarterly*, 3d. ser. 62 (2005): 3–112.

[280] John Brooke, "Ancient Lodges and Self-Created Societies: Voluntary Association and the Public Sphere in the Early Republic," in Hoffman and Albert, eds., *Launching the "Extended Republic,"* 273–359, quotation at 277; Brooke, "'To Be Read by the Whole People': Press, Party, and Public Sphere in the United States, 1789–1840," *Proceedings of the American Antiquarian Society* 110, part 1 (2000): 44–118; Brooke, "Consent, Civil Society, and the Public Sphere in the Age of Revolution and the Early American Republic," in Pasley, Robertson, and Waldstreicher, eds., *Beyond the Founders*, 207–50; and Brooke, "On the Edges of the Public Sphere," *William and Mary Quarterly*, 3d. ser. 62 (2005): 93–98.

of political discourse beyond the confines of the political system itself, including the newly emerging political parties. In a variety of social locations—political celebrations and demonstrations but also voluntary associations, clubs, coffeehouses, and salons—and in written sources—books, periodicals, and private, even secret, correspondence—people participated in the formation and contestation of public opinion. On the whole, the intellectual possibilities inherent in the concept of the public sphere gave historians an innovative approach to bringing disparate groups into a lively political tableau—above all, one that drew its inspiration and energy from the liberating implications of the Revolution.

Historians have particularly used the notion of the public sphere to give us a greater appreciation of the ways women engaged in political and social activities and brought their own perspectives to bear on what had been largely male-dominated discourse. To offset the greater gendered weight inherent in the political associations and institutions of men, and above all to diminish the traditional separation of a male public sphere of politics and a female private sphere, Brooke and others have suggested the use of an alternative term, "civil society," as a more inclusive notion that helps move beyond the bifurcated categories of "public" and "private."[281] Mary Kelley's definition of civil society as "any and all publics *except* those dedicated to the organized politics constituted in political parties and elections to local, state, and national office" seems almost to surround if not absorb the traditional political process.[282] In general, by highlighting alternative sites of women's political engagement—the reading circles, salons, and other "institutions of sociability" that existed apart from but adjacent to the formal workings of politics dominated by men—Kelley calls for broadening our view of post-Revolutionary politics to encompass a greater variety of political influences and behaviors, in which women's assume a position closer to men's. If women still could not vote and hold office, they nonetheless moved into a more central spot on the political stage.

Though intellectually engaging, the constructs of the expanding "public sphere" and "civil society" have their limits. Like the term "middle ground" in Native American studies, both offer the great advantage of giving us a fresh way of looking at fundamental political relationships, but they also run the risk of being applied too broadly, becoming a conceptual catch-all,

[281] See, for instance, "Women and Civil Society: A Symposium," *Journal of the Early Republic* 28 (2008): 23–82.

[282] Kelley, *Learning to Stand and Speak*, 5; emphasis added.

or indeed, perhaps not catching enough. David Waldstreicher has argued, for instance, that the notion of the public sphere never fully resolves the distinction between political engagement and political entitlement: there remains "a vagueness, an indeterminacy about who were 'the people' and who were 'the citizens,' or true political actors."[283] Even though women "broadened their own influence and importance in the post-Revolutionary public sphere," their involvement remained most often not acknowledged by men or, if acknowledged, became assigned to a nonpartisan periphery seemingly "above" the competitive political arena. Men in partisan political organizations often celebrated the selfless civic virtue of women, invoking in their ceremonial toasts "women's influence as the path back to the pure republicanism of the Revolution." Their point, though, was to use that apparent respect for female virtue as a means of palliating their own partisanship: "In a political culture that mixed appeals to partisan action with encomia to national unity," Waldstreicher explains, "women helped make that unity possible." That sense of national unity, of course, did not extend widely enough to embrace women as full citizens. In that regard, he argues, women paid "the price of their extraordinary engendering: the heightening of their gendered difference whenever they entered the male-dominated public sphere."[284]

An additional critique challenges us to consider those who were still excluded from even that degree of participation in the public sphere, not only by gender but by race and class as well. To say the least, Native Americans and African Americans tended to be seen as uninvited outsiders in a public sphere defined by discourse among educated white people. The emphasis on education itself formed a formidable class-based barrier to participation. Educating young women for their participation in a post-Revolutionary public in intellectual terms was one thing, but that did not necessarily prepare them for sharing that participation with a more inclusive public in human terms. As Susan Branson has observed, the larger population of elite and middle-class women—those who perhaps read Judith Sargent Murray or Mary Wollstonecraft with considerable relish—"did not necessarily articulate the aspirations, values, or ideologies of the wives and daughters of mechanics and tradesmen, nor of women of the laboring classes." It may well have been, she suggests, that some women of the lower classes read

[283] Waldstreicher, *In the Midst of Perpetual Fetes*, 37–38. See also Waldstreicher, "Two Cheers for the 'Public Sphere' . . . and One for Historians' Skepticism," *William and Mary Quarterly*, 3d. ser. 62 (2005): 107–12.

[284] Waldstreicher, *In the Midst of Perpetual Fetes*, 166–72, 234–41, quotations at 234, 235, 241.

the same books and pamphlets, took part in the same public events and protests, and shared the same ideas and aspirations of their more socially prominent sisters, but too often our only evidence is inference. "Identifying their contributions and hearing their voices is difficult," Branson admits, and "poorer women, for the most part, remain silent."[285]

And perhaps more socially prominent republicans, both male and female, did not care to hear them. In a generally sympathetic response to Kelley's notion of "civil society," Jeanne Boydston has nonetheless noted that the term "civil" can easily become conflated with "polite," whether in the sense of polite letters or, more broadly, polite society. "Some gatherings of citizens were far more desirable than others—more refined, more estimable, more equal," she points out, but equal only for those of a similar background based on class or race. "Put bluntly," she asserts, "Kelley's subjects would not have been caught dead in a mob or as a member of the 'outdoors' classes, even if everyone else present were a woman." Indeed, Boydston argues that the very ability of elite and middle-class women to share a place in civil society with elite and middle-class men depended on their making accommodation to their shared social status: "the women Kelley studies eventually proved indispensable to the class wars of the early republic."[286]

But that intergender class alliance in a "civil" society cannot fully define the final point. Boydston usefully posits the possibility of a more inclusive view of the "public," which was "the property of just about anyone who cared to speak up or act out—in the form of editorials, historical novels, parades, processions, public lectures, sermons, revivals, tavern debates, street brawls, and theater performances."[287] This more expansive—and certainly more energetic—image of an eclectic and often rowdy public reminds us that people of all ranks in post-Revolutionary America still asserted their rights and demanded a place in politics just as passionately as did their pre-Revolutionary counterparts. They came out of the Revolutionary era just as they went into it, with a mixture of motives and interests, variously united and divided in a host of frequently intricate and sometimes shifting ways. Many may have read the same books and broadsides, taken part in the same demonstrations and celebrations, engaged in the same debates

[285] Branson, *These Fiery Frenchified Dames*, 8.

[286] Jeanne Boydston, "Civilizing Selves: Public Structures and Private Lives in Mary Kelley's *Learning to Stand and Speak*," in "Women and Civil Society: A Symposium," 47–61, quotations at 57, 59.

[287] Ibid., 52.

and battles, and ultimately accepted the same laws and leaders in the new nation. Many, of course, did not, and many others—Native Americans and African Americans above all—were not offered the opportunity to participate in that public sphere. And that may be the most important point. The inhabitants of the new nation did not march in a political lockstep marked by a consensual spirit or a common identity. They remained engaged in a continuing struggle to defend their rights—and to do so not just in the loftiest economic and intellectual levels of society but in an ever-expanding sphere that included a mixture of different ranks and races.

Afterword

Gregory H. Nobles

If J. Franklin Jameson were alive again today, he might well want to revise his metaphor for the American Revolution. It may still be fine to say, as he did in 1925, that the "stream of revolution, once started, could not be confined within narrow banks, but spread abroad upon the land," but even that image hardly captures the thrust and power of recent research. Instead of an overflowing stream, the description now needs to portray the rapidity and turbulence of the revolutionary waters. Indeed, modern scholarship would suggest that there is not a single stream but a confluence of currents coming from different directions and flowing into —and often against—the "mainstream" narrative of the American Revolution as a unified movement for independence. The result is a roiling mix of people and political issues, with constantly surging struggles in several fast-flowing movements that left almost no one untouched by the tumult.

Whose American Revolution was it? It is impossible to assign primary identity, much less possession, to anyone. Certainly, the men who assumed and exercised formal leadership of the patriot movement can no longer hold the sole focus as "Founders" on their own. However much some scholars may still like to see them as members of an elite political brotherhood, these leaders did not by any means form a united front, nor could they act as isolated statesmen making policy in a socially enclosed setting. Rather, as much as they debated and negotiated with each other, which has been the main preoccupation among some of their recent biographers, they also had to engage in different forms of debate and of negotiation about the outcome of the Revolution with different sorts of people—yeomen, artisans, and other white men who worked with their hands; women of all classes; African Americans, both free and enslaved; and Native Americans, both allies and enemies. Taken together, the multiplicity of political relationships that came into play in a quickly changing, truly revolutionary environment helps us understand what the Revolution meant to people living at the time, and as much as anything else, those political relationships now define the founding.

Throughout the Revolutionary era, from before the drafting of the Declaration of Independence to well after the framing of the federal Constitution, political leaders had to consider the recurring pressure coming from what they called the "people out of doors," Euro-American farmers and artisans whose insistence on greater social and political equality provided an undercurrent to the movement for national independence. The Revolution's leadership needed these men, who helped propel the anti-imperial protest movements before the war and who formed a large part of the American military force that eventually helped defeat the British. But throughout the war and on into the peace, many ordinary folk felt overburdened by the sacrifices required of them and underrepresented by the new political order that governed them. As these disaffected citizens expressed their grievances, political leaders at both the state and federal levels had to do something to address the unrest. In some cases, most notably in Massachusetts and Pennsylvania, the initial political response resulted in a show of military power. More often, however, political leaders found it wiser, and certainly safer, to make necessary concessions to people's demands for more responsive representation, more equitable taxes, and more accessible land. The resurgence of class as a category of analysis has enabled us to see the larger political significance of many such local struggles. At a time when the post-Revolutionary settlement still seemed anything but secure, this process of accommodation seemed most likely to make some measure of social peace possible.

At the same time, Revolutionary-era leaders showed little interest in offering similar political concessions to white women, nor, in the absence of an organized women's movement, did they feel nearly as much pressure to do so. Except for a few farsighted women writers, people in Revolutionary-era America considered the formal participation of women in politics, and certainly voting, all but unthinkable. That is not to say, however, that women had no role in politics. Like many of their male counterparts, they appeared on the political scene as active participants in street demonstrations, riots, and other forms of protest; as providers of critical support services to the army and, in a handful of cases, as combatants; and in other instances, as well-read and articulate contributors to political discourse with men. Men in positions of power sometimes celebrated women's virtue even as they patronized their positions, but men could hardly ignore women as women began to carve out their own approach to an expanding public role. Given the upsurge of innovative scholarship that has come on the scholarly scene in recent decades, it is now equally unwise for anyone to patronize or ignore the importance of women in the Revolutionary era.

As much as men and women in white society proved problematic for the Revolutionary-era leadership, African American men and women proved to be even more of a political challenge. From the very beginning of the military conflict, for instance, George Washington and other political and military officials had to pay close attention to the push of African Americans to be part of the army, and Washington eventually realized he had to accept them as soldiers. Escaped slaves affected the strategy of both the Americans and the British, not just by disrupting the stability of white society but by taking up arms to fight for their own freedom on whichever side seemed most likely to offer the better prospects for immediate emancipation. Their actions helped highlight the longer-term issue of emancipation for all enslaved people, making clearer the contradiction of slavery in a revolutionary movement for liberty and equality. The framers of the new federal Constitution failed to resolve that contradiction for the nation as a whole, but antislavery advocates, both black and white, pushed northern states to take the first steps for the eventual abolition of slavery. Above all, the various challenges to slavery during the Revolutionary era have become an increasingly significant issue among historians of the African American experience, and recent scholarship has given emancipation and equality an inescapable place in the political debates of the new nation.

The emphasis on these critical social issues within American society offers us a useful internal perspective on the political emergence of the United States, but the inclusion of Native Americans, people who lived outside that society, adds a broader imperial dimension to the Revolutionary-era narrative. Taking the view from Indian country leads us to look beyond the political and conceptual boundaries of the new nation and to gain a better appreciation of the competing empires in North America, both Euro-American and Native American. Here again, the designs and desires of Euro-American leaders ran up against the interests of Native American leaders, and no one at the time could easily dictate the outcome. We can now, however, better discern the pattern of expansionist policy that became such a central aspect of the history of the United States. Taking this broader view of imperial competition causes us to take a longer view of time, locating the American Revolution on a longer time line of the "long war" for the North American interior—again, a process that extended far beyond the chronological confines of the traditional narrative of the Revolution. The long war lasted well over a century and eventually covered the continent, only ending, some scholars would argue, with the United States' military conquest of Indians in the West at the end of the nineteenth century. But in the context of the late eighteenth century, when the outcome was still very much in doubt, the history of these frontier struggles now commands our attention by locating the origins of American imperialism in the Revolutionary era. The warfare of that period brought forth an emerging tendency on the part of white Americans to make explicitly racial distinctions between themselves and Native Americans, and this embrace of racism increasingly energized the expansionist sentiment for removing Indians from the landscape.

On the whole, the writing on the Revolution in recent years is both extensive and impressive, and it certainly poses a daunting challenge to put it all together in a coherent synthesis. Historians have so extended the reach of Revolutionary-era scholarship that it may seem to exceed anyone's ability to grasp it all. The task of telling the story used to have a clear narrative direction, a well-defined time frame, and a familiar cast of characters, so that historians could limit themselves largely to looking at the actions of Euro-American people along the eastern seaboard in the period between 1763 and 1787. That cannot be done these days, or it certainly should not. Writing about the Revolution now all but requires taking account of the recent research that addresses the people formerly disregarded, even dismissed, in the once-standard narrative. Finding a new narrative strategy, however, also requires new ways of embracing the various stories of many different people in many different places and weaving them together in a way that makes historical sense. That may well become an intellectual sticking point for the rising generation of historians.

It should thus come as no surprise that the major efforts at synthesis in the past decade and a half have come from senior historians whom Alfred Young singled out in the first essay in this book, scholars who began their explorations of the Revolution at a time when they had to confront J. Franklin Jameson's thesis. Edward Countryman's *The American Revolution*, first published in 1985 and expanded in a revised edition in 2003, provides a clear and concise analysis of the growing unrest over imperial issues, the turbulent movement for independence, and the creation of a new nation. Countryman pays considerable attention to the political roles of the prominent men who have long dominated the Revolution's narrative, but he also brings African Americans, Native Americans, and ordinary white men and women into the story of nation making. Countryman's *Americans: A Collision of Histories* offers an engaging and metaphorically imaginative way of bringing together the histories of Euro-Americans, African Americans, and Native Americans, taking them well beyond the American Revolution to the next great national collision, the American Civil War.[1]

Gary Nash, whose earlier work had already laid a strong foundation for looking at the Revolutionary era from the perspective of people outside the main positions of power, published two books in the first years of the twenty-first century that synthesized the central issues of his scholarly career. *The Forgotten Fifth: African Americans in the Age of Revolution* puts forth a brief but sweeping analysis of critical issues in African American experience in the Revolutionary era: the agency of black people in creating a "revolution within a revolution," the failure of white political leaders to embrace emancipation within their own revolution, and black people's continuing struggle for citizenship in the post-Revolutionary era.[2] In *The Unknown American Revolution: The Unruly Birth of Democracy and the Struggle to Create America*, Nash tracked the many parallel strands of radical struggle taking place between the 1760s and 1785, a period that ended, he argues, in "the taming of the Revolution." Instead of narrow and neat-seeming political narrative, he gives us a "messy, ambiguous, and complicated" story of a "seismic eruption from the hands of an internally divided people, . . . a civil war at home as well as a military struggle for national liberation."[3] Nash reminds us that the Founders themselves understood the Revolution that way, and it makes sense for us to do so as well.

The use of energetic language such as "collision" and "eruption" in these books speaks to the political energy of the various sorts of people on the scene, even as it does not overstate the success of their efforts. While both Countryman and Nash underscore the significance of social conflict that suffused the Revolutionary era, they also underscore the compromised nature of the revolutionary settlement. "The republic that the Founders created did not suit everybody's needs equally well," Countryman concludes,

[1] Edward Countryman, *The American Revolution* (New York, 1985; rev. ed., 2003); and Countryman, *Americans: A Collision of Histories* (New York, 1996).

[2] Gary B. Nash, *The Forgotten Fifth: African Americans in the Age of Revolution* (Cambridge, MA, 2006), 67.

[3] Gary B. Nash, *The Unknown American Revolution: The Unruly Birth of Democracy and the Struggle to Create America* (New York, 2005), xvi, 1.

"but its very structure permitted and encouraged people to define themselves and their interests and to seek to pursue those interests, even against the greatest odds and at the risk of their own lives, fortunes, and honor." Thus invoking the language of the Declaration of Independence, he suggests that no matter how much the Revolution might have been tamed by those at the top, people throughout American society still embraced its original spirit.[4]

Gordon Wood has chosen to focus his synthesis not on the Revolutionary era traditionally defined as 1763 to 1789, but in *Empire of Liberty: A History of the Early Republic, 1789–1815*, he extends into the early nineteenth century his emphasis on emerging republicanism, the theme he addressed almost two decades earlier in *The Radicalism of the American Revolution*. Leaders of the new political parties take center stage for the first part of this newer work, leading up to the election of 1800 and the liberating effects of the victory of Thomas Jefferson's liberal Republicanism over John Adams's conservative Federalism. The new republican society Wood describes abounds with expansionist energy and movements for reform that make the early republic seem a progressive expression of the Revolution's democratizing legacy. Noting that "historians now tend to conceive of the Revolution much more broadly than they did in the past," Wood himself has given us in effect a massive argument for the "long" American Revolution.[5]

Looking back at the historical scholarship discussed in the two essays in this book should certainly put to rest any suggestion that the study of the American Revolution has somehow reached a saturation point, much less an intellectual dead end. It also answers the charge that the inclusion of formerly underrepresented or excluded groups in the Revolution's narrative is primarily a concession to modern political concerns or, even worse, mere academic fashion. Instead, it makes it all but impossible for us to take a complacent approach by portraying the American Revolution as a socially

[4] Countryman, *American Revolution*, 235. Other recent syntheses of the Revolutionary era include Ray Raphael, *Founders: The People Who Brought You a Nation* (New York, 2009); Barbara Clark Smith, *The Freedoms We Lost: Consent and Resistance in Revolutionary America* (New York, 2010); and T. H. Breen, *American Insurgents, American Patriots*. Moreover, the 2009 reprinting of two of Staughton Lynd's earlier books, *Class Conflict, Slavery, and the United States Constitution* (1967) and *Intellectual Origins of American Radicalism* (1968), brought these important works of interpretation back to the bookshelf.

[5] Gordon Wood, *Empire of Liberty: A History of the Early Republic, 1789–1815* (New York, 2009), 741. For Wood's briefer overview of the Revolution, 1763–91, see *The American Revolution: A History* (New York, 2002).

unified, much less historically inevitable, event. Historians now give us a picture of the Revolution that is complicated, to be sure, but also intellectually compelling. They make us understand that taking these different perspectives—from the coastal capital *and* the treaty ground, from the plantation house *and* the slave quarters, from the prominent townhouse *and* the plebeian tavern, from the top down *and* the bottom up, not to mention from the middle as well—gives us a better, more historically realistic view of the past, much like the view people in the past took themselves. Seeing things that way matters to us now, because it mattered to them at the time. It should continue to matter to those of us who study the Revolutionary era in the future. In the end, the question "Whose American Revolution was it?" can only be answered by taking account of all the people who struggled in so many ways to make it their own.

Acknowledgments

The authors are greatly indebted to our editor at NYU Press, Deborah Gershenowitz, for her wise counsel, reassurance, and good cheer, particularly in the latter stages of writing. Gabrielle Begue very helpfully managed the manuscript at the press, and Despina Papazoglou Gimbel provided outstanding support during the editing and production processes. Andrew Katz did a very careful job of copyediting, and the authors accept responsibility for any remaining errors.

Alfred F. Young wishes to repeat his thanks expressed when this essay first appeared, in 1995, to Ronald Hoffman, Jesse Lemisch, and Gary B. Nash for their astute critical comments on the manuscript; to Staughton Lynd, Jackson Turner Main, Morey D. Rothberg, and Peter H. Wood, who read sections of it, correcting errors and adding to the author's knowledge; to Paul Buhle, Stephen Foster, Mary Furner, and James M. Smith, who answered queries; and to James A. Henretta, who criticized an early version. The University of Virginia Press has generously granted permission to reprint the essay.

Gregory H. Nobles is very grateful to several generous colleagues—Susan Branson, Carla Gerona, Woody Holton, Daniel Richter, and Billy G. Smith—who read and responded to various sections of this essay with smart comments and very helpful suggestions. Al Young read each of the sections, and the essay owes a great debt to his wisdom and commitment to getting things right.

Index

About the Authors

A historian of the American Revolution for over fifty years, Alfred F. Young is Emeritus Professor of History at Northern Illinois University and was Senior Research Fellow at the Newberry Library, 1990–2005. His most recent books include *The Shoemaker and the Tea Party* and *Liberty Tree: Ordinary People and the American Revolution* (NYU Press).

Gregory H. Nobles is Professor of History at Georgia Institute of Technology. His books include *Divisions throughout the Whole: Politics and Society in Hampshire County, Massachusetts, 1740–1775* and *American Frontiers: Cultural Encounters and Continental Conquest.*